BORROWINGS IN
ENGLISH CHURCH MUSIC
1550–1950

BORROWINGS IN ENGLISH CHURCH MUSIC 1550–1950

Judith Blezzard

STAINER & BELL : LONDON

Printed in Great Britain by Galliard (Printers) Ltd, Great Yarmouth

Set in Garamond

British Library Cataloguing in Publication Data

Blezzard, Judith
Borrowings in English Church music, 1550–1950
1. English Church music, history
I. Title
783'.02'6

ISBN 0 85249 784 9

Contents

Preface

Church music enters the lives of most English-speaking people at some point, whether or not they attend a place of worship. Songs used at school assemblies, anthems that appear as concert items rather than as part of a church service, carols that are virtually ubiquitous around Christmas: all these, with numerous further examples, are likely to be part of current experience or retrievable memory. To many people the concept of English church music brings to mind the idea of a musical entity complete in itself, unique in many ways, insular and possibly retrospective, having almost no connection with other kinds of music or with matters of everyday life. To some this music means a great deal, to others very little. But few people, whatever their level of interest in church music, may realize that many of the usual preconceptions about it have little foundation. In reality, the history of English church music from its inception throughout its growth in the four hundred years up to the middle of the present century shows it to have been almost constantly a reflection of the latest developments in music, both British and European, from outside the church, and at times the subject of heated controversy. Far from being insular, archaic and remote, English church music has for the most part constituted a lively reflection of current musical activity.

This contention can be taken a stage further. Not only have contributors to the English church music repertory been very much aware of contemporaneous influences in their own compositions, they have also borrowed and adapted other musical material for use in church. At first glance, plagiarism of this kind may not seem to be an important element in the development of English church music, but further investigation shows that a far greater proportion of the church music repertory uses borrowed material than might actually be supposed. These borrowings can be divided into three main areas, each of which this book explores in detail. First, there is the vast amount of music borrowed from that of other churches, including plainsong, Latin polyphony, the German chorale and sacred music from other mainland European areas. Second, almost every kind of secular music has been appropriated at some stage to provide music for use in the English church. This music ranges from popular melodies borrowed for worship in Tudor times, through the use of material from opera, secular vocal and instrumental music, to the recasting of folksongs and other melodies as hymns in the twentieth century. Finally, borrowing of a musical style (as distinct from the re-use of actual musical material) has had a widespread influence. It is apparent in the earliest sacred compositions, both monophonic and polyphonic, with English texts. It persists through the absorption of mainland European styles into English music in general throughout the seventeenth, eighteenth and nineteenth centuries, culminating in the pursuit of popular secular styles for use in worship up to the early years of the present century. This tenacious and almost universal fashion in church music for drawing on styles that did not originate in church naturally provoked adverse reactions, particularly in the nineteenth century when there was an influential movement towards deliberate archaism in church music in some quarters that persisted until well after 1900.

This kind of reaction is one manifestation of the controversies and conflicts which have typified the development of English church music at every stage and which emerge constantly in discussions of it in relation to other music. Put very broadly, there are two extreme and opposing views. One view is that any music, irrespective of its origin, can be used as a vehicle for worship. This view is enshrined in the aphorism 'Why should the devil have all the best tunes?', attributed variously to the evangelical preacher Rowland Hill (1744-1833), to the German Protestant leader Martin Luther (1483-1546), to the founders of Methodism John (1703-91) and Charles (1707-88) Wesley, and even to the composer Ralph Vaughan Williams (1872-1958), all of whom put the principle behind the idea into practice. The other view is that music for use in church ought to be separate and distinct from music of any other kind, particularly secular music. This view, supported by opinions as to the nature of music that was considered apt for use in church, has found expression in many ways in the period under discussion, but perhaps most significantly as part of the aims of the Tractarian movement in the nineteenth century, whose recourse to deliberate archaism in church music has already been mentioned.

Between these two extreme views lies the broad spectrum of attitudes that have been reflected by the development and acceptability of the large and varied corpus of English church music. Other factors have been influential also. Popularity, fashion, expediency and commercialism as well as the pursuit of artistic integrity and culturally esoteric ideals: all these have played significant parts. In this book, not only are borrowed material and styles surveyed, but the means by which they have been adapted and brought into church use are also investigated. No less important than these aspects are the reasons behind the borrowings and the results that it was hoped they would achieve, as well as contemporaneous and later reactions to these external influences on church music. In these ways, the book is more than merely an explanation of what lies behind the fragments of information such as those found in some hymnals, that describe a tune as no more than 'trad.' or 'ancient melody'. Its aim is to show how borrowing, far from being merely an expedient or a substitute for originality, has acted instead as a stimulus for ingenuity and a pivot for musical inspiration. All types of English Protestant vocal music are investigated: hymns, anthems, psalms, service music and carols. These are treated in parallel because their functions, relationships, character and importance change substantially in the four centuries under discussion. A starting date of approximately 1550 reflects the emergence of texts for worship in English with the consequent need for music to adorn them. A closing date of 1950 is marked by the publication of *Hymns Ancient and Modern Revised* and its consolidating effect on much English hymnody; also, perhaps in reaction to this, the proliferation shortly afterwards of a number of new movements in church music. Some of these have had more enduring effects than others and to have included discussion of them would have placed undue weight on the most recent developments at the expense of the longer span that forms their essential antecedent.

Inevitably, much church music from the four hundred years in question has had to be omitted. Not every borrowing can be dealt with, but it is hoped that text, references and examples will together be enough to act as the stimulus and first steps towards further enquiry. Footnotes have been kept to a minimum and signify groups of references for each section. Organ music, specifically Scottish church music, colonial and American church music, music for the Roman Catholic church in England and for the individual Nonconformist churches as distinct from the corporate movement and from the Methodist church as a whole, are touched upon only as they relate to the main topic. Nor is it possible to take account of the enormous number of publications, particularly of hymnals and psalters, that furnished the repertory of church music in the period in question: a few examples must suffice. Much useful background on the history of the church and its music can be found in Nicholas Temperley's absorbing and comprehensive study *The Music of the English Parish Church,* two volumes, (Cambridge, 1979). Church music of the period is discussed in a series of books by Peter le Huray, Christopher Dearnley, Arthur Hutchings, Bernarr Rainbow and Erik Routley. Reference books for individual items include those by Percy Dearmer and

Archibald Jacob, Edmund H. Fellowes, Maurice Frost, John Julian, James T.
Lightwood and Erik Routley. All these are listed in full in the Bibliography.
Where references are given in the text to individual hymn tunes, abbrevia-
tions refer to hymnals as follows:

EH   *The English Hymnal with Tunes* (1906)
A&MR   *Hymns Ancient and Modern Revised* (1950)
MHB   *The Methodist Hymn Book with Tunes* (1933)
SP   *Songs of Praise,* full music edition, revised and enlarged (1932).

Other references are given in full. Much, though not all, the music mentioned is accessible in modern editions to which references are given in footnotes; only where no modern edition is available is an older reference given.

   Thanks are due to the Dean and Chapter of Liverpool Anglican Cathedral,
to Mrs Mary Dunlop and to Mrs Ursula Vaughan Williams for allowing me
to quote from unpublished letters written by the late Colin Dunlop and the
late Ralph Vaughan Williams. Permission to quote extracts from musical
works, which I acknowledge with thanks, has been granted as follows: Stainer
and Bell Ltd. and The Musica Britannica Trust for John Stevens's edition of
William Cornysh's 'Blow thy horn, hunter' in *Music at the Court of Henry
VIII,* Musica Britannica, 18; the Society for Promoting Christian Knowledge
for part of John Merbecke's Magnificat in J. Eric Hunt's facsimile edition of
Cranmer's First Litany and Merbecke's Book of Common Prayer Noted and
for a music example by Myles Coverdale from Maurice Frost's book *English
and Scottish Psalm and Hymn Tunes;* Oxford University Press for an ex-
tract from Thomas Tallis's motet 'O nata lux de lumine' in *Tudor Church
Music* 6 and for Frederick A. G. Ouseley's anthem 'Is it nothing to you?' in
The Church Anthem Book edited by Henry Walford Davies and Henry G.
Ley; A-R Editions, Madison, Wisconsin, USA, for extracts from *The Tudor
Church Music of the Lumley Books,* Recent Researches in the Music of the
Renaissance, 65; Bärenreiter-Verlag, Kassel, West Germany for Heinrich Isaac's
tune 'Innsbruck, ich muss dich lassen' from Walter Lipphardt's edition in
Gesellige Zeit 1.

   I owe a debt of gratitude to the staff at the British Library, the Church
Information Office Archive and the Vaughan Williams Memorial Library, Lon-
don; the Library of the Royal School of Church Music, Croydon; the Bodleian
Library and Christ Church College Library, Oxford; the City Library and the
University's Brotherton Library, Leeds; the Henry Watson Library and the
University's John Rylands Library, Manchester; the City Library and the
University's Sydney Jones Library, Liverpool, for their tolerance and

11

resourcefulness in helping me track down elusive but essential items. The authorities at Liverpool University generously granted me a period of study leave and funds to finance most of the necessary research. I should like to thank Miss Valerie Curtis for compiling the Index, which was made possible by an award kindly given to me by the Pratt Green Trust. The individuals who have helped me are too numerous to mention: I hope that in singling out a few, the rest will not feel that my gratitude towards them is in any way less sincere. Special mention must be made of the following for help, encouragement and information: Mr Bernard Braley, Miss Dorothy Chapman, Miss Elizabeth Danbury, Dr Barbara Douglas, Mr Julian Elloway, Miss Joyce Horn, Emeritus Professor Arthur Hutchings, Mr Michael Kennedy, Dr Richard Rastall, Revd. Canon Ken Riley, Emeritus Professor Basil Smallman, Mr Anthony Smith, Professor Michael Talbot, Mr Ian Tracey, Revd. Tom Tyler, the late Mr Eric Whittome, Dr James Wrightson and Miss Gillian Yeatman. Most of all I am indebted to my family for their patience, understanding and practical help throughout this project and the enormously enjoyable years of music-making and study that preceded it. It is too late, alas, to thank my parents personally for their unobtrusive yet constant support, but in continuing appreciation of their kindness I should like this book to stand as a tribute in memory of them.

Judith Blezzard
July 1989

PART I

MUSIC BORROWED FROM SACRED SOURCES

1
A Musical Challenge

The Reformation in England

As the 1540s drew to a close, acute problems faced all those whose livelihoods depended on the church in England. Not the least among these were church musicians: mostly singing men and boys bereft, at the dissolution of the monasteries, of the musical routine of services that had governed their daily lives. In general there is no further trace of their musical activities, since very few of them were able to find posts at the handful of choral establishments that remained or were refounded. Some, however, were composers for the church as well as singers, organists or teachers of the choristers. Pre-eminent among a host of lesser names are distinguished composers such as John Merbecke (c.1505–c.1585), Christopher Tye (c.1505–c.1572) and Thomas Tallis (c.1505–85). Their surviving work, together with that of their contemporaries whose names and backgrounds are lost to us, provides a fascinating glimpse of a turbulent but innovatory period in the history of English church music in which borrowed material had an essential part to play.

English composers of church music in the late 1540s were confronted by two main problems. The first was that of language. The entire corpus of church music with which they were familiar consisted of settings in Latin, central to which stood the text of the Ordinary of the Mass. Starting from 1544 with the Litany in a translation by Thomas Cranmer, English translations of the liturgy were brought into use and disseminated largely by means of primers. These were books intended for private rather than corporate devotion, but their influence was widespread and they paved the way for the introduction and enforcement of the first Book of Common Prayer in 1549. Various parts of the liturgy in English translation were tried out with music, chiefly at the Chapel Royal. Following the accession of Edward VI in 1547, restrictions were increasingly imposed on the use of Latin musical settings at choral foundations elsewhere, with the mandatory substitution of settings in English. Liturgical changes occurred frequently — sometimes as often as every month — and until 1549 there was little guidance as to what was authorized liturgical practice and what was forbidden. In particular the Communion and its associated beliefs provoked controversy and confusion. Mass and Communion coexisted unofficially for a period, even in some of the larger establishments. In the face of such uncertainty in an age when unorthodox religious conduct was likely to have dire consequences for the individual, it is not hard to understand why composers were reluctant to commit themselves to setting the new English material. The English prose of the liturgy was unfamiliar and uncongenial; English metrical material (chiefly psalms) even more so. This, and the risk that a setting, once composed, would rapidly be rendered obsolete or incur official disapproval, would be enough to deter the most intrepid composer.

The second problem was that of musical style. It was customary for Latin settings, especially festal ones, to be massive and complex, with five or more voice-parts. Pieces (or movements, in the case of the Ordinary of the Mass) were divided into sections in which fewer voice-parts were used, the whole group coming together for climactic points. Individual voice-parts consisted of long and rhythmically intricate lines to which the Latin texts were underlaid so that each syllable was sung to a string of musical notes, sometimes with rests in the middle of a syllable. Many pieces were based on plainsong appropriate to a particular occasion. A common method of using plainsong was to allocate it to a single voice, often a Tenor part, while the other voices wove a complex web of polyphony round it. In such cases the plainsong (known as the *cantus firmus*) could be given out in long notes, elaborated or fragmented into shorter notes, allowed to migrate from voice to voice, or omitted altogether for a period.

Although this style of composition was highly developed, fostering magnificent work from composers such as John Taverner (c.1490–1545) and Thomas Tallis, its drawback in the climate of the 1540s was that the texts, festooned with long and complicated patterns of notes, could not be clearly perceived and understood. The move towards simplification of the style which had begun to occur in the shorter Mass settings of Taverner and others was insufficient to satisfy the more radical outlook of the 1540s. There was a growing demand for services that the laity could understand and in which there was the possibility that they could participate. Thomas Cranmer led the way by setting his translation of the Litany to the traditional plainsong, but with only one note to each syllable. In a letter to Henry VIII, written in 1545, he suggested that this method should ideally be adopted for further English settings. At this stage, therefore, composers were not under official constraint. But by 1548, official attitudes towards church music, where it was tolerated at all, had hardened. Injunctions to the Dean and Chapter of Lincoln Cathedral in April that year show that English settings only, with no more than one note for each syllable, were to be permitted. Latin settings, together with any music in praise of the Virgin Mary or other saints, was specifically forbidden. An injunction couched in these terms amounted to an official mandate to composers, forcing them to abandon an elaborate and sophisticated style of composition in favour of an inflexible ideal which had hardly begun to exist, let alone develop. The enforcement in 1549 of the first Book of Common Prayer, despite its aim of standardization, did little to reassure composers or inspire them to produce musical settings in line with the prevalent constraints on language and musical style.

Yet surviving sources show that, even in the face of such conditions, some composers were willing to come to terms with the kind of music that was being imposed on them. Much of what survives is anonymous, although relative newcomers such as Thomas Caustun (?c.1520/25–1569) and John Brimley (c.1502–76) are to be found alongside Tallis and Tye, already well established as church composers. The texts they could set were far fewer in number than those available from the recently-abandoned Latin rites. Composers could use material from the 1549 Book of Common Prayer or from the primers that immediately preceded it. The earliest English metrical psalters were similar in purpose to the prose primers; they often contained other versified material as well as psalms, such as prayers and canticles. All these devotional texts, both prose and metrical, provided potential material for musical setting. The issue of a second Book of Common Prayer in 1552 had little impact on church music because the following year Edward VI died and the accession of the Roman Catholic queen Mary Tudor put an immediate stop to all reforming activities. When Elizabeth came to the throne in 1558 she took prompt action to reinstate the English church as a separate entity from that of Rome. But the situation did not simply revert to that at the end of Edward VI's reign in 1553. Considerably more freedom of religious conduct was allowed, and this in turn gave composers of church music a modest but increasing degree of latitude.[1]

How musicians responded

It was natural that composers working under new and severe constraints should look first at any means that could be salvaged from the style they had been forced to abandon, and second at any means from elsewhere that could be used as the basis for new compositions. These methods had the advantage of utilizing concepts that were already familiar to performers and listeners as well as to the composers themselves. Such means fell into two main categories: the direct borrowing and, where necessary, adaptation of material; and the copying of a pre-existent musical style (as distinct from the borrowing of specific material). Techniques falling into the latter category will be discussed in Part III (see below, pp.160ff.). Into the former category come a variety of musical borrowings from different backgrounds. Those from secular music will be discussed in Part II (see below, pp.100ff.). Those from sacred music, whether from the earlier polyphonic style of Latin settings in England or from Protestant music elsewhere, will be discussed here. There are three main types of material borrowed from sacred sources: plainsong, polyphony and European Protestant hymns. All three exerted a strong influence on most types of English church music until well into the seventeenth century. Remarkably, it was to these three sacred repertories that church musicians turned once more in the mid nineteenth century and later, to furnish much of the material that acted as a catalyst in the revival of church music.

Plainsong: Cranmer and Merbecke

In England the liturgies and their associated plainsong were mostly those of the Salisbury (Latin abbreviation: Sarum) use. These differed in many ways from those of the Roman and other uses that prevailed elsewhere in Europe. Plainsong was familiar to English church musicians in two forms, monophony and as part of polyphony. As monophony it was the musical means by which substantial sections of the Latin services were transmitted, sung by an individual or by a choir in unison. As part of polyphony it often formed the basis for settings of the liturgy, sometimes acting as a *cantus firmus* which would designate a polyphonic composition as being appropriate to a feast with which the particular plainsong was associated. In these respects, therefore, the conduct of English church music up to the 1540s was similar to that in Europe.

Within both the monophonic and the polyphonic traditions of plainsong in Europe and England, there were precedents for borrowing that were to provide appropriate guidelines for English composers faced with new and stringent requirements. In the thirteenth and fourteenth centuries a large number of new feasts had been established in the Roman Catholic church. When liturgies for these new feasts were compiled they were sometimes very closely based on pre-existent liturgies, to the extent that in verse-forms (such as the sequence) only a few words might be changed to make the text appropriate to the new feast. It was then a simple matter to borrow all or most of the pre-existent plainsong, making minor adaptations where necessary to accommodate the material for the new feast.

Where plainsong was incorporated as part of polyphony, borrowing was not merely a matter of musical convenience. Although the plainsong melody had a liturgical function in associating a polyphonic setting with a particular occasion it had a formal musical function too, giving a piece or series of movements a unity, sense of structure and point of reference. The borrowing of plainsong as part of polyphony acted as an artistic stimulus to composers, and by the mid sixteenth century it had given rise to a number of diverse and highly-developed styles of church music in Europe and England.

It is likely that Thomas Cranmer's setting in 1544 of his translation of the ✓ Litany into English was the first English church music to use borrowed plainsong. Cranmer compiled this version of the Litany at the command of Henry VIII in the face of his impending invasion of France. The laity were to be instructed in the use of the Litany in processions. Cranmer set the English words to the traditional chant for the Latin Litany, but with only one note to each syllable. This version remained current even after the processions that it had accompanied had fallen into disuse. The chant with its English text became the basis for a harmonized version soon after its publication but this harmonization has not survived except possibly for a fragment in a manuscript in the British Library, London. This manuscript, Additional 34191, also contains a Tenor part adapted from plainsong of the Nicene Creed, other parts of the Communion service, and a Te Deum. This partbook is the only remaining book from a set containing harmonizations of these plainsongs. Of subsequent harmonizations of the Litany probably the best-known is that by Tallis who, unlike most other composers in the genre, used Cranmer's chant as the topmost voice in his five-part setting, rather than as a Tenor part. Having met with royal approval of his Litany, Cranmer undertook further experiments using English texts set syllabically to plainsong, but (unless those in British Library Additional manuscript 34191 can be shown to be by Cranmer) these have not survived.

Cranmer's work in borrowing plainsong for the monophonic setting of his English translations undoubtedly provided a model for others to follow. Some of their monophonic settings may now survive only in harmonized versions, disguising their original intention. But the best-known and most enduring example of the borrowing of plainsong for monophonic use is John Merbecke's *The booke of Common praier noted* (original spelling; hereafter modernized) published in 1550. It was intended to be used in parish churches rather than cathedrals, but only by the priests and clerks, not by the congregation. The endurance and wide dissemination of the material in Merbecke's book, especially in later centuries, is in some respects paradoxical. It is a musical setting of material from the 1549 Book of Common Prayer;

consequently it was rapidly rendered obsolete by the issue of that book's successor in 1552 and the official reversion to Roman Catholicism the following year.

For his book, Merbecke devised a simple system of notation which, with its four-line stave, clef-shapes and predominantly square and stemless notes, resembled that of plainsong. But the main difference was that Merbecke's four note-shapes, as he explained in his Preface, corresponded directly to the breve, semibreve which could be dotted, minim, and breve with a pause for use only at cadences. This meant that, unlike plainsong neumes with their freer rhythm, Merbecke's notes bore a proportional relationship to each other and so his music, although derived from plainsong, was intended to be sung in strict rhythm.

Merbecke's aim was to produce music that was simple and familiar in style, while at the same time conforming to the principle of only one note to each syllable. Accordingly he adapted plainsong for use with some of the texts, composing chants of his own in a similar style for the remainder. Merbecke's own compositions included substantial sections of the Communion service: the Gloria, Creed, Offertory sentences and Post-Communions. These borrowings of the plainsong style will be discussed in Part III (see below, pp.160ff.).

The remainder of the material consists of Merbecke's own adaptations of plainsong for use with English texts. All the following texts are set to music in this way: Preces and responses; Matins (Venite, Te Deum, Benedictus); Evensong (Psalms, Magnificat, Nunc dimittis); Benedicite; Athanasian Creed; Communion (Introit, Kyrie, Sanctus, Benedictus, Agnus Dei); Burial of the Dead (Responds, Psalms); at the Communion when there is a burial (Kyrie, Sanctus, Agnus Dei). Other material, such as the Lord's Prayer in Matins and Evensong and the Prefaces at Communion, is set to a monotone.

Predictably, the well-known plainsong tones feature prominently in Merbecke's borrowings, since their flexibility is such that they require a minimum of adaptation to accommodate appropriate English texts. That most frequently used is the eighth tone in a very much simplified form. The Venite, introits to Communion and Communion when there is a burial, and psalms at the burial of the dead all use this tone with almost no departure from its reciting-note: the intonation is absent and the ending is the simplest possible. The Magnificat and a second (alternative) setting of the Matins Benedictus use the eighth tone in a more nearly complete form. The following example, in which the plainsong and Merbecke's notation are reproduced with modern staves and clefs, and juxtaposed, shows how Merbecke's mensural notation and syllabic underlay relate closely to the plainsong original:

The fifth tone is used for the first settings of the Nunc dimittis and Matins
Benedictus with little change except in the text underlay. The second (alternative) setting of the Nunc dimittis uses a slightly simplified version of the
seventh tone. The Communion Sanctus and Benedictus are derived from the
second tone but, unlike the Magnificat shown above, the plainsong underwent a good deal of modification in the process. The Benedicite is set to
the English version of the 'Peregrinus' tone. The Athanasian Creed is set to
the fourth tone. In some cases, such as the latter, Merbecke's choice of tone
was probably influenced by the occurrence of particular tones for corresponding sections of the Sarum rites.

There are few borrowings of plainsong that do not relate directly to these
tones. The Te Deum is a contraction of the single Te Deum melody in Sarum
antiphoners, and it may possibly be related to an Ambrosian melody. The
Agnus Dei at Communion is based on a Sarum melody that seems to be uni-

que to Sarum use. The music for the burial of the dead makes the widest use of material apart from the tones. The Kyrie, Sanctus and Agnus Dei are simplified versions of Sarum chants for the daily Mass for the Dead. The Responds seem to fall on the borderline between borrowed material and new material composed in a borrowed style. Their openings resemble those of some Sarum respond melodies but their continuations diverge to a greater or lesser extent from those of any identifiable Sarum respond melodies.

In comparison with the elaborate Sarum rites the 1549 Book of Common Prayer presented very few opportunities for musical setting, giving no guidance as to when music would be appropriate. Merbecke's book met with official approval and was the most comprehensive attempt to come to terms with the new constraints. For the short period of its currency it fulfilled a need, at the same time forming a link with the familiar musical language of plainsong. But it is doubtful whether its influence up to 1552 spread beyond a few parish churches in London, or beyond the ranks of the priests and clerks for whose use it was intended.[2]

Plainsong: early harmonized settings

Cranmer's Litany and sections from Merbecke's *Book of Common Prayer Noted,* most frequently the Preces and Responses, were used by composers from Edward VI's reign and early in Elizabeth's reign as the basis for their own harmonizations, some of which have survived into present-day use. But it is likely that Merbecke's monophonic settings were used as part of improvised harmonization also. The tradition of improvised harmonization, known as faburden, was well established in sixteenth-century England. It consisted of the improvisation at sight, according to certain rules about intervals, of up to three simultaneous additional voice parts to a plainsong melody. Well-known melodies such as the psalm tones were obvious subjects for faburden and it is possible that Merbecke and Cranmer chose some of their plainsong borrowings with this possibility in mind. Sometimes a faburden melody would establish its own existence, independent from the plainsong upon which it was originally based. Some of these faburden melodies themselves then gave rise to new compositions. This is particularly true of keyboard music, for example 'O Lux on the faburden' by John Redford (died 1547), which survives in the *Mulliner Book* (London, British Library Additional manuscript 30513), compiled between about 1545 and about 1585. A few faburden melodies are also to be found as the basis of polyphonic settings of English liturgical texts. Although some surviving plainsong-based polyphonic settings of English liturgical texts show attributes of a probable faburden style, it is impossible to take full account of this style since such improvisations were neither written down, nor were they intended to be preserved.

Concurrently with adaptations of plainsong for monophonic use with English texts, plainsong borrowings were used also to form the basis of polyphonic compositions. Unlike later elaborations of Merbecke's and Cranmer's work, whether improvised or written down, these compositions were designed as polyphony from their inception: they are unlikely to have been the result of grafting harmony on to pre-existent adaptations. The earliest of these polyphonic settings date from about 1547 in manuscript; some were published between that date and the accession of Mary Tudor in 1553 and a few further ones are found in publications around the closing years of the sixteenth century. Increasingly by that stage, however, the simple homophonic style of these plainsong harmonizations was declining in favour of freely-composed music in the forms of anthems, services, psalms and hymns. The shift of importance away from the Tenor as the principal melodic voice part hastened this decline. Nevertheless these harmonized borrowings of plainsong are important because they demonstrate one aspect of composers' ingenuity in meeting fresh needs while at the same time incorporating familiar material. Furthermore, their simplicity of style had a distinctive influence on freely-composed sacred music in England. For example, sustained repetition of a single triad with a reiterated pivot note governing any harmonic departure from it, is a particular feature of these plainsong harmonizations. This device is sometimes used effectively in freely-composed music, especially in contrast to passages in which the harmonic pace is rapid or the movement more florid. The later Latin works of Tallis provide several examples of which perhaps the best known occurs in the closing passage of the hymn 'O nata lux de lumine', shown in the example on page 24, in which the Contratenor D forms the pivot.

Apart from the fragment of a possible polyphonic setting in British Library Additional manuscript 34191 (discussed above, p.19), the earliest polyphonic settings of English sacred texts incorporating borrowed plainsong date from about 1547 or 1548. There survive two main sources, both manuscript. Neither is complete: as well as the absence of certain leaves, each set of partbooks has one book missing, meaning that music throughout the set is rendered incomplete by its loss.

The longer of these two sources, known as the Wanley partbooks (Oxford, Bodleian Library MSS. Mus.Sch.e.420–22), contains a large repertory, all anonymous, including anthems, canticles and Communion services, mostly for men's voices only. Some of the composers may be identified in cases where a piece has a concordance in another source where the composer is

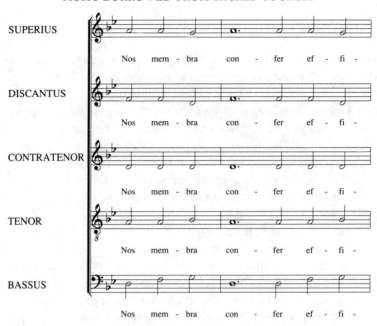

SUPERIUS

Nos mem - bra con - fer ef - fi -

DISCANTUS

Nos mem - bra con - fer ef - fi -

CONTRATENOR

Nos mem - bra con - fer ef - fi -

TENOR

Nos mem - bra con - fer ef - fi -

BASSUS

Nos mem - bra con - fer ef - fi -

ci Tu - i be - a - ti cor - po - ris.

ci Tu - i be - a - ti cor - po - ris.

ci Tu - i be - a - ti ___ cor - po - ris.

ci Tu - i be - a - ti cor - - - po - ris.

ci Tu - i be - a - ti cor - po - ris.

named. Identifiable composers in the Wanley books include Tallis, Shepherd, Johnson, Caustun and Stone. The books were copied out between 1549 and 1552, probably for a London parish church. The possibility that some of the compositions may date from a few years earlier than this arises because certain of their texts are known to antedate the 1549 Book of Common Prayer. Among the wide variety of styles in the Wanley books are a few non-metrical pieces based on borrowed plainsong or faburden. Identification of these borrowings is made more difficult by the loss from the Wanley set of the Tenor partbook — the part that almost always carried the borrowed material — but the Tenor line can sometimes be extrapolated from the remaining voice parts.

The plainsong and faburden borrowings in the Wanley books are restricted to canticles and psalms. Their four-part harmony is simple, sometimes homophonic almost throughout and, particularly at the frequent cadences, limited by the prescribed ending of the plainsong. Repeated harmonies are rarely alleviated by variety of texture. The rhythm, insofar as mensural notation permits, is governed entirely by the words: stressed syllables and important monosyllables such as 'God' being given longer notes. It follows from this that the stresses rarely fall into regular patterns. This is the reason why modern editorial attempts to add barlines (whether regular or irregular) to this music are seldom successful in outcome. It is this lively and varied rhythmic element, combined with brief moments of melodic climax, that give this music its momentum despite the very limited means it uses.

The other main manuscript source of polyphony incorporating plainsong and faburden borrowings is the Lumley partbooks (London, British Library Royal Appendix manuscripts 74-76). This set, from which the Bass book is missing, contains predominantly four-part music for men's voices only. The remainder of the books' content includes instrumental dance music set out in score; this music was probably copied in some time later than the sacred section. All the sacred pieces except one, a setting of the Matins Benedictus by Tallis, are anonymous in the source. Concordant sources reveal that one further Lumley piece is by Tallis; another is by Tye. All three attributable pieces are freely-composed. The Lumley sacred music may have been copied for a private chapel, but there is also the possibility that it may have come into private hands after having been copied and first used at the Chapel Royal or Westminster Abbey. Copying of the Lumley sacred music probably took place over the period 1547 to 1552 but some of the compositions may antedate this period. The importance of the Lumley set depends, not only on its content, but also on its somewhat dilapidated state of handling and repair. Unlike the Wanley books, there are clear signs that the sacred music

in the Lumley books was used repeatedly in performance, a fact which
enhances the status of this source as a possible means of disseminating and
influencing church music.

Most of the Lumley pieces based on identifiable plainsong use material from
the eight psalm tones. There are settings of both metrical and prose texts.
Although the scope for musical invention is severely limited because of the
psalm melody in the Tenor, there are cases where a degree of ingenuity has
been exercised to give the piece as a whole a greater feeling of coherence
and sustained momentum. It is obvious that composers were beginning to
look beyond the borrowed plainsong towards other musical devices that
would create balance and interest. The Lumley prose psalm-setting entitled
'Laudate pueri Dominum' (a setting of Psalm 113) provides a clear example,
even though the Contratenor and Bass parts have to be editorially
reconstructed because of material missing from the source. In this piece the
text is organized into eight verses including the doxology. The Tenor repeats
the fifth psalm tone throughout. Musically, the verses work in four pairs so
that the Treble melody of each verse is repeated once and then succeeded
by a different melody. As the piece progresses, the melodies become a little
more adventurous, increasing in range and mobility. The opportunity is taken
to modulate briefly and to vary the harmony around the Tenor reciting-note,
as comparison of the following examples from the first and third verse-pairs
demonstrates. Note values have been halved and spelling modernized
editorially.

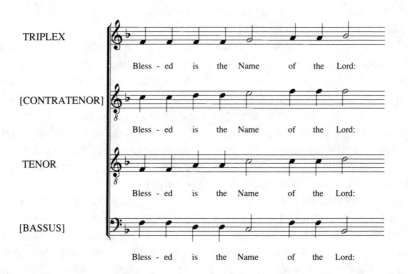

The fourth pair of verses rounds off the piece by restating almost exactly the music of the first pair, but with some lengthening at the end to reinforce the effect of the last of so many closed-ended cadences.

    The Lumley metrical pieces based on plainsong follow a scheme in which two sections of music, each based on a modified version of a chant, are sung alternately to successive text verses. In the source, problems of underlay caused by metrical anomalies in the cumbersome and stilted text are avoided by copying out every repetition of the music for each verse. In the metrical setting of the Matins Benedictus the fourth tone is used, without intonation, but it is not strictly adhered to throughout. As in some of the other plainsong-based pieces in this source, accidentals are added to the chant in the Tenor where this will facilitate appropriate harmony, and the chant is apparently abandoned altogether at cadences. In this particular piece the use of a melodic sequence in the Treble adds a point of interest to the otherwise rather un-prepossessing tune.[3]

Plainsong: metrical psalters

Two printed metrical psalters from Edward VI's reign make use of borrow-ed plainsong as part of polyphony, but the musical schemes of these settings are more rudimentary and less resourceful than some of the more enterpriz-ing plainsong-based pieces in the Wanley and Lumley sets. On the other hand, simplicity may have ensured a wide popular appeal. Unlike the manuscript pieces discussed above, these printed psalm tunes were designed to be sung with any of a number of different psalms. All the versifications in each volume worked in the same metre so there was no need to underlay every verse to music. Publication of settings based on borrowed plainsong was not solely a feature of Edward's reign. A few settings, both prose and metrical, from Elizabeth's reign continued to resort to this device, probably in the cause of familiarity and retrospective homage, and isolated examples appear even after 1660.

In 1549 Robert Crowley published *The psalter of David newely translated into Englysh metre*. This was the first publication of all 150 psalms in English metrical verse and also the first published English psalter with harmonized music. Only one tune is printed, intended for use with any of the psalms. It is for four voices, the second lowest of which (labelled 'Playnsonge' in the source) carries the seventh psalm tone. The compactness and simplicity of Crowley's chant together with its bipartite form give it obvious parallels with later Anglican double chants of which it is a precursor. Although in-tended for parish church use it seems that Crowley's book met with little success. One reason may have been his lack of an influential patron. But perhaps the more likely reason lies in the work itself. The verses work bet-ter read than sung, and the astringent minor-key setting, though entirely apt for a penitential or supplicatory psalm, may have seemed inappropriate for a jubilant one.

Francys Segar's *Certayne Psalmes select out of the Psalter of Dauid,* published in 1553, is smaller in scope than Crowley's psalter but musically more enterprizing. There are only nineteen versified psalms but two tunes are provided; even so, the tunes are similar to each other in style and subdued character. Both are for four voices. The first is apparently freely composed although there is a canon almost throughout between the topmost and lowest voices. At the final cadence there is a modest elaboration departing briefly from strict syllabic word-setting. The second borrows the plainsong of the sixth psalm tone to provide the Tenor line and is strictly syllabic throughout. It is unlikely that Segar's psalter received wide circulation, and only after Elizabeth's accession did psalters with printed music come more widely into use in England.

From early in Elizabeth's reign, a few composers continued the tradition of borrowing plainsong as the basis for English psalm settings. Tallis did so as part of a cycle of Christmas festal psalms composed probably for the Chapel Royal. These prose psalm settings are for five voices in a simple syllabic style. Three have survived in full and they include harmonizations in the Tenor of the first and seventh psalm tones to sections of Psalm 119. The fact that these very simple settings were composed for the most important feast in the church's year at England's most highly-renowned establishment for church music is a vivid reminder of the severity of constraints governing church music. Thomas Morley briefly explored the method of setting the eight psalm tones as Tenor parts in simple four-part harmonizations in his didactic work *A Plaine and Easie Introduction to Practicall Musicke,* published in 1597. The collections of Edward Lowe (1661) and James Clifford (1664) also use the psalm tones as part of mensural monodic and simple polyphonic settings. It is clear that these two isolated examples are deliberate attempts to resurrect former practices, rather than to reflect current methods or new ideals.

Elizabethan metrical psalters did not in general continue with the kinds of plainsong borrowing found in Crowley's and Segar's metrical versions. However, one of the eleven harmonizations contributed by Richard Brimle to John Day's publication *The Whole Psalmes in Foure Partes* (1563), using verses by Sternhold and Hopkins, shows a vestige of this method. In the 1560s it was becoming increasingly common for metrical psalters to include other versified material such as the canticles. Brimle's four-voice setting of the Magnificat quotes the first phrase of a Magnificat plainsong tone at the start of the Tenor part. Although direct quotation ends with this first phrase, the rest of Brimle's Tenor line maintains chantlike characteristics. A quotation like this is unusual, partly because it is late in comparison with similar techniques in other metrical psalters and partly because it occurs in a canticle rather than a psalm. It is out of the ordinary also in being only a partial quotation, but it would certainly have been recognizable and can hardly have been inadvertent on Brimle's part. It may show that Brimle wrote this setting or an earlier version of it in 1553 or before, but that it was not published until a decade later.[4]

Polyphony: techniques and early examples

Latin sacred settings by English composers provided material for adaptation to English texts. In pieces of this kind, unlike those in which only a plainsong was borrowed and a new composition was devised to fit it, entire polyphonic settings were borrowed and adapted only to the extent of accommodating the English words. Thus no new composition was involved. Borrowings from polyphony are found in English sources from the late 1540s and the practice continued until early in the seventeenth century. The identification of borrowings from polyphony is sometimes problematic. For example, a piece may show characteristics suggesting that it may be an adaptation, such as numerous repeated text-phrases for no apparent reason other than to give syllabic underlay under an original melisma, or (conversely) the rapid dispatch of several text-syllables to what may have originally been a single long note. Yet no Latin original may be extant. Where models have not survived it is difficult to do more than surmise that certain pieces of English church music may be adaptations rather than original compositions.

On the continent especially, there was already a well-established tradition in the early sixteenth century of borrowing from one piece of sacred polyphony to provide material for another. The most usual scheme was for sections from a motet to be used as part of a mass-movement in such a way that the beginning and end of the mass-movement, at least, were almost the same as the beginning and end of the motet. Intermediate material in the mass-movement was freely composed but might make reference to features of the motet such as imitative points. By this method, known as parody technique, an entire mass could be unified by its relationship to a pre-existent motet. Parody-masses are prominent among the works of composers such as Giovanni Pierluigi da Palestrina (c.1525–94), Orlande de Lassus (1532–94) and Tomás Luis de Victoria (c.1548–1611). The English composer John Taverner (c.1490–1545) also made use of parody technique in his masses 'Mater Christi' and 'Sancti Wilhelmi Devotio' (the latter also known by the names 'Small devotion', 'In all devotion' and 'Christe Jesu'), both based on antiphons by him. One anonymous English example, a setting of 'Christ rising again' based on a shorter setting of the same text, occurs in the Wanley manuscripts, and a piece by Tye in the Lumley manuscripts was apparently the subject of a later parody (see above, pp.25–26). However, despite a substantial element of borrowing, parody technique remains essentially a method of composition rather than adaptation because the borrowed material, as well as being reproduced, acts as a stimulus to further musical creativity.

Parody technique, despite making use of borrowed material, should not be confused with *contrafactum,* which is the much more limiting and less creative process of substituting one text for another in a piece of vocal music. This was a frequent practice in early English church music and, like parody, it had numerous continental precedents. The most usual continental method was to borrow from secular music to produce sacred pieces with Latin texts. But Protestant reformers on the continent were quick to grasp the advantages of borrowing traditional Latin sacred music and substituting their own vernacular devotional texts in accordance with Protestant views. English church musicians did likewise, drawing on music that was probably already familiar to singers and adapting it to prescribed English texts.

Where a change of language was involved, such as Latin to German or Latin to English, there were inherent problems of sense, stress and syntax in the new text and these inevitably detracted from the musical expression. Luther, with his profound knowledge and love of music, was well aware of this. Despite the enthusiasm of his followers for the obvious advantages of borrowing and adapting polyphony, Luther was not wholeheartedly in favour of the practice. His misgivings, expressed in 1525 in the following lines, say much that is true of adaptations in early English as well as German church music:

> Although I am willing to permit the translating of Latin texts of choral and vocal music into the vernacular with the retention of the original notes and musical settings, I am nevertheless of the opinion that the result sounds neither proper nor correct; the text, the notes, the accents, the tune, and likewise the entire outward expression must be genuine outgrowths of the original text and its spirit; otherwise, everything is nothing more than an apish imitation.

Problems of this nature are apparent in the earliest adaptations of polyphony for the English church, found in the Wanley partbooks (Oxford, Bodleian Library MSS. Mus.Sch.e.420–22, discussed above, pp.23–26). The most important of these adaptations are two anonymous settings of the English Communion service borrowed from masses by Taverner. The choice of these particular Taverner masses, 'Sancti Wilhelmi devotio' and 'Sine nomine' (the latter also known as the 'Meane' mass) is significant because, of Taverner's eight extant masses, these two are among the most nearly syllabic settings of the Latin mass text, and their music tends to fall into compact, shapely phrases. Thus they are good candidates for adaptation; even so, certain structural rearrangements were necessitated by the adaptation process and the degree of success was erratic.

A few further adaptations of polyphony can be traced in the Wanley books, including an adaptation of Taverner's antiphon 'Mater Christi' to a text beginning 'O God be merciful unto us'. Like the two Taverner masses mentioned above, this antiphon is ideal for adaptation; moreover, its widespread use and popularity as an antiphon is attested by its dissemination in a large number of manuscripts. It is not surprising, therefore, to find this particular antiphon used as the subject of more than one English borrowing: it was certainly current as late as c.1580 in the guise of 'O most holy and mighty Lord' together with 'I will magnify thee' adapted from Taverner's antiphon 'Gaude plurimum', in a manuscript of that date in the library of King's College, Cambridge (Rowe Music Library, MS. 316, Meane partbook from an original set of five).

The adaptations in the Wanley partbooks were first and foremost matters of expediency. Like the seven freely-composed Communion settings in the same source the adaptations were designed to meet the need in the late 1540s for English settings on syllabic principles, and the Taverner settings probably had the added advantage of familiarity. It is all too easy to disparage borrowings such as these as no more than musical stopgaps. Yet even when the immediate need for new English settings had subsided, the tradition of borrowing from Latin polyphony continued. The prolongation of this practice, particularly with its later concentration on the provision of anthems rather than services, suggests a desire to increase the number of situations in which especially highly-esteemed Latin pieces could be used, rather than a temporary measure to appropriate pre-existent music for use with an unfamiliar liturgy.

A good example of the adaptation of such a piece is provided by an anthem by Thomas Caustun (?c.1520/25–1569) entitled 'In trouble and adversity'. This piece, first published in 1560 in John Day's *Certaine Notes set forthe in foure and three partes,* is an adaptation from the Benedictus section of Taverner's mass 'Gloria tibi Trinitas'. The mass is for six voices and takes its name from the plainsong that acts as its *cantus firmus*. The second section of the Benedictus, starting with the text 'In nomine Domini', is for four voices. This section became very popular in its own right and was frequently copied into manuscripts as a separate piece. It underwent various arrangements for lute, keyboard and instrumental consort. These, together with later instrumental compositions based on the same *cantus firmus,* acquired the generic title 'In Nomine', and In Nomines were produced in large numbers up to and including some by Henry Purcell (1659–95). The arrangement of the piece as an English anthem, seen in this context, is an obvious means of diversifying the use of this popular piece still further. Caustun's piece is one of the few English borrowings from polyphony for which the identity of the arranger is known. At least one further adaptation of Taverner's 'In nomine Domini' section as an English anthem was current in the late sixteenth century.[5]

Polyphony: later examples

Other composers whose polyphonic Latin works were adapted as English anthems include Robert Whyte (c.1538–74), Thomas Tallis (c.1505–85) and William Byrd (1543–1623). It is perhaps surprising that, apart from one piece by each composer for which *contrafactum* is no more than a conjecture, there appear to be no English adaptations of Latin works by John Sheppard (c.1515–c.1560) or Christopher Tye (c.1505–c.1572), both of whom wrote at least some Latin settings that may have suited this purpose. Two adaptations traceable to Latin models by Whyte are 'O Lord, deliver me' (from 'Manus tuae fecerunt me') and 'Praise the Lord, O my soul' (from 'Domine, non est exaltatum'). Both these Latin originals are extensive psalm-motets with much florid melismatic counterpoint that does not lend itself easily to English adaptation. The resultant rather inept underlay in the arrangements begs the question of why these particular Latin models were chosen. Scrutiny of English anthems by Whyte that are presumed to have originated as such rather than as Latin pieces, such as 'Lord, who shall dwell in thy tabernacle', reveals similar problems. It is possible, therefore, that more of Whyte's anthems are adaptations based on models since lost. Two anthems ('I will wash my hands' and 'Let thy merciful ears') are apparently considerably later adaptations of 'O how glorious art thou', thought to be by Whyte, and there are two versions of his 'O praise God in his holiness', one for four voices and one for eight, the latter of which may be the original version. It is possible that William White (before c.1585 – before c.1667) was the composer of 'O praise God in his holiness'.

There are at least thirteen instances of borrowings from the Latin sacred polyphony of Thomas Tallis for use as English anthems, a measure of the high regard in which Tallis's music was held as well as of its comparative suitability for this purpose. All except one of the Latin originals date from Tallis's Elizabethan period, by which time his music had acquired a conciseness and intensity of expression lacking in his typically more florid Henrician and Marian works. Most of the adaptations appear to date from Tallis's lifetime or shortly thereafter. They include two large-scale pieces: the recently discovered composite psalm-adaptation derived from parts of the large pre-Elizabethan antiphon 'Gaude gloriosa Dei Mater' and 'Sing and glorify', an adaptation of the forty-part motet 'Spem in alium' devised to be sung in 1610 at the banquet for the coronation of Prince Henry as Prince of Wales. Most of the smaller-scale pieces appeared in print as Latin originals in *Cantiones sacrae*, Tallis's joint publication with William Byrd dating from 1575. In one case ('O sacrum convivium') the English version ('I call and cry to thee, O Lord') may have antedated the Latin, but the remainder are demonstrably adaptations from Latin to English. A total of ten English adaptations comes from just six of Tallis's short Latin pieces. The adaptations are much more adept than those of Whyte's music and they may have been undertaken by Tallis himself although, unlike the Latin versions, they apparently did not find their way into print in Tallis's lifetime. Perhaps the best-known example is 'With all our hearts and mouths', an adaptation of the first setting of 'Salvator mundi'. The English text, in praise of the Trinity, is unusual in the present context, for it is neither a translation nor a reflection of the sentiment of the Latin text. Even so, it suits the slightly-amended Latin music well in language, shape and spirit although nothing can detract from the superiority of the original.

A handful of pieces from William Byrd's substantial output of Latin music was adapted for use with English texts, but these form an almost insignificant proportion of Byrd's legacy of English anthems and other sacred pieces of similar types. Fourteen adaptations survive, of which the majority were taken apparently during Byrd's lifetime from early works. The best-known of the adaptations, 'Bow thine ear', is one of two adaptations of 'Civitas sancti tui', the second part of the motet 'Ne irascaris, Domine', composed before 1581.[6]

Continental sources (excluding plainsong)

This category includes all the music that found its way to England from Protestant communities in mainland Europe, chiefly from about 1539 to the mid 1560s. Most of the music consisted of unaccompanied melodies to metrical psalms in the vernacular; less often, metrical canticle or prayer settings, or tunes with four-part harmony were borrowed. Many of these European psalm tunes were themselves borrowings. Some were derived from medieval vernacular hymns or from plainsong. Others were adapted from music with secular texts. Some were composed expressly for Protestant use but were then borrowed and adapted by various Protestant communities over a wide area.

The intention behind these settings, that everyone should be able to sing and understand them without any special knowledge or expertise, suited the prevailing Puritan-influenced outlook of Elizabethan England particularly well.

The texts alone could be used for private devotion. The borrowed musical settings, alongside well-known native tunes to which metrical texts could also be sung, could be used in a gathering of any size, from a small family group at prayer to a vast church or outdoor congregation. Although the borrowed tunes, chiefly from France and Germany, never supplanted the native product, they held their place in the repertory of English congregational music to the extent that some of them might almost be regarded as folk music. Unlike most of the English music borrowed from plainsong or Latin polyphony in the sixteenth century, the use of this imported music has persisted in one form or another until the present day. Although there were few further borrowings in this category between the sixteenth and nineteenth centuries, many of the early borrowings endured as part of the hymn repertory throughout this period and beyond.

Coverdale and Lutheran tunes

The earliest borrowing of non-native Protestant music for English settings occurred about 1539 with the publication of Myles Coverdale's *Goostly psalmes and spirituall songes*. As well as metrical psalms, Coverdale's book contains metrical settings to unharmonized melodies of canticles, prayers, the Ten Commandments and various hymns which, like the majority of the tunes, have Lutheran origins. Many of the tunes are known from a variety of sources chiefly from the 1520s and 1530s, but the pre-eminent source upon which Coverdale seems to have drawn is Johann Walther's *Geystliches gesangk Buchleyn,* first published in Wittenberg in 1524. Walther, who collaborated with Luther in laying the foundations of German Protestant hymnody, may have been the composer or arranger of some of these hymns. Some of the pieces chosen by Coverdale are more familiar nowadays in the form of chorales harmonized by Johann Sebastian Bach. One such is 'Mit Fried' und Freud' ich fahr' dahin', appropriated by Coverdale from Walther's book to carry a metrical version of the Nunc dimittis. Coverdale's version is rhythmically less complex than Walther's, but the most striking feature of both Coverdale's and Walther's versions is the freedom of rhythm and phrase-structure in comparison with Bach's version, a vehicle for harmony. This progressive ironing out of the characteristically buoyant rhythms and asymmetrical phrasing of early Protestant hymns is typical, and the early forms of these melodies are a revelation to those whose first acquaintance with them is through the more widely-known Bach chorales. The most familiar of the tunes borrowed by Coverdale is 'Ein' feste Burg ist unser Gott', to a metrical version of the Book of Common Prayer Psalm 46:

Oure God is a defence and towre, a good armoure and good weapen;
he hath ben euer oure helpe and sucoure, in all the troubles that we haue ben in;
therfore wyl we neuer drede for any wonderous dede, by water or by londe;
in hilles or the see sonde; our god hath them al in his hond.

Again, Coverdale's tune (probably taken from a source dating from 1529) shows a rhythmic vitality absent from the later harmonized version. A Lutheran tune taken from the plainsong melody 'Christe qui lux es et dies' undergoes a second borrowing by Coverdale to accommodate an English metrical hymn: 'O Christ that art the lyght & day'. The tune 'Erschienen ist der herrliche Tag' (also known as 'Hermann', in modern use with the hymns 'Our Lord is risen from the dead' and 'Lo, when the day of rest was past') appears in Coverdale's book to a metrical version of the Book of Common Prayer Psalm 128: 'Blessed are all that feare the lorde'. The tune as it appears in later hymnals is attributed to a collection first published by Nicolaus Hermann in 1560, with a French folk song as its possible antecedent. The version harmonized by Bach, with strong triple metre and terse, angular modal melody, is the one usually given. However, the inclusion of the tune in Coverdale's book shows that it was in circulation as a hymn long before its appearance in Hermann's collection. Coverdale's version (shown in the music example) is much longer, largely because of the repetition of several phrases, and the subsequent drastic pruning of this music (as shown at A&MR 609, MHB 222, SP 159) is far from atypical of the later treatment of many of these early melodies.

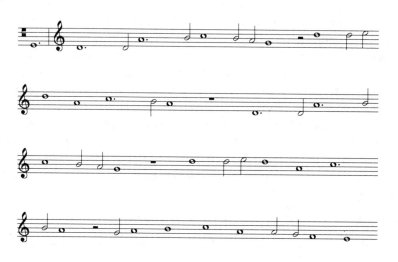

Coverdale's book had only limited success. Although it appears to have been published during the brief period when Lutheranism was in favour with Henry VIII, the climate of official opinion soon changed and the book, an isolated example of its kind at that time in England, was banned and ceremonially burnt in 1546.

Apart from Coverdale's book there were no substantial further attempts to introduce Lutheran music into English worship in the sixteenth century. In Scotland the brothers John, James and Robert Wedderburn occasionally named a tune composed or adapted for Lutheran use as the melody to be sung to one of the metrical texts in their publications of the 1560s and 1570s. The fact that no music was printed alongside their texts suggests that some such tunes were common knowledge, but there is no way of knowing how frequently the verses to Lutheran tunes were sung to the prescribed melodies. Most of the tunes chosen by the Wedderburns were secular, and their work will be discussed in detail in Part II (see below, pp.111ff.). It is likely that there was some interchange of tunes between Lutheran and Genevan Protestant communities, or at least that some musical phrases were 'common property' to both traditions. Hence a few Lutheran melodies may have come into the English repertory at second hand, by way of sources such as the Genevan psalters. The tune sung nowadays to 'Joy and triumph everlasting' (EH 200, A&MR 523, SP 291) is an example of this. Possibly adapted from a Lutheran source for Psalm 42 in the Geneva Psalter of 1551, it was used for Psalm 27 ('The Lord my light and health will be') in the Anglo-Genevan Psalter of 1561. From there it became part of the Scottish, rather than the English psalm tradition, and it was eventually turned into a hymn in *The Yattendon Hymnal* of 1899.[7]

Sternhold, Day and the Anglo-Genevan Psalters

One of the earliest attempts at versifying the psalms in English was made by Thomas Sternhold, who earned his living as Groom of the Wardrobe to Henry VIII and Edward VI (see below, p.101). Encouraged by the success with which his verses had met at the royal court, Sternhold published a collection of nineteen psalms in metre in 1549. All were in metres that could easily be fitted to well-known secular tunes. Several further enlarged editions appeared which included work by collaborators, the first of whom was John Hopkins. No music was printed in these editions, and still only 44 of the psalms in verse were published. From 1553, with the accession of Mary Tudor, many English Protestants went into exile abroad and established communities in several cities including Frankfurt, Strasbourg and Geneva. The psalter they took with them was that of Sternhold and Hopkins.

The English community in Geneva came under the influence of the Protestant reformer John Calvin, whose views on music in worship were much more stringent than those of Luther. Calvin deplored the appropriation of secular music for sacred use (see below, p.100). Consequently, when the English exiles published their first metrical psalter with music in 1556 for their own use they borrowed to a considerable extent, in both substance and style, from the music of pre-existent Genevan psalters dating from 1539. Many of the texts from the Sternhold and Hopkins volume had to be heavily modified in order to reach a compromise between their metres and the less regular French ones. Some new English versifications were compiled in order to admit existing Genevan tunes to the exiles' repertory, and some tunes appeared that had possibly been in use by English Protestant exiles in other cities. In all, 51 psalms with music appeared in the 1556 Anglo-Genevan Psalter.

The best-known survivor from the 1556 Anglo-Genevan Psalter is the tune known as the 'Old Hundredth' (EH 365, A&MR 166, 370, 621, MHB 2, 3, SP 443). The tune first appeared in the Genevan Psalter of 1551 set to Psalm 134. Its opening was borrowed by the English exiles as the start of a very heavily adapted version for Psalm 3 ('O Lord, how are my foes increased') in the 1556 Anglo-Genevan Psalter, where the metre was altered to fit that of the English text. However, by 1561 this version had been supplanted by 'All people that on earth do dwell', a metrical version of Psalm 100 composed to fit the original Genevan 1551 tune, and it is this version that survived in most Anglo-Genevan, English and Scottish psalters in various harmonizations.

The second Anglo-Genevan Psalter, published in 1558, omitted some of the 1556 material in favour of texts apparently written especially to accommodate more French tunes. The influence of the English Protestant community in Strasbourg and its strong links with the Frankfurt exiles is shown by the inclusion of the Strasbourg leader Richard Cox's metrical version of the Lord's Prayer ('Our Father which in heaven art') to the tune 'Vater unser im Himmelreich'. This tune first appeared in 1539 in a Lutheran source and, linked to Cox's text or to a version of Psalm 112, it appeared in most Anglo-Genevan, English and Scottish psalters to the end of the seventeenth century. It survives as a hymn (EH 462, 539, MHB 683, 723, SP 566), sometimes with the harmony by Johann Sebastian Bach. The hymn melody, though with a few added passing-notes and shorn of the longer notes with which every phrase started and ended, is almost the same as the Lutheran version and suffered little alteration despite being repeatedly borrowed.

After Elizabeth's accession in 1558 some of the exiles stayed abroad and produced at least one further Anglo-Genevan psalter, that of 1561. This later version was a principal source for material in the Scottish psalters. Meanwhile, with the return of most of the Protestant exiles to England, psalm singing in the Genevan manner rapidly became a popular means of devotion for gatherings large and small. Queen Elizabeth is said to have referred to these versions of the psalms as 'Geneva jigs' but this may have been an allusion to popular English tunes that were sung to some of the psalms, rather than to the borrowed Genevan melodies. It was usual for the psalms to be sung in unison as they had been in Genevan services: harmonization of these melodies was a separate development, probably for private rather than public use in the first instance at any rate. There may have been some organ accompaniment to congregational use of the psalms in England.

The compilers of English psalters were quick to capitalize on the popularity of psalm singing and the wealth of musical material that could be appropriated to go with it. Numerous editions of metrical psalms with tunes were published from 1560 onwards. The first complete metrical psalter with music to appear in Elizabethan England was John Day's *The whole booke of psalmes, collected into English metre by T. Starnhold I. Hopkins & others* published in 1562. There were 65 tunes in all (some tunes served for more than one psalm) and several of these were from the previous Anglo-Genevan psalters. The first harmonized version came out in 1563: John Day's publication *The whole psalmes in foure partes.* Composers such as Thomas Caustun and William Parsons supplied harmonizations. The tunes were drawn largely from the Anglo-Genevan psalters. These, together with some new tunes and some alternative settings that placed the tune in the Treble or Bass instead of the usual Tenor, made a total of over 140 pieces. This harmonized version may well have been intended for domestic rather than public congregational use, and it was the 1562 monophonic edition that was probably the most widely circulated.

By the late sixteenth century the pattern of borrowing non-native psalm tunes had altered so that fewer new tunes were taken direct from contemporary foreign sources: most were survivals of earlier borrowings in previous English psalters. An isolated exception is Henry Ainsworth's *The book of psalmes Englished both in prose and metre* published in Amsterdam in 1612. In addition to tunes from Anglo-Genevan psalters there are ten tunes newly taken from the French psalter and set to English metrical psalms. Ainsworth's book was intended for the use of an English Separatist community in the Netherlands. Although it may have had some very limited use in England, it is doubtful that its newly-borrowed musical material would have been at all widely disseminated.

John Day's 1562 psalter with tunes went into a total of several hundred editions in just over a hundred years. The texts, by Sternhold, Hopkins and others, were later referred to as the 'Old version' to distinguish them from the 'New version' of Tate and Brady which came out in 1696. The tunes as printed by Day in 1562 acquired the status of 'official' tunes which the Puritan faction preferred to the 'common' tunes, popular melodies to which metrical psalms were also often sung. Both types of tune found their way into the many subsequent metrical psalters, containing both harmonized and unharmonized music, that were published up to the end of the seventeenth century, and some tunes were sufficiently well entrenched to survive beyond the decline in popularity of metrical psalm singing that began in the eighteenth century. [8]

2

Changes in Style: I

Baroque treatment of earlier material

Music borrowed from plainsong and from non-native music other than plain-song retained a secure but not highly significant place in the development of English church music from the 1660s to about 1830, when new ec-clesiastical influences began to take effect. By the early seventeenth century, fashionable taste in music was moving away from polyphony and towards a style in which there was greater variety of texture and enhancement of the importance of treble and bass lines at the expense of inner parts. In church music this is evident in the verse anthems of composers such as Orlando Gibbons (1583–1625), in which instrumental accompaniment in support of vocal solos is an essential feature.

After the restoration of the monarchy in 1660 there was an acceleration in the influence of new Italian and French styles on English music. Some English composers had been trained abroad, such as Walter Porter (c.1587 or c.1595–1659) in Italy and Pelham Humfrey (1647–74) in France. These, together with composers such as John Blow (1649–1708), Henry Purcell (1659–95) and Matthew Locke (1621/2–77), composed church music which, like their theatre music, was much indebted to fashionable continental styles. Their verse anthems in particular are characterized by virtuosic affective vocal solos with a high incidence of word-painting, extended ritornello passages for strings and organ, and choruses in which interest in the part-writing is of markedly less importance than the overall dramatic effect of the harmony. But the indebtedness of these composers to continental influences was one of style rather than substance, and very little borrowing and adaptation of musical material took place at this stage in English anthems and services.

However, the same was not true of metrical psalms. Well-known psalm tunes were borrowed and subjected to extreme adaptation to suit contem-porary fashion, emerging into print as curious incongruities of style in which the original material is sometimes almost unrecognizable. Adaptations of this

kind persisted until well into the nineteenth century. A case in point is the
chequered history of Tallis's eighth psalm-tune, the last of the set written
for Archbishop Matthew Parker's metrical psalter and published in 1567 or
1568. This tune, known as 'Tallis's canon', was originally in double long metre
(entailing a repetition of every phrase) but was turned into long metre (by
omitting the repetitions) in Thomas Ravenscroft's *The whole booke of psalmes*
published in 1621. This is the canonic form in present-day use as a hymn
(EH 267, A&MR 23, MHB 943, SP 45). But by the eighteenth century the tune
was festooned with ornaments and passing-notes so that it became more like
a miniature aria than a psalm tune. In this form it was clearly intended for
a solo vocalist with instrumental accompaniment. Other adaptations
presented the tune curtailed from long metre to common metre. In both cases
the adaptation meant that the canonic property of the tune was lost, chiefly
because of the substitution of an open-ended cadence to the third line. By
the beginning of the nineteenth century Tallis's tune was being perpetuated
under the names 'Brentwood', 'Berwick', 'Suffolk', 'Magdalen' and 'Cannon'
(sic, amazingly, since the canon had disappeared) and attributed to Brent-
bank, of whom nothing seems to be known. Such versions can be found
until at least the mid nineteenth century. The following example, from *A
Collection of Psalm Tunes....compressed into two Lines for the Organ or
Piano Forte* published by Samuel Webbe (junior) c.1808, is typical of the
florid treatment of the tune:

From a twentieth-century point of view it would be natural to deplore adaptations of this kind as inartistic and lacking in respect for the original material. But such a view is tenable only with a twentieth-century sense of historical perspective backed up by a wealth of information and a quest for understanding which, certainly as far as music was concerned, were absent from the prevailing attitudes of the seventeenth and eighteenth centuries. In those days there was little regard for the past: people esteemed only what was currently in fashion. The manifestations of religion, such as its music, were no exception. Thus, if an old but familiar tune seemed tedious, musicians would not have had the slightest hesitation about adapting it to popular taste and the means of performance at their disposal, just as they were content to appropriate other, more up-to-date material. If the matter were considered at all, such borrowing would be seen as a compliment rather than an insult to the original composer, and any adaptation would be perceived as an 'improvement' for a particular purpose, such as a hymn. The idea of a deliberately archaic and artificial 'church style' had not become widespread by this stage.

The practice of borrowing the music of Latin polyphony and adapting it for use with English texts faded out soon after the beginning of the seventeenth century. This was a natural consequence of the change in style of church music towards the more instrumentally-based harmonic style in which treble and bass were distinctly polarized, and in which polyphony had little place. However, the practice was revived towards the end of the century by Henry Aldrich (1647–1710), dean of Christ Church Cathedral, Oxford from

1689 until his death. For his time Aldrich was exceptional, even within the cultivated circle of the university. Despite distinguished activities in many fields of learning he took his deanship seriously and promoted orderliness, discipline and good musicianship in the Christ Church choir at a time when such principles of conduct were not usually practised in choral foundations. He was interested in Italian music and collected examples of it; also he had an unusual liking for polyphonic music which, with an enthusiastic and well-trained choir at his disposal, he was in a good position to indulge. Accordingly he adapted a number of Latin-texted polyphonic works by Palestrina, Victoria, Tallis and Byrd for use as English anthems. He also reshaped and gave new texts to some pre-existent English anthems, and adapted pieces by Carissimi and possibly music by other Italian composers for which the models have not been traced. He took considerable liberties with his adaptations, as a comparison between his anthem 'We have heard with our ears' and its model, Palestrina's 'Doctor bonus et amicus Dei' demonstrates. Aldrich excised some short repeated passages, altered the tonality of the final cadence and densified some of Palestrina's light textures. He also introduced deliberate word-painting on falling and rising melodic lines. In places, Aldrich's adaptation for solos and chorus is scarcely recognizable as Palestrina's motet. Although Aldrich's adaptations were primarily for use by the Christ Church choir, they retain a degree of importance as borrowings in the present context because they won the respect of other more able choirs in later years and achieved wider dissemination through publication. Aldrich himself was much revered as a musician, and was seen in academic church music circles as a worthy successor to Tallis, Byrd, Gibbons and Purcell.[9]

German music

As the seventeenth century progressed, metrical psalm-singing began to lose its appeal, partly because of the largely moribund state of congregational music-making that resulted from disinterest and a lack of musically literate leaders. But the main problem lay in the texts rather than the music. Many of the metrical psalm texts lacked the elegance and expressiveness of contemporary devotional poetry: moreover, the psalms reflected Old Testament values rather than Christian beliefs. Accordingly, freely-composed hymn texts began to be added to metrical psalters. There was no impediment to the informal or domestic use of these hymns even though the established church stedfastly resisted their formal introduction into services. As late as the start of the nineteenth century the prevailing attitude in the established church was one of tolerance rather than wholehearted acceptance of hymns as a means of worship. The new hymn texts used predominantly the same metres as the psalms, so the same tunes could be used to sing them. The most influential of the early hymn writers was Isaac Watts. His collections of hymns, published in the early years of the eighteenth century, marked a radical shift away from the literal and objective interpretation of the psalms and towards a more subjective reflection of the thoughts of the individual Christian worshipper.

Once hymn singing became firmly established, the demand grew for tunes that provided a livelier and more up-to-date reflection of the new type of text, and yet were suitable for congregational use. Some attempt was made to meet this need by recourse to German hymnody, perhaps given greater impetus by the accession of the Hanoverian King George I to the English throne in 1714. A small collection of German hymn-tunes entitled *Lyra Davidica* was published anonymously in 1708, with the purpose of offering material that could replace the more staid psalm tunes. It contained several items that are now well known in England, although it cannot be credited with having led to the introduction of items such as 'Ein' feste Burg' (EH 362, 567, A&MR 183, MHB 494, SP 436) and 'In dulci jubilo' which were known much earlier even though they may have fallen into disuse by the eighteenth century. The best-known tune from *Lyra Davidica* to have survived into present-day use is that sung to 'Jesus Christ is risen today' or 'Christ the Lord is risen today' (EH 133, A&MR 134, SP 145 as 'Easter Hymn', MHB 204 as 'Easter Morn'). The reasons for its immediate acceptance are obvious. It is a strong and memorable tune that is suitable for unison singing. When harmonized, its wide compass calls for a variety of chord-spread within four-part harmony, and this produces interesting inner part-writing. Its refrain, 'alleluia', is florid but not to the extent of defeating a congregational purpose. The ornate and colourful nature of this tune, in line with fashionable musical style, was sufficient to ensure its early and continuous success. Other collections of German hymns were published in England, including the substantial series *Psalmodia Germanica* (1722-1765) compiled by Johann Christian Jacobi, Keeper of the German Chapel in St James's Palace. The tune 'Innsbruck' (EH 86, 278, A&MR 34, MHB 946, SP 57), sung to 'The duteous day now closes' and itself a borrowing from a German secular melody (see below, pp.98–99), came into general use in England by way of a late (c.1765) edition of *Psalmodia Germanica* long before it won final acceptance by virtue of its status in Johann Sebastian Bach's St Matthew and St John Passions.

The dissenting churches that came into being after the restoration of the monarchy in 1660 were responsible to a large extent for the evolution of hymn singing. Although there were constraints on the freedom of dissenters to hold meetings there were, of course, no establishment constraints on the conduct of worship in such meetings, so hymns could be freely used to the extent that they eventually became the central feature of the worship of several dissenting bodies. Of these bodies, the Methodists made the most important and enduring contributions to English hymns and their tunes. Both John and Charles Wesley were greatly influenced by the hymns of the German Moravians with whom they travelled as missionaries to the USA. The German Moravian communities attained a high musical standard. Their repertory included the polyphonic singing of chorales and hymns from collections such as those compiled by Johann Anastasius Freylinghausen, which included much material in the elegant aria-like style that was a feature of much late baroque German hymnody. The Wesley brothers were deeply impressed by this music and by the fervour and liveliness with which it was sung by the Moravians. This led John Wesley to borrow and adapt music from Moravian hymnals for use in his own early publications, which were sold very cheaply and aimed at as broad a social spectrum of potential users as possible. These German tunes, together with adaptations from secular music and hymns composed in similar styles, soon became extremely popular. Despite disapproval by the established church of the supposed frivolity, theatricality and secular associations of these tunes in contrast to those of the old metrical psalms, many of these Methodist tunes outlasted older melodies and found permanent places in the English hymn repertory. One such borrowing from the Moravians is the tune sung to 'Love's redeeming work is done', a text by Charles Wesley. The tune (EH 135, A&MR 141, MHB 87, SP 160) is usually entitled 'Savannah' but John Wesley called it 'Herrnhut' after the headquarters of the Moravians and the location of their manuscript hymn book from which he took the tune. John Wesley first printed it in *A Collection of Tunes Set to Music, As they are commonly Sung at the Foundery* published in 1742, and it was perpetuated in numerous subsequent collections. Its short, graceful phrases, simple structure and climactic final line give it a facility of appeal in profound contrast to the staider attributes of the older psalm tunes, and it is easy to see why borrowed German tunes like this one became firmly established in the affections of English congregations.[10]

Handel

There was one German influence on eighteenth-century music in England that was more far-reaching than the Wesleys' Moravian borrowings or the publications whose specific purpose was to introduce German hymns as such to English worshippers. The consequences of the German composer Georg Friederich Handel's sojourns in England from 1710 were to affect aspects of English music, and in particular sacred music, until around the beginning of the twentieth century. It was very much a case of a composer being in the right place at the right time: the existing social, religious and musical framework in England was such that it was receptive to what Handel had to offer. Handel, for his part, drew on aspects of existing English musical forms and styles, combining them with German baroque and Italian operatic techniques to produce works that were accessible yet forward-looking, so that his music held its place at the pinnacle of English esteem for many years after his death.

Above all it was Handel's oratorios to English texts that endeared him to public taste. His Italian operas were enjoyed by the upper classes of society but the appeal of the oratorios was wider. They offered everything that the emergent English middle classes wanted in music: English narratives based most often on compelling Biblical events, a variety of affective contemplative arias in which soloists could shine, colourful instrumental passages and, to crown the sense of dramatic occasion, grandiose and vivid choruses in which word-painting abounds and in which tension and momentum are often made to increase towards a final majestic climax. Listeners were moved by this music and could identify with the feelings and predicaments of the characters depicted. Moreover, there was the chance to participate: by the 1780s the tradition of performing Handel's oratorios, in particular *Messiah,* with massive choral and orchestral forces had been established, and this meant that larger numbers of musically literate people than ever before could experience the music as performers rather than as listeners. In the early years of the nineteenth century the spread of musical literacy widened the pool of potential performers to include women, for whom public performance in oratorio (as opposed to opera) was considered respectable. The proliferation of choral festivals and choral societies that typified mid nineteenth-century English corporate music-making was largely based on Handel's oratorios.

Whether or not the oratorios on Biblical texts can properly be regarded as sacred music is another matter. Their roots were in theatre music and their aim was to provide entertainment rather than a means of devotion. Attitudes towards *Messiah* in particular, on its first London performance in 1743, were ambivalent. Some thought the subject too sacred to allow performance in the theatre. Others felt that a theatre audience, however profane, was bound to be uplifted and improved by the experience. Evangelical clergy such as the Revd. John Newton, the former slave-trader who became incumbent of St Mary Woolnoth, London, in 1780, were highly critical of *Messiah.* Newton made the scriptural passages set by Handel the subjects of a whole year's sermons in order to redeem them from supposed secular associations. He warned his congregation regularly against supposedly sacred pieces which people went to hear for primarily secular reasons. Whatever the original intention of Handel's oratorios had been, they were soon elevated to the status of sacred music and as such commanded a position of respect and reverence — not to say adulation — that remained unparalleled in England before or since. Perhaps, strictly speaking, they should be considered as secular music together with other works by Handel, particularly the operas, from which English church music was to borrow material. But the important point here is that they were *perceived,* rather than conceived, as sacred music, and borrowings from them were undertaken from that point of view.

Handel himself was no stranger to musical borrowing. He borrowed from his own and from other composers' works: over half the choruses in the oratorio *Israel in Egypt* incorporate borrowings adapted by Handel in an age when plagiarism and 'improvement' were regarded by the perpetrators as ingenuity rather than theft. By the same token, sections from Handel's own works, particularly the Italian operas produced in England, were considered fair game for appropriation by his commercial rivals in theatrical circles. In this context it is hardly surprising that Handel's oratorios on sacred subjects, as well as his substantial anthems, should have provided material for use as hymns, anthems and psalms in the English church.

Oratorio choruses were the obvious choice for use where there was even the semblance of a choir, and Handel's scoring could be adapted for the forces available. Sometimes this meant the omission of one or more parts: inevitably some such omissions had to be coped with on the spot but there were editions that catered for limited forces by stripping the part-writing down to the absolute minimum number of musicians needed to utter the piece at all in a barely recognizable form. Adaptations of duets and arias were much in vogue when soloists were available. The aspirations of soloists may well have on occasions exceeded their musical abilities, but it was not unknown for soloists or a group of singers to be imported to a church or chapel for a special occasion that would be enhanced by music. Sometimes adaptation affected not only the disposition of the part-writing, but the shape of the music itself. The church music historian John Skelton Bumpus, writing in 1908, describes with thinly-veiled acrimony some late eighteenth and early nineteenth-century extracts from Handel's oratorios, mutilated for church use. These include the adaptations made by Thomas Pitt of Worcester and published in 1789. Pitt took selections from Handel's oratorios and put them into groups so that these groups could then be used as verse anthems. He shortened some of the movements 'to obviate any objection which might arise from prolixity', arranging for 'diapasons' what remained of the instrumental writing. From *Messiah* Pitt took the chorus 'For unto us a child is born' as the last movement of a verse anthem for Christmas Day, cutting over a quarter of its total length and omitting its short opening symphony altogether. He used the 4/4 version of the aria 'Rejoice greatly' to begin another anthem, reducing it to less than half its usual length and rendering the opening symphony so short that it does little more than give the note and tempo for singing to begin. Another editor, Hugh Bond of Exeter, treated Handel's Chandos anthems likewise. Not all editors went to the lengths (or rather, brevities) described above in their adaptations, and many remained relatively faithful to their originals.

During the late eighteenth and early nineteenth centuries collections of psalm tunes proliferated, often compiled by a local music teacher (who probably also directed the music in church) for use in a particular area. Adaptations from Handel's oratorios often figured prominently in these collections, the aim of which was to breathe new life into psalm singing that had become sluggish and slovenly and in which ornamental flourishes for the organ between each sung line had become increasingly common. One such psalm adaptation, based on the aria from *Messiah* 'I know that my redeemer liveth' and simply entitled 'Messiah', appears in the popular and influential volume *Psalms of David* published in 1790 by George Hay Drummond and Edward Miller. In this adaptation, the distinctive opening phrase of the aria is used twice, with a conventional cadential phrase added to each occurrence to make a common-metre (8 6 8 6) tune. The text is part of Psalm 146:

> The Lord who made both heav'n and earth,
> And all that they contain,
> Will never quit his stedfast truth,
> Nor make his promise vain.
>
> (Three further verses)

Another, based on the aria 'He shall feed his flock', also from *Messiah,* appears in *A Collection of Psalm Tunes* of c.1808, compiled by Samuel Webbe junior. In this example Handel's music is presented in an extremely condensed form without any of the repetitions from the aria. Yet, despite some changes, Handel's harmony and a semblance of his accompanimental part-writing are mostly retained. So are the characteristic lilting rhythm and above all Handel's irregular groupings of two-bar sequential phrases, which give the music its life and individuality:

Seventy years later the sentiment of part of the aria's text had been restored but at heavy cost to the music, as the next example shows. William Walsham How, the co-editor of *Church Hymns*, supplied the dynamic markings for each line. In the musical adaptation by Sir Arthur Sullivan or one of his collaborators dating from 1874 (in *Church Hymns with Tunes* which by 1905 had sold 62,000 copies) the vestiges of Handel's aria are forced into a metrical straitjacket by the curtailment of phrases and the substitution of conventional nineteenth-century hymn closes for Handel's elegant cadences. The lilting rhythm and intriguingly asymmetrical phrase groupings have gone and the melody is grossly mutilated, yet enough has survived to make this a popular hymn with congregations for whom the annual performance of *Messiah* was probably the musical highlight of the year.

p   'Come unto Me, ye weary,
        And I will give you rest.'
m   Oh, Blessed voice of Jesus,
m   Which comes to hearts opprest!
        It tells of benediction,
        Of pardon, grace, and peace,
f   Of joy that hath no ending, ⎱
f   Of love which cannot cease. ⎰ twice

        'Come unto Me, ye wanderers,
        And I will give you light.'

m Oh, loving voice of Jesus,
    Which comes to cheer the night!
pp Our hearts were filled with sadness,
    And we had lost our way,
cr But morning brings us gladness, ⎱
f And songs the break of day. ⎰ twice

(Two further verses)

Other borrowings from Handel's oratorios were adapted initially as psalm tunes and subsequently found their way into the anthem and hymn repertories, often at first by way of the dissenting churches. One or two bordered on the bizarre, such as the bass aria 'The people that walked in darkness' from *Messiah,* current by 1829 as a bass hymn with upper harmonies. The common-metre tune 'Solomon' (EH 80, MHB 561, SP 110) usually sung to 'My God, I love thee; not because I hope for heaven thereby' is an adaptation of the aria 'What though I trace each herb and flower' from *Solomon,* first performed in 1749. 'Brunswick' (EH 555, SP 297, 450) is an adaptation of 'Sin not, O king', an aria from *Saul.* The oratorio was first performed in 1739 and the adaptation had appeared in print by 1760. The adaptation is less than half the length of the aria, omitting all repetitions and all the brief instrumental linking passages that make the phrasing of the aria less ponderous than that of the hymn tune. Apart from that the hymn version is relatively faithful to the original, retaining the mixolydian modal element that characterizes the first two phrases of the aria. One of the most popular Handel borrowings, 'Maccabeus' (MHB 213), the tune to 'Thine be the glory', is an adaptation of the chorus 'See, the conquering hero comes' from *Judas Maccabeus,* first performed in 1747. John Wesley approved the adaptation of this chorus to 'Christ the Lord is risen today'. Its straightforward harmony, memorable melody and refrain form make this chorus an obvious candidate for adaptation as a hymn of jubilant nature, in contrast to many of the other Handel borrowings. It is noticeable that borrowings from Handel (as distinct from hymn tunes composed as such by him) have only rarely appeared in volumes of *Hymns Ancient and Modern.* This is unlikely to reflect disapproval of borrowed music, since borrowings from secular and other sacred sources have appeared there.[11]

Later sacred sources

Borrowings from Handel's works headed a spate of borrowings from other music with sacred texts, particularly the large choral works of composers such as Joseph Haydn (1732-1809), Wolfgang Amadeus Mozart (1756-91),

Ludwig van Beethoven (1770–1827) and in later years Felix Mendelssohn (1809–47), Franz Liszt (1811–86) and Johannes Brahms (1833–97). Most sources for such borrowings came from the German tradition or some derivative of it, the most frequent exceptions being music by Gioachino Rossini (1792–1868) and Charles Gounod (1818–93). Many anthems were, and still are, almost note-for-note transcriptions of choruses from large choral works, with English texts underlaid and with orchestral accompaniments adapted usually for organ. Most of these, largely because of their size, entered the anthem repertory rather than that of the hymn or the psalm. Some, such as 'The heavens are telling' from Haydn's *Creation,* reflect the sentiment of the original piece despite the impoverishment of effect that is the result of taking them out of their larger contexts. Others, like 'Hear me when I call', an anthem fashioned from the Kyrie of Hummel's first mass in B flat op.77, show scant regard for the original context by the incongruous texts that are used.

The growth of the anthem repertory coincided with and was stimulated by an increase in the availability of inexpensive editions of choral music, many of which were published by the London firm of Novello. This firm also published the monthly journal *The Musical Times* from the journal's inception in 1844. With every issue of the journal a vocal music supplement was provided free of charge to purchasers. Often the supplement consisted of an anthem, which might be an adaptation from a choral work by Handel, Haydn, Mozart or Beethoven. As supplements to a widely-read journal these choral pieces achieved a breadth of dissemination that would have been less likely in other circumstances. Smaller pieces, such as Mendelssohn's motets, were also published for use in the English church, although it seems that almost none of even these smaller pieces with a sacred origin ever made the transfer from anthem or psalm to hymn, as some of the earlier borrowings from Handel did.

Hymns and metrical psalm-settings that consisted of borrowings from sacred sources in the nineteenth century had, unlike anthems, usually originated as self-contained pieces rather than as sections of larger works. Some came about as part of the revival of interest in music for the Anglican church that began about the middle of the century. In the Nonconformist churches, too, there was increasing dissatisfaction with some of the lighter eighteenth-century tunes used for psalms. A notable attempt to remedy this was made by Henry Allon, minister at the Union Chapel, Islington in London. His organist was Henry John Gauntlett, a man of diverse musical knowledge who was personally acquainted with Mendelssohn and Samuel Wesley and who was an advocate of early music, including plainsong and the organ works of Bach. Allon and Gauntlett established a psalmody class at Islington, and collaborated in the publication of the *Congregational Psalmist* in 1856. In this work, tunes were revived from the early psalters, and some French and German tunes were brought in. The latter included the tune for 'We plough the fields, and scatter' (EH 293, A&MR 483, MHB 963, SP 14), entitled 'Dresden' but usually known in hymn-books as 'Wir pfluegen', by Johann Abraham Peter Schulz, which had first appeared in a German school songbook of 1800. Sometimes Gauntlett took the start of an older tune that appealed to him and then devised a different continuation to make a new hymn tune. This entailed a degree of composition that places some of Gauntlett's work on the border between borrowing of existing material and composing in a borrowed style.

A monumental collection of psalm and hymn tunes that included much material borrowed from sacred musical sources was published in 1872. This was Samuel Sebastian Wesley's *The European Psalmist,* which can be seen as the culmination and in some ways the conclusion of a long and diverse musical tradition of metrical psalmody, although it contains numerous hymns also. It took Wesley over twenty years to compile the collection, during which time church music in England had begun to branch out in new directions including the revival of plainsong and Latin polyphony, developments with which Wesley had little sympathy. By the time Wesley's collection was published the first complete edition of *Hymns Ancient and Modern* of 1861 had already become established in church use. As the most comprehensive book of tunes then available it rapidly supplanted most of its rivals and made Wesley's collection virtually redundant, despite its different purpose.

It was unfortunate that changing tastes and circumstances should have over-taken Wesley's volume, for it had much to offer despite its retrospective nature. Everything about it militated against the unthinking acceptance of the then modern Victorian hymn tune. The title reflected the stress on psalms rather than hymns, and the layout was that of some older psalters in which the tune with its bass was set out for organ and the inner vocal parts given separately above so that in verses after the first, all singers would have had to refer to a separate book of words. Music by popular Victorian hymn composers such as Dykes and Monk was pointedly omitted, and substitutes offered for some of their best-known tunes. About a quarter of the tunes are by Wesley himself but most of the total of 615 are borrowings, almost exclusively from sacred sources. To many of these tunes Wesley added his own harmonies and then put 'S. S. W.' at the top as though he had been responsible for the entire composition, so not all his borrowings are easy to detect. Most of the tunes have German origins: in some cases they are designated merely as 'German', in others Wesley was more specific although his assertions are not always reliable. The names that Wesley assigned apparently arbitrarily to some tunes are apt to confuse matters further.

Many tunes in *The European Psalmist* are taken from hymn books of the United Brethren (Moravians) whose music had so deeply impressed John and Charles Wesley; from their books Samuel Sebastian Wesley selected German sixteenth-century Reformation hymns and wherever possible gave them with harmonies by Johann Sebastian Bach, whose music he revered. One example is the tune known nowadays as 'Passion Chorale' (EH 102, A&MR 111, MHB 202, 768, SP 128), which appears as no.393 in Wesley's collection to words beginning 'Lord, grant me thy protection, remind me of thy death', entitled 'Dresden', drawn from 'Hy. U. B. 102' and attributed 'H. G. Haszler. 1610. Sebn. Bach'. Sometimes several harmonizations of this kind of tune are given. Many of the harmonizations in *The European Psalmist* are by Wesley himself. The fact that he rarely lapsed into fashionable mellifluous blandness in these harmonizations demonstrates his keen perception and understanding of the styles of material he had borrowed from former times. Despite his intolerance of much church music it is clear that Wesley was prepared to forgive in Bach what he might condemn in others. In a comment accompanying one of Bach's harmonizations in *The European Psalmist* Wesley administered the mildest possible rebuke: 'The [consecutive] 5ths in this beautiful passage may have escaped Bach's notice'. Wesley acknowledged his debt to other collectors, notably Catherine Winkworth (see below, pp.73–74), who were doing much to make the use of German hymns in England more widespread. Apart from German hymns *The European Psalmist* included tunes from sixteenth-century English psalters, from Handel (including 'Brunswick' cited above) and from Orlando Gibbons (his settings in George Wither's *Hymns and songs of the church* of 1623), sometimes adapted in order to change the metre or to smooth out rhythmic irregularities.

Although Wesley amassed an impressive array of subscribers to support his venture and even resorted to bribery in order to secure good reviews for it, *The European Psalmist* did not accomplish its part in his mission to reform English church music, and by the end of the nineteenth century it was virtually forgotten. Subsequent developments vindicated many of Wesley's aims if not his methods of achieving them, particularly his attitude to the presentation and use of borrowed material. But his collection, though valuable, was in many ways idiosyncratic. Far from sowing the seeds of a new movement in church music as Wesley had hoped, *The European Psalmist* marked the end of an era.[12]

3

The Romantic Revival

Introduction

One of the effects of the nineteenth-century Romantic movement was a change in intellectual attitude towards works of art, literature and music of former times. This came about partly as a reaction to the secularization, mechanization and materialism that went hand in hand with the increasing prosperity of all but the poorest classes in Victorian England. Many cultured people conceived the romantic idea of a distant past; of medieval times in which the pace of life was slower and more serene, and in which works of art of all kinds were the pure, high-minded productions of innocent beings untainted by the pursuit of fashion, social favour or money. Although this sentimentalized and idealized view of medieval life embodied a good deal more fantasy than reality, one of its lasting benefits was the dawning of a sense of historical perspective and the beginnings of respect for the artistry of the past. With this went a zeal for collecting, cataloguing, investigating and imitating the art, literature and music of the remote past, given greater impetus by new attitudes towards education and self-improvement, activities that many affluent and benevolent Victorians were keen to promote.

In music, notwithstanding a few notable exceptions such as Henry Aldrich at Oxford (see above, pp.45-46), scant attention had been paid before the nineteenth century to composers of the past apart from descriptions by chroniclers such as Charles Burney (1726-1814) and Sir John Hawkins (1719-89), whose attitudes were bigoted and sometimes derisive. From the early 1830s, however, a new and more objective attitude towards music history began to prevail. Research into the sources of early music started in earnest and the results were published, marking the beginnings of the discipline of musicology. But there were pitfalls which, in retrospect, seem obvious but which early musicologists and editors could hardly have been expected to take into account. First, they were mostly scholarly amateurs working in isolation and without training, so their efforts were limited in scope and not co-ordinated towards any universally-accepted standards. Second, they did not recognize the importance of authentic performance practice, relying more on idealized supposition than on historical evidence. Third, they fell prey to an evolutionary view of music which denied that the pinnacles of achievement in any one artistic movement were worthy of esteem on their own terms, and which assessed them only as part of a stream of continuous development culminating in the music of the nineteenth century. Thus they wrote patronizingly of composers such as Tallis, whose work they saw as little more than a primitive striving towards the sophistication of nineteenth-century harmony — the kind of music the early composers would have written if only they had known how. Accordingly, early editors felt it their duty to smooth away earlier composers' 'mistakes', substituting bland musical platitudes in a somewhat faceless academic contrapuntal style that they thought was the means of expression aspired to by all early polyphonic sacred music. These attitudes affected many musical editions and performances of early music, including those produced for English church use in the nineteenth century (see below, pp.183ff.).

The Romantic movement had its effect on the conduct of worship in the English church. In parallel with an idealized view of the distant past in the arts, the idea grew up that much would be gained by the revival of ecclesiastical practices of former times. The problem for the Protestant church of England was that any such revival inevitably entailed conduct that was reminiscent of Roman Catholicism, a persuasion whose manifestations were abhorrent to many worshippers. Much heated controversy grew out of this dilemma, which persisted well beyond the close of the nineteenth century in its effect on the choice of music for worship. Antiquarian predilections began to influence church music early in the century and some of the old metrical psalm tunes were deliberately revived and sung in four-part harmony. Plainsong, because of its medieval associations, was once more put to use, edited with English words. Early church music (which in this context means unaccompanied polyphony and plainsong) was considered to represent the 'sublime' style: the ideal to which all music for church use should aspire. This theory of a single 'sublime' style took no account of the rich diversity of polyphonic composition, and gave rise to the artificial and almost characterless type of counterpoint that early editors believed to represent the best in church music (see below, pp.176ff.).

In these ways a start had been made in the borrowing or revival of early music for use in the English church before the rise of the Tractarian movement, which was influential from the 1830s. Among the widespread concerns of the Tractarians was the reverend and dignified conduct of ceremonial customs in church, based as far as they could determine on pre-Reformation usage but with English rather than Latin texts. An altar cross became the focus of worship, and the use of vestments and incense enhanced the atmosphere of holiness. In addition, the practice grew in Tractarian-influenced churches large and small of putting the choir at a distance from the congregation at the approach to the altar. Members of the choir wore robes and were placed in choir-stalls if possible. Both choir and congregation learnt to regard beautiful, disciplined music-making as a fitting adjunct to worship. The Society for Promoting Church Music, with its monthly journal *The Parish Choir* which ran from 1846 to 1851, advocated Tractarian ideals. The journal contained advice on the organization and training of choirs together with useful material for choirs to sing. These included settings of plainsong, to be sung by the congregation in unison supported where possible by a choir singing in harmony.[13]

Plainsong: the beginnings

Attempts in the late 1830s to introduce the Gregorian plainsong tones for the congregational chanting of psalms met with only limited success. Even where a trained choir could lead the singing the congregation found it difficult to come to terms with the unfamiliar idiom. In the 1840s plainsong psalters began to be published for congregational use. They were generally unharmonized, and presented the chant in a heavily adapted form. The following example shows Richard Redhead's adaptation of the fifth plainsong psalm tone from an 1841 supplement to his *Church Music: a Selection of Chants, Sanctuses and Responses* of 1840, parallel to the plainsong tone (given above), transposed down a tone:

Where harmonized settings were published they were sometimes of a colourful Victorian cast. In churches with an organ it is not unlikely that the
organist would have supported unison plainsong with improvised harmonies
in a similarly modern style. Barlines were used in these adaptations of plainsong, suggesting a lack of understanding of its unmeasured nature on the
part of the editors. For example in another publication by Redhead in 1859,
the Magnificat is set to the eighth psalm tone used as the treble to a four-
square harmonization replete with chromaticisms and changes in texture
almost like a partsong, which obliterate all the natural stresses of the chant.
It is easy to condemn this adaptation of borrowed plainsong as a travesty
but in its own time it was an expedient, just as Robert Crowley's and similar
settings of psalm tones had been at the time of Edward VI. Probably the most
significant contribution to a better understanding of plainsong in the mid
nineteenth century was the work of William Dyce, who in 1843 published
The order of daily service ... with plaintune. This was an adaptation of
Merbecke's 1550 *Book of common prayer noted* for use with current services. In a preface and appendix to it published in 1844 Dyce discussed the
adaptation of plainsong to English words, advocating a method that echoed
what Merbecke had sought to do three hundred years earlier. Dyce's work
provided the impetus for the later widespread adoption of Merbecke's music,
and laid the foundations for unmeasured settings of English texts to plainsong.

The brothers Thomas and Frederick Helmore did a great deal to promote
the understanding of plainsong and to disseminate its use in English churches. While a student at Oxford in 1845, Frederick Helmore had been hor-
rified to find that settings to plainsong at a local church were sung so that
every note was counted out to its exact face value of a breve, making the
music inordinately slow and exhausting to sing. Thereupon he organized
study groups for plainsong, and spent the rest of his life training choirs all
over Great Britain in the revival of plainsong and other early church music.
Thomas Helmore, a passionate advocate of the 'sublime' style in church
music, was in charge of the music at St Mark's College, Chelsea, London;
where teachers for church schools were trained. By the mid 1840s students
at the college were proficient in the singing of polyphony and plainsong,
and their expertise aided the spread of these skills to churches and schools
where they subsequently found employment. From 1843 Thomas Helmore
published his own editions of plainsong, at first with barlines and harmony
but later without, following the method put forward by Dyce. *The Psalter
Noted*, published in 1849, was incorporated the following year into *A Manual
of Plainsong*, which included other service music also. Helmore presented
plainsong unaccompanied, on a four-line stave in stemless notation, with

every syllable given its own separate note (even dividing up the reciting notes in this way) to avoid ambiguity in performance by congregations or choirs unpractised in pointing the psalms. *A Manual of Plainsong* rapidly became the standard book where plainsong was used in the English church and it went through numerous editions and revisions, not being superseded in authority until around the start of the twentieth century.[14]

Plainsong: dissemination

The revival of plainsong by the English church was not an isolated occurrence. Similar revivals were taking place concurrently in Europe, most notably in Bavaria, Belgium and France, and in the Roman Catholic church in England. The fruits of these revivals had a small but lasting influence on English church music. For example the group of 'Mechlin melodies', brought to England in the late nineteenth century and used in *The English Hymnal* of 1906 (2, 154 ii, 326 and SP 280) are from a series of plainsong books published at Mechlin (Malines) in Belgium in the mid nineteenth century. Some of the 'French church melodies' in *The English Hymnal* are ultimately derived from plainsong (for example EH 191, SP 28 ii); the revival of plainsong in France antedated that in England by about forty years and culminated in the enormously influential work of the Benedictines of Solesmes. It is noticeable that these hymns borrowed into the English repertory by way of plainsong revivals in Europe sometimes transmit little more than an echo of the plainsong melody. The phrases tend to be more regular and the melodies less diffuse than those of the chants from which they are reputedly derived, showing a high degree of compromise between an early version and one that would win popular acceptance centuries later.

The revival of plainsong in the Roman Catholic church in England owed much to the work of Vincent Novello who, starting in the 1840s, collected many Latin plainsong hymns and published them with piano accompaniments, presumably with the intention that they should be used by families at home as well as at church. His piano accompaniments were in a typical mid nineteenth-century style with mild chromaticisms and, where possible, modulations. For example Novello's version of the Whitsuntide hymn 'Veni Creator Spiritus', published c.1850, has different colourful harmonies for each of its four verses, with an alternative harmonization to the fourth verse for use at Paschal time. Novello's work influenced some of the pioneers of the plainsong revival in the English church. During the 1840s, the revival was widened in Tractarian circles of the established church by the addition of Latin hymns. This was a bolder step at that time than it would appear to be nowadays. Hymns, since they were neither psalms nor part of the liturgy and thus had no recognized authority in church, were associated with non-conformity, and the doctrines expressed in many Latin hymns were considered highly suspect. But precisely because they were non-liturgical, they could be incorporated without altering the framework of the English service, at the same time opening up a vast repertory from the traditions of a distant past.

Of those who worked on translating the texts of Latin medieval hymns into English, John Mason Neale (1818–66) was clearly the most outstanding and many of his translations are still in use. He favoured a recourse to pre-Reformation hymns and his gifted and scholarly translations into English retain their original metres and rhythms so that they could be used with their original melodies. Neale's work was embodied in *The hymnal noted* published in two parts: the first, containing 46 hymns mostly from the Sarum Use, in 1851; the second, containing 59 hymns from various medieval sources, in 1854. In these volumes he collaborated with Thomas Helmore, who was responsible for transcribing and editing the plainsong. The music is presented in two parallel forms of notation. The plainsong melody is given on four lines in unmeasured stemless notes using the archaic C clef. The accompaniment, clearly for keyboard, is given in modern notation: unlike some later plainsong accompaniments it adopts a fairly rapid harmonic pace but unlike some contemporaneous ones it is modal, reflecting the character of the plainsong as far as possible without forcing it into a key or bedecking it with incongruous chromatic harmonies. Both Latin and English texts are underlaid. Although Neale's collection was not widely adopted at the time of its publication its value and integrity were demonstrated by its repeated use as a source for hymns some fifty years later when plainsong achieved a degree of wider understanding and acceptance in the English church. Perhaps its best-known legacy is the Advent hymn 'O come, O come, Emmanuel' (tune at EH 8, SP 66, but only A&MR 49 and MHB 257 use Neale's translation, slightly altered). This appeared in the 1854 volume where the tune was stated by Helmore to have been copied by Neale with the 'Veni, veni, Emmanuel' words from a French missal in the National Library, Lisbon. This missal has never been traced.

The path towards a wider acceptance of plainsong was not without obstacles. Some eminent church musicians, among them Frederick Ouseley (see below, pp.178ff.), disapproved of its use because it admitted the congregation, and not the choir only, to worship in song. Samuel Sebastian Wesley disliked plainsong chanting, advocating instead the use of mainly German and English psalm tunes as demonstrated in *The European Psalmist* (see above, pp.57–58). Many of the laity were antipathetic towards plainsong:

some found its austerity uncongenial in contrast to the familiar idiom of contemporary hymn tunes, others found plainsong and its accompanying ceremonial uncomfortably reminiscent of Roman Catholicism. At its worst extreme this latter attitude precipitated mob violence, but even where reactions fell short of this the use of plainsong or its eschewal reinforced the divisions between so-called 'high' and 'low' factions in the English church.

Meanwhile, efforts continued to render plainsong acceptable to congregations. Many churches used adaptations of Merbecke's settings, editions of which proliferated after the start made by Dyce. Another compromise was the elaboration of organ accompaniments surrounding plainsong sung by the congregation, particularly at moments when chanting on a monotone took place. At these moments it was not uncommon for organists to indulge in successions of harmonies with a scalic bass-line, sometimes actually incorporating modulations in which the monotone provided a pivot as a kind of upper pedal note. In principle this is reminiscent of the method of composition around a *cantus firmus* that church musicians had used centuries beforehand. Books on the art of organ accompaniment expounded methods for accompanying plainsong and monotones. This use of the organ provided a means of stabilizing the pitch and pace of congregational chanting, at the same time mitigating the austerity of the plainsong with harmonies which, though totally out of keeping with the plainsong, had some appeal for those who were singing it.

The use of plainsong in this way as a thread running through a more elaborate musical texture found a place also in music for choirs. For example Charles Wood (1866–1926) used plainsong melodies as the basis of canticles and anthems. The usual pattern in the canticles, such as the Magnificat on the sixth tone and the Nunc dimittis on the fifth tone, published in 1911, is to present the chant initially in unison against a sparse organ texture, introducing greater complexity for both organ and voices as the piece progresses. Wood treats the chant itself freely, allowing contractions, simplifications and deviations where these will enrich the texture or overall harmonic scheme. The anthem 'In exitu Israel' of 1924, based on the Tonus Peregrinus, is stricter in its use of the chant melody. Two plainsong melodies are used in Wood's *St Mark Passion* (1921), his largest work for church use.[15]

Plainsong: presentation

Leaving aside the use of plainsong as the basis for elaboration at the organ or as part of music for choir use, its position by the 1860s was established as the sole or topmost musical part rather than as an inner melody, as had been predominantly the case in the sixteenth century. This was largely the result of principles used by Neale and Helmore: in their accompanied editions the keyboard part gives the chant greatest prominence, providing only a subdued harmonic background to unison singing by a large body of people. It was this method of presenting and performing plainsong that was taken up in the first complete edition of *Hymns Ancient and Modern* (1861), which contained 132 versions of Latin hymns, many drawn from *The hymnal noted.* In later editions these hymns were less predominant. Various experiments were tried, both with the use of barlines and forms of notation, and with different harmonizations. Interestingly, these changes reflect a shift in the stance of the book. In the 1875 revision the plainsong harmonizations are modified in line with popular taste, but in the 1904 revision the plainsongs are presented more accurately and re-harmonized in a more austere manner, the aim of the book being not to appeal to popular taste but to elevate it. But the 1904 revision was a failure and demand continued for the 1875 version. *A plainsong hymnbook,* based on the 1904 revisions and published in 1932, although accurate and scholarly, similarly made almost no impact on congregations. *Hymns Ancient and Modern Revised*, published in 1950, reinforced the standards of the 1904 edition in the presentation of plainsong. The 43 plainsong melodies are given in modern notation but without conventional barlines so that no metrical stress is implied. The keyboard accompaniments are sparse in texture and smooth in movement, to the extent that the bass is more like a countermelody than the product of chordal harmonization. The musical preface to the book provides detailed instruction on notation, method of singing and accompaniment; however, it is impossible to say to what extent the inclusion of plainsong in the various editions of *Hymns Ancient and Modern* has been reflected in its utilization in church.

A different method of commending borrowed plainsong for use in the English church was tried out in *The Yattendon Hymnal,* edited by Robert Bridges and Harry Ellis Wooldridge, published in 1899. This book was uncompromising in its intellectual and aesthetic approach. Extravagantly presented in an archaically-styled typeface with decorative motifs, its quarto size (most hymnals with music are sextodecimo) may indeed have been chosen to make its use at the keyboard difficult and by the congregation impossible: the latter were to use only a wordbook if they sang at all. *The Yattendon Hymnal* contains 100 hymns of which thirteen are plainsong. The texts are given in Latin and in English translations by Bridges. The plainsong music takes obvious pride of place in the book: it is printed on red four-line staves in unmeasured stemless notation with ligatures and old forms of C and F clefs. The underlaid texts start with large red initial letters. On the facing page, the same plainsong is given as the topmost voice of an unaccompanied harmonization for four voices, in measured notation but without barlines except to mark phrase-endings, and in C clefs (rather than G and tenor G clefs) for the inner parts. The harmony is in a very simple note-for-note modal style reminiscent of some plainsong borrowings in sixteenth-century England, yet lacking the character and poise of those by composers such as Tallis and Byrd. The book's preface and detailed notes to each hymn give some idea of the editors' point of view. Harmonies are supplied 'with some attempt towards the particular qualities of workmanship upon which much of the beauty of the old vocal counterpoint depends'. Harmonies to plainsong are given to help choirs that find unison singing wasteful to get to know plainsong tunes, and it is suggested that all parts should memorize the tune first to understand the essential rhythmical freedom. As to the style of the harmonizations, '.... the best harmonic treatment which they can have is the Palestrinal'. The editors considered the 'Palestrinal' (sic) to be the earliest 'complete' system that nevertheless depended on modality. Accordingly their workings are pastiche, not so far removed from the so-called 'sublime' style (see below, pp.176ff.), of what a sixteenth-century composer might have done with plainsong, rather than an attempt to present plainsong on its own terms shadowed by an unobtrusive modal harmonic background. Understandably, *The Yattendon Hymnal* did not commend itself to ordinary parish use, so its practical influence was narrow. Its importance lies rather in its position as a precursor to other hymnals which made some of its borrowings more accessible.

Two further important hymnals presented borrowed plainsong in a deliberately archaic fashion. *Songs of Syon,* edited by George Ratcliffe Woodward and first published in 1904 was musically diverse and ambitious. Woodward adopted an Anglo-Catholic stance, organizing the book in terms of the feasts of the church's year including some for the Virgin Mary. At the start of each section, unharmonized plainsong in archaic notation takes obvious precedence: the notation and use of decorated initials distinguish it from other material. It is left unharmonized on the grounds that opinions differ over the correct style of harmonization and that organists may prefer to devise their own harmonies, although the absence of an accompaniment is recognized as better than an incompetent one. Latin texts are not given. Woodward supplied some of the translations himself, others he drew from Neale's work. *The Oxford Hymn Book,* published in 1908, was prepared by a group of Oxford dons and clerics. Basil Harwood, organist of Christ Church, edited the music. Like *The Yattendon Hymnal* it is historically well documented and uses a deliberately archaic style of typeface, although the layout is much more practical and the possibility of organ accompaniment is admitted. *The Oxford Hymn Book* has a number of plainsong hymns including a group of fifty in Latin only, in plainsong notation with organ accompaniment beneath. Where English translations are given (including several by Neale), a second tune appears as an alternative to the plainsong, a policy also adopted in *The English Hymnal*. The plainsong harmonizations are for accompaniment only. Although it is of considerable historical interest *The Oxford Hymn Book* seems esoteric in outlook and had little influence in promoting plainsong for general church use.

The same cannot be said of *The English Hymnal,* first published in 1906. Like *The Yattendon Hymnal* and the 1904 revision of *Hymns Ancient and Modern* its aim was to elevate popular taste as well as appealing to the intellectual, but it succeeded in winning acceptance where they failed. This was largely because of the enterprizing diversity of the material used and the practicality of its presentation. Ralph Vaughan Williams, who edited the music, believed passionately in the ability and the right of congregations to join in musical performance, with the proviso that they should sing only in unison. Thus plainsong was an obvious candidate for inclusion in *The English Hymnal,* although Vaughan Williams modestly disclaimed understanding of it and obtained editorial help from William John Birkbeck for the 1906 edition and John Henry Arnold for that of 1933. The plainsong items, with English versions by a number of translators, are mostly given for use on the occasions appropriate to them: particular feasts in the church's year, or as part of 'Sacraments and other rites'. In most cases an alternative modern tune is given, but the majority of these tunes are 'modern' only in the sense that they postdate the chants appearing alongside them. The plainsong is drawn wherever possible from English sources and presented in a clear, simplified form similar to that revived by the Benedictines of Solesmes, which is practical in use. Parallel to the plainsong notation, the melody is set out as the topmost line of a keyboard harmonization in which the aim has been to shadow the plainsong melody with unobtrusive harmony in which there is relatively little movement in the inner parts but in which the mobile bassline, changing with nearly every note of the melody, is sometimes more reminiscent of conventional nineteenth-century hymn bass movement. Where necessary the music of the keyboard version, from the top line of which the congregation would generally sing, is transposed from the plainsong version to bring it easily within the compass of most untrained voices. Barlines indicate phrase-ends only, and the keyboard notation, in minims but with beams where the plainsong has ligatures, is a workable solution to the difficult problem of representing unmeasured music in notation that is essentially measured. In the 1933 edition the notation and harmonizations are brought into line with those of *Songs of Praise* except that plainsong notation is retained in a separate upper line parallel to the keyboard accompaniment.

Songs of Praise, first published in 1926 with Ralph Vaughan Williams and Martin Shaw as musical editors, has a smaller proportion of plainsong melodies and adopts a different style of presentation for them. Plainsong notation is not used; instead, the melody is presented only as the topmost part of the keyboard accompaniment, thus abandoning the principle of showing where material has been transposed. The accompanying harmonies, mostly by John Henry Arnold, are sparser in both texture and degree of movement than those in the 1906 *English Hymnal,* allowing the contours of the plainsong melody a greater degree of prominence. The bass moves only when necessary to underpin an essential new harmony, and angular bass movement is kept to a minimum. The music is notated in quavers. Beaming represents ligatures but flags are used for the rest of the notes, giving the *Songs of Praise* plainsong borrowings a somewhat cluttered appearance. Although *Hymns Ancient and Modern* in its various editions outweighed in sales and popularity all other hymnals including *The English Hymnal* and *Songs of Praise,* these latter two were more influential in widening the scope of hymns in congregational use. Plainsong, as presented in them, is made as accessible as possible with the minimum degree of compromise.

Some attitudes to the use of plainsong

Opinions continued to differ, not only about the best method of presenting plainsong for congregational use, but about whether or not it should be used at all. The 'high' or 'low' stance of churches came to be judged partly on their attitudes to the admissibility of plainsong and there were sharp disagreements, both on musical and ecclesiastical grounds. Official views sometimes owed more to expediency than to direct allegiance. For example the report of the church music committee to the Worcester Diocesan Conference of 1904, faced with deprecation by some members of the spread of plainsong, recommended 'that a knowledge of plainchant, with that of ancient ecclesiastical music generally, should be part of the equipment of every church musician'. This refers to knowledge only and takes no account of practice: in effect it meant that the use of plainsong was a matter for decision by individual churches. Some musical disagreements turned on the practicality of plainsong for congregational use. The learned Robert Bridges felt that the public taste for 'catchy' tunes meant that congregational plainsong was like casting pearls before swine. Walford Davies and Harvey Grace in the 1930s took the more moderate view that what was appropriate for the monastery, and indeed for the monks of Solesmes, was not necessarily so for the parish church. They advocated a practical approach, laying down principles for organ accompaniment that should be 'modal, or at least diatonic' and 'neither dull nor distracting'. For the same reason they were against the use of elaborate plainsong melodies with long decorative melismas. Some writers, while recognizing the qualities of plainsong as devotional music, doubted its efficacy as a medium for worship by a public accustomed to music with a rhythmic framework. At least one commentator in the 1930s scorned the translations from Latin that brought so many plainsong melodies into *The English Hymnal,* preferring instead the native products of English writers such as Charles Wesley. Feelings about plainsong and its associations continued to be contentious, and the delicacy of the matter is shown by the following section of a letter from the domestic chaplain to the bishop of one diocese to the dean of another after a visit to the latter's cathedral in 1932:

> Plainsong psalms might of course lead to a riot in the diocese ... but why not try to train the choir to recite them really well and deliberately? The effect of this in your Cathedral would be very impressive, and it would be an admirable example for parish churches to follow.

The context indicates a preference for plainsong rather than Anglican chants, but no mention is made of congregational participation, either in the cathedral or the parish churches that were supposed to act on the cathedral's example. It points to the essential dilemma that overshadowed plainsong revivals for English church use in both the sixteenth and nineteenth centuries: the suitability (or otherwise) of borrowed plainsong and how best to adapt it as a medium for worship by English-speaking people most of whom, inevitably, were untrained in its use.[16]

Polyphony

The investigation and revival of Latin polyphony that began around the 1840s was primarily intellectual rather than ecclesiastical in background, although it was seen in Tractarian circles as a welcome means of improving the standard of English church music. Bodies such as the Musical Antiquarian Society and the Motett Society were set up and in the 1840s began to publish editions of early sacred music, both English and Latin. These were sometimes heavily edited to smooth away what the editors considered to be the composers' 'mistakes'. Both William Dyce and Thomas Helmore were active in bringing material adapted to English texts from music by composers such as Palestrina, Victoria and Lassus into wider practical use. Dyce made several such adaptations and Helmore tried them out with his choir of student teachers at St Mark's College. Palestrina's music in particular was considered to represent the 'sublime' style in church music, and it seems to have been on Palestrina's style more than any other that composers and editors drew when they aspired to a 'church style' (see below, pp.173ff.). The motets of continental composers were adapted as anthems and the masses as settings of the Communion service. Particularly in the latter, the adaptations were often very far-reaching in order to accommodate the English Communion text. In some cases, mass-movements were adapted as anthems rather than as services. Longer movements such as the Credo and Gloria were partition-ed into sections to be sold separately. These sections were given anthem texts that often bore no relation to the Latin original, partly to increase the poten-tial market for the music and partly because the use of a Roman Catholic mass in direct translation was still a contentious matter among some con-gregations.

Although the use of adapted Latin polyphony flourished in some churches under Tractarian influence from the 1850s it was still a minority taste. Unlike plainsong, there was no possibility of its use by the congregation and so it remained the province of church and other gatherings where there were skill-ed singers to perform it. Where adaptations were used as anthems and ser-vices, the general preference was for the more highly-coloured masses and other sacred works of classical and romantic composers from mainland Europe. The idiom of these works was by no means exclusive to the church and it could hardly have been further removed from the 'sublime' style ad-vocated for church music by many Tractarians. Sometimes there were at-tempts at compromise: for example Joseph Barnby's arrangement of *The breces and responses with litany according to Tallis* has colourful organ har-monies in the *Quicunque vult* and some adjustment of Tallis's part-writing in the four-voice sections. As with so much nineteenth-century church music of every kind, whether freely-composed or adapted, dynamic markings are frequently and painstakingly inserted. It is clear from catalogues of music publishers such as Novello in the late nineteenth century that adapted polyphony formed only a small proportion of the repertory. But more re-cent continental music was plundered with enthusiasm: even for 'Responses to the Commandments' the Novello catalogue was able to offer 'Beethoven in C; Gounod in D, G; Hummel in B flat, D minor; Mendelssohn in G, A; C. M. von Weber in E flat; F. Schubert in C, G, C, F, E flat, A flat' all in inex-pensive leaflets for use by church choirs.

The use of borrowed polyphony as English church music did not become firmly established until the present century, but still largely as part of the repertory of cathedrals or other churches where an expert choir was available. By the 1920s the music of Palestrina, Victoria, Lassus and Sweelinck, all in English translations, was still regarded in influential church circles as an ideal medium for worship where its use was possible. The preface to *The Church Anthem Book*, a collection of one hundred anthems published in 1933 as a representative selection of good-quality material for use by church choirs, speaks of renewed interest in choral music stimulated by the invention of broadcasting and the proliferation of competitive music festivals. Even so, only a very small proportion of this collection consists of adapted polyphony: most of the adaptations are from the sacred works of Bach, Mozart, Brahms and — above all — Mendelssohn. Increasingly after the 1930s, polyphonic works were sung as anthems in the language (usually Latin) for which the music had first been composed. Thus adaptation into English became rarer although polyphony still continued to be borrowed, retaining a modest though not insignificant place in the anthem and service repertory.[17]

The German influence

The marriage of Queen Victoria to Albert, Prince of Saxe-Coburg-Gotha in 1840 further enhanced public interest in German culture and customs and particularly in music, at which the Prince himself showed talent. Music in the prevailing German and Viennese styles was pre-eminent in England, and a period of study in Germany was considered almost obligatory for aspiring English composers or performers. Church music was no exception: notwithstanding the efforts of the Tractarians, the inclination of public taste was towards the music of Haydn, Mozart, Schubert, Brahms and Mendelssohn or native music in similar styles, with the works of Handel retaining their special place at the pinnacle of musical respectability. Mendelssohn's influence in promoting the music of Bach, and particularly the *St Matthew Passion* in England, had a greater bearing on the repertory of the concert hall than that of the church. Despite the veneration accorded to Bach's music from the mid-nineteenth century, it was not at this stage appropriated for church use in the way that Handel's music continued to be.

As part of the predilection for German styles in music there was a renewed interest in German hymns. Some hymns of German origin were already part of the English repertory having survived as psalm tunes; others had been brought in as part of the work of John and Charles Wesley, Henry John Gauntlett and similar compilers. Many of these latter were of the more florid type that became current in Germany in the eighteenth century, and they were sometimes heavily adapted to fit existing regular metres of English texts. But from the 1840s there began a succession of collections for English use devoted also to early Lutheran hymns, many with increasing regard for the irregular rhythms and metres that often characterized them. The first of these collections was Frances Cox's *Sacred hymns from the German* published in 1841, which became the basis for several similar and larger collections including one in four volumes by Jane Borthwick and Sarah Findlater: *Hymns from the land of Luther* published from 1854 to 1862. Some of the German hymns in William Henry Havergal's publication *Old church psalmody* (1847) have survived into modern use, but Havergal's tendency to choose later and more rhythmically staid German versions of some chorales, adapting them further where he thought fit, meant that his work was restricted in scope. An example is provided by the tune 'Narenza' (EH 518, 627, A&MR 229, MHB 112) often sung to 'Ye servants of the Lord'. The earliest known version of this tune goes back to a collection of 1584 where it provides a rhythmically free and metrically irregular setting to the text 'Ave Maria klare'. In seventeenth-century collections, however, the phrase-lengths had been regularized and the rhythm made uniformly triple throughout. A version like this was probably Havergal's source: he then shortened the melody and further adapted the rhythm from triple to duple to give the present hymn tune which, though it probably reflects the source from which Havergal took it, bears almost no resemblance to the earliest known version of the tune.

The work of the translator Catherine Winkworth was of far greater importance in the promotion of German hymns as part of the English repertory. In 1833 the German hymnologist Christian Karl Josias von Bunsen (1791–1860) published a collection of 900 Lutheran hymn texts. Catherine Winkworth chose selections from these, translated them into English and published them in 1855 and 1858 under the title *Lyra Germanica*. But her most significant contribution was *The Chorale Book for England*, published in 1863. This consisted of 200 hymns with music from mainly Lutheran sources. It was intended for church as well as family worship. In the prefaces to her collections she remarked on the wide variety of metre in the hymns which was so different from the preponderance of a few regular metres in current English hymnody. These unaccustomed metres perhaps hindered early acceptance by congregations of her translations, just as the lack of metrical organisation hindered acceptance of plainsong. Winkworth's main concern was with older hymns rather than with those that had already been successively modified. Instead of adapting tunes and texts to conform to conventional existing English hymn metres, she devised new hymns and translations that used the metres of these early tunes as well as reflecting as far as possible the mood and meaning of the early German texts. For *The Chorale Book for England* Winkworth had two musical collaborators, William Sterndale

Bennett and Otto Goldschmidt, each of whom harmonized some of the hymn melodies. They strove to 'preserve period character' but their harmonies were nevertheless bland, and in many cases owed more to Johann Sebastian Bach's style than to earlier harmonizations, some of which appeared in an appendix.

Although *The Chorale Book for England* was not widely used as a hymn book, it is important because it increased awareness of the nature and diversity of Lutheran hymns which soon afterwards became a fruitful source for the compilers of other more influential hymnals; also it added several new hymn texts by Catherine Winkworth to the repertory, many of which are still in use. Robert Bridges favoured the use of German Reformation hymns, and some of his selections for *The Yattendon Hymnal* (1899) followed the principles of text translation and music transcription exemplified by Catherine Winkworth, although he used very little of the material that she had published. Similar principles were followed by George Ratcliffe Woodward in *Songs of Syon* (1904). Several translations by Winkworth appeared in *The English Hymnal* (1906) and subsequent books influenced by it. One of the best-known tunes and texts from *The Chorale Book for England* is 'Praise to the Lord, the Almighty' (EH 536, A&MR 382, MHB 64, SP 626), with harmony by William Sterndale Bennett. This tune is thought to have appeared first in 1665 but there are many versions of it. Another is 'Deck thyself, my soul, with gladness' (EH 306, A&MR 393, SP 267). Although Winkworth gives Crüger's version of the tune in an appendix, it is the 1863 editorially regularized and harmonized version that has survived as a hymn. Catherine Winkworth took the texts for both these hymns from Bunsen's collection of 1833.[18]

The Swedish 'Piae Cantiones'

As well as German sources, collections of sacred music of various kinds from other countries awakened the interest of musical antiquaries in the mid nineteenth century. It was from the results of their work that compilers of later volumes, particularly of hymns, drew much material, sometimes revising what the earlier researchers had done by looking again at the sources they had used. Many pieces first made available in England in the mid nineteenth century became firmly entrenched in the English repertory although sometimes in modified form. Not all the pieces from foreign sources that were tried out in English versions established themselves. Many passed into oblivion, either because tune or text lacked immediate appeal or was supplanted by another version that became more popular, or because they did not outlast changes in fashion. From this time onwards the progress of borrowing from sacred sources into English church music is remarkable for its constantly increasing resourcefulness and diversity, often encompassing groups of pieces from large collections as well as isolated individual items.

Apart from nineteenth-century revivals already discussed, probably the most important rediscovery of a foreign collection of sacred music in terms of its lasting influence in England was that of *Piae Cantiones*, a Swedish songbook first published in 1582 by Theodoricus Petri Nylandensis, at that time a student at the university in Rostock. The book contains 74 songs and was intended for church and school use. Most of the contents are Swedish or Finnish; some are German, Bohemian or Moravian. Almost without exception, the texts are Latin. The book underwent several later revisions and enlargements and copies of the original edition became exceedingly rare. However, such a copy came into the hands of an Englishman who was Queen Victoria's envoy in Stockholm. Not later than early 1853 the envoy gave the book to John Mason Neale who, with Thomas Helmore, published selections from it in 1853 and 1854 under the titles *Carols for Christmastide* and *Carols for Eastertide*. The *Piae Cantiones* pieces chosen by Neale and Helmore were mostly specific to those seasons, but there was a further reason why their choice of music for Christmas was especially propitious. English interest in German culture was increasingly widespread and some German Christmas traditions, introduced by Prince Albert and the royal family, were adopted by English families too. These included the setting up of decorated fir trees and the singing of popular Christmas religious songs. The romanticized association of Christmas with snow seems also to have originated in Germany and to have become fashionable in England in the 1840s. Circumstances were exactly right, therefore, for pieces like Neale's 'Good King Wenceslas', devised specially to fit a tune in *Piae Cantiones*, to win popular acceptance, widened still further by publication in the highly successful anthology *Christmas Carols New and Old* (1871). Neale's picturesque text combines morality and melodrama with Christmas snow as background. It has no connection whatsoever with the original Latin text 'Tempus adest floridum', which is a poem of uninhibited rejoicing and praise to God for the coming of spring. The sprightly melody is reproduced at it stands in *Piae Cantiones* but the addition of text and harmonies in the Victorian manner, combined with the usual slow performance tempo of 'Good King Wenceslas', weighs it down unduly and gives it an inappropriate level of decorum. Strictly speaking 'Good King Wenceslas' is neither church nor Christmas music, but in popular perception and use it fulfils both these functions. Much has been written deploring the incongruous alliance between the jaunty dancelike tune and Neale's solemn text, and attempts have been made to displace the latter in favour of direct translations of the Latin poem. But intellectual considerations have proved to be no match for popular approval. Neale's carol has retained its place in the repertory, attaining, together with its borrowed tune, virtually the status of folk-music in its own right.

Of the *Piae Cantiones* songs specific to Christmas, 'In dulci jubilo' is probably the most widespread. Although its macaronic text appears in *Piae Cantiones* as Swedish interpolated with Latin, it is of German origin and both German text and tune probably date from the fourteenth century. As a Lutheran tune it was used with English texts in the mid sixteenth century by John, James and Robert Wedderburn in the *Gude and godly Ballates* of c.1540 (see below, pp.111ff.), and was named to be sung with metrical texts in their publications of the 1560s and 1570s. It also appeared in *Lyra Davidica* (1708). However, there seems to be no evidence of its special popularity in England until Neale and Helmore turned the *Piae Cantiones* version into their carol 'Good Christian men, rejoice' (MHB 143). This first appeared in their 1853 collection and, like 'Good King Wenceslas', was further popularized in the widely-used volume of carols edited by Bramley and Stainer and published in 1871. The flow of Neale's text is disrupted by a two-syllable line (for example 'News! news!' in the first verse) between the third and fourth lines of each eight-line verse. This was the result of a misreading of the music at this point by Helmore. The old German line 'layt in presepio' had a single note on 'layt' but this had to be divided into two equal notes to accommodate the equivalent Swedish line 'ligger in presepio'. Helmore mistook these two minims for two longs, perhaps because both minims and longs have stems, unlike the breves and semibreves in which the rest of the piece is notated in *Piae Cantiones*. The version by Neale and Helmore with the extra notes remained current for many years and retained a separate existence from versions with the correct melody and macaronic text in Latin and English. Among the latter, the arrangement of 'In dulci jubilo' based on a German source of the tune by Robert Lucas Pearsall, composed in 1834 and later adapted by Reginald Jacques, became widely used, as did the harmonizations by Bartholomew Gesius and Johann Sebastian Bach in *The Oxford Book of Carols*.

In addition to the two examples already discussed, *Piae Cantiones* continued to be a fruitful source of borrowings, not only for Neale and Helmore but for their successors. For the most part it was the Christmas pieces that established an enduring hold on the repertory and became current as concert and domestic as well as church music. Attempts to promote repertories of carols for similar use at other seasons such as Easter and Ascensiontide met with little success. George Ratcliffe Woodward took a substantial proportion of *Piae Cantiones* material for use in *The Cowley Carol Book* first published in 1902: one of his most notable successes was 'Unto us is born a son', a faithful rendering of the *Piae Cantiones* version of the 'Puer nobis nascitur' melody and text. The *Oxford Book of Carols* text 'Unto us a boy is born' (also at SP 385) uses the same melody. Woodward used Neale's texts 'Christ was born on Christmas day', to the *Piae Cantiones* tune 'Resonet in laudibus', and 'Let the song be begun' to 'Personent hodie'. However, Woodward's harmonization of 'Personent hodie' is demure and conventionally hymnlike in contrast to Gustav Holst's strident and deservedly popular version of 1924 entitled 'Theodoric', with its agile bass-line and asymmetrical seven-note introduction, a notorious trap for unwary singers. The text used to Holst's borrowing is 'God is love: his the care' (SP 502). Woodward used further *Piae Cantiones* material in both *The Cowley Carol Book* and *Songs of Syon* (1904) but few of these borrowings became firmly established, perhaps because of the indirect and rather precious nature of some of the texts that Woodward devised for them. 'Up! good Christen folk, and listen', with harmonization, interpolation of 'Ding-dong, ding' to fill an original opening melisma, and quaint macaronic text all devised by Woodward, was a version for *The Cowley Carol Book* of a *Piae Cantiones* song on the significance of unity: 'O quam mundum, quam iucundum, vivere concorditer'. The *Piae Cantiones* tune 'Divinum mysterium' appears in *Songs of Syon* in a translation by Richard Prosser Ellis beginning 'Unity in Trinity, majesty unbounded' and at EH 613 as a procession: 'Of the Father's heart begotten'. The latter version, specifically for Christmas, attained wider currency, perhaps because of its Christmas association but more probably because of recent arrangements for unison singing which liberate the spirited melody from the rather sluggish four-part harmonizations with which it was earlier saddled and present it in its rhythmically correct form, given in *Songs of Syon* and at MHB 83 but not in *The English Hymnal* (1906): apparently another case of notational misreading. Woodward's 1910 edition of *Piae Cantiones* perpetuates the rhythmic error by dividing a ligature indicating two semibreves so that it appears to indicate two longs, yet his own transcription, which has supplanted the version in *The English Hymnal,* transmits the rhythm of the 1582 original.[19]

Christmas music

The anthology *Christmas Carols New and Old* edited by Henry Ramsden Bramley and John Stainer, published complete in 1878, was the most influential nineteenth-century medium in popularizing Christmas carols in the broadest sense, for many of its contents are really no different from hymns specific to the season. Apart from the *Piae Cantiones* borrowings derived from the work of Neale and Helmore, nearly all the tunes in the anthology are either 'traditional' (the implication being that they are traditional English) harmonized by Victorian composers, or newly written by these composers. Two tunes, no longer familiar, are stated to be 'old French' but beyond that their origins are obscure.

The only serious rival in popularity to the anthology by Bramley and Stainer was that compiled by Richard Robert Chope and first published in 1875: *Carols for use in church during Christmas and Epiphany.* The musical editor was Herbert Stephen Irons, who was responsible for harmonizing most of the tunes. Many of them are stated to be 'traditional' from various parts of the British Isles, but the term 'traditional' seems to be used as a catch-all for any whose origins are uncertain. Every tune, whatever its origin, is overloaded with ingenious but frequently inapt harmony. This applies to the borrowed material too, most of which is stated to be Flemish: 'from the stock pieces of the carol singers of Dunkerque'. A few of the pieces are given as French in origin, yet one well-known French tune appears in Chope's book categorized among the English traditional tunes. This is the French carol melody 'Les anges dans nos campagnes' which first appeared in print in France in 1867 but may have originated there around 1800. In recent decades the tune has generally been sung to the words 'Shepherds in the fields abiding' (A&MR 594) or 'Angels, from the realms of glory' (MHB 119 ii, SP 71) but in Chope's book the words begin 'When the crimson sun had set' and use a 'Gloria' refrain. It is clear from Chope's title and from reviews of his anthology that all the material was considered appropriate for congregational use in church. The *Manchester Guardian* review provides a glimpse of the Victorian attitude to the propriety of carols and Christmas hymns:

> Our immediate forefathers seem to have been more pleased to sing of the crackling log and bowl of beer, than to turn their thoughts to Bethlehem, and meditate on the Incarnation.

A few further carols are the results of nineteenth-century borrowings from sacred music. Predictably, several came from German-speaking countries. Among the best known of these, 'Silent night' originated in the village of Hallein in the Austrian Salzkammergut. On Christmas Eve in 1818 the church organ broke down, and the carol 'Stille Nacht' was hurriedly concocted by the local priest Josef Mohr and choirmaster-composer Franz Xaver Gruber to be sung with guitar accompaniment at Christmas services. Its use spread rapidly and it was translated into English in the 1850s. Its unashamedly sentimental lilt did not commend it to the more austere compilers of hymn and carol collections but its undoubted popularity shows the limitations of such collections as arbiters of public taste. 'As with gladness men of old' (EH 39, A&MR 79, MHB 681, SP 83) is sung to a hymn melody by Conrad Kocher in his 1838 collection *Stimmen aus dem Reiche Gottes*. The melody was adapted and shortened from seven phrases to six by the Victorian hymn-composer William Henry Monk. Although 'Three kings from Persian lands afar' found its way into the English repertory much later, in an arrangement by Ivor Atkins in 1930, it deserves mention here as a double borrowing. The German composer Peter Cornelius (1824–74) used a simple harmonization of the much older and well-known chorale 'Wie schön leuchtet der Morgenstern' (How brightly shines the morning star) as the piano accompaniment to his solo song 'Die Könige' (The kings), the third of his set of six Christmas songs, op.8, of 1856. In the arrangement with English words the piano accompaniment is slightly adapted to provide the subdued choral background to Cornelius's melody which, as in his song, is performed by a soloist. The English adaptation is an inspired piece of work, but not more so than Cornelius's own borrowing and transformation of the chorale. All six of his Christmas songs deserve to be better known.

A notable feature of carol and hymn collections from the early twentieth century is the increasing diversity of sacred sources for borrowings. Apart from pieces already mentioned, *The Cowley Carol Book* (first published in two series, 1902 and 1919) is notable for two pieces translated by George Ratcliffe Woodward and harmonized by Charles Wood from Dutch sources. 'King Jesus hath a garden' is taken from 'Heer Jesus heeft een Hofken' in *Geestlijcke Harmonie* published in 1633 but originally dating from 1609. An English translation was published in 1860 but Woodward's picturesque version has become established. 'This joyful Eastertide' uses the melody of 'Hoe groot de vrugten zijn' in *David's Psalmen* published in 1685. The text 'How great the harvest is' to the same tune (SP 169) is a closer reflection of the Dutch original, the melody of which ultimately derives from a popular song.

The Cambridge Carol Book, published in 1924, also the work of George Ratcliffe Woodward and Charles Wood, continued and widened the tradition of borrowing established in *The Cowley Carol Book*. Some further German chorales from the sixteenth century or earlier are introduced, including one ('Lobt Gott, ihr Christen alle gleich') to Nahum Tate's words 'While shepherds watched their flocks by night'. Not surprisingly, the chorale did not supplant the English version. The Flemish or French carol 'Quittez, pasteurs' appears to a text by Woodward beginning 'Hail! holy child'; a later version by Percy Dearmer carries the same melody at SP 98. With their stress on the appropriate musical presentation and meticulous documentation of borrowed material, these collections by George Ratcliffe Woodward and

Charles Wood are to carols what *The Yattendon Hymnal* and *Songs of Syon* are to hymns: a reaction against insularity and the indiscriminate imposition of the Victorian style on texts and music alike.

Percy Dearmer, Ralph Vaughan Williams and Martin Shaw, the editors of *The Oxford Book of Carols* first published in 1928, cast the net still further in their discerning quest for worthwhile material. They borrowed more widely from early Dutch sacred sources and also incorporated a high proportion of French carol tunes, many with fanciful narrative texts which are loose modern paraphrases of the original versions. But perhaps the most significant borrowings from foreign sacred sources were the two carols from Czechoslovakia, of which the better-known, the 'Rocking' carol ('Little Jesus, sweetly sleep'), has become firmly established as a children's carol. Although their original texts have a sacred theme in common they were more akin to folk music inasmuch as they were transcribed from singers as part of the oral tradition, rather than being discovered in manuscript or printed sources. Spanish, Basque and Russian tunes are also introduced in *The Oxford Book of Carols*. These have not been influential in their own right, but all these borrowings have served to increase awareness of other carol repertories that have enriched the English tradition. Like its two predecessors, *The Oxford Book of Carols* was intended as an antidote to entrenched Victorianism and as such it enjoyed greater success because it was more broadly based and less esoteric in approach. It was not intended as a representative selection of carols in English use at the time it was published, but most subsequent carol collections that claim this function owe something to its influence.[20]

Hymn-anthems and hymns

The hymn-anthem flourished briefly early in the twentieth century as a hybrid form intended to amalgamate the contributions to worship of choir and congregation, so that both could feel that they had an important musical part to play. The usual scheme was for the congregation to sing a well-known hymn in unison with organ accompaniment, and for choral harmonies to be woven around some of the verses. The hymn melodies chosen by composers for this kind of treatment were often revivals borrowed from other, much older repertories than that of current English hymnody. For example, Charles Wood composed 'How dazzling fair' (published posthumously in 1929), using the Genevan melody for Psalm 1 as the basis for an anthem in which the organ provides most of the elaboration. Henry George Ley based 'The strife is o'er' and 'Lo round the throne' on the German hymns 'Gelobt sei Gott' (A&MR 135 i) and 'Erschienen ist der herrliche Tag' (see above, pp. 37–38). Edward Bairstow's 'The day draws on' uses a French church melody

(EH 123 ii). The best-known example is Ralph Vaughan Williams's setting
for the coronation in 1953 of Queen Elizabeth II of the 'Old Hundredth',
a tune that was first borrowed for English use in the 1556 Anglo-Genevan
Psalter (see above, p.39). Composed for a splendid public occasion rather
than the conventional congregational service, this setting relies largely on
the simple but effective device of extending the final note of each phrase
with unexpected harmonies, rather than the more obvious ploy of modifying the implicit harmonies of the melody itself.[21]

The Post-Victorian Reaction

Challenges to Victorian hymnody

By the end of the nineteenth century *Hymns Ancient and Modern* was in use in a large and increasing proportion of Anglican churches. Although it contained some borrowed material from older traditions, its content of hymns by contemporary composers such as Joseph Barnby and John Bacchus Dykes was the feature that endeared it at once to most congregations. It is hardly surprising, therefore, that this trend provoked a reaction that was influential in the stance taken by books such as *The Yattendon Hymnal* (1899), *Songs of Syon* (first published 1904), *The English Hymnal* (first published 1906) and *The Oxford Hymn Book* (1908). Particular aspects of their borrowed material have already been discussed but each of these volumes as a whole was effective in extending the range of borrowings and thus influencing the contents of subsequent widely-used hymnals.

The chief object of *The Yattendon Hymnal,* as stated in its preface, was to restore old melodies to use. Most of the sources were already well known but the melodies in question had either been overlooked previously or else had been presented only in altered forms to suit English common metre. In cases where only the melody was extant but harmony was needed, the editors supplied harmony 'in a suitable manner, and with some attempt towards the particular qualities of workmanship upon which much of the beauty of the old vocal counterpoint depends'. Most of the borrowed material comes from the work of Louis Bourgeois as composer or arranger of melodies for the succession of Genevan psalters between 1541 and 1577. A good example is the tune to 'Bread of the world in mercy broken' (EH 305, A&MR 409, MHB 756, SP 265) which is presented in *The Yattendon Hymnal* without barlines, with Reginald Heber's words altered by Robert Bridges and with austere harmony by Harry Ellis Wooldridge. Later hymnals reverted to Heber's text but retained the tune from Bourgeois, substituting harmony that is somewhat more fluent and urbane than that by Wooldridge. Other

Bourgeois melodies are offered by Bridges and Wooldridge for 'Abide with me' and 'When I survey the wondrous cross'. Further material draws predominantly on early French and German psalters and settings by Johann Sebastian Bach of chiefly earlier melodies. Most of the music in *The Yatten-don Hymnal* is borrowed but none is taken at first hand from a secular source and none postdates the music of Bach. Material from *The Yattendon Hymnal* appeared in later collections but some or all aspects of the idiosyncratic manner of its presentation by Bridges and Wooldridge were usually excluded.

George Ratcliffe Woodward acknowledged his debt to *The Yattendon Hymnal* in the compilation of his own volume, entitled in full *Songs of Syon: a Collection of PSALMS, HYMNS & SPIRITUAL SONGS set, for the most part, to their ANCIENT PROPER TUNES*. He greatly extended the borrowings from French psalters to include several of Claude Goudimel's settings and frequently printed alternative versions of the same tune with the melody as the treble or the tenor. Woodward's own texts were designed to accommodate unfamiliar metres, and barlines were omitted from these settings. The range of borrowings from early German hymns was also widened, and *Songs of Syon* includes complex settings by Bach, with continuo, that are more in the nature of anthems than hymns. *The Oxford Hymn Book* pursued a policy that was similar in many ways, but without the inclusion of complex anthem-like settings like those in *Songs of Syon*. The musical editor, Basil Harwood, drew heavily on Samuel Sebastian Wesley's collection *The European Psalmist* (see above, pp.57ff.) for tunes that Wesley had borrowed or composed. Tunes from early English psalters were used and one astounding borrowing consists of Edward John Hopkins's tune 'Oundle', a colourless adaptation of the motif at 'God is gone up with a merry noise, and the Lord with the sound of the trumpet' from the eight-part anthem 'O clap your hands' by Orlando Gibbons.

Both *Songs of Syon* and *The Oxford Hymn Book* were less influential than might otherwise have been the case because their functions were largely superseded by *The English Hymnal,* which first appeared in 1906. Its music editor was Ralph Vaughan Williams, who in later years wrote as follows:

> .... I have no real connection with anything ecclesiastical and no longer count myself as a member of the Church of England. I drifted into hymns more or less by accident (chiefly to prevent someone else doing it and making a mess of it).

Despite his modesty and apparent reluctance to allow involvement with hymns to become more than a minor part of his work, Vaughan Williams was responsible for many of the most influential and refreshing innovations in the history of the English hymn repertory. Like *The Yattendon Hymnal*, *The English Hymnal* aimed to restore old tunes to modern use in versions as close as possible to their early forms. It brought to light many tunes, some from sources previously untapped, and gave with each of them at least a modicum of historical documentation. But whereas the impact of *The Yattendon Hymnal* on English hymns extended little beyond its theoretical importance as a historical document, *The English Hymnal* had a wide-reaching and enduring practical influence that brought revivals of worthwhile music within the reach of all, not just the unusually musical or literary minority. Throughout, Vaughan Williams's main consideration was the needs of the congregation, and the preface to *The English Hymnal* outlines his firm approach to practical matters such as pitch, tempo, pauses, organ accompaniment and choral harmony. But his precepts extend beyond the practical to the educative. In a tactful but forthright note on the choice of material, Vaughan Williams deplores familiar tunes that are 'quite unsuitable to their purpose', being 'positively harmful to those who sing and hear them'. It is not difficult to guess the objects of his invective, especially since these 'old favourites' are later described as 'dating at the earliest from the year 1861' — the year in which the complete *Hymns Ancient and Modern* was first published. 'It is indeed' he said 'a moral rather than a musical issue'. Accordingly Vaughan Williams selected tunes that were 'beautiful and noble'; regarding these attributes as the only criteria of the 'musically correct', whatever historical period the tunes represented. The appeal of the book lay not only in the choice of tunes and texts but in the way in which they were presented to ensure maximum usefulness to churches at all levels of musical accomplishment.[22]

The English Hymnal

The tunes that Vaughan Williams chose came from a wider variety of sources than had ever been drawn upon before for a single collection. The preface to *The English Hymnal* gives a regional and chronological outline of the sources used. Apart from plainsong and English sources, Welsh and Scottish psalm and hymn melodies were borrowed, as well as tunes by Irish composers. There were also a few American hymn tunes. From mainland Europe the principal recourse was to German hymns but in the broadest sense: not only sixteenth and seventeenth-century Lutheran hymns were used but also material from Roman Catholic songbooks of the same period, as well as eighteenth-century and later German tunes. French and Swiss material was represented chiefly by music from the sixteeenth-century Genevan psalters and ecclesiastical melodies from various French uses. An assortment of tunes came from Italian, Spanish, Flemish and Dutch sources and there are melodies of Russian, Hebrew and even supposed Indian origin. The aim was to include the best specimens of every style and to print the finest version of every tune, not necessarily the earliest.

There was no selfconscious attempt to provide pastiche archaic harmony for tunes whose old versions were extant as melodies only but which needed harmonization for practical use in *The English Hymnal*. Yet the editorial harmonies provided do not obtrude: they do not draw attention away from the melody but at the same time they furnish a stable musical environment for it. An example is provided by 'Alta Trinità beata' (EH 184, slightly altered version at SP 669), a tune that came originally from a fourteenth-century Florentine source of Italian spiritual songs for communal singing, the style of which depended partly on plainsong and partly on popular influence. The melody as it was taken into *The English Hymnal* was a version transcribed from the source, probably in the 1770s, by Charles Burney, who misread some of the fourteenth-century notation. Even so, the melody is good, and Vaughan Williams was content to use Burney's version rather than attempting to seek out and retranscribe its fourteenth-century original. Although the melody is directed to be sung in unison, a lively and effective harmonization is given which neither overwhelms the melody nor cowers behind it. Nor, by any stretch of the imagination, is the harmonization remotely connected with anything the fourteenth century might have produced. The result is a thoroughly workable and memorable congregational hymn tune which is close in spirit, if not in musical manifestation, to its fourteenth-century purpose of communal devotion. A similar example is provided by the melody 'Lasst uns erfreuen' (EH 519, A&MR 172 as 'Easter song', MHB 4, 28 as 'St Francis', SP 157), which was slightly modified by Vaughan Williams from a book of sacred songs published in Cologne in 1623 and transformed by the addition of strong but not over-colourful harmony into a worthwhile enrichment of the English hymn repertory.

It is possible to argue that borrowings like these are travesties of fine originals, in the same class as those in which irregular rhythms are flattened out or phrases regularized to fit conventional English hymn metres. The previously-discussed adaptation of Handel's *Messiah* aria 'He shall feel his flock like a shepherd', mauled into the shape of a hymn (see above, pp.53–55), is a spectacularly bizarre example of this widespread practice. Yet Vaughan Williams did not favour adaptations like the latter, and indeed sought to restore the original metres of tunes such as 'Innsbruck' (EH 86, 278, A&MR 34, MHB 946, SP 57), although what he restored in that particular case was not the metre of Heinrich Isaac's late fifteenth-century original song (see below, p.99) but that of its adaptation as a hymn, as harmonized by Johann Sebastian Bach. But where an adaptation previously made had produced a worthwhile melody that was already well established, Vaughan Williams allowed this version to stand. When faced with a choice between two versions of a tune, either of which would work in congregational use, his priority was historical accuracy and the restoration of an earlier version if it were musically superior. In introducing a tune new to the repertory, however, his concern was above all for the needs of the congregation, although his attitude was not condescending and he did not shrink from presenting challenging material that required effort on their part. Adaptations like that of 'Alta Trinità beata' and 'Lasst uns erfreuen' reflect Vaughan Williams's wish above all to bring good melodies back into use, even if this made necessary some compromise over historical accuracy in style and presentation to facilitate maximum usefulness.

The English Hymnal did not win immediate acceptance in all quarters, chiefly because some of the texts and possibly some of the tunes were considered to be too reminiscent of Roman Catholicism. But the book established important principles about the sources from which hymn tunes might be borrowed and about the treatment and presentation of borrowed material. These principles, as well as much material from *The English Hymnal,* were absorbed to a greater or lesser extent by subsequent hymnals. Although in terms of circulation *The English Hymnal* and its revisions achieved widespread use, the true measure of its impact exceeded that reflected merely by sales figures, so great was its influence on English hymn usage.[23]

Hymnals c.1918–1950

The First World War had a profound effect on the practice of English church music at every level. Many parishes where there had been cathedral-style choirs were obliged to reconsider their musical outlook and accept simplification and a greater degree of participation in the choice of music and its performance by members of all social classes. *Songs of Praise,* first published in 1926 under the same editorship as *The English Hymnal* with the addition of Martin Shaw, was designed to fulfil the needs of parishes whilst at the same time extending and reinforcing the stated aims of *The English Hymnal.* It was intended to be non-denominational, and the wide choice of texts was an attempt to sweep away the pomposity and undue solemnity that was thought by many to reflect an undesirable separation of church worship from everyday life. The music was drawn from a wide range of sources: there were further borrowings and these were treated in a similar manner to those in *The English Hymnal,* always with an eye to practical application. Many of the tunes newly introduced in *Songs of Praise* were incorporated into later editions of *The English Hymnal.*

Songs of Praise promoted further a practical idea tried out with a few tunes in *The English Hymnal:* the provision of descants and so-called fa-burdens, a way of admitting vocal harmony without the necessity of a four-part choir. In this context fa-burden was the name given to an arrangement in which the melody was sung by the tenor, harmonized by treble, alto and bass. None, any or all of these latter three parts could be sung, or their harmony could be played as keyboard accompaniment. An example is the treatment of the 'Vater unser' tune (SP 566, MHB 683, 723), given as harmonized by Bach and with a rather unwieldy fa-burden arrangement by Sydney Nicholson as an alternative. A descant consisted of a treble countermelody to the tune, in conjunction with which the tune was to be sung in unison by all other voices, with keyboard accompaniment. For example the tune 'Stuttgart' (SP 84, MHB 242) is given as it was adapted from its eighteenth-century German source, and then an alternative version is offered with a descant by William Henry Harris for treble voices: in this case the opportunity is given for further harmony parts to be sung around the main tune if the full range of singers is available. In these ways, *Songs of Praise* further increased the range of worthwhile and interesting music available to congregations with limited resources and expertise. For this reason it found much favour as a book for school use.

In 1943 Ralph Vaughan Williams and Martin Shaw produced a booklet entitled *Tunes selected from Songs of Praise (enlarged edition) to be sung to familiar hymns.* Thirty tunes were given, each of which was cross-referenced to an item in *Hymns Ancient and Modern.* The aim was to 'improve' church music without the expense of providing a new hymn book for members of the congregation. Many of the *Songs of Praise* borrowed melodies were included. Although the preface stated that the booklet could be used with any hymn book, it was clearly intended as a direct challenge to some of the material in *Hymns Ancient and Modern,* made available in the cheapest and most accessible manner.

In 1950 *Hymns Ancient and Modern Revised* was published. This was a revision of the standard edition of 1922, but in general outlook it was conservative, with no attempt at the kinds of radical changes encouraged by *The English Hymnal* and *Songs of Praise.* Nevertheless it did incorporate borrowed material as they had done, and there were further borrowings (though mainly from a similar range of sources) that the latter two volumes did not include. Some arrangements of borrowed material were copyright and this prevented their inclusion in *Hymns Ancient and Modern Revised.* Some of the borrowings first introduced in *The English Hymnal* and *Songs of Praise* owe their popularity to *Hymns Ancient and Modern Revised,* which had a broader if less exalted appeal and consequently a wider circulation. Revisions and supplements to all these volumes over the years have demonstrated that the ploy of borrowing material from other repertories of sacred music is not outworn, and that it has been a source of enrichment to the English repertory rather than a makeshift substitute disguising inadequacy of invention.[24]

Part II

MUSIC BORROWED FROM SECULAR SOURCES

5

A Conflict of Interests

Introduction

About 1930, Ralph Vaughan Williams received a letter from Percy Dearmer (his collaborator in editing the revised version of *Songs of Praise*) to whom a clergyman had written objecting to the use of the American tune 'Covenanters'. Vaughan Williams's reply to Dearmer is worth quoting almost in full because it shows how strongly Vaughan Williams felt about worthwhile borrowings from secular sources for hymns. Never one to waste words, he nonetheless launches into a considerable tirade on the subject, reaffirming the attitude he had taken throughout his influential work on hymns which began in 1904. In support of his argument he gives the background to several borrowings from secular music of a variety of types and historical periods, showing something of the extent to which the practice of such borrowing had become part of English church music: [Square brackets denote material added to Vaughan Williams's letter for the purpose of the present study.]

We had already decided long ago (in deference to someone's objection) to exclude the tune "Covenanters" [MHB Additional Tunes 5] from the new S. P. [*Songs of Praise*]. Personally I am sorry as I consider it a fine vigorous tune and well suited to the words.

   Your correspondent calls it "Jazz" — but there is no hint of "Jazz" characteristics in the tune — but perhaps your correspondent uses the epithet "Jazz" like many people use the word "Bolshie" to designate anything they disapprove of.

   As to its "origin" I care nothing — If your correspondent enquires closely into the credentials of every tune he admits into his church I fear his congregation will be cut off from all the noblest hymn tunes in the world — Is he aware that "O Filii et Filiae" [EH 626, A&MR 130, SP 143] is adapted from a presumably pagan song in praise of spring "Voici venir le joli mois"? that "Innsbruck" [EH 86, 278, A&MR 34, MHB 946, SP 57] was originally a secular song? That the "Old hundredth" [EH 365, A&MR 166, 370, 621, MHB 2, 3, SP 443] is an adaptation of a love song? That the splendid solemn "Helmsley" [EH 7, A&MR 51,

MHB 264, SP 65] is probably an adaptation of a stage song (sung by a female actor) "Where's the mortal can resist me"? — That "Jesu meine Freude" [MHB 518, SP 544] was originally "Flora meine Freude" — that the tune "St. Theodulph" [EH 545, 622, A&MR 98, 597, MHB 84, SP 135] is first cousin to the dance tune "Sellenger's Round" — that "Amsterdam" [MHB 17, SP 286] is similarly derived from a dance tune? These adaptations have always been the principle of every church, and I believe quite rightly — so that the "Devil may not have all the pretty tunes".

Otherwise we shall be reduced to the lucubrations [i.e. studies or their product] of the Rev. J. B. Dykes — doubtless very pious but decidedly anaemic.

However the discussion is an academic one for we have decided, rather unwillingly to omit the tune.

In 1956 Vaughan Williams repeated much of what he had said here in a pamphlet marking the fiftieth anniversary of *The English Hymnal*. Even at this stage, he still found it necessary to defend in this way his policy of using adapted secular music for hymn purposes.

This correspondence is an illustration of the continuing conflict of interests that has surrounded borrowings from secular music for church use since long before the Reformation. Church musicians have frequently borrowed secular music: for use as the basis of their own church compositions, for straightforward adaptation for devotional use by the substitution of sacred texts for secular, or (in the case of instrumental music) the application to it of sacred texts. A number of linked suppositions and aims lie behind the use of secular music by the church. Perhaps the most overriding supposition is that familiarity with a piece of music in its secular form leads to the easier acceptance and assimilation into the repertory of a sacred version. Whether it be a mass into whose counterpoint a secular melody is ingeniously woven, or a metrical psalm sung to a well-known air, the aim is to establish recognition and communication between sacred and secular in place of ignorance, apathy or even antipathy. Although the use of a secular melody in complex counterpoint may have been for the delectation of performers rather than listeners, it follows from this that all those who worship by means of music with sacred texts need material that they are capable of singing. Professional singers had their counterpoint but the musically uneducated worshipper, perhaps using metrical psalms in a domestic or family environment, perforce fell back on memorized 'common property' melodies the majority of which were probably secular.

A further supposition, but one of which the truth is very much to be doubted, is that the application of sacred texts to secular tunes may eventually bring about abandonment of secular versions and universal adoption of only sacred ones. This was an aim much favoured by compilers and publishers of metrical psalters in the sixteenth century, often being made clear to potential users by a statement in the preface or on the title page. The preface to Myles Coverdale's *Goostly psalmes and spirituall songes* of c.1539 is unique by virtue of its metrical cast and early date, but the aims described in this extract from it typify those outlined by a number of other metrical publications with English texts:

> Go lytle boke, get the acquaintaunce
> Amonge the louers of Gods worde
> Geue them occasyon the same to auaunce
> And to make theyr songes of the Lorde
> That they may thrust vnder the borde
> All other balettes of fylthynes
> And that we all with one accorde
> May geue ensample of godlynes

Whether or not this idealistic notion ever worked in practice is impossible to determine. It seems highly unlikely that sacred texts would ever have supplanted 'wanton ditties' although they might have existed alongside them. In later years, the successful supplanting of secular texts (such as 'Our captain calls all hands') by sacred ones (In this case 'He who would valiant be', EH 402, MHB 620 as 'Who would true valour see', SP 515) came about only because the secular versions of songs like this had almost died out of everyday use. Perhaps the earlier idea of displacing lewd songs was no more than an apparently exalted disguise for expediency, the real aim being to maximize the use of the sacred material by allying it to the familiar, fashionable and already popular. Indeed, it seems just as likely if not more so that borrowing in the opposite direction took place, particularly in contexts such as the nineteenth-century music-hall sketch. One of the mildest secular parodies of a well-known sacred piece (although the origins of its *tune* are in fact secular, see below, pp.135–36) is the following, current around Christmas 1936:

> Hark! the herald angels sing, Mrs Simpson's pinched our king.
> Peace on earth and mercy mild, wasn't Mr Baldwin wild!

Vaughan Williams, in common with a number of other editors involved in church music around the same time, was concerned in his secular borrowings not to present the familiar or fashionable but to present the worthwhile in music, no matter what its source. His aim was to elevate public taste using the supposition that 'the average congregation likes fine melody when it can get it' (EH preface); even so, he took care not to use melodies with secular associations that were still current, in the way that earlier compilers had often done. Thus his view represents a shift of opinion away from those who believed that the popularity of a melody was what mattered most.

In conflict with these ideas there were the views of those like the clergyman who wrote to Percy Dearmer deploring the use of a piece of so-called jazz as church music. The use of secular music by the church has been a constant source of misgivings and contention, and there have been many moves by the church to rid itself as far as possible of secular influences in its music. Such misgivings have by no means been confined to the Protestant church. Calls for the reform of Roman Catholic church music had been made for at least a century before the Council of Trent took place, from 1545 to 1563. The Council of Trent made several pronouncements in 1562 concerning church music. One of these dictated that nothing 'lascivious or impure' could be tolerated, and in the context of its circumstances this meant any secular melody used as a *cantus firmus* in counterpoint, or any harmonized secular song used in whole or in part to form a sacred piece by the parody technique of composition. The pronouncement deplored the use of 'frivolous or sometimes wicked melodies': clearly no *melody* by itself can be frivolous or wicked, it is only by association with particular words or background that it can be considered so, but this was sufficient to unleash condemnation by the Council of Trent. However, since it was left to individual bishops to implement pronouncements like this as they thought fit, techniques of church music composition using secular material were not banished, merely made less blatant.

In the English Protestant church, particularly in the eighteenth and nineteenth centuries, a frequent objection to the adaptation of secular material was that it betrayed 'theatrical' associations, a connection that was abhorrent to those who felt, perhaps idealistically, that in terms of conduct and attitude the church should be the antithesis of the theatre. Just as it was felt that the subject-matter of *Messiah* made it too sacred for performance in a theatre, so it was felt that the associations of some secular music put such music beyond the pale for church use. As well as its associations, the nature of the music itself was sometimes seen as a cause for concern. Increasingly with the influence of the Tractarian movement from the 1830s, dignity and fitness for its purpose was seen as the paramount quality of church music and this ruled out the use of many a good secular tune. Adaptations were sometimes deplored on grounds of incongruity as well as those of impropriety: scarcely anything could be more innocent of undesirable associations than Mendelssohn's *Songs without words* for pianoforte, but the adaptation of one of them as a hymn (A&MR 463, based on part of *Songs without words* no.9, op.30 no.3) provoked an outcry of disapproval in learned quarters. In a paper entitled *Music in cathedral and church choirs* read before the Church Congress in London in 1899, the distinguished composer Charles Villiers Stanford (1852–1924) condemned the practice of adapting as anthems compositions that were 'foreign' to the English church in any sense, advocating a movement in church composition that did not depend on material imported from other genres or styles. Direct secular borrowings were excluded from *The Yattendon Hymnal* of 1899, although the remote secular origins of some of the tunes used there were acknowledged. In the present century, the policy of using secular music and in particular folk music as the basis for hymns in *The English Hymnal* and *Songs of Praise* did not meet with universal approval, a situation to which Vaughan Williams's words in his pamphlet of 1956 about *The English Hymnal* were intended as a response. Where borrowings from secular music are concerned, the arguments of expediency on one hand and impropriety on the other have remained controversial throughout the history of English church music.[25]

Precedents

The long-established tradition of using secular material as the basis for church music, either as *cantus firmus* or for sacred parody use, was what lay behind the pronouncement against 'impure and lascivious' material by the Council of Trent in 1562. The practice of borrowing secular material in these ways was principally a Continental one. Even though some English examples may remain undiscovered it is unlikely that the use of secular tunes as *cantus firmi* in England was widespread, or that English church composers resorted to the sacred parody of secular music before the Reformation. Isolated but well-known English secular *cantus firmus* examples from the sixteenth century are the masses based on a single tune entitled 'Western wind', used as a *cantus firmus* by John Taverner (c.1490–1545), John Sheppard (c.1515–c.1559) and Christopher Tye (c.1505–c.1573). There is some confusion about this tune. It is undoubtedly secular but no text is known for it. It seems to bear almost no relationship to another tune, current in the sixteenth century, that has these words:

> Westron wynd, when wyll thow blow the smalle rayne downe can rayne? Cryst,
>   yf my love were in my armys & I yn my bed agayne

It is not known for certain how the title 'Western wind' came to be applied to the three composers' *cantus firmus*, nor why they chose this particular tune, nor why they took the unusual step (for English composers) of using a secular tune. All three masses use the tune as the basis for elaborate variations. Taverner's mass is the most accomplished; he gains an effective degree of contrast by varying the texture within the four voices, and by allowing the 'Western wind' tune to migrate among three of the voices. Sheppard's mass is shorter and less resourceful. Tye's mass may have been in some way a response to Taverner's because Tye restricts the 'Western wind' tune throughout to a single voice — the one voice to which Taverner never gives the tune throughout his mass. The reasons behind this, like those governing the choice of tune, remain a mystery.

Borrowing from secular music was a well-established principle among Continental composers for the church. With the advent of the Reformation and its new ideals for church music, the principle was continued but it was practised in additional ways to reflect the wish for increased clarity and simplicity, and to accommodate vernacular texts rather than Latin ones although Latin remained in use in many Protestant churches, especially in Lutheran Germany. Luther himself loved music: he favoured Latin church music, German folksong and music for dancing. Only lewd songs met with his disfavour because he felt that they were a debasement of God's gift of music. Accordingly he was not at all averse to the borrowing of secular melodies and their adaptation for use as hymns. He saw this as a means of preserving old melodies, of giving people material that he hoped would displace unwholesome songs, and of appropriating beautiful melodies for sacred use — Luther is credited in various sources as having originated the question 'Why should the devil have all the best tunes?'.

Numerous Lutheran hymns have melodies that can be traced to secular origins. Some of these hymns later enriched the English hymn repertory at various stages, culminating in the widespread interest in German hymns that grew up in England in the second half of the nineteenth century. A good example of this kind of Lutheran secular borrowing is provided by the tune set to several German hymn texts but usually known in England as 'Passion chorale' (EH 102, A&MR 111, MHB 202, 768, SP 128). This tune, in jaunty irregular rhythm instead of duple, was originally composed or appropriated by Hans Leo Hassler (1562–1612) for a love song for five voices entitled 'Mein G'müt ist mir verwirret' ('My mind is in turmoil — and a young woman has made it so'). This seems startlingly at odds with its eventual use as a chorale: 'O Haupt voll Blut und Wunden' ('O sacred head, sore wounded') given prominence by Johann Sebastian Bach at the most solemn moments in the *St Matthew Passion,* but it shows that the tune itself, rather than its associations, was what mattered most to church musicians.

An earlier example, involving one of the most beautiful tunes in the history of either sacred or secular music, is provided by 'Innsbruck' (EH 86, 278, A&MR 34, MHB 946, SP 57). This tune, with irregular metres and phrase-lengths and a repeated final phrase with a florid cadence, was written by Heinrich Isaac (c.1450–1517), possibly as counterpoint to an existing melody. It first appeared in print in 1539 although it was current by about 1475. The text 'Innsbruck, ich muss dich lassen' tells of the poet's sorrow at leaving the city with which there is clearly some amorous connection. The tune was transmitted in numerous forms, both vocal and instrumental, over a long period and wide geographical area. It is thought to have been first borrow-ed for sacred use during the sixteenth century as 'O Welt, ich muss dich lassen', substituting earthly mortality for the city as the subject of the poet's farewell. Later it became 'Nun ruhen alle Wälder' ('Now all the woodland is at rest'), an evening hymn freely translated as 'The duteous day now closeth' by Robert Bridges for *The Yattendon Hymnal*. The tune was used by Bach in both the *St Matthew Passion* and the *St John Passion*. Robert Bridges, in *The Yattendon Hymnal*, commented that it was the fate of this tune to have become lighter and more trivial as the words to which it was set became more sacred. The truth of this can be judged by comparing the regularized, four-square hymn version (references above) with Isaac's elegant and evocative melody to which he composed three additional voice-parts. The melody is given here in modern notation:

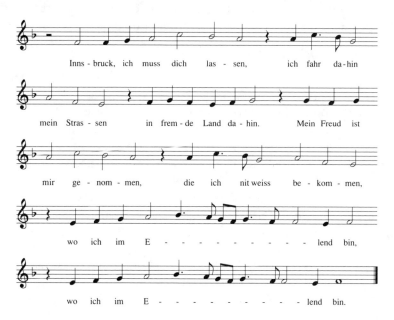

Elsewhere in mainland Europe, Reformation attitudes towards borrowed secular music were more restrictive than those of Luther and his compatriots. Unlike Luther, Calvin felt that it was inappropriate to borrow for church use tunes to secular love songs because of their inevitable sensual associations. Even so, several such borrowings took place. In some cases it is difficult to tell whether the melodies used for metrical psalms by composers such as Bourgeois and Goudimel were newly composed or taken from currently popular tunes, since melodies of either origin have so many stylistic features in common. Some secular borrowings can be ascertained through other extant versions of individual tunes. In this way it can be shown that several of the tunes in the Genevan Psalter of 1562 were based on folksongs and popular chansons, and that these had been in simultaneous secular and sacred use for many years before their appearance in this important collection. The borrowing of chansons continued: in the 1570s even those by Lassus were appropriated for use with Calvinist devotional poetry. Particularly in Switzerland, Lutheran hymns (some of which were of secular origin) were used and their texts adapted and translated where necessary. The Lutheran tradition also informed the hymn and psalm repertories of the Netherlands, Geneva and Strasbourg together with melodies native to those areas. There was much interchange of material among the various European Protestant communities by the mid sixteenth century and this probably had some influence on secular borrowings for English sacred music, both in the type of material and in the ways in which it could be used.[26]

The earliest English popular tunes

In mid sixteenth century England, as in other European countries, there existed a large repertory of secular tunes in current popular use. Some had attributes that favoured them as dance tunes; some were the melodies to familiar songs. Tunes like these were 'common property' melodies in the sense that they were used as the basis of numerous arrangements and (chiefly later in the century) sets of variations. Compositions using these 'common property' melodies could be for almost any combination of instruments, voices or both, or in the case of variations often for a solo keyboard instrument. Especially in the case of arrangements for group rather than solo music-making, there was often no strict division between vocal and instrumental music so that 'common property' melodies could appear in a wide variety of musical contexts. From there it was but a short step to put some of these familiar melodies to use with sacred texts. Settings like these were ideal for private or family devotion as well as for corporate worship by larger groups of people.

Another factor, of particular relevance to England, made circumstances especially favourable towards the borrowing of secular music for sacred use. This was the existence of the English carol, in the present context a specialized musical and literary form, often in a mixture of English and Latin, that flourished in the fifteenth century and did not necessarily have any relevance to Christmas nor even to anything sacred at all. The carol was characterized by its form, in which a repeated burden alternated with successive verses. In its early stages particularly, it was strongly associated with dancing, with witchcraft and with the many pagan ceremonies and symbols (such as holly and ivy) that were taken over by the Christian church but which persisted also in traditional customs not associated with Christianity. Carol melodies tended to be appealing and colourful, with lively triple rhythms. The carol reached a peak of sophistication in the late fifteenth century, by which time the repertory included numerous carols on sacred themes such as the Incarnation or semi-sacred ones like that of the Agincourt carol ('Deo gracias, Anglia'), a vivid description of England's triumph at the battle of Agincourt but with emphasis in the repeated burden on thanksgiving to God for the victory. By the mid sixteenth century the carol as a form for new expression was in decline and it was condemned by some English Protestant reformers as papist or heathenish. But carols persisted, many retaining their secular connections and blurring the distinction between sacred and secular by virtue of their dual associations. In this way the existence and development of the English carol helped to lay the foundations for further interchange between secular and sacred material as the sixteenth century continued.

The regular patterns and phrase-lengths of much secular music current around the mid sixteenth century did not lend themselves easily to use with sacred vernacular texts in prose. But for poets such as Thomas Sternhold, who made early attempts to devise metrical versions of sacred texts such as psalms, the ploy of setting their verses to familiar secular tunes was an obvious recourse. All nineteen metrical psalms that Sternhold published in 1549 used metres that matched those of many well-known secular tunes from the repertory of 'common property' melodies. Although this collection was the first publication of Sternhold's work it is likely that metrical psalms like his had been in circulation for some time. There may have been other minor poets engaged in similar activities whose work is now lost. Unlike the metrical psalm publications by Myles Coverdale, Robert Crowley and similar compilers, Sternhold's publication neither gives music nor names tunes to be used. There was no need: the metres of Sternhold's verses would have revealed at once that each of them could be sung to an assortment of current popular melodies that potential users knew from memory. These attributes were probably the most important in ensuring the wide dissemination and increasing popularity of Sternhold's and his collaborators' verses, to the exclusion of almost all others for a considerable period. On the other hand, the adoption of only a small selection of metres at this stage had a limiting effect later on the music available for metrical psalms and, subsequently, hymns. Put very broadly, it meant that there was a tendency to compose and adapt music to conform to texts in conventional metres, rather than modifying the metres to fit music that did not conform. This tendency has already been seen in borrowings and adaptations of other sacred music for use with English metrical texts. There were exceptions, such as the new texts composed for the Anglo-Genevan psalters for the purpose of bringing irregular Genevan tunes into the English repertory. But in general, the stultifying grip of standard metres showed few signs of being relaxed until the end of the nineteenth century, when new texts and translations began to take account of irregularities in the music instead of flattening them into rigid conformity.

Because secular tunes borrowed for metrical psalm settings were usually part of a memorized rather than a written repertory, examples that show exactly how these tunes were used in a sacred context are rarely to be found. No identifiable examples occur in the mid sixteenth-century Wanley partbooks (see above, pp.23–25, 32–33). The few surviving examples present a problem already encountered with supposed adaptations from other sacred music: where no model is extant it is often impossible to tell whether a piece actually uses borrowed material or whether it is an original composition in a borrowed style. This question surrounds some of the supposed secular borrowings in one of the more prolific sources of music of this type: the Lumley partbooks (London, British Library Royal Appendix manuscripts 74–76), which have already been mentioned in connection with borrowings from sacred music (see above, pp.25ff.). Four anonymous metrical pieces in the Lumley partbooks show characteristics such as homophonic textures and regular rhythm and phrase patterns that suggest origins in secular music. Three of them are laid out in a manner suggesting performance with alternating burden and verses, a form reminiscent of the carol repertory.

For one of these Lumley pieces the secular model has been discovered. This piece, entitled 'Domine Dominus noster', is a metrical version of Psalm 8, which in the Lumley books is set to music that is clearly borrowed from a well-known song by William Cornysh (died 1523) entitled 'Blow thy horn, hunter', shown in the following example as it appears for verse 1. Cornysh's piece, to a pastoral text with thinly-disguised amorous allusions, achieved wide circulation and may itself have been based on a pre-existent popular melody. The text of Psalm 8 is ideal for application to a secular tune in carol form because its first and last verses are the same, giving a hint of an analogy with the burden-verse-burden principle. In the Lumley versification this principle is extended so that every verse concludes with the same reminder of the substance of these first and last verses: 'O Lord our Lord, how marvellous is thy great name most glorious'. There are eleven verses in all (including doxology) in this somewhat unwieldy metrical version, the poetry of which is colourful but not, by any stretch of the imagination, of high quality. In this example note values have been halved, barlines inserted and spelling modernized editorially. The Bass part of the sacred version is an editorial reconstruction.

hun - ter, now blow thy horn, jol - ly hun - - - ter!

hun - ter, now blow thy horn, jol - ly hun - - - ter!

hun - ter, now blow thy horn, jol - ly hun - - - ter!

TRIPLEX

CONTRATENOR

TENOR

[BASSUS]

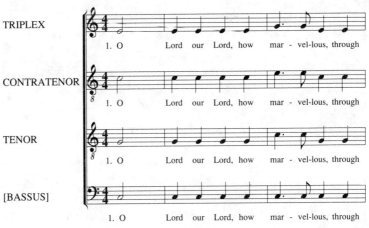

1. O Lord our Lord, how mar - vel-lous, through

1. O Lord our Lord, how mar - vel-lous, through

1. O Lord our Lord, how mar - vel-lous, through

1. O Lord our Lord, how mar - vel-lous, through

all the world so wide, is thy great name most glo - ri - ous, prais-

all the world so wide, is thy great name most glo - ri - ous, prais-

all the world so wide, is thy great name most glo - ri - ous, prais-

all the world so wide, is thy great name most glo - ri - ous, prais-

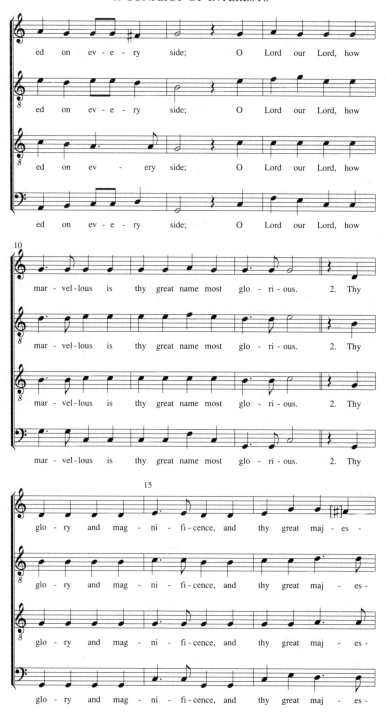

ty,   sur - mount - eth   all   in - tel - li - gence a -

ty,   sur - mount - eth   all   in - tel - li - gence a -

ty,   sur - mount - eth   all   in - tel - li - gence a -

ty,   sur - mount - eth   all   in - tel - li - gence a -

bove the hea - vens high;   O   Lord our Lord, how   mar - vel - lous is

bove the hea - vens high;   O   Lord our Lord, how   mar - vel - lous is

bove the hea - vens high;   O   Lord our Lord, how   mar - vel - lous is

bove the hea - vens high;   O   Lord our Lord, how   mar - vel - lous is

thy great name most   glo - ri - ous.   11. Glo - ry, hon - our and

thy great name most   glo - ri - ous.   11. Glo - ry, hon - our and

thy great name most   glo - ri - ous.   11. Glo - ry, hon - our and

thy great name most   glo - ri - ous.   11. Glo - ry, hon - our and

The music for the odd-numbered verses is a *contrafactum* of Cornysh's three-part setting slightly modified and adapted for four voices. This is used for all the odd-numbered verses and is shown in the example as it appears for verses 1 and 11. No model for the music of the even-numbered verses has been identified but it is similar in style and mood to Cornysh's song, giving welcome harmonic relief from Cornysh's predominant use of C major. The music for the even-numbered verses, shown in the example as it appears for verse 2, was probably composed or adapted as a 'lead-in' to the repetitions of Cornysh's tune, for it is harmonically open ended rather than self contained. This theory presumes that every verse of 'Blow thy horn, hunter' was sung to the same music. However, it is possible that 'Blow thy horn, hunter' was in carol form so that its first verse was used as a burden alternating with all subsequent verses, and that Cornysh's music carried the burden only, the other verses being sung to a different unnamed tune now forgotten. Such a scheme would match that of other material in the principal source of the song. In this case the music to the even-numbered verses in 'Domine Dominus noster' in the Lumley partbooks may have revealed the lost verse-music to 'Blow thy horn, hunter', since the music can be made to fit both sacred and secular texts.

The resemblance of the Lumley setting to Cornysh's piece is very marked and it is difficult to imagine that the composer did not use the secular tune consciously. Assuming that *contrafactum* was intentional, it shows that the emphasis had shifted from the Tenor (round which Cornysh presumably wrote his tune) to the Treble, which predominates in the sacred version. In the Lumley books every verse is underlaid to music, rather than the music appearing only once for all the verses. The reason for this is probably the awkwardness of the text. This entails rhythmic modification of the music in some verses which would not be clear without detailed underlay for each of them. This, combined with the change in the number of voice-parts from three to four, was probably the reason why such well-known music had to be written out rather than being sung from memory to sacred words. This Lumley psalm may have been an experimental piece and as such may not typify a larger, lost repertory of sacred *contrafacta* from harmonized metrical secular originals at this early stage apart from the few possible examples in the Lumley collection. However, it is an illustration of the lengths to which the early English Protestants would go in order to adapt harmonized secular music for sacred use, and it marks the start of a tradition that diversified later to include non-metrical texts and non-vocal secular music.[27]

Memorized melodies, named tunes and sacred parodies

Each of Thomas Sternhold's metrical psalms could be sung to any one of an assortment of well-known melodies which in general were probably left unharmonized vocally, although they may have been accompanied instrumentally. A more specialized aspect of the same practice involved the naming of a particular tune which the author of a text intended for use with his work. This meant, in theory, that a wider variety of metres could be introduced in both texts and music, but at the same time it limited the number of tunes available for use with any one text if the metre were in any way unusual. Although there is apparently no written evidence as to how some of these sacred borrowings of secular tunes worked, it is at least possible to speculate how they might have sounded in cases where a known tune is specified.

Most examples of this kind of borrowing come from the seventeenth century. Although psalms and canticles still formed the basis of much religious verse, the range of topics for devotional poetry that could be set to music had grown much wider to include moral themes, narratives and meditative material. Many of these verses were sung to borrowed ballad tunes, for by this time the ballad was well established as a type of popular (as distinct from courtly) song. Ballad texts told vivid stories of crime, disaster or the misfortunes of love. Some recounted stories of Biblical characters in order to point to a moral that was relevant to everyday life. Many ballads were legendary but some were topical, and among the latter were political ballads with religious connotations, the product of a strife-ridden era in which religion and politics were closely linked. Examples included mock litanies in which pleas for release from contemporary political ills bore the refrain 'Good Lord, deliver us'. Sometimes several versions of the same ballad coexisted. The relationship between the following eighteenth-century text and its sacred counterpart used nowadays as a Christmas carol is obvious:

> God rest you, merry Gentlemen, let nothing you dismay;
> Remember we were left alive upon last Christmas Day,
> With both our lips at liberty to praise Lord Castlereagh
> For his practical comfort and joy.

Examples like these show that there was very little distinction between secular and sacred material of a popular nature, and that borrowings for sacred use were part of a natural and continuing interchange and evolution of texts and tunes. This was enhanced, rather than instigated, by deliberate borrowings in one direction only: from secular to sacred.

In this atmosphere, sacred pieces to named ballad tunes flourished and
different versions proliferated, giving some individual tunes a long and varied
history of borrowing. For example 'Wigmore's Galliard' started life as a dance
tune although it seems that ballads were sung to it in Elizabethan times. By
1588 the tune was specified for use with solemn verses and it was used for
a ballad licensed in 1591 entitled 'A right excellent and godly new Ballad
... vncertainctye of this present lyfe' with text beginning 'All carefull Christians, marke my Song'. In 1642 the same tune was named for use with 'A
Caroll for Saint Stevens day' and by around 1675 the tune itself had become
known as 'Dying Christians Exhortation', an indication of how thoroughly
it had been absorbed into the devotional repertory. Perhaps it was tunes like
'Wigmore's Galliard', coupled with metrical psalms, that called forth Queen
Elizabeth I's reputed description of psalm-singing as 'Geneva jigs'.

Although borrowings like these were evidently widely used, especially in
domestic circles, they had no official sanction and did not enter the repertory of printed psalm tunes. Indeed, the subject-matter of texts associated
with some of the tunes provided sufficient reason in the eyes of some Puritan
factions to rule out the use of such tunes with sacred words in any circumstances. In the early 1630s William Slatyer published a book entitled
Psalmes, or songs of Sion in which he specified well-known tunes such as
'Barow Faustus dream' and 'Goe from my window' for use with particular
metrical psalms. Slatyer was severely reprimanded for this, but the practice
was hard to suppress. It seems that in 1642 Slatyer's work was republished
without the references to specific popular tunes. However, in the copy of
the 1642 edition that survives in the British Library, London, an early owner
has annotated some of the psalm texts with titles of tunes that would fit them:
for example 'Crimson velvet' is specified for Psalm 43 ('Judge my cause, O
Lord; and give sentence for me'), and a title already mentioned but transmitted by the annotator as 'Barbara Forster's dream' is given for Psalm 19.
Although it is perhaps the most frequently cited, Slatyer's work is by no means
unique in this respect, and it is clear that the practice of fitting named popular
tunes to metrical psalms and other devotional poetry was widespread and
tenacious, despite objections to it in some quarters.

Even closer links between some sacred texts and their secular counterparts
can be seen in the practice of sacred parody. The coexistence of several versions, both sacred and secular, of popular ballads in particular has already
been noted, and it is likely that one tune or variants of it would have been
common to all versions of a particular text. Adaptations from sacred to secular
and vice versa were abundant, especially in the seventeenth century. Some

secular texts could be 'moralized' with almost no difficulty. For example a song by Thomas D'Urfey published in 1683 beginning thus:

> State and Ambition, alas! will deceive ye,
> There's no solid Joy but the Blessing of Love

was soon afterwards parodied as:

> State and Ambition, alas! will deceive ye,
> There's no solid Joy but in Blessings above

Entries in the Stationers' Register show that a ballad beginning 'Row well, ye mariners', first licensed about 1565, had by about a year later been 'moralized' as 'Stand fast, ye mariners'. By about 1568 there were several versions, including 'Row well, Christ's mariners', 'Row well, God's mariners' and one entitled 'Row well, ye mariners, moralized, with the story of Jonas'. The evidence in this case survives only in the registers and neither tune nor full texts are known, but the successive modifications of this piece are a measure of its apparent success as both secular and sacred poetry as well as of the ease with which parodies of this kind could be devised.

In cases of sacred parody like these, it was usual for the sacred text to match the secular one fairly closely, so this meant that it was impractical to use the technique for material with predetermined form or subject-matter such as psalms. Consequently the texts of sacred parodies tend to be more in the nature of devotional or moral poetry, but with very strong allusions to their secular origins. This meant that the reader had no difficulty whatsoever in identifying the parallel secular verse, and hence its tune in whichever variant the tune was locally current.

The most important and interesting work in the field of sacred parody was carried out in Scotland by the brothers John, James and Robert Wedderburn. They were fanatical Protestants and their writings betray profound distaste for every aspect of Roman Catholicism and most of all for the Pope. John Wedderburn fled Dundee for Wittenburg in 1539 and was there influenced by the Lutheran practice of borrowing popular tunes for use with hymn texts. In the 1540s he and his brothers published the first of a series of volumes, each more comprehensive than the last, containing metrical versions of sacred texts ranging from parables to graces before and after meat. Commonly known as the Wedderburns' *Gude and godlie Ballates* after the edition of 1567 reprinted in 1897 edited by Alexander Ferrier Mitchell, the full titles of the various editions reveal more about the origins of some of the material. For instance an edition of the 1570s (from which the following examples are drawn) was entitled *Ane compendious buik of godlie psalmes and spirituall sangis collectit furthe of scripture, with diveris ballatis changeit out of prophane ungodlie sangis, for avoyding of sin and harlatrie. With augmentation of sindrie [gude] and godlie Ballates not contenit in the furst edition.*

In many of these versifications the language is full of picturesque similes such as poisoned snakes and cankered carrions, and there are subversive texts about supposed corruption in the Roman Catholic church. Some of the texts are direct sacred parodies of well-known secular poems. A particularly daring example is the parody on 'John, come kiss me now', an amorous song manipulated by the Wedderburns so that the singer is made to represent 'the Lord thy God' and 'John' mankind. The kiss was a symbol of reconciliation. The complete text runs to four pages and opens thus:

> Iohne cum kis me now, Iohne cum kis me now
> Iohne cum kis me by and by, and mak no moir adow.
> The Lord thy God I am that Iohne dois the call,
> Iohne representit man be grace celestiall.

The tune was widely known, both as a dance and a song, and one version of it formed the subject of a substantial set of variations by William Byrd in *The Fitzwilliam Virginal Book.*

In the Wedderburns' sacred parody of 'Goe from my window', the situation of a lover being refused admittance at an unfaithful wife's window because her husband is at home is transformed into that of a sinner who, after entreaties lasting 22 verses, is finally admitted to forgiveness in the presence of God. The repeated interrogations and dismissals from the window retain the reminiscence of carol-form in the original. The Wedderburns' version begins the dialogue thus:

> Quho is at my windo, quho, quho,
> Go from my windo, go, go
> Quho callis thair, sa lyke a strangair
> Go from my windo go.
>
> Lord I am heir, ane wratchit mortall
> That for thy mercy dois cry and call
> Unto the my Lord celestiall
> Se quho is at my windo, quho.

The tune existed in several versions and, with its accompanying amorous verses in which the lover was variously a sailor or a collier, was popular in England as well as in Scotland. A set of variations on one version of 'Goe from my window' appears twice in *The Fitzwilliam Virginal Book*, attributed first to Thomas Morley and later to John Munday.

An example of the Wedderburns' vivid invective against Rome can be seen in their sacred parody of 'The hunt is up', like 'Blow thy horn, hunter' a pastoral song with possible amorous allusions. It was popular in Tudor times and three variants of it appear in *The Fitzwilliam Virginal Book* as the subjects of sets of variations by Giles Farnaby, William Byrd and John Bull. The title could be applied to any tune intended as a morning wakening song, but the tune to the following words was probably the one borrowed by the Wedderburns:

> The hunt is up, the hunt is up
> And it is well nigh day,
> And Harry our king is gone hunting
> To bring his deer to bay.

This poem became the basis of mild 'moralizings' by other poets, but in the hands of the Wedderburns it seethes with gruesome vituperation:

> With huntis up, with huntis up,
> It is now perfite day,
> Jesus our King, is gaine in hunting
> Quha lykis to speid thay may.

> Ane cursit Fox, lay hid in Rox,
> This lang and mony ane day,
> Devouring scheip, quhill he micht creip,
> Nane micht him schaip away.

> It did him gude to laip the bluid
> Of young and tender lammis,
> Nane culd he mis, for all was his,
> The young anis with thair dammis.

> The hunter is Christ, that huntis in haist,
> The hundis ar Peter, and Paull,
> The Paip is the Foxe, Rome is the Rox,
> That rubbis us on the gall.

Subsequent verses of this long poem continue in a similar manner. However, enough has been quoted to give some idea of the mood, as well as of the strict adherence to the poetic scheme of the secular model. Also, the allegory of the Pope as the fox, explained in the fourth verse, suggests a possible wider implication for verses like this. In an age when symbolism and particularly animal symbolism was a common means of verbal and visual expression, it would presumably have been possible for apparently innocent songs such as 'Tomorrow the fox will come to town' (given with the 'Trenchmore' tune in Thomas Ravenscroft's *Deuteromelia,* 1609) to take on hidden, symbolic meanings of a political, religious or amorous nature.[28]

Polyphonic secular models

Although the adaptation to a sacred psalm text of Cornysh's secular partsong 'Blow thy horn, hunter' may not be an indication of the existence of a large repertory of similar adaptations, there are isolated surviving examples show-ing that the tradition of adaptation from secular polyphony persisted until the early seventeenth century at least. Even at this comparatively late stage there was no rigid distinction between sacred and secular music. The in-cidence of cultivated domestic music-making and its utilization for worship meant that there was nothing unusual or incongruous about collections of vocal or mixed consort pieces such as Thomas Tomkins's *Songs of 3. 4. 5. & 6. parts* (1622) that contained both secular and sacred madrigals. Sacred songs also occur in some early seventeenth century collections of lute ayres such as John Dowland's *A Pilgrimes Solace* (1612). These kinds of pieces were equally at home in both secular and sacred contexts, and so it is hardly surprising that pieces of a similar cast but with avowedly secular texts were adapted for sacred use alongside them.

There are at least two sacred adaptations from secular partsongs in a set of five partbooks dating from Elizabeth I's reign (London, British Library Ad-ditional manuscripts 30480–4). These partbooks are known to contain fur-ther adaptations including some from other sacred sources (Tallis's 'With all our hearts and mouths' from his first setting of 'Salvator mundi' is one, see p.35 above) and there may be yet more in this source whose models remain untraced. These partbooks are the sole source for Tallis's four-part anthem 'Purge me, O Lord' which is almost certainly an adaptation of his simple part-song 'Fond youth is a bubble'. The partsong may date from Henry VIII's reign but like the adaptation it could have been composed in Edward's or early in Elizabeth's reign. 'Fond youth is a bubble' survives only in a keyboard source (the *Mulliner Book*, London, British Library Additional manuscript 30513) from the same period, where no text beyond the title itself is given. It is possible that the secular version was an adaptation of the sacred one rather than vice versa, but in any case it may well be that the two versions originated almost contemporaneously and maintained a parallel existence. A four-part song from Henry VIII's reign by John Sheppard, 'O happy Dames', survives in a vocal source (London, Public Record Office, State Papers 1, Henry VIII, Vol.246 f.28v) giving its text, as well as in a keyboard arrange-ment in the *Mulliner book*. Its style is simple and direct, with brief closely-knit imitative passages reminiscent of many early English anthems by composers such as Christopher Tye. It comes as little surprise, therefore, to find 'O happy Dames' adapted to a sacred text: 'I will give thanks unto the Lord' in the same partbooks as Tallis's 'Purge me, O Lord'. This collation provided the means of attributing 'I will give thanks unto the Lord' to Sheppard, since the sacred version is known from only one source and was previously regarded as an anonymous anthem.

Given the close relationship between the early sixteenth-century partsong and the early anthem as background, the later mutual influence between the English madrigal and the late sixteenth and early seventeenth-century full anthem can be seen as less of an isolated or remarkable phenomenon. There are abundant examples of an intermingling of style between madrigal and anthem, especially in the works in both repertories of composers such as Thomas Weelkes. However, there seem to be few adaptations of secular material for sacred use, although those that are known serve to illustrate further the affinities of style between sacred and secular polyphony around the close of the sixteenth century.

John Wilbye (1574 or earlier – 1638) was chiefly a composer of madrigals, and 'Draw on, sweet night' for six voices is possibly his finest work. It is a substantial piece, but despite its length it is highly integrated and there is no lapse in its intensity of expression. Its text is a melancholy one, yearning for the relief from daily cares that darkness brings. The piece first appeared in Wilbye's *Second Set of Madrigals*, published in 1609. By 1614 Wilbye had reworked some of the material from this madrigal from six voices to five, using a sacred text beginning 'O God, the rock of my whole strength'. This piece, one of only a handful of anthems by Wilbye, was composed in response to a commission from Sir William Leighton, who had written a number of devotional metrical texts and engaged several distinguished English composers to set them to music. The results were published in Leighton's *The Teares or Lamentacions of a Sorrowfull Soule* (1614). The adaptation uses material from the madrigal in a heavily condensed form. Rhythmic intricacy is increased but the anthem lacks the sustained intensity of its model. Three further madrigals by Wilbye for three voices from his set published in 1609 occur with sacred texts in a manuscript dated c.1620 (Oxford, Christ Church Library, music manuscripts nos.1074–77), but these adaptations are not known to be Wilbye's work; nor, like the adaptation to Leighton's text, can it be certain that they were widely used in their sacred versions.

Unlike John Wilbye, Thomas Tomkins (1572–1656) was chiefly a composer of church music, with only a small known output of madrigals. One of his five-part madrigals, 'See, see the shepherds' Queen', first published in 1622 in his *Songs of 3. 4. 5. & 6. parts,* was adapted as an anthem to words begin-

ning 'Holy, holy, holy, Lord God of Sabaoth' and published with organ accompaniment in Tomkin's *Musica Deo sacra et Ecclesiae Anglicanae* of 1668.
At first glance the madrigal seems to be a strange choice for adaptation,
especially since there are several other madrigals by Tomkins that seem to
offer much more promising material for this purpose. 'See, see the shepherds'
Queen' is a lively piece of the ballett type but with the form extended to
provide three repeated sections (with interchange of the upper two voices)
instead of the more usual two. All sections have the characteristic ballett 'fa-
la' refrain, which in this madrigal is used as a catalyst for much of the contrapuntal, textural and climactic interest in the piece. The text is of a light,
pastoral nature. In its adaptation to sacred words the piece loses none of the
verve of the original. The sacred version is an almost exact *contrafactum*
of the madrigal. The 'fa-la' passages are given over to jubilant repetitions of
'alleluia' in a manner similar to Weelkes's musical use of this word in his anthem 'Alleluia, I heard a voice'. The adaptation may have been the work of
Tomkins's son Nathaniel, who after his father's death in 1656 prepared *Musica
Deo sacra* for publication. His standard of editorship was not above reproach
and perhaps because of this he has been criticized for having made this particular adaptation, chiefly on the grounds that certain word-stresses in the
piece are falsified as a result. But this criticism is hardly justified whether
or not Nathaniel was the arranger: the intrusion of the modern concept of
barlines is all that falsifies the word-stresses in anthem and madrigal alike,
and as an anthem the piece is remarkably convincing. Thomas Tomkins's
output of polyphonic madrigals and full anthems virtually concluded the era
of polyphonic composition in England. He showed little interest in the new
influences, chiefly from Italy and France, that were beginning to affect English
musical style in the seventeenth century. In both vocal and instrumental music
the ascendancy of harmonic elements and the consequent polarization of
melody and bass at the expense of the more amorphous contrapuntal textures led to new means of musical expression in both secular and sacred fields
that opened up further possibilities for interchange between them.[29]

6

Changes in Style: II

Theatre and instrumental music

The rise in predominance of theatre and instrumental music, particularly after
the restoration of the monarchy in 1660, opened up fruitful areas for sacred
borrowings. These borrowings tended to owe more to the assimilation of
the newly-fashionable treble-dominated style than to the use of actual borrowed material. The new style won immediate favour, not only among congregations who were impressed by its light textures, shapely melody and
unashamed virtuosic display, but by church musicians also. Trained singers
could exercise their talents as soloists (as, indeed, many of them were already
doing in the theatre). Less highly-trained singers, such as the children from
charitable institutions, could be taught unison melodies with continuo accompaniment on the organ. The organist, in turn, had the opportunity for
skilled technical expression in accompaniments and in solo pieces and interludes. The attention thus directed towards individual musicians led to a
curious by-product in the field of borrowing. This was a kind of inverse borrowing in which a piece of music could be given added prestige by being
ascribed (often without foundation) to a famous composer such as Purcell
or Handel. In this way the name was borrowed but not the music, instead
of the other way round.

But musical material of secular origin continued to be appropriated for
sacred use in both home and church. The principal trend, in line with the
diversification of types of instrumental music and the flourishing of various
kinds of theatre music, was the use of music from a greater variety of secular
origins to form works for sacred use. This trend continued until well into
the nineteenth century, when it was overtaken by a variety of factors including newly discovered or rediscovered sources for borrowings, and a
change in attitude partly influenced by the Tractarians which called into question the practice of allowing sacred music to be influenced by secular,
whether directly borrowed or not.

Since theatre music reflected one aspect of musical fashion and popular taste, it was natural that it should be drawn upon to provide material for devotional use at home or in church. This can be seen as an extension of the principle of using courtly songs, and later ballads, to sacred words. There is evidence to suggest that, even as early as Elizabethan times, some ballads may have originated as theatre music. Henry Purcell (1659–95) borrowed material originally for the theatre for re-use as music to accompany a religious ceremony, even if not strictly as church music. The March and Canzona for brass instruments and kettledrums, used in the funeral procession of Queen Mary in March 1695, is still regarded as one of the most apt and solemn works ever composed for such an occasion. Yet it started life as part of the music by Purcell to *The Libertine, or the Libertine Destroyed,* a tragi-comedy by Thomas Shadwell based on the Don Juan legend, to which Purcell wrote music in 1692. Brass instruments are a prominent feature in Purcell's music for the tragi-comedy, and so the music was ideal for processional use without any change of instrumentation. Music from other works composed by Purcell for the theatre was adapted for sacred use in the years that followed. As late as 1736 an adaptation to sacred words was published of a duet sung by Bacchus and Cupid in a masque written about 1694 by Purcell for Shadwell's adaptation of Shakespeare's *Timon of Athens.* The original version:

> Come, let us agree, there are pleasures divine
> In wine and in love, in love and in wine.

was changed in the 1736 sacred version to the following:

> Come, let us agree, there are pleasures and charms
> In anthems and hymns, and also in psalms.

In this case the bathos of the sacred version is heightened by the sprightly, beguiling nature of the duet music, but the example is not so very far removed in type from the 'moralizings' of secular ballads that were current in the seventeenth century. Adaptations of this kind from theatre music are descendants of that tradition. Despite objections in some quarters to the use for devotional purposes of any music, or even musical instruments, that had connections with the theatre, the practice of borrowing from theatre music continued, receiving further impetus in particular from the work of John and Charles Wesley in the eighteenth century.

One field in which borrowings could be undertaken from any source of popular melodies, whether vocal or instrumental, was that of the improvised organ voluntary. In this area the organist reigned supreme; his skill, knowledge and audacity were tempered only by the capabilities of his instrument and, on occasions, by what clergy and congregation would tolerate. Organists were quick to capitalize on the possibilities. The taste for light, melodious music rich in technical display sometimes overflowed into frivolity. By the end of the seventeenth century there were several recorded instances of organists being reprimanded for turning 'common ballads' or 'light gay tunes' into voluntaries — and then immediately flouting authority by doing likewise shortly afterwards. In the eighteenth century an increasing number of organ voluntaries were published that were arrangements of other music, particularly of Italian music originally for harpsichord, and of sections from fashionable Italian operas and concertos. The works, including those solely for instruments, of Giuseppe Tartini (1692-1770), Francesco Geminiani (1687-1762), Arcangelo Corelli (1653-1713) and of course Georg Friederich Handel (1685-1759) were considered particularly fruitful sources of thematic material also, upon which capable organists could improvise voluntaries that were more likely to induce devotional feelings in the congregation than the frivolous tunes that were sometimes used for this purpose.

The ornamentation of existing psalm tunes in the fashionable Italian style and the borrowing of further material for psalms, hymns and anthems from popular sacred music, particularly that of Handel, has already been noted (pp.43-44, 50-55, above). As editions of devotional music proliferated, so too did borrowings and adaptations, and alongside the borrowings from sacred sources there were a few from secular instrumental music. In these cases the transfer from an instrumental medium to a vocal one meant often that radical changes were necessary to adapt thematic material to a pre-existent metre, so that sometimes only a barely-recognizable vestige of the original remained. This is perhaps one reason why adaptations from purely instrumental music are generally outnumbered by those from vocal forms, which were sometimes more susceptible to satisfactory adaptation.

The following example of borrowing from a piece by Corelli demonstrates the problem of adaptation from instrumental music. It is taken from a volume published about 1808 that was largely a compendium of music that was current earlier, so the arrangement may well date back to at least the mid eighteenth century. Corelli's music was enormously popular in England, and his op.5 set of sonatas for strings and harpsichord, written in Rome in 1700, was especially favoured. Here the theme from the opening of Corelli's Trio Sonata op.5 no.12, the 'Folia' variation movement, is the subject of adaptation. The 'Folia' tune itself was well known in England: even before Corelli composed his variations the tune had appeared in England as the basis of works for recorder and for violin. In the sacred adaptation entitled 'Dunbar' in this publication, the 'Folia' tune is heavily truncated to meet the requirements of the short-metre (6 6 8 6) text. Corelli's theme falls naturally into four-bar phrases but the psalm phrases (except for the third) are only two and a half bars in length. Consequently the psalm's main caesura is in the middle of one of Corelli's phrases, the phrase-end at the imperfect cadence marking the main caesura in the 'Folia' theme occurs in the middle of the psalm's longest phrase, and the remaining psalm words have to make do with a perfunctory ending manufactured to resemble Corelli's cadence. Moreover, Corelli's elegant dotted rhythms are eliminated in favour of a series of staid minims. The melody lines are given in this example:

The result is far from satisfactory, yet arrangements like this coexisted with more satisfactory ones such as that in the same volume of psalms set to the opening of 'The flocks shall leave the mountains' from Handel's *Acis and Galatea,* entitled 'Bewsey' in the psalm collection.[30]

Current popular music

Most borrowings from secular music for the purpose of sacred adaptation until the mid eighteenth century occurred as isolated instances in collections consisting mainly of other material. After the reforming zeal of the sixteenth century, when the ploy of secular borrowing was used explicitly for the purpose of displacing 'wanton ditties', popular preferences in church music changed so that the emphasis was on music that was fashionable, elegant, easy to listen to and rewarding to perform rather than solemn, profound or idealistic. The old psalm tunes that still predominated, albeit sometimes in fashionable disguise, were considered by many to be dull and outmoded, and the usual uncaring manner of their performance did nothing to endear them to the musically perceptive worshipper. Yet this was the staple musical diet on offer in the established church in the eighteenth century for congregations to sing, with the chance for those of somewhat greater musical ability to take part in anthems in current popular styles.

Hymn singing had no formal place in the worship of the established church but increasingly it became a central feature in the worship of the dissenting bodies upon whose conduct of worship there was no official constraint. With the growth of hymn singing and the diversification beyond metrical psalm texts of devotional poetry for this purpose by writers such as Isaac Watts, there was increasing demand for new tunes that would provide a more convincing means of expressing these texts whilst at the same time staying within the musical capabilities of the congregation. Although other leaders and musicians were active in this field and sometimes furthered their aims by similar means, the demand for new tunes of this kind was met to the most significant extent by the efforts of John and Charles Wesley in the Nonconformist movement. Those of Rowland Hill and William Gardiner in the Evangelical movement (which came near to dissent with the established church) were also important in the shorter term but their lasting effects were much more limited. All these men of radical ideas made deliberate and co-ordinated attempts to influence church music, and particularly hymn singing, by copious direct borrowing and adaptation for sacred use of music from currently fashionable secular sources.

The contribution made by the brothers John (1703–91) and Charles (1707–88) Wesley to the development of English hymnody as a result of their contacts with the Moravians has already been noted (pp.47–48, above). The Wesleys were inspired by the heartiness and sincerity of the Moravians' singing, and felt that this was the kind of impetus that was needed to counteract the moribund state and slovenly conduct of English musical worship. Accordingly the Wesleys advocated the use of simple, appealing tunes, neither dreary and outmoded as some considered earlier psalm and hymn tunes to be, nor festooned with excessively complex 'fuging' and repetition like some of the settings that were beginning to gain favour in the established church. As a deliberate policy the Wesleys borrowed music from currently fashionable secular sources and adapted it for use in worship. Like Luther (but unlike Vaughan Williams, later) they had no misgivings about using material that still retained its secular associations. Charles Wesley even went so far as to advocate the Wesleys' policy in the words of one of his own hymns, a plea for musicians to rise up, 'plunder the carnal lover' of the 'moving strain' and 'melting measure' of music and rescue it for use in 'virtue's cause': a verse clearly inspired by the sentiment behind the aphorism 'Why should the devil have all the best tunes?'. This policy shocked conservative people particularly in the established church, who deplored the devotional use of any music that might summon profane or frivolous thoughts to the minds of worshippers. But the Wesleys themselves drew the line at the flippant or indecorous performance of music in worship, whatever its origin. They favoured hearty but devout singing, and deplored the florid tunes and elaborate anthems that by the 1760s had begun to infiltrate Nonconformist services.

The secular music used by the Wesleys came from a variety of sources. Some tunes were known only in particular areas of the country, and John Wesley noted them down on his travels. This may well have been the origin of the hymn tune 'Stella' (EH 417, A&MR 203 ii, MHB 452), known as the tune to a children's round-game in certain areas of northern England and incorporated under the name 'Coventry' into some Wesleyan books, being taken up as the tune for a Roman Catholic hymn in the 1850s. Other tunes were of theatrical origin. These include 'Jericho' (abridged as 'Milites', EH 1933 381, MHB 819, SP 343) which was adapted from the march in Handel's opera *Riccardo Primo, Re d'Inghilterra,* first performed in England in late 1727 in honour of the new king George II. The shape and character of Handel's triumphant tune were faithfully retained but, like so many hymn tunes, the music was made to modulate to the dominant at the ends of certain phrases. This was one of the Wesleys' earliest secular borrowings, appearing in *A Collection of Tunes Set to Music, As they are commonly Sung at the Foundery* (published in 1742). In 1761 Charles Wesley's famous hymn text 'Love divine, all loves excelling' appeared in John Wesley's *Sacred melody: or a Choice Collection of Psalm and Hymn Tunes* to the tune 'Fairest isle, all isles excelling' from Purcell's semi-opera *King Arthur* (composed in

1691), on the text of which the first stanza of Charles Wesley's hymn was clearly a sacred parody. As late as 1788 the Wesleys were continuing the practice: the hymn tune at first called 'Melisse' was borrowed from a comic opera by Jean Jacques Rousseau (1712–78), *Le devin du village* (The village soothsayer), first performed in 1752, and it later acquired the title 'Rousseau's dream' (MHB Additional Tunes 26). This hymn tune is borrowed from a lively gavotte, the first of a series of rustic dances forming the pantomime that concludes the opera. Although hymn and gavotte share a similar harmonic scheme the hymn melody is simpler, perhaps in this case suggesting borrowing by memorization and oral transmission rather than by direct copying. Surprisingly, this appealing tune was not one of those chosen by Charles Burney for his adaptation (published 1766) of Rousseau's opera as *The Cunning Man*.

Still other hymn tunes were based by the Wesleys or their associates on popular catches and melodies. Some of the models for these hymn tunes can be identified but others, in common with many of those that may have furnished sacred borrowings in earlier periods, are lost. This means that it is sometimes impossible to ascertain whether a particular hymn tune is a direct borrowing, or an original composition in a secular style. A case in point is the tune used for Charles Wesley's text 'Lo, he comes with clouds descending'. Known nowadays as 'Helmsley' (EH 7, A&MR 51, MHB 264, SP 65) and attributed to Thomas Olivers, one of the Wesleys' helpers, it is a typical eighteenth-century tune with a florid melody line, some emphasis on repetition and sequence, and the possibility of modest antiphony between high and low voices in the harmony. In the mid nineteenth century steps were taken to banish this tune from worship on the grounds of its supposed secular origin: 'Miss Catley's Hornpipe, danced at Sadler's Wells'. Although the tune first appeared with Wesley's words in 1769 and the hornpipe in question was not printed before 1774, the hornpipe is one of a number of similar popular tunes that Thomas Olivers might have heard whistled in the street, for he claimed a melody familiar to him in this way to have been the origin of his tune now known as 'Helmsley'. How far the tune by Olivers was original and how far derivative will probably never be known. But tunes like these, with their strong popular appeal, were a significant factor in attracting congregations to the Nonconformist movement at the expense of the established church. Many of these tunes, like 'Helmsley', have held their ground, attaining a circulation far in excess of their original Nonconformist origins.

Rowland Hill (1744–1833), like the Wesleys, was well aware of the power of music to influence people's minds, and as a church leader he pursued a

deliberate policy of direct borrowing from familiar secular music for adaptation as hymn tunes. One of the most charismatic and controversial preachers
of his day, he was refused priest's orders in the established church because
of his irregular preaching, and the first twelve years of his ministry were spent
in itinerant evangelism. With the help of rich and titled people who were
influenced by his ideals, he founded the Surrey Chapel in Blackfriars Road,
Southwark, London, in 1783, a licensed proprietary chapel in which he was
the minister for the next fifty years. He attracted large congregations to the
Surrey Chapel and administered Sunday schools for over 3,000 children.

Hymn singing featured strongly in services at the Surrey Chapel and its
associated institutions, and Rowland Hill's work in popularizing hymn singing had some effect on other churches too. He published collections of hymns
in the 1770s and 1780s but his main publications were in co-operation with
Benjamin Jacob (1778–1829), whom Hill engaged as organist at the Surrey
Chapel in 1794, a post which Jacob held for over thirty years. Hill believed
strongly in the sacred use of popular melodies and, like Martin Luther and
John and Charles Wesley, is asserted to have been the first person to have
stated that 'he did not see any reason why the devil should have all the best
tunes'. Whether or not he can be so credited, he put this belief enthusiastically
into practice. In *A Collection of Hymn Tunes, for 3 & 4 voices composed
for the use of Surry* [sic] *Chapel, by Dr Arnold, Messrs. Breillat & Dixon
etc.* published in 1797 by Benjamin Jacob and dedicated to Rowland Hill,
several popular melodies were adapted for use with sacred texts. But the best
known of Hill's hymns was a fairly free but instantly recognizable parody
of the patriotic song 'Rule, Britannia', the tune of which was clearly intended to be borrowed for use with the following words:

> When Jesus first at Heaven's command,
> Descended from His azure throne,
> Attending angels joined His praise,
> Who claimed the kingdoms for His own.
> Hail, Immanuel! Immanuel we'll adore,   } Repeated at the end
> And sound His fame from shore to shore.   } of all six verses.

This appeared, entitled 'The Kingdom of Immanuel, exalted', in a large collection of texts which went through several editions from 1783 to 1830 under
Hill's editorship. Tuneful, stirring material like this, sung by a large congregation, exerted a compelling influence on rich and poor alike and helped to
win adherents to Rowland Hill's ministry, despite disapproval from the more
conservative factions in the established church.

William Gardiner (1770–1853) of Leicester was active as a musician, not as a church leader. His interest in hymns was musical rather than ecclesiastical: he deplored the state of hymn singing in England, including the borrowing for devotional purposes of what he considered to be trivial secular melodies. Unlike the church leaders John and Charles Wesley and Rowland Hill, he had no particular interest in musical ploys designed to attract large and enthusiastic congregations. The motive for his efforts at reform was the desire to introduce good modern music into the church for congregational use without necessarily having recourse to material of bygone days, such as the old psalm tunes. In his wish to introduce modern material his views were in direct conflict with those of church musicians who came under the influence of the Tractarian movement in the nineteenth century (see pp.60–61, 70 above) and who felt that the only way to redeem church music from its degenerate state was to bring music from the distant past, such as plainsong, back into use.

Gardiner's hosiery business afforded him the funds he needed to travel abroad and make the personal acquaintance of Beethoven, whose music he promoted in England and from whom he tried to commission an overture. Gardiner was highly esteemed nationally as composer, writer and musical executant, and was thus in a good position to make his publications widely known in influential circles. His *Sacred Melodies, from Haydn, Mozart and Beethoven* published in six volumes between 1812 and 1838, included adaptations of passages from Viennese classical works for use with psalms and hymns. Both sacred and secular works were used and the volumes included a wider selection of composers, many of whose works are now almost forgotten, than those named in the title.

In general Gardiner chose slow, lyrical sections as his models although scherzo and minuet movements were not altogether avoided. He tended to retain original keys and was largely faithful to the textures of his models even where this produced partwriting that was inapt for the scoring he used, as in his vocal arrangement of the variation movement of Haydn's so-called 'Emperor' string quartet op.76 no.3 in C, in which the inner vocal parts have to cope with isolated words and long rests at one moment and florid arpeggios at another (see also below, pp.129, 133–35). From Beethoven's instrumental music the opening of the funeral march from the second movement of Symphony no.3 in E flat, op.55 ('Eroica'), composed in 1804, was used as a funeral hymn scored for three-part chorus, organ and kettledrums, and the second movement of Beethoven's Violin Concerto in D, op.61, composed in 1806, gave a hymn with the words 'We beseech thee' repeated to the opening rhythmic figure.

Although little of Gardiner's work survived beyond the nineteenth-century hymn repertory it is important in the history of church music borrowed from secular sources for three reasons. First, it showed that popular evangelism was not necessarily the main reason for using secular melody for sacred purposes. Second, it showed that (apart from original composition) there was a way of providing worthwhile music for church use that satisfied current needs but did not depend upon an idealistic recourse to music from the past. Third, it marked the beginning of the nineteenth-century fashion, continued by Vincent Novello and others, for adapting instrumental classical pieces for devotional use. In retrospect it is easy to dismiss this fashion as one of the many supposed aberrations of nineteenth-century church music. Despite the efforts of the Tractarians, however, works from the concert hall continued to influence church music, both in direct borrowings and in style, until the beginning of the twentieth century.[31]

7

The Nineteenth Century

Instrumental music and opera

William Gardiner's publications were the earliest sustained attempt at wholesale borrowing from contemporary secular music for use with English sacred texts. As such they were a landmark in a practice that had been in piecemeal but tenacious existence since near the beginning of the eighteenth century. As the nineteenth century progressed, further borrowings of this kind proliferated. Their dissemination was undoubtedly helped by the increasing availability of cheap printed music for use both at home and in church, and by the spread of musical literacy beyond the confines of the richer classes of society. Music, mainly for use as hymns, was borrowed from orchestral and chamber works, piano music and opera. Composers from whom material was borrowed included Haydn, Mozart, Weber, Beethoven, Schumann, Mendelssohn and Spohr, with occasional recourse to the secular works of earlier composers such as Handel. For obvious reasons there was a tendency for borrowings to be taken from themes that were sustained and lyrical rather than motivic or complex in rhythm or texture. Slow movements from symphonies, chamber music and piano music in classical forms, themes from variation movements, simple operatic arias and piano music with a compact but prominent melody were the sources most frequently used.

Many such adaptations appeared in *The Psalmist,* a collection of four volumes each containing 100 tunes, edited by Vincent Novello (1781–1861) and published from 1835 to 1843. Although these volumes contained a great deal of material apart from adaptations of the kind under discussion, they were undoubtedly among the most influential collections in widening the range of borrowings. Many of the adaptations were by Novello himself, but others in *The Psalmist* were by distinguished musicians such as Henry John Gauntlett (1805–76), remembered now as the composer of 'Once in Royal David's city', and Sir John Goss (1800–80), known now chiefly for his splendid familiar tune to 'Praise, my soul, the King of heaven'. Sir Henry Walford

Davies (1869–1941), whose reputation rested upon teaching rather than composition but whose most enduring contribution to English hymnody was probably the tune to 'God be in my head', continued to make sacred adaptations from classical sources until well into the twentieth century. All these musicians would probably have been acutely embarrassed, in retrospect, at being credited with some of their arrangements from classical masterpieces. In use as sacred music, most of the arrangements under discussion did not outlast the nineteenth century, persisting for longer in some Nonconformist and evangelical collections. The practice of such adaptations was deplored by many writers as the twentieth century approached. Yet it continued, with examples appearing not only in *Hymns Ancient and Modern Revised* (1950) but, amazingly, in *The English Hymnal* (1906) and *Songs of Praise* (1926). The examples in the latter two collections were of new adaptations from instrumental music and opera, and will be discussed in a later section (see below, pp.144, 148).

From the repertory of symphonies, those of Beethoven seem to have been most favoured by Novello, Gauntlett and others for arrangement as hymns. Gauntlett's tune entitled 'Alsace' which appeared in Novello's *The Psalmist* (no.250) and in the *Congregational Hymnary* of 1916 (no.97) is an arrangement of the opening of the second movement of Beethoven's Symphony no.2 in D, attributed in *The Psalmist* to 'Louis Beethoven'. An obvious target for the arranger, the familiar 'Ode to joy' theme from the last movement of Beethoven's choral symphony no.9 in D was adapted by Henry Walford Davies for use as a hymn in the *Fellowship Hymn Book* (1933) to a text giving thanks for comradeship at summer camps. Beethoven's harmony is modified to admit further pedal-points, and even his melody is made more suave and demure. But perhaps the most astounding guise in which a Beethoven symphonic fragment appeared was that of a double psalm chant. Sir John Goss's arrangement of the opening theme from the second movement of Beethoven's Symphony no.7 in A appears below:

In this example, Beethoven's well-balanced theme is disfigured almost beyond recognition. From its eight short phrases, Goss has made what appears to be an almost arbitrary selection of the first, third, fourth (so that the main intermediate cadence is included), fifth, sixth and seventh. The eighth, final phrase is thus embarrassingly conspicuous by its absence, and to sing or hear this fragment repeatedly in the context of a chanted psalm or canticle must have been scarcely tolerable, with or without prior knowledge of the Beethoven model. Furthermore, the harmony is altered. Sometimes this is because of the changes in rhythm necessary to turn the music into a chant, but sometimes it happens for no apparent reason, exemplified by the gratuitous dominant seventh that appears in Goss's third bar. This adaptation is a particularly lamentable one, and it shows the lengths to which even distinguished musicians were prepared to go in their quest to press classical masterpieces into the service of the church.

The best-known example of an apparent borrowing from chamber music is that of the tune 'Austrian hymn' (EH 393, 535; A&MR 'Austria' 257, 368, 632; MHB 16, 228; SP 500) which is the melody used by Joseph Haydn as the theme for variations in the second movement of his string quartet op.76 no.3 in C, known as the 'Emperor' quartet, published in 1797. But since this theme had been used in the previous year by Haydn in his choral piece 'Gott erhalte Franz den Kaiser' ('The Emperor's hymn') it is probably more accurate to consider the well-known hymn tune as a borrowing from a secular cantata (see below, pp.133–35, also above, p.125) rather than from chamber music. Beethoven's chamber music was the source for the hymn tune 'Bonchurch' which appears arranged by Vincent Novello in *The Psalmist* (no. 390) and as no.314 ('Hail to the Lord's anointed') in *The Congregational Hymnary* of 1916: its model was the variation theme from the fourth movement of Beethoven's Septet in E flat, op.20, for strings and wind instruments, composed in 1799 and 1800. The densely-harmonized hymn version turns Beethoven's delicately-scored caprice into something much more ponderous.

The theme from the second movement (Andante con variazioni) of Louis Spohr's string quartet in A minor op.58 no.2, composed in 1821 or 1822, was used as the source for the tune 'Lebanon', also known as 'Flensburg' (MHB 602 ii). Spohr's elegant and lightly-scored melody is reduced to three quarters of its original length by the extraction of the third section which carries most of the harmonic interest. Consequently the hymn modulates only to the dominant and back. The melody is further altered to make it more compact and, presumably, easier to sing. Spohr's music was a favoured source for chant melodies as well as hymn tunes: some of each survive in *The Bristol Tune Book,* of which several editions were published between 1863 and 1891.

Piano music, particularly the piano sonatas of Beethoven, gave plenty of material for borrowing and arrangement as sacred music. The arrangement of the theme from the slow movement of Beethoven's piano sonata op.13 in C minor, (the 'Pathétique'), completed about 1798, as a psalm chant which survives in *The Cathedral Psalter,* first published with music in 1878, is mercifully more respectful to Beethoven's original than the chant adapted from his seventh symphony (see above, p.128). Even so, 'Beethoven in D', as this popular chant was labelled, bears only an unhappy resemblance to its model. It must be one of the few examples of a borrowing for English sacred use in which the music has to be performed at a more rapid tempo than the original, instead of being slowed down to achieve what was considered to be an appropriate degree of decorum for church use.

The hymn entitled 'Hayes', taken in the following example from *The Bristol Tune Book* edition of about 1876 but surviving also in several other sources, demonstrates how even the most subtle, intimate and good-humoured music of a lively nature could be rendered practically immobile in the cause of the Victorians' concept of penitence:

He dies, the Friend of sinners dies;
Lo! Salem's daughters weep around;
A solemn darkness veils the skies;
A sudden trembling shakes the ground.
Ye saints, with contrite hearts, review,
How He beneath your burdens groaned,
Not tears, but blood, He wept for you,
And for a guilty world atoned.

In this arrangement (credited in *The Bristol Tune Book* to W. R. Braine), the theme of the variations in the second (Andante) movement of Beethoven's piano sonata, op.14 no.2 in G, composed about 1799, is used in a truncated form as the basis of a solemn hymn tune. Its pace was presumably slowed down to fit Isaac Watts's lugubrious text, the nature of which bears added witness to the total incongruity of this adaptation. All Beethoven's wit and ingenuity, particularly in his handling of rhythmic stress, has been swept away. The result is a specimen of cheerless uniformity pressed into alliance with an equally cheerless text. Faced with adaptations like this, the indignation of those who favoured a Tractarian point of view on church music is easy to understand.

One of Mendelssohn's *Songs without Words* for piano, op.30 no.3 in E, published in 1835, provided material for a somewhat less startling adaptation as a hymn tune. Adapted at first by Adolphus Levy as a hymn tune called 'Epiphany' in Edward John Hopkins's *The Temple Church Choral Service* of c.1867 (no.146), it was adapted again by Sir Sydney Nicholson (1875–1947) especially for inclusion in *Hymns Ancient and Modern Revised* (1950). The tune, entitled 'Felix' (A&MR 463), provides a relatively harmless but insipid setting for the wedding hymn 'O perfect Love', retaining Mendelssohn's phrasing and characteristic harmony with its extended bass pedal-points at the cadences. It is surprising to find this kind of adaptation appearing afresh in so late a collection, and predictably it provoked some disapproval. Another of Mendelssohn's *Songs without Words*, op.19 no.1 in E, adapted c.1867 by Edward John Hopkins complete with closing *rallentando* and 'Amen', provided a tune formerly sung to 'It came upon the midnight clear' (see also below, p.142).

A few adaptations were made from operatic music, perpetuating a tradition of adaptation from theatre music that had been in sporadic existence for two centuries. In the nineteenth century, in line with the English predilection for music in the prevailing German and Viennese styles and the fashion for adapting such music for sacred use, the models were the operas of composers such as Mozart and Weber. Later, even Wagner's music was used, but that was part of a separate development that did not contribute to the nineteenth-century spate of wholesale and almost indiscriminate adaptations (see below, pp.144–45).

Two of Mozart's operas with libretti by Lorenzo da Ponte evidently provided material for hymn tunes, both of which seem almost amazingly inapt when their origins are known. One of these was made by Mozart's pupil Thomas Attwood (1765–1838) for Vincent Novello's collection *The Psalmist*. Attwood, who wrote much original music for the church including a well-known tune to the hymn 'Come, Holy Ghost, our souls inspire', was induced by contemporary attitudes into adapting as a hymn tune Zerlina's aria 'Batti, batti, o bel Masetto' from Act I of Mozart's *Don Giovanni,* composed in 1787. In the opera, this winsome but agitated piece is Zerlina's attempt to appease her lover Masetto after her flirtation with Don Giovanni. Entitled 'Norwood' *(The Psalmist* no.86, not the tune 'Norwood' at MHB 666), the bland, innocuous hymn version, with its contrived final cadence, loses all the urgency of Mozart's original and stands as the antithesis of a fitting posthumous tribute to Attwood's teacher.

The origins of another apparent Mozart borrowing are more obscure. The hymn tune 'Hursley' (EH 274, A&MR 24, MHB 942) caused disapproval on its inclusion in the first edition of *Hymns Ancient and Modern* (1861) and in subsequent editions, because of its resemblance to Figaro's aria 'Se vuol ballare' in Act I of Mozart's *The Marriage of Figaro,* composed in 1785 and 1786. Indeed, the resemblance of the hymn tune to the opening of Mozart's almost wickedly tongue-in-cheek portrayal of Figaro's attitude to his master Count Almaviva is striking. The description of the hymn as an 'execrable spoliation' of the aria would be justified if this hymn were, in fact, an adaptation. But direct derivation is unlikely in this case. The tunes diverge by the end of the hymn's second phrase, and after that its resemblance to the aria is slight except in metre. The beguiling, lilting character of 'Hursley' is seen in better perspective as a borrowing of style rather than substance, a probability borne out by evidence which attributes its origin to a melody in a Viennese *Katholisches Gesangbuch* of about 1774. Thus the tune was current in sacred use before Mozart wrote his opera, and the close affinities of style between theatre and church music in late eighteenth-century Vienna would have made Mozart's composition of a similar melody for an aria seem to be nothing out of the ordinary. 'Hursley' may well have entered the English hymn repertory by way of hymnals in German use in the early nineteenth century. Later writers objected to its lilting character, especially when allied to solemn words, and its resemblance to an operatic aria served only to add fuel to the fire of their invective.[32]

Contemporary secular cantatas

At first sight the secular cantata may appear to have been a potentially less fruitful field for English church music, although a small number of nineteenth-century borrowings consisted of adaptations from earlier music of related types, particularly that of Handel. However, two nineteenth-century borrowings from contemporary secular cantatas proved to be enormously successful almost from the moment of inception, and they have remained as familiar and worthwhile enrichments of the English church music repertory. As such they stand in complete contrast to some of the adaptations discussed immediately above which can for the most part be seen as travesties, both of the music from which they originated and of the purpose which their presumably well-intentioned devisers meant them to serve. Those who, for whatever reason, deplore sacred borrowings from secular music, would nevertheless be unlikely to dismiss as travesties the hymn tunes 'Austrian Hymn' (commonly sung to 'Glorious things of thee are spoken') and 'Mendelssohn' (the tune now sung to 'Hark! the herald angels sing'). Perhaps the durability of these hymn tunes and the respect in which they are held reflects the wisdom of the policy later adopted in general by Vaughan Williams: that of borrowing for sacred use only music that no longer has current secular associations. For this purpose, as exemplified by the somewhat bizarre adaptations from Beethoven discussed above, such associations include a secular context (such as a symphony) as well as secular words (such as an operatic aria). The Haydn and Mendelssohn tunes are adaptations of portions of secular cantatas that in their own times were relevant chiefly to particular sets of circumstances. These circumstances had no special relevance either in England or after the celebrations for which the cantatas were composed. Consequently the models for these hymn tunes were hardly known in England and the adaptations from them retained almost no incongruous associations.

The hymn-tune 'Austrian hymn' (EH 393, 525, A&MR 257 as 'Austria', MHB 16, 228 as 'Austria', SP 500) may have begun as a Croatian folksong, but Joseph Haydn (1732–1809) wrote it first in 1796 as a solo song with keyboard, a few months later setting it for what at the time would have been considered a large orchestra to form a miniature solo cantata. The words, 'Gott erhalte Franz den Kaiser' ('God save Emperor Franz') are by Lorenz Leopold Haschka (1749–1827), linking divine invocation with praise for the goodness and wisdom of the emperor himself. The piece was intended as a tribute to the Holy Roman Emperor Francis II (1768–1835) on his birthday in February 1797. In September of that year the tune appeared as the theme for variations in the second movement of Haydn's so-called 'Emperor' string quartet op.76 no.3 in C, and by the end of 1799 Haydn had composed an arrangement of this string quartet movement for keyboard. The tune was subsequently used as the national anthem of Austria, Germany, and the German Federal Republic. Its use as such by Germany in World War II led to a degree of ambivalence towards its status as an acceptable hymn tune on the part of those whose memories of wartime suffering remained all too vivid. The tune seems to have first been used as a hymn in Germany in 1804, but its use as such in England apparently began earlier than this. Although it was printed in an English collection of c.1802, it also appeared in an undated pamphlet which may antedate this. The pamphlet formed a supplement to *Psalms, hymns and anthems for the Foundling Chapel* (1796), and gave the tune as that which was to be sung to the anonymous metrical version of Psalm 148: 'Praise the Lord! ye heavens, adore him'. The hymn tune with its usual harmonization is close to Haydn's vocal version. There is slight adjustment in rhythm and ornamentation and the phrasing is altered: Haydn's tune is based on an anacrusis at the half bar whereas the hymn tune proceeds in neat two-ba

phrases with the stress at the start of each phrase coinciding with the barring. Haydn's harmonization is for the most part sparser, and the hymn tune
dispenses with the repetition of Haydn's final musical phrase which carries
the refrain 'Gott erhalte Franz den Kaiser, unsern guten Kaiser Franz' ('God
save Emperor Franz, our good Emperor Franz') at the end of each of Haschka's
four verses.

The tune 'Mendelssohn' (EH 24, A&MR 60, MHB 117 as 'Berlin', SP 74),
used almost exclusively for Charles Wesley's Christmas hymn published in
1739 beginning 'Hark! the herald angels sing', is an adaptation of part of
Festgesang, a secular cantata composed in 1840 consisting of a group of
choruses by Felix Mendelssohn (1809–47). Wesley's text originally began with
'Hark! how all the welkin rings, Glory to the King of kings', a version still
occasionally encountered. It was printed with the tune 'Dent Dale' (EH 23,
MHB 804, SP 88), an adaptation by Ralph Vaughan Williams of an English
folksong. The better-known opening, with some further material added to
Wesley's original text, became established in the 1750s. At some time in 1847
or more probably as late as the mid 1850s, William Hayman Cummings
(1831–1915), a highly-respected English church musician with a profound
knowledge of Mendelssohn's music, adapted a section of *Festgesang* for use
with 'Hark! the herald angels sing'. Whether or not Cummings's efforts to
adapt this section of Mendelssohn's piece to sacred words were the first, cannot now be ascertained. Some other versions were published around the same
time as his, c.1856. The possibility that earlier attempts were at least considered is suggested by Mendelssohn's own assertion, apparently made in
1843, that he believed the music to be unsuitable for sacred words, although
Elizabeth Poston has noted a strong resemblance between Mendelssohn's
tune and a martial aria by Johann Christoph Pepusch first performed in London in 1715.

Mendelssohn's *Festgesang* (a work without opus number) was written in
1840 as part of a commission for the Leipzig Festival to celebrate the 400th
anniversary of Johann Gutenberg's invention of the printing press. It is scored
for male chorus and two separate and predominantly antiphonal brass groups,
one large, one small and directed to be placed at a distance from the main
body of performers. There are four movements, the outer two being set-
ings based on the German hymns 'Es ist das Heil uns kommen her' ('Salva-
ion has come to us') and 'Nun danket alle Gott' ('Now thank we all our God'),
but with different texts (by A. E. Prölss) substituted for the usual hymn texts.
Thus the cantata has some sacred allusions even though its principal sen-
iments are secular. The second movement, upon the first part of which Cummings based his adaptation, is entitled 'Lied' ('Song'). The male chorus sings

the well-known tune in unison almost throughout. The adaptation intercalates a fragment of the trumpet melody at the brief moments in Mendelssohn's piece where the voices are static on a dominant pedal, and the harmony throughout is close to that which Mendelssohn scored for brass instruments. The text of this movement is overtly secular and patriotic. It is easy to understand Mendelssohn's consternation at any sacred use of the music, which moves at a fairly rapid pace befitting the lively, festive text. The first two verses (the extent of Cummings's adaptation) are given here:

1. Vaterland, in deinen Gauen brach der gold'ne Tag einst an,
    Deutschland, deine Völker sah'n seinen Schimmer niederthauen.
    Gutenberg, der deutsche Mann, Gutenberg, der deutsche Mann,
        Zündete die Fackel an,
    Gutenberg, der deutsche Mann, zündete die Fackel an.

2. Neues allgewalt'ges Streben wogt im Land des Lichtes auf,
    Seinem raschen Siegeslauf folgt ein allbeglückend Leben.
    Gutenberg, der grosse Mann, Gutenberg, der grosse Mann,
        Hat dies hehre Werk gethan,
    Gutenberg, der grosse Mann, hat dies hehre Werk gethan.

(Fatherland, once, when the golden day dawned in your regions,
Germany, your people have seen his glimmer of light emerge.
Gutenberg the German has set the torch ablaze.

A new, supreme endeavour has stirred in the land of light,
His life of good fortune follows a swift course of victory.
Gutenberg the Great has attained this sublime achievement.)

Lest Mendelssohn's music in Cummings's adaptation were thought to be too secular, an alternative tune was offered in the first complete edition of *Hymns Ancient and Modern* (1861). But Cummings's adaptation soon supplanted any rival tune. Apart from its intrinsic merit, its success may have been due in part to the limited relevance and appeal of this particular Mendelssohn occasional piece to the English consciousness, so that its secular origins were not well known and therefore not obtrusive and apparently incongruous. At any rate, despite its patriotic German text, it was sufficiently well entrenched as the tune for Charles Wesley's Christmas hymn to survive the English anti-German sentiments of two world wars, finding an enduring place as one of the best-known English Christmas carols.[33]

Glees, partsongs, solos, hymns and anthems

From the middle of the eighteenth century onwards, music from the English partsong repertory furnished material for borrowing as hymns and anthems

Given an established tradition of borrowing secular music for sacred purposes this is hardly a surprising development, since from this time until around the end of the nineteenth century the principal English composers of secular choral songs were also often the most highly-respected church musicians. Examples included John Wall Callcott (1766–1821) who wrote numerous glees and a few anthems, and was responsible jointly with Samuel Arnold for the collection of tunes entitled *The Psalms of David for the Use of Parish Churches,* published in 1791. Jonathan Battishill (1738–1801), still remembered for his massive anthem *Call to Remembrance,* was also famous as a prize-winning writer of glees.

The glee was a type of simple unaccompanied partsong, usually for three or four male voices but sometimes for a small mixed group of singers. The subjects of the texts were secular. They could be serious or cheerful, touching on any of the pleasures of life: a pipe of tobacco, a pastoral scene or the joy of music itself. The singing of glees was usually a pastime of the cultivated amateur musician, and societies were formed for this purpose. Renewed interest in the madrigal in the mid-eighteenth century led to the formation of similar groups to promote madrigal singing, but the glee retained its separate status as a more readily appealing and less cerebral form of music-making. Both the glee and the madrigal in this period provided sources from which English church music was borrowed. Of the two forms, the influence of the glee on church music was the more widespread, largely because it had more affinity with current styles of church music. Its influence was deplored by Samuel Sebastian Wesley, who in 1849 wrote a tirade on the current state of church music in which he complained that the reduced size of choirs meant that the resulting ensemble pieces that predominated were 'more like *glees* than church music'.

Earlier examples of sacred music borrowed from madrigals (see above, p.115–16) showed that because of their texture they were restricted to the anthem repertory, and these borrowings did not survive into modern use. This applies to similar later attempts also. In his three-volume collection entitled *Harmonia Sacra* published in 1800, John Page (c.1760–1812), a London vicar choral, included an adaptation of a madrigal for four voices by the Italian Luca Marenzio (1553 or 1554–99): 'Dissi a l'amata mia lucida stella', first published in 1585. This adaptation, by Thomas Bever, an academic lawyer and amateur musician, works relatively well since the madrigal is one of Marenzio's less characteristically vivid or idiomatic pieces. It is an almost exact *contrafactum,* to a text beginning 'Save, Lord, hear us when we call', with figured bass added. Marenzio's piece was also popular in Thomas Oliphant's secular version 'Lady, see on every side'.

The simpler glee, on the other hand, offered material that was thought suitable for borrowing as hymn tunes. Identifiable borrowings of this kind that have survived into modern use include the tune 'Harington', also known by its original title 'Retirement' (EH 85, MHB 593, SP 613). This tune was originally a glee for three voices beginning 'Beneath the silent rural call', composed about 1775 by Henry Harington (1727–1816), an amateur musician who had no professional connection with church music. This glee was adapted as a hymn tune for four voices. Its original form has not been greatly obscured in the borrowing: the elegant melody and the mellifluous harmony emphasizing movement in thirds between the upper two voices still typify the style and texture of many eighteenth-century glees.

In the first half of the nineteenth century the spread of musical literacy to an increasing range of social class meant that unaccompanied part-singing was no longer exclusively the pastime of well-to-do cultivated amateur musicians. Apart from the aristocratic glee societies there grew up a tradition of recreational church and domestic part-singing among working people, particularly in the north of England. The glee itself survived in this broader context, but it was superseded by less ephemeral and more versatile types of partsong under the influence of fashionable German and Viennese composers in the partsong repertory such as Schubert and particularly Mendelssohn. Later in the century there were striking parallels of style between the secular partsongs of composers such as Barnby and Sullivan, and some of their hymns and anthems. These are not, strictly speaking, borrowings of material but rather of style.

In a musical climate which, as far as the domestic market was concerned subsisted to a large extent on 'arrangements', the appropriation of partsongs to swell the fast-growing hymn repertory was not the isolated aberration which, in retrospect, it may appear to have been. Such borrowing was a mark of respect and approval, and in this area no composer met with greater respect or approval than Mendelssohn. Equally at ease in the vocal forms of oratorio, cantata, unaccompanied church music and partsong, Mendelssohn wrote with a facility of style in which there are strong similarities in the vocal writing in all these forms. Many of his partsongs were intended as recreational ('open air') music and were published as such in England; nevertheless, they were sometimes elevated inappropriately to the status of formal concert pieces and a few of the less boisterous ones met an even more sombre fate as hymns. The following example, current in other hymnals but taken in this case from *The Bristol Tune Book* edition from c.1876 (no.116), is the kind of piece that sullies Mendelssohn's musical reputation, whereas in reality it is only a vestige of a much more interesting partsong:

This tune, entitled 'Sherborne', consists of extracts from Mendelssohn's partsong 'Ruhetal' (op.59 no.5), composed in 1843. Published in England as 'The vale of rest', the partsong begins with four-part harmony over a tonic pedal, a device much favoured by Mendelssohn and those under his influence. This gives way to a texturally varied and harmonically more mobile central section that accounts for about half the total length of the piece. The closing bars, in four-part harmony with an extended cadence, act as an appropriate gathering-point after the comparative waywardness of the central section. The adaptation uses only the beginning of the first section and the final ex-ended cadence. Consequently half the hymn tune has a tonic pedal as an undertow, after which the long-drawn-out cadence is of little relevance. The omission of the most interesting section of the partsong (doubtless for prac-ical reasons because four-part harmony is largely in abeyance in this sec-ion), combined with the diligent flattening out of Mendelssohn's dotted rhythms, leaves no more than a forlorn reminiscence of the original music. Other borrowings of hymns from Mendelssohn's partsongs adopt similar pro-cedures. In some cases a little more variety of texture, such as unison writing for a brief passage, is retained.

Solo songs, too, provided material for hymns. Adaptations for this pur-pose even incorporated the mainstay of the popular repertory, 'Home sweet home'. This song, dating from 1823 in an opera by Henry Rowley Bishop 1786–1855), was subjected to arrangements and variations so numerous and diverse that it was still being reprinted in some form in the 1920s. Undoubted-ly some pre-existent music of a similar kind (described in relation to its time as 'present-day urban folksong') was borrowed for use with the gospel hymns

of the Salvation Army and revivalists such as Moody and Sankey. But their
music was based largely on borrowed secular styles rather than identifiable
material. By the end of the nineteenth century the practice of almost indiscriminate borrowing of secular music for sacred purposes had become
so deeply entrenched that some reaction against it was inevitable. The Tractarian movement was significant in this respect but, partly because many of
their precepts were reminiscent of Roman Catholicism, their influence on
music was chiefly confined to the so-called 'high' Anglican church and scarcely touched other forms of worship. Some writers and musicians condemned the entire practice of borrowing from secular sources, including even the
earliest examples that entered the English sacred repertory from Genevan
and Lutheran sources in the sixteenth century. In few cases was borrowing
seen as beneficial, for no account was taken of affinities of style between
sacred and secular music.

   In a pamphlet dating from 1897 reprinted from an article in *The Chur-
chman,* doubts were expressed about the validity of 'Old Hundredth' and
'Passion Chorale' as hymn tunes because of their distant secular associations.
From the category of 'good' hymn tunes the writer of the pamphlet also
sought to exclude '.... all the whole tribe of 'adaptations' or endeavours to
press into the service of the Church music not written for such use. No doubt
these endeavours are well-intentioned ... but ... the ingenuity has been misapplied'. The composer Charles Villiers Stanford (1852–1924), who wrote much
notable church music most of which has outlived his even larger secular output, expressed concern but in even broader terms. He wished to rule out
all adaptations 'imported from sources, foreign in more senses than one,
foreign to our buildings, to our services and to our tastes'. It is clear from
his mention of 'a vulgar modern anthem of foreign origin' that he deplored
adaptations to English of sacred music as well as secular. Although the fashion
that led to a flood of adaptations had subsided by the end of the nineteenth
century, some elements of it persisted until well into the twentieth. But by
this time, new movements had begun to influence English church music.
These movements brought with them radical changes in attitude towards
the borrowing of secular music for use in worship, sweeping away the
wholesale and musically indiscriminate appropriation for this purpose of
secular material that had been a particular feature of nineteenth-century
church music.[34]

8

New Trends in the Twentieth Century

'The English Hymnal'

The appointment of Ralph Vaughan Williams as musical editor of *The English Hymnal,* which first appeared in 1906, was a propitious move on the part of its instigators which was to have a profound effect on English church music. Like some other hymnals that appeared around the same time, *The English Hymnal* had an educative purpose. But whereas the success of other hymnals with a similar purpose was limited in scope or short-lived, *The English Hymnal* maintained a widespread and tenacious influence, largely because of its straightforward practical approach that ensured wide congregational utility. As well as introducing music borrowed from other sacred repertories, Vaughan Williams incorporated a large proportion of secular borrowings into *The English Hymnal.* But these borrowings were very different from those that had entered English church music in previous centuries. The sources for secular borrowings explored by Vaughan Williams showed a preponderance of traditional melodies, mainly from England but also from Scotland, Wales, Ireland and mainland Europe. In many cases these tunes were on the verge of extinction and had lost for the twentieth-century congregation any secular associations they may previously have had. Traditional tunes from foreign sources, likewise, would have lacked direct secular associations in England. Thus, in his choice of material, Vaughan Williams turned his back on the policy of previous compilers, which had been to choose familiar, fashionable material for use in sacred collections. Only a very few new arrangements from music of other secular genres were admitted to *The English Hymnal* and, on the whole, these have not survived in common use as hymns. Some secular adaptations that had already gained popular currency as hymns, such as 'Harington' (also known as 'Retirement', EH 85, MHB 593, SP 613, see above, p.138) were retained if the result was a worthwhile tune. Quality, not popularity, was the main criterion for selection.

Vaughan Williams's editorship of *The English Hymnal* coincided with his active interest in the preservation and revival of English folksong. He first began to note down folksongs as sung to him by gipsies and elderly rural working-class people late in 1903, and by 1913 he had amassed over 800 songs from all over England. As well as making his own collection Vaughan Williams took an interest in similar work undertaken by observers such as Cecil Sharp (1859–1924) and Lucy Broadwood (1858–1929). By the early twentieth century many of these folksongs, current only among a handful of largely elderly people who had learnt them in childhood, were at risk of passing unrecorded from living memory. As Vaughan Williams stated, 'The collector of folksongs gives them back again to the world'. His way of achieving this aim was to incorporate folk tunes into *The English Hymnal* for congregational use. In cases where these tunes proved popular, his aim was fulfilled.

Vaughan Williams was not the first compiler to realize the potential of folksongs as hymn tunes. Henry John Gauntlett (1805–76) adapted a characteristic Silesian sacred folksong, 'Jesu über alles', as a hymn entitled 'Ascalon' (MHB 115) in 1842. Sir Arthur Sullivan (1842–1900), who wrote dozens of hymn tunes, is remembered now chiefly for just one: his adaptation, made for publication in 1874, of a folksong as the hymn tune 'Noel' (EH 26, A&MR 66, MHB 130, SP 76), used with the Christmas hymn 'It came upon the midnight clear'. This text had previously been sung to an adaptation from a piece by Mendelssohn for piano (see above, p.132). The origin of Sullivan's 'traditional air' was clearly one variant of 'Dives and Lazarus', a tune later incorporated by Vaughan Williams into *The English Hymnal* under the name 'Eardisley' after the Herefordshire village where it was collected. The extent to which Sullivan manipulated the tune to comply with orthodox hymnody can be assessed by comparing 'Noel' with Vaughan Williams's adaptation (EH 601, SP 393 iii), which retains the striking melodic shape and rhythmic vitality of the folksong.

In using over thirty folk tunes in *The English Hymnal,* Vaughan Williams made the first systematic attempt to give these tunes a new lease of life. Some of the tunes he chose became so firmly established that it is hard to imagine that they once had an existence separate from the hymns with which they were first allied by Vaughan Williams. For example the tune 'Forest Green' (EH 15, A&MR 65, MHB 897, SP 79 i) has almost displaced in current usage at least two other tunes to the Christmas hymn 'O little town of Bethlehem'. The 'Forest Green' melody was originally a folksong called 'The Ploughboy's dream', about an apparition of an angel that frightened a ploughing team. Vaughan Williams noted the tune in December 1903 from an elderly labourer at Forest Green in Surrey. The tune was presented in *The English Hymnal* almost exactly as Vaughan Williams had heard it, but with harmonies added for the use of choirs or organists. The tune 'Herongate' (EH 597, MHB 854, SP 602) is an almost exact representation of the folksong about a lost love, 'In Jesse's city', sung to Vaughan Williams in December 1903 by 'a maid at Ingrave Rectory'. Its gentle simplicity, together with the unobtrusive editorially-added harmonies, accords well with the nineteenth-century catechism hymn 'It is a thing most wonderful'. 'Monks Gate' (EH 402, MHB 620, SP 515), the tune to 'He who would valiant be', the words for which Percy Dearmer based on John Bunyan's text 'Who would true valour see', was taken from the folksong 'Our captain calls all hands on board tomorrow'. This tune was sung to Vaughan Williams by a lady at Horsham in December 1904. Another variant of it had been noted four years earlier but Vaughan Williams used the version sung to him. In this case, a considerable degree of adaptation was undertaken to turn the folksong into a hymn. One repeated phrase was excised, another intercalated. But although some of the stresses were changed, the rhythm was for the most part left intact: there was none of the ruthless elimination of rhythmic subtleties that had so often been a feature of earlier borrowings for sacred use.

The most comprehensive reference work on Vaughan Williams's folksong borrowings for hymn tunes is Michael Kennedy's book *The works of Ralph Vaughan Williams* (1964). This contains, in tabular form, details of all such tunes in *The English Hymnal, Songs of Praise* and *The Oxford Book of Carols,* with the names of their folksong models where these are known. The book also contains a chronological list, with locations, names and circumstances of singers, of the folksongs collected by Vaughan Williams. Transcriptions of many of these songs appear in early volumes of the *Journal of the Folk-Song Society.* Comparison of these transcriptions with their hymn versions reveals in general a remarkable degree of editorial integrity and faithfulness, usually to one identifiable variant of a tune where several variants exist. It also reveals a breadth of knowledge of British and European secular folk music and carols extending far beyond Vaughan Williams's own experience in gathering folksongs from the oral traditions of localities he visited. A few tunes have eluded identification with secular models but two of these can be shown to owe their origins to the first and last pieces in *The Fitzwilliam Virginal Book*, an important manuscript collection of keyboard pieces compiled by Francis Tregian (1574–1619). Many of the pieces in *The Fitzwilliam Virginal Book* are sets of variations on particular variants of well-known tunes. The first of these, 'Walsingham', the subject of variations by John Bull (?1562/3–1628) and (later in the book) William Byrd (1543–1623), provided Vaughan Williams with the tune 'St Issey' (EH 388, SP 490) which he set to

John Mason Neale's translation of an eighth-century poem, 'Fierce was the wild billow'. The last piece in Tregian's collection, variations by Richard Farnaby (born c.1594) on the tune 'Hanskin', gave Vaughan Williams the hymn tune 'Farnaby' (EH 591, 654, SP 362), which he used for the children's litany 'God the Father, God the Son', and for the first part of 'Gentle Jesus, meek and mild'.

Of the borrowings from secular music in *The English Hymnal,* those from folksongs were easily the most successful, and in almost every case the editorial harmony is sufficiently unobtrusive not to obscure the character of the original tune. However, one or two borrowings from other secular sources did not attain the same degree of success. One such is 'Deo gracias' (EH 249 ii, A&MR 501, 516 ii as 'Agincourt', SP 684). This tune originated in the fifteenth century as a medieval carol now known as the 'Agincourt song' (see above, p.101), a spirited celebration of England's triumph at the battle of Agincourt. Early sources of this piece show that it abounded in lively and complex rhythms, and that it was sung in two-part harmony with a burden for three voices. In the hymn adaptations (the harmony in A&MR differs from that in EH and SP) the tune is retained but loses its character because of the addition of an unwieldy bass line and harmonies that substitute dense homophony for fast-moving transparent texture. Presumably because of its complex rhythms the burden is dispensed with altogether, although its verbal tag 'Deo gracias' would have been an apt conclusion to the verses of the hymns to which it is allied in these hymnals. Another secular borrowing in *The English Hymnal* is remarkable in view of Vaughan Williams's policy of omitting tunes with current secular associations. This is the tune 'Da zu dir der Heiland kam' (EH 313, SP 271 as 'Meistersinger chorale'), used for a Communion hymn with text by Percy Dearmer. The tune is a direct transcription of the chorus at the start of Act I of Richard Wagner's opera *Die Meistersinger von Nürnberg,* first performed in 1868. But the context in the opera is that of a church service in which this chorus depicts congregational worship. This, and the intrinsic quality of the music, probably provided the reasons for the inclusion of the tune in *The English Hymnal,* although its use as a hymn seems incongruous on acquaintance with the opera. The banal final 'amen', editorially added to the *English Hymnal* version, was mercifully dispensed with for the tune's appearance in *Songs of Praise.*[35]

Other early twentieth-century collections

Although *The English Hymnal* was pre-eminent in promoting worthwhile borrowings from a wide variety of secular sources as hymns, significant contributions in this area were made by other collections also. Both George Ratcliffe Woodward's *Songs of Syon,* which first appeared in 1904, and Basil Harwood's *The Oxford Hymn Book* (1908) took a scholarly approach to secular borrowings as Vaughan Williams had done, but their efforts in this direction were less systematic, enterprizing or practically presented than those which distinguished *The English Hymnal.* In the area of the carol in its broadest sense *The Cowley Carol Book* (1902 and 1919) and *The Cambridge Carol Book* (1924), both edited by George Ratcliffe Woodward and Charles Wood, added some worthwhile secular borrowings to the repertory. One particular borrowing that achieved some popularity as an unaccompanied Christmas anthem was 'Come to Bethlehem and see the new-born King'. This was an arrangement by Dom Gregory Murray of the 'Pieds-en-l'air' movement from the *Capriol Suite* for string orchestra or piano duet by Peter Warlock (1894–1930), which in turn was taken from pieces in the social etiquette and dance manual *Orchésographie* by Thoinot Arbeau (an anagram on his real name Jehan Tabourot) first published in Langres, France, in 1588. However, only the tune is reminiscent of a sixteenth-century dance; the harmonic clothing in both suite and Christmas piece is very much Warlock's own.

George Ratcliffe Woodward's *Songs of Syon* (see above, p.84) was first published during the period in which *The English Hymnal* was in preparation but it was much more esoteric, particularly with regard to its borrowings from secular music which occupy only a small proportion of the collection. Like Vaughan Williams, Woodward included 'Da zu dir der Heiland kam' from Act I of Wagner's *Die Meistersinger von Nürnberg,* together with two further Wagner borrowings. These were 'Wach auf!', the assembly's greeting to Hans Sachs before the song contest in Act III of *Die Meistersinger,* and 'Der Glaube lebt', a chorus from the Temple of the Grail scene in Act I of *Parsifal* (first performed 1882), to which Woodward added opening and concluding 'amens' and an organ introduction derived from related but not adjacent material in the opera. These two Wagner borrowings are more in the nature of anthems than hymns and would not have been practicable for congregational worship. All the Wagner borrowings are to texts by Woodward. The other secular borrowings in *Songs of Syon* are from a mixture of origins. 'Potsdam tune' (MHB 635), an anonymous tune based on the opening of the ninth fugue from Part II of Johann Sebastian Bach's *Das wohltemperierte Klavier,* is set to one of John Mason Neale's translations. From earlier English secular music come a lute ayre, 'Now, O now I needs must part', by John Dowland (1563–1626), a sixteenth-century 'common property' melody 'In pescod time', which was the subject of keyboard variations by William Byrd (1543-1623) and others, and the 'Agincourt song' (see above, p.144). The latter is more faithful to its model than the version used in *The English Hymnal* and later collections, but with the addition of four-part harmony almost throughout as well as the retention of most of the original complexity of rhythm, the music is overloaded and impractical at anything quicker than an inaptly sedate speed. In some cases Woodward gave no more than a hint as to the origins of his tunes: 'French chanson', 'old Spanish melody' and even 'ancient Japanese melody'. Most of the editorial harmonizations are by Charles Wood. Many of the texts by Woodward were designed especially to carry his chosen tunes. Despite their literary quality many of them seem better read than sung, and it is not surprising that only a few ultimately established themselves.

In terms of secular borrowing, *The Oxford Hymn Book* (1908) was less resourceful than either of its immediate predecessors. The music editor, Basil Harwood, deliberately avoided adaptations from 'modern secular melodies' and almost all the borrowings were at second hand from material with secular origins that had already won acceptance in the hymn repertory. There are no ambitious anthem-like pieces like those in *Songs of Syon.*

The two carol books edited by George Ratcliffe Woodward and Charles Wood (see above, p.79) broadened the scope of secular borrowings beyond that of *Songs of Syon* but with less emphasis on complex set pieces requiring a high level of musical expertise from the singers. In *The Cowley Carol Book* (published in two series, 1902 and 1919), the use of Scots airs and English sixteenth-century 'common property' melodies was a novel feature. Woodward supplied texts in order to admit several such tunes, including 'Western wind' (not the mass *cantus firmus* version but that with a known secular text, see above, p.97) and 'The woods so wild', the subject of keyboard variations by Orlando Gibbons (1583-1625) and William Byrd (1543-1623).

The Cambridge Carol Book, though only half the size of the combined *Cowley* series, was much more resourceful and many of the pairings of carol texts with secular music seem less inapt, cumbersome or contrived. Where secular melodies had extant harmonies these were used (sometimes with modifications), but most of the harmonizations were by Charles Wood. More 'common property' melodies were incorporated: the 'Walsingham' tune (see above, pp.143-44) became a sacred parody with the substitution of the text 'As I went to Bethlehem' (translated from the Latin 'Quem pastores laudavere') for its secular version 'As I went to Walsingham'. In this case the highly-concentrated sacred text overbalances the tune, obscuring its appealing simplicity. The more successful and well-known carol 'Past three o'clock' was devised by the editors from its pre-existent refrain and the tune 'London Waits' from William Chappell's collection *Popular Music of the Olden Time* (two volumes, 1855–59). This collection also provided the tune 'We are poor frozen-out gardeners' as an apt pairing with the sixteenth-century poet Robert Southwell's words 'Behoulde a sely tender babe', later set by Benjamin Britten as 'In freezing winter's night'. Even the ebullient 'Old King Cole' tune was utilized to provide the vehicle for a remarkably jolly text by Woodward about Moses praising Christ the King. The chorus is as follows:

> Yea, merry merry merry merry merry merry may we be,
> As birds upon the berry of the may or cherry tree,
> While as we stand with harp in hand
> On the shore of the Red Red Sea.

In addition to indigenous secular melodies *The Cambridge Carol Book* included borrowings from Basque and Flemish folk music. But probably the most successful secular borrowings in the book are four tunes from Thoinot Arbeau's *Orchésographie* (see above, p.145). All four tunes are lively, direct and memorable, although Woodward's texts to them are sometimes heavy-handed. 'Air de la Gavote' was turned into 'Christ is at thy portals'. The other three tunes were all branles — rustic round-dances that found their way into aristocratic circles in the sixteenth century. 'Branle des sabots' provided music to the Easter carol 'Thus on Easter morrow' and the slightly wistful minor-key 'Branle de la torche' became 'Blest, withouten match' — the pun must have been unintentional on Woodward's part. The best-known of the *Cambridge Carol Book* borrowings is 'Ding dong! merrily on high', to the tune of a kitchen steward's dance, 'Branle de l'Officiel'. Charles Wood's setting does not overwhelm the tune and Woodward's text has outlasted many of his other more intricate, precious or lengthy ones. The exuberance of the dance is retained in this carol, an important factor in its popular survival in sacred form.

'Songs of Praise' and 'The Oxford Book of Carols'

Like *The English Hymnal, Songs of Praise* (first published 1926) was edited by Percy Dearmer and Ralph Vaughan Williams, with Martin Shaw as additional music editor. Its aim was to provide a non-denominational means of musical worship for congregations, and to this end an unusually wide selection of devotional poetry was drawn upon for use as hymns. As far as the music was concerned the policy continued that of *The English Hymnal*. Most of the newly-borrowed material came from an increased range of sacred sources but a few items were secular. A large proportion of the *English Hym-*

nal folksong borrowings were retained in *Songs of Praise* but any comparable impetus to adapt additional ones seems to have been lacking; the effect, perhaps, of the First World War and of Vaughan Williams's own diversification of musical interests beyond folksong as social and musical history. Only a handful of new folksong adaptations by Vaughan Williams appears: an example is 'Stalham' (SP 393 i) which originated as a folksong collected at Sutton in Norfolk.

Martin Shaw and his brother Geoffrey were responsible for a few further adaptations from similar material. Among these, one of the best known is 'Royal Oak' (A&MR 442 i, MHB 851, SP 444), one of a number of tunes to 'All things bright and beautiful'. This tune appeared in *Old English Popular Music* edited by Harry Ellis Wooldridge and published in 1893, a revision of William Chappell's *Popular Music of the Olden Time* of 1855. Martin Shaw's tune 'Royal Oak' was known as a dance tune under several different titles, and appeared in collections of popular dance tunes from at least as early as 1686. Geoffrey Shaw's adaptations included 'Robyn' (SP 467), a greatly altered version of a song by William Cornysh (died 1523). Unlike his roistering 'Blow they horn, hunter' (see above, pp.102–8) Cornysh's song 'Ah Robin, gentle Robin' is a graceful love lyric: musically its form is complex, consisting of a repeated canon for two voices, in counterpoint with which alternating third and fourth voices sing refrains and varied verses. In Geoffrey Shaw's version the imposition of four-part harmony, the redistribution of some of the tune's phrases and the elimination of others sweeps away the artistry behind Cornysh's piece. The replacement of the insistently repeated pleading phrase 'Ah Robin' by the stern exhortation 'Watch and pray!' serves only to make the transition from secular to sacred seem even more uncomfortable

A few hymns were taken from lute ayres: 'Galliard' (SP 461) is a shortened form of a piece by John Dowland (1563–1626) in *The Firste Booke of Songes or Ayres* published in 1597. The first book of ayres of 1613 (*Divine and Morall Songs*) by Thomas Campion (1567–1620) gave material for two hymns 'Song of Joy' (SP 639) and 'Weather-beaten sail' (SP 587), both with harmony only slightly adapted and using Campion's own texts, a measure of the breadth of devotional poetry that the editors of *Songs of Praise* sought to bring into regular use as hymns. Two adaptations from the twentieth-century instrumental repertory became hymns in *Songs of Praise*. 'Thaxted' (A&M 579, MHB 900, SP 319 i), the main tune in the 'Jupiter' movement from Gustav Holst's suite *The Planets,* op.32, composed 1914–16, was set to the patriotic hymn 'I vow to thee, my country'. 'Marathon' (SP 302), the march from Vaughan Williams's incidental music written in 1909 to *The Wasps* by Aristophanes, provided a somewhat ungainly but not inapt setting for Percy

Dearmer's lengthy missionary hymn 'Servants of the great adventure'.

The Oxford Book of Carols (see above, p.80), first published in 1928 and edited by Percy Dearmer, Ralph Vaughan Williams and Martin Shaw, was nothing less than an attempt to redefine the carol for modern use and within its terms to present a wide range of material in a practical way for use as carols. The aim was threefold: first, to extract the carol from the narrow confines of the formal Christmas hymn; second, to show that in the popular traditional carol any borderline between sacred and secular is artificial; and third, to extend the use of a single large repertory of carols for the whole year to schools, churches, concert halls, private houses and door-to-door singing. Thus the concept of the carol put forward in *The Oxford Book of Carols* was nearer to that of the fifteenth and sixteenth centuries (see above, pp.100-1) than to the wholly secular festive eating or drinking song or the exclusively sacred Christmas hymn of more recent times. Throughout, the emphasis in *The Oxford Book of Carols* was on informality, spontaneity and popularity, but not at the expense of quality in either texts or music.

Within the area encompassed by *The Oxford Book of Carols,* therefore, there could be no borrowing from secular to sacred: all carols, whatever their subject matter, were eligible for inclusion although carols on Christian themes predominated in the book. No music from outside the repertory was borrowed. 'The tunes in this book' stated the editors, 'are real carol tunes. We have made it a principle not to attempt to provide words for other traditional music'. The editors would not admit newly-contrived carol pastiches even if they were based on folksong. Only in cases where a tune had been associated for a long time with both a carol and a folksong could it rightly be classified as a carol. In practice, the editors relaxed this rule somewhat so that the tune 'Forest Green', derived from a folksong and first used as a hymn in *The English Hymnal* only two decades previously (see above, pp.142-43) could be used in *The Oxford Book of Carols* with 'O little town of Bethlehem'. This is the most familiar of a small group of exceptions allowed by the editors.

Many of the borrowings in *The Oxford Book of Carols* had long been established in what might best be described as the semi-sacred folk repertory. In some cases, several versions of a piece coexisted to what was essentially the same melody. For example the tune 'Greensleeves', current from at least as early as 1580 and used to carry ballads, political texts and sacred 'moralizings', appeared in *Christmas Carols New and Old* of 1878 (see above, p.77) to a text by William Chatterton Dix (1837–98) beginning 'What child is this?'. In *The Oxford Book of Carols* a much older text with sacred and festive elements was restored to use with the tune. This text, 'The old year now away is fled', was published for use with the 'Greensleeves' tune in 1642 and was one of many carol versions of it that proliferated from that date if not earlier. But in modern use this carol for the new year failed to supplant Dix's text, probably because carols for seasons other than Christmas did not establish themselves in popular use despite the efforts of Dearmer, Vaughan Williams and Shaw.

An example of borrowing from within the carol repertory occurred for the carol of the Holy Innocents: 'Rise up, rise up, you merry men all', otherwise called 'The miraculous harvest'. The tune was collected by Lucy Broadwood in 1893 from a family of gipsies in Surrey. They sang it to a semi-sacred apocryphal folk legend beginning 'King Pharim sat a-musing'. Vaughan Williams had already borrowed the tune for *The English Hymnal,* where it appears as 'Capel' (EH 488, MHB 845, SP 248), and used it again in *The Oxford Book of Carols* to provide the tune for the traditional versified legend about the outwitting of Herod by Christ and a faithful husbandman.

The inclusion in *The Oxford Book of Carols* of similar items from all periods and on a variety of topics promoted greater informality in the use of carols, just as *Songs of Praise* had sought to do with hymns. The carol repertory was further widened by the incorporation of traditional music from Ireland, Wales and several European countries, and in all cases the tunes used came from folk carols or folk music that enshrined both sacred and secular elements. However, only a few of the contents of *The Oxford Book of Carols* have survived in regular popular use. There may be several reasons for this. Some of the musical arrangements, though practical, seem cumbersome and tedious, and have not retained their appeal. The texts, despite their literary quality, are sometimes too complex for comfortable singing, or else embarrassingly precious to later twentieth-century perceptions ('darling, darling little man' from the 'Rocking' carol is an example). Perhaps the main reason is the failure of carols apart from those specific to Christmas to establish themselves, or to become the focus of the kinds of social gathering throughout the year that the editors of *The Oxford Book of Carols* idealistically envisaged. Nevertheless, *The Oxford Book of Carols* was influential, largely in opening up a fresh approach to carols that freed them from the constraints of nineteenth-century ideals and showed in particular their legitimate and close relationship with secular music.[36]

Some twentieth-century attitudes

The spate of borrowings for sacred use of secular melodies, principally from art music, in the nineteenth century, aroused disapproval in many quarters. Despite the intentions of some of its advocates who sought to provide better music for church use than that which was currently to hand for the purpose, such borrowings were seen in retrospect as just one of the numerous supposed aberrations in the apparently wholly debased area of nineteenth-century English church music. Few could have disapproved more strongly of this kind of secular borrowing than Ralph Vaughan Williams, who sought an antidote to this and other entrenched Victorian practices in sacred music by resurrecting much older secular tunes, chiefly English folksongs, for sacred use. His policy of borrowing only from much earlier secular sources eliminated one of the principal objections to borrowings by avoiding music that had current secular associations. Music that had lost such associations would be unlikely to subvert its users' thoughts from concentration on worship, but would at the same time restore for use many items of worthwhile music that would otherwise have passed from living memory.

Yet even this much more discriminating policy met with opposition, mainly from those who felt that the church was a unique and separate entity in which matters of everyday life had no place. Robert Bridges, writing in 1899 and again in 1912, condemned the merger of distinction between sacred and profane. He stressed the importance of music, asserting that a worthwhile tune can elevate a weak text or lower a good one. 'On entering a church' he said, 'we wish to hear music different from that heard elsewhere'. His views, epitomized in *The Yattendon Hymnal* of 1899 in which the only secular borrowings were those that had entered the sacred repertory in the distant past, were extreme but influential in cultivated circles. They were echoed to a greater or lesser extent by reports and occasional papers on church music that were current before 1914. But the First World War brought about many changes. In parish churches the demand increased for simple, practical music that no longer took that of the cathedral service as its model. Thus Vaughan Williams's aims were vindicated, although changes in congregational practice in this direction were far from rapid.

Thereafter, the attitudes of influential writers on church music towards secular borrowings became in general less extreme, but some still held misgivings. George Gardner and Sydney Nicholson, in a book published in 1923, addressed the problem of balancing the 'popular' with the 'good' in church music. They advocated the use wherever possible of plainsong, Merbecke and sixteenth-century anthems, noting the ancient precedents for using folk tunes as hymns but warning against those with lingering secular associations. Henry Walford Davies and Harvey Grace, writing in 1935, took a similar view on the use of folksongs as music for worship. But they expressed misgivings about 'some of the more jingling of the *English Hymnal* folk-melodies' (without giving examples) and felt that the use of folksongs as hymns was a vogue that would eventually pass. They cited the example of the folk tune 'Lodsworth' (SP 336) which had failed to displace John Bacchus Dykes's popular tune 'Melita' (EH 540, A&MR 487, MHB 917) to 'Eternal Father, strong to save'. They believed that whereas folk tunes are independent of harmony, hymn tunes are not, and that despite its better melodic line 'Lodsworth' offered only a weak and repetitive alternative to Dykes's tune — one of his strongest, which fits the text admirably. Their views represented a judicious balance among extremes, showing tolerance of the best products of all movements, whether those of Victorian hymnody, adapted plainsong or borrowed secular music of the past.

In contrast to the firm and well-reasoned approach of Henry Walford Davies and Harvey Grace stood the opinions of Bernard Manning, Fellow of Jesus College, Cambridge and writer on hymns whose seminars on the subject were published in 1942. He claimed complete musical ignorance, yet inveighed against hymns set out in what he called 'the jazz music of Vaughan Williams'. He deplored the 'self-conscious preciosity' of Songs of Praise, and described Vaughan Williams's own composition 'Sine nomine' (EH 641, MHB 832, SP 202) to 'For all the Saints who from their labours rest' as 'a feeble dance tune'. Although Manning's attitude to the contents of The English Hymnal and Songs of Praise may in retrospect seem ill-informed, his work was widely cited and reflected the views of many who were deeply concerned about what they saw as the increasing encroachment of secular music of any kind upon the music of worship. A similar attitude is apparent in the letter (discussed above, pp.93–94) from a clergyman to Percy Dearmer, objecting to the inclusion of a particular tune in the revised Songs of Praise.

Charles Henry Phillips, writing in 1945, took a more conciliatory view of secular borrowings, neither laying down sweeping guidelines nor making value judgments on general usage. He noted with approval borrowings such as the 'vigorous Old English melody' ('Monks Gate', EH 402, MHB 620, SP 515) for 'He who would valiant be', but seemed to consider himself on safer ground in approving borrowings from sacred rather than secular sources. On the surface, the Archbishops' Committee's report Music in Church, first published in 1951, seems to take a stronger line:

> Music that is in keeping with the spirit of the liturgy will be characterized by qualities of nobility and restraint; by freedom from sensationalism or mawkishness, and from all suggestions of secularity.

When the report was published it caused much strife about the apparent gulf between what was 'good' and what was 'popular' in church music. But it is not easy to determine what the statement quoted above actually means in practice: words like 'nobility' and 'restraint' when applied to music are hard to define, and 'sensationalism' to one person may be 'inspiration' to another. 'Freedom ... from all suggestions of secularity', if strictly applied, would condemn not only all direct secular borrowings (including those from the remote past that had long been established in the sacred repertory), but also all church music in which there is any evidence of the borrowing (intentional or otherwise) of a secular style. Not a great deal is left.

Although the 1951 report expressed an ideal rather than commenting upon an existing state of affairs, it did nothing to settle the controversy over the kinds of music that were admissible to church services. Vaughan Williams remained a firm advocate of his own earlier policy on the borrowing of secular tunes, restating his case in 1956 in a publication marking the fiftieth anniversary of *The English Hymnal.* The inclusion of some of the more successful folksong borrowings in *Hymns Ancient and Modern Revised,* published in 1950, was a measure of the success of his policy, although the 1950 revision as a whole was far from radical. Attempts by writers to influence the course of church music proved to be no match for public taste in the area of borrowings from secular music. Although, like many hymns of all kinds, some of the twentieth-century borrowings have passed into obscurity, many have won an enduring place in the repertory without any compromise in quality or in apparent fitness for sacred use. In this area *The English Hymnal* and later volumes from the same editors influenced all subsequent collections of hymns and carols, enriching the repertory with material that few people nowadays would condemn as secular in origin even if they recognized it as such.[37]

Part III

BORROWINGS OF
MUSICAL STYLE

9

Derivative Musical Styles

Introduction

The purpose of this section is to outline some of the ways in which borrowings in English church music extended beyond the use of specific and usually identifiable material from outside its own repertory. It is mainly concerned with the borrowing of styles, whether or not as a deliberate strategy, from music outside that of the English church. In theory, such borrowing could be from music of any kind, either sacred or secular, and for any medium, but in practice only limited areas of music are relevant. Nevertheless, numerous diverse musical styles influenced English church music for a variety of reasons. These influences did not always run parallel to the changes in style that affected the direction of European art music as a whole in the four centuries under discussion.

As with music in general, it would be possible to go to almost infinite lengths in observing points of style in English church music that are ultimately derivative rather than original and thus, in theory at least, constitute borrowings of style. But the aim here is not to accumulate detail but to identify and account for particular trends. Some examination of style is essential so that borrowings may be seen in their proper perspective as part of a larger context. Lest it be thought that the borrowings from sacred and secular material discussed in Parts I and II were little more than minor elements in English church music, the developments outlined here suggest that many such borrowings were important in helping to determine the direction of apparently free composition for the English church. Not surprisingly, trends in the development of styles in English church music and in the choice of outside material for adoption into the repertory mirror each other. At every stage there are parallels between borrowed material and borrowed styles: that which is borrowed is also imitated, and vice versa.

Conflicts of interest permeate beyond those surrounding the use for worship of borrowed musical material, whether sacred or secular. One approach is to view ideal church music as an outgrowth of popular music-making analogous to the use of music as entertainment, and to exploit music that is familiar in substance, idiom or allusion in the service of the church. Such music may be fashionable and up to date, or it may be in a deliberately slightly outdated or diluted idiom with which the majority of its users and listeners are conversant. In this way, music can be seen as a means of demonstrating that worship in church relates strongly to matters of everyday life. This philosophy is enshrined in borrowings of style and substance such as the mid sixteenth-century sacred *contrafactum* of a secular song by William Cornysh (see above, pp.102–8) and similar compositions that copy its style; also the work of John and Charles Wesley in introducing Moravian hymns into the English repertory (see above, pp.47–48).

In opposition to this approach lies the belief that the church should offer an atmosphere that is distinct and separate from that of everyday life, and that church music should be a manifestation of that separateness. Particularly in the nineteenth century, this ideal concurred with the wider Romantic notion of religious conduct which was in part a reaction against the overt secularity of the preceding era. In Tractarian-influenced church music it led to the deliberate avoidance of fashionable or sensual idioms and a recourse instead to music of the remote rather than the immediate past. At a more popular level, the retention of counterpoint with similarities to that in Handel's oratorios was equated with the decorum and respectability of a supposedly separate 'church style'. Borrowings of style and substance in this category include the revival of plainsong and the perpetuation of its characteristic stepwise lines in the melodies of meditative passages of sacred music by Stanford, Wood, Elgar and others. They include adaptations to English texts of motets by composers such as Palestrina, pastiches of similar music in the so-called 'sublime' style, and the harmonizations used in some nineteenth-century revivals of early music, most memorably if not entirely accurately described as 'Palestrinal' by the editors of *The Yattendon Hymnal* of 1899 (see above, pp.66–67, 83–84).

These opposing arguments represent two extremes, and in between them comes a vast quantity of church music in which borrowings of style or substance are the results of other circumstances and ideals. Expediency was probably the principal factor behind Merbecke's borrowings of plainsong and his own chants in similar style, and behind mid sixteenth-century *contrafacta* of Latin music by Taverner (see above, pp.32–33) and the English pieces in polyphonic style that occur in sources such as the Wanley and Lumley partbooks. Artistic integrity combined with practicality in church music was the aim of William Gardiner (see above, pp.124–26) and Ralph

Vaughan Williams (see above, pp.84–87, 141–44, 147–49), both of whom sought to elevate the standard of English church music by introducing borrowings from outside its repertory, Gardiner from up-to-date Viennese classical music and Vaughan Williams largely from almost-forgotten folk music in which sacred and secular elements were often intermixed. Although their methods and results were very different, they were both governed by considerations that were mainly musical. In the case of Vaughan Williams these considerations extended to become a stimulus for his own creativity in sacred music, which often made some reference to the styles of earlier music that he had borrowed.

The church music of composers like Vaughan Williams, in which there is a degree of apparent deliberate archaism or at least some measure of fusion between old and new styles, has given rise to the sometimes derogatory supposition that English church music is essentially retrospective in character. It is true that few leading progressive twentieth-century composers have written for the English church and that composition for it has not kept pace with contemporary developments in musical style. For example, the works of Herbert Howells (1892–1983) and Edmund Rubbra (1901–86), though individual, are strongly rooted in tradition, and even the relatively innovative and significant church music of Charles Villiers Stanford (1852–1924) owes a debt to the past; not least to Johann Sebastian Bach, to whose *Magnificat* Stanford's own setting in B flat, dating from 1918, bears conspicuous affinities. But in earlier centuries, notwithstanding the effects of movements such as Tractarianism, English church music was far from retrospective, as its assimilation of contemporary and fashionable styles from the sixteenth century onwards demonstrates.

The same qualifications apply to insularity, a term that is sometimes used to account for particular points of style that can be attributed, justifiably or otherwise, to English music. The prominent use of flattened sevenths, melodically and harmonically, is one such feature although it is by no means exclusive to English music, still less so to English church music. Some degree of insularity is inevitable because of the unique course followed by the English Protestant church, and its use of the English language in musical settings, in the four centuries under discussion. But English church music has always been open to foreign influence: the prompt and effective assimilation of the Italian melodic style by church composers such as Matthew Locke (c.1621–77) and the adoption by a whole host of nineteenth-century English anthem and hymn composers of chromaticism and modulation in a manner used most notably by Schubert in Vienna are just two examples. To dismiss the entire repertory of English church music as insular and retrospective is unrealistic, and takes no account of its enrichment from many outside sources together with its development which has, with certain significant exceptions, mirrored that of contemporaneous music from outside the church.

The earliest borrowings of style

Among the earliest borrowings of style in English church music were those by John Merbecke (c.1505–c.1585). In *The Book of Common Prayer Noted,* published in 1550 as a monophonic musical setting of material from the 1549 Book of Common Prayer, Merbecke's aim was to present familiar elements of plainsong and its associated characteristics in a way that was compatible with the prevailing constraints on English church music. These constraints meant that the emergent style of setting for the new vernacular liturgy used only one note to each syllable. Accordingly, Merbecke's adaptations of plainsong compiled with this principle (see above, pp.20–22). Merbecke was not the only mid sixteenth-century composer to experiment with the adaptation of plainsong for the English liturgy, but his work is the most important in retrospect because it achieved wide dissemination especially later in the sixteenth and in the nineteenth centuries, partly because of its versatility, ease of use and susceptibility to further adaptation.

A surviving small output of Latin sacred polyphonic settings and a single short carol-like English setting for three voices demonstrate Merbecke's accomplishment as a composer. On a much more limited level, he composed some further melodies for *The Book of Common Prayer Noted* in a style similar to that of his adapted plainsong in the same book. For a church composer in an age when plainsong had recently been the normal vehicle for musical worship, the composition of material in a similar style would have presented no problem and would have been a natural recourse in the climate of musical experiment with the new English liturgy. It would have provided an element of familiarity to performer and listener, whilst at the same time exploring a possibly fruitful means of musical setting without contravening the principle that there should be only one note to each syllable.

Merbecke's own compositions in the style of his adapted plainsong included sections of the Communion service, namely the Gloria, Creed, Offertory sentences and Post-Communions. All these exhibit a variety and mobility that often exceeds that of the plainsong-derived pieces in Merbecke's book. It is true that there are reminiscences of particular fragments of plainsong, but for the most part Merbecke's compositions are more condensed and colourful. This may be due in part to the necessary rapid despatch of syllables, but the careful attention that Merbecke paid to details of phrase shape and individual word setting are clearly a factor also. For example in his setting o the Creed, climactic points represented by the use of relatively high-pitched phrases occur at 'the onely begotten sonne of God', 'he arose again', 'ascended in to heauen' and similar places. Merbecke's precise use of proportional note values made it possible for him to emphasize particular words in the midst of his normal declamatory writing by the use of longer notes for important words such as 'Christ' and 'glory'. Also, the use of varied note values enhances the resemblance of the chanted material to normal speech, with its stressed and unstressed syllables. It was possibly this factor that led some later exponents of Merbecke's monody to interpret his proportional note values very loosely so that the effect would be more like unmeasured recitation than measured song.

Merbecke's skill as a composer, despite severe externally-imposed constraints and the necessity of dealing with relatively unfamiliar texts, enabled him tentatively to explore ways of giving his English monodic settings some degree of musical shape and sense of direction. But Merbecke was neither the first nor the only composer of English church music to attempt to do this. Certainly by the late 1540s, composers had already recognized the possibilities of using plainsong as the basis of polyphonic English sacred settings. Several compositions of this type survive in the Lumley and Wanley partbooks, mostly anonymously, and show that attention was being directed towards ways of giving the music a greater degree of interest and overall form than that which would merely derive from repeated harmonizations of plainchant (see above, pp.26–28).

In the same way that Merbecke borrowed and adapted plainsong for English use and then extended the repertory by similar compositions of his own in the borrowed style, so other composers adapted plainsong for the purpose of harmonization and then wrote further music in a similar style. For example, a handful of the anonymous pieces in the Lumley partbooks (London, British Library Royal Appendix manuscripts 74–76, see above, pp.25–28) exhibit features that are reminiscent of plainsong without using identifiable sections of plainsong or faburden. The metrical version of Psalm 19, 'Celi enarrant' beginning 'The heavens in their excellence, O God, they utter thy glory' is very similar in style to some of the pieces from the same source based on identifiable plainsong. Its treble and tenor lines in particular exhibit chantlike characteristics. The construction of the cadences, in which the tenor always descends to the final note even where, in terms of the harmonic style, it might reasonably be expected to rise to the third, is further evidence of the borrowing of a chant-based style. Similar allusions to this kind of style occur sporadically in other pieces from the Lumley collection, and there is no way of knowing for certain whether these allusions were deliberate or whether they crept in as a normal element in the composers' musical vocabulary. In either case these borrowings of plainsong style show that plainsong itself was influential in early English sacred settings in a way that went beyond the appropriation of actual plainsong material. It strengthens the case for the existence of a style based on the practice of improvised faburden, but in four parts instead of the more usual three. The apparent influence of harmonized plainsong can be detected in later freely-composed polyphony by English composers, such as the motet 'O nata lux', a late work by Thomas Tallis (c.1505–85). The closing passage (quoted above, p.24) uses largely static harmony around a reiterated pivot note, a device that often occurs in early English plainsong-based compositions.

Other borrowings of style that extended from borrowed material were also influential in this very early experimental period. As well as *contrafacta* and adaptations to sacred use from pre-existent secular material (see above, pp.102–9), composers also worked in a borrowed secular style. The main difficulty here is that it is not always possible to determine whether a sacred piece merely copies the characteristics of contemporary secular music, or whether it is an actual *contrafactum* or adaptation of a particular secular piece that has not survived and so cannot be identified. A further difficulty relates to the definition of a secular style at a period when sacred and secular music had structures, idioms and textures in common, and when the textual substance of the carol in particular obscured the distinction between sacred and secular with its blend of Christianity, folklore and celebration (see above, pp.100–1). Some of the metrical pieces in the Lumley books exhibit strong, regular rhythmic patterns, evenly-balanced phrases, fairly wide-ranging and easily-memorable melodies, and entirely homophonic textures. These pieces may be based on secular models as yet unidentified (compare p.102–8, above), or they may merely give particular prominence to features that can be associated with contemporaneous secular song, constituting a borrowing of style. The distinction between sacred and secular music remained tenuous: from the mid sixteenth century onwards, partsongs with religious texts appeared in sources alongside those with secular words. Collections of this kind were used for recreational music-making and it is an open question as to how much of the material with devotional texts found its way beyond the domestic environment into the private chapel, the church or the cathedral. Although the borrowing of secular music or of an overtly secular style was perhaps at first a deliberate expedient, it would probably be more accurate to consider the assimilation of a secular partsong style into early English sacred music as merely an extension of that style to cope with further vernacular material which, because of the new circumstances affecting religious conduct, was sacred.

Some aspects of the style of Latin polyphonic music had a strong influence on church music with English texts from an early stage. The practice of adapting sacred Latin polyphony for use with English texts was established in the late 1540s. The earliest examples include those in the Wanley partbooks (see above, pp.32–33). The practice of *contrafactum* from Latin pieces continued until well into the seventeenth century, long after the immediate need for church music to fulfil the requirements of a new English liturgy had subsided (see above, pp.33–35). Most of the music adapted in this way was of a fairly compact, syllabic nature in the original, beginning with some of the later masses by Taverner in which these characteristics had begun to supersede his earlier, more expansive style, and continuing with Latin works by composers such as Robert Whyte, Thomas Tallis and William Byrd.

Material of this kind presented an obvious recourse, not only for adaptation but also for imitation. From the 1540s onwards aspects of this style were borrowed for use in freely-composed English sacred music. Within what may broadly be termed the polyphonic style a great deal of variety was possible, from simple chordal homophony to elaborate use of textures and complex imitative patterns. English music in this polyphonic style often exhibits a blend of these elements to create a finely-balanced whole appropriate to the function of the piece concerned: a simple psalm setting might be predominantly chordal whereas an elaborate festal piece might be somewhat more resourceful in technique. Composers writing such music included Thomas Tallis (c.1505–85), Christopher Tye (c.1505–c.1572), Richard Farrant (c.1525 to 1530–80) and John Merbecke (c.1505–c.1585). Merbecke's single surviving piece of English polyphony, the apparently incomplete carol section 'A Virgin and Mother' for three voices probably composed around 1550, has strong affinities with his Latin polyphonic style. The handful of pieces in four-voice polyphony, mostly anonymous, in the Lumley partbooks dating from around the same time show a remarkable degree of ingenuity and self assurance in their handling of the English texts and musical structures. Perhaps the best-known example from this collection is Tallis's setting of the Matins Benedictus for four men's voices, a long but well integrated piece in which the adept use of diverse musical ideas sustains interest throughout, despite the predominantly sombre close texture.

As the English anthem and its associated sacred forms developed further in the Elizabethan period, it was influenced by features borrowed from styles outside the English sacred repertory. The verse anthem with accompaniment (usually for organ) epitomized in Elizabethan times by the works of composers such as William Byrd (1543–1623), Thomas Morley (1557 or 1558–1602) and Orlando Gibbons (1583–1625), owed its origin partly to current types of solo song. In a secular context vocal solos were performed with accompaniment either by instrumental consort (such as a group of viols) or by a solo instrument (such as the lute). Vocal solos were often a feature of contemporary drama. Song texts ranged from the frivolous to the moralistic or devotional, and collections of songs included material of all these kinds, intended for recreational purposes. Composers such as those mentioned above were active both in the field of songwriting and in that of music intended specifically for church use, and the mutual influence of style which contributed to the development of English-texted sacred music in particular was a natural consequence of these conditions. The solo passages in verse anthems such as Byrd's 'Christ rising again', Morley's 'Out of the deep' and Gibbons's 'This is the record of John', among the best-known examples from each composer, allow the texts due prominence against accompaniment that virtually amounts to a web of instrumental polyphony as background.

The development of the full anthem and its associated forms gained much from the parallel ascendancy of the English madrigal. The full anthems of Thomas Weelkes (1576–1623) often borrow typically madrigalian features such as close imitation and stretto particularly among high voices, lively rhythms and vivid use of rapidly-changing textures. Perhaps the best example is his anthem for five voices 'Alleluia, I heard a voice' in which the sense of drama and excitement is sustained throughout by the colourful interplay of voices within the complete ensemble. The intensity of expression in some of the sacred music of Thomas Tomkins (1572–1656) matches that of his finest madrigals. His full anthem 'When David heard that Absalom was slain' is a masterpiece in the graver polyphonic madrigal style, with calculated dramatic use of chromaticism throughout and a striking transition from minor to major modality at the approach to the final cadence. The first publication of this piece in 1622 as a 'sacred madrigal' and its appearance in a collection of pieces with predominantly secular texts underlines the absence of any strict distinction during the sixteenth and early seventeenth centuries between the styles of sacred and secular music. It demonstrates also that the use of English sacred music was not confined to church worship, and that such music was not exclusively transmitted in sources designed for church use.[38]

Church music and European styles

From the beginning of the seventeenth century, English music of almost every kind was affected by newly-fashionable styles from mainland Europe. A predominance of polyphonic writing began to decline in favour of a more open style in which treble and bass lines were more conspicuously polarized and the inner parts fulfilled a harmonic rather than a contrapuntal purpose. The verse anthem, in which solo vocal writing with instrumental accompaniment was an essential feature and which had already undergone significant development at the hands of composers such as Orlando Gibbons, was the ideal vehicle for further cultivation in the new style, especially after the re-establishment of church music on a formal basis after the restoration of the monarchy in 1660. Accordingly, the verse anthem and its associated forms achieved a pre-eminence which affected almost all church music in one way or another. Such pieces became the exclusive province of professional solo singers and instrumentalists. For these musicians, church music-making sometimes came a poor second to theatre work for which the rewards, in both public esteem and private wealth, were potentially greater. Several composers, among them Henry Purcell (1659–95) were active in both church and theatre music, so some cross-fertilization of style and idea between church and theatre music comes as no surprise. Where non-professional singers were concerned, newly-composed anthems, psalms and hymns adopted the fashionable style to a certain extent, incorporating an increasing degree of florid melody-writing. Some of the old psalm tunes underwent adaptation so that by the addition of ornaments and the substitution of elegant and fashionable cadential figures they became more like solo anthems in an aria-like style (see above, pp.43–45).

The most potent and enduring influence on English church music until well into the eighteenth century came from Italy. Of the numerous English composers who spent periods working abroad from the early seventeenth century, most visited Italy and some went there to study. Walter Porter (c.1587–1659) was almost certainly a pupil of Monteverdi and his output of both church music and madrigals with continuo bass and instrumental sections reflects the emergent Italian concertato style that rapidly became fashionable in England. William Child (1606 or 1607–97) was almost exclusively a church musician, well versed in the vivid polyphonic style that had its background in the work of composers such as Weelkes and Tomkins. As well as grafting some Italianate mannerisms on to his polyphonic style in numerous anthems, he also made a deliberate attempt to borrow the Italian concertato style in his collection *The First set of Psalmes of. III. Voyces. Fitt for private Chappells or other private meetings with a continuall Base either for the Organ or Theorbo newly composed after the Italian way* published in 1639. This collection, reissued by John Playford in 1656 as *Choise Musick to the Psalmes of David,* consists of prose psalm settings that are in essence miniature anthems for two treble voices and one bass voice, accompanied by a figured organ part that does little more than underpin the florid melodic lines. These lines are sometimes almost like recitatives, with word painting at passages such as 'fly like a bird unto the hill' (Psalm 11) and colourful turbulent chromatic writing at 'Why do the heathen so furiously rage together?' (Psalm 2). These anthems have much in common with the Italian trio sonata in form, idiom and relationship among the voice-parts, and represent comparatively early developments in the borrowing of this style into English church music.

The re-establishment of church music at the Chapel Royal in 1660 led to the formation there of a new group of men and boy singers under the tutelage of Henry Cooke (c.1615–72). Cooke was himself a fine singer: he had trained under Walter Porter and was recognized as a supreme exponent of the 'Italian manner' of singing, an accolade of high esteem for a soloist at that time. He used Italian and Italianate material in his teaching of both composition and performance. His pupils included John Blow, Michael Wise and Pelham Humfrey, all of whom absorbed the Italian style to a high degree that was manifest in their later compositions. Other composers associated with the Chapel Royal whose work reflects the fusion of Italian idioms with English church music included Matthew Locke (c.1621–77) and Henry Lawes (1596–1662), both of whom were active also in secular theatrical and instrumental music. Composers such as these laid the foundations for the work of Henry Purcell, whose church music represented a synthesis of the native idiom with the more progressive aspects of the imported styles. As late as 1752, the distinguished musician and writer Charles Avison (1709–70), who had studied under Francesco Geminiani (1687–1762) in London, wrote a controversial *Essay on Musical Expression* in which he advocated the supremacy of Italian styles, promoting the works of Giacomo Carissimi (1605–74) and Benedetto Marcello (1686–1739) as ideal models for English church music.

Pelham Humfrey (1647–74) was largely responsible for the influence of French instrumental music on the emergent English post-Restoration baroque style, and particularly on the verse anthem. Possessed of a precocious musical talent and a commensurate degree of vanity, Humfrey was sent to Italy and France to study music when his time as a Chapel Royal boy chorister came to an end. Although there are no extant details of his study period it is clear from his subsequent music that he had become well acquainted with the work of Carissimi in Italy and Jean-Baptiste Lully (1632–87) (a native Italian) in France. Humfrey's absorption of the most innovative aspects of their styles concurred with the tastes of the king, Charles II, who preferred the lighter newly-fashionable European styles to the denser textures and graver demeanour of the native product. The king established an orchestra of stringed instruments of the violin family (as opposed to a group of viols) at court. He ordered that anthems composed for occasions when he was to attend the Chapel Royal should include symphonies and ritornellos, which in the present context signify introductions and recurring sections for instruments only.

Humfrey's training had given him first-hand experience of the emergent style of French instrumental writing that was being fostered at court in France by composers such as Lully. The presence there of a well-trained string orchestra contributed towards the growth of an ensemble-orientated string style, as distinct from the more solo-orientated style that was predominant in Italy. The period of Humfrey's stay in France coincided with Lully's increasing interest in sacred music and particularly in the *grand motet* with its large instrumental and vocal forces and consequent opportunities for dramatic elaboration of sacred texts. In these pieces Lully was beginning to develop the use of tonality as a structural device, a technique already adopted by some of his Italian contemporaries. The possibility of introducing some of these ideas to the English verse anthem must have struck Humfrey forcibly, and the climate of fashionable English taste was favourable to their introduction. The innovations in Humfrey's verse anthems, especially in the creation of longer pieces in which some essence of a unified structure is conveyed by tonal organization, repetition and development, are a classic example of the enrichment of English church music by the borrowing and absorption of styles from outside its repertory.[39]

Handel in England

Not all those involved with English church music found it easy to accept the allegiances to fashionable European styles introduced by composers such as Pelham Humfrey and developed into a characteristic personal style by Henry Purcell, the supreme composer of the Restoration period. Moreover, the opulence and receptivity to new music of the Chapel Royal (which itself later fell into a musical decline) did not typify the situation in other establishments where church music was practised. By the beginning of the eighteenth century there was a widening gulf in cultivated perception between sacred and secular music. This was partly the result of the growing dominance of theatre and concert music as arbiters of public taste, so that church music composed in similar style was sometimes perceived as inappropriate for its purpose. As a reaction against what was considered to be undesirable secularity and triviality in church music, various writers sought to keep the older polyphonic tradition alive. With this aim in view, some musicians compiled anthologies that made a feature of earlier music: Thomas Tudway's manuscript collection (London, British Library Harleian manuscripts 7337–42) compiled between 1714 and 1720, and William Boyce's *Cathedral Music,* published in three volumes from 1760 to 1773, are two examples. Other musicians composed in a manner that attempted to reconcile modern idioms with grave and stately polyphony. Many of their efforts made adept use of the polyphonic idiom but lacked musical distinction. Some church pieces by Henry Aldrich (1648–1710) (see above, pp.45–46) paid homage to the past in this way and remained part of the cathedral repertory for many years. Probably the best work in this deliberately conservative style is that by William Croft (1678–1727), whose anthems of this type have an intensity that exceeds the mere competent handling of the medium.

Into this divisive and largely slovenly state of affairs in English church music came Georg Friederich Handel (1685–1759), whose successful blend of Italian operatic techniques and German baroque idioms with pre-existent English forms and styles ensured for him a unique position in the history of English sacred music. But it was not the music that Handel wrote specifically for use in worship that was influential in this respect. The eleven anthems written in 1717 and 1718 for performance at Cannons, the home of the Duke of Chandos; the anthems written for the Chapel Royal and the settings for specific occasions such as the four coronation anthems (including *Zadok the priest),* did not establish themselves in the general anthem repertory. Their status as pieces for specific occasions combined with their relatively elaborate scoring probably inhibited wide dissemination and acceptance. Two of the three tunes that Handel wrote specifically for use with hymns (as distinct from those borrowed for this purpose from his other works, see above, pp.50–55) have remained in the repertory ('Cannons', EH 66 ii, A&MR 84, SP 337; 'Gopsal', EH 476, A&MR 216, MHB 247, SP 632), but did not engender borrowings of style. Rather, it was the music of Handel's operas and oratorios that gave rise to borrowings, not only of material but also of style and form. His musical language was essentially an individualized version of that currently in favour throughout Europe, which was principally Italian in origin. English church composers aspired to this language with varying degrees of success, and in doing so they were almost inevitably influenced to some extent by Handel's work as part of this borrowed style.

The impact of Handel's work was as much a social phenomenon as a musical one. His oratorios, in particular, appealed to people from a wide range of social class and Protestant persuasion. They combined an element of religious expression with a personal appeal and immediacy that was largely absent from music of the established church, utilizing dramatic techniques that were more akin to opera. Handel's arrival on the English musical scene was propitious: circumstances were favourable to the enthusiastic acceptance of his work, while Handel himself was sufficiently astute to draw on existing musical styles, blending and developing them in a way that gave his music an overwhelming influence on English taste (see above, pp.48–50). By the end of the eighteenth century, attendance at or participation in oratorio, particularly *Messiah,* was regarded by many people at least as an eminently respectable pursuit and at most as a profound religious experience. The fashion for performing Handel's oratorios with vast forces of musicians held sway. Performances proliferated throughout Great Britain, and societies and festivals were established with the aim of performing oratorios, chiefly those of Handel. Further oratorios were compiled by adapting and juxtaposing material from Handel's other works.

It was not until the nineteenth century that other composers began to produce oratorios in any great numbers that owed allegiance to Handel's innovations. But in smaller forms with sacred texts, such as the hymn and the anthem, there were sometimes parallels of style that reflect the tuneful and elegant nature of Handel's arias or the dramatic impetus of the choruses in his oratorios. The use of the organ to add not only harmony but colour and ornament to these smaller forms grew partly from the desired emulation of Handel's similar use of the oratorio orchestra. In effect, Handel's influence during his lifetime was to accelerate the adoption into English church music of the predominantly Italianate style that suffused most European music to a greater or lesser extent. The English borrowing at this stage was not so much of Handel's style as of elements of a universally favoured musical language of which, in England, Handel was the principal exponent. The following hymn provides an example. It is taken from the second edition of *Hymns on the Great Festivals and Other Occasions* with texts by Charles Wesley and music by John Frederick Lampe (c.1703–51), published in 1753. Most of Lampe's music is for the theatre, but he was involved with the Methodist movement and co-operated closely with Charles Wesley in the production of hymns. Entitled 'On the corpse of a Believer', this piece is an apt demonstration of the urbane and almost extrovert attitude to death that was common in the eighteenth century, an attitude that seems incongruous to twentieth-century perceptions and that would have shocked many a Victorian churchgoer with its absence of solemnity:

The five subsequent verses continue in a similarly positive spirit. Although the piece is set out as a hymn, the prevalence of musical ornamentation (to which more may have been added in performance) makes it unlikely to have been successful in congregational use. In organization it is like a miniature aria, with digression and recapitulation in the key structure, and development by means of sequence, modification and extension of a single principal phrase. The graceful melody is underpinned by harmonic progressions and cadential structures that are conventional to solo-orientated music of the period, including much of Handel's own. The idiom of this piece is typical of those in the collection, and shows the extent to which composers of music for worship and entertainment strove to speak the same musical language.

This conformity was shared to a large extent by Handel's English contemporaries in their production of church music. Inevitably their reputations suffered by comparison with Handel's genius. If some of their work appears vapid and devoid of inspiration alongside Handel's, it is because they were less adept than Handel at working in the largely borrowed style of the period, not because they deliberately tried to copy Handel and failed. For example the anthems of Maurice Greene (1696–1755) are for the most part fluent and accomplished, although occasional passages seem perfunctory. They show many affinities with Handel's style, but the level of inspiration is less consistent than Handel's. 'My God, my God, look upon me' (first published in 1743) is not atypical of Greene's output: it is a verse anthem for tenor solo, five-part chorus and organ. The dramatic recitative at 'they shoot out their lips and shake their heads' shows effective use of chromatic colour, and the chorus that follows, 'He trusted in God, that he would deliver him', is vivid and well wrought: it lacks the impact of Handel's setting of the the same text only because of its more modest size and weaker imitative subject which is much less angular and forceful than Handel's. Greene's pupil William Boyce (1711–79) wrote in a somewhat more personal style than his master but his music is sometimes pedestrian by comparison. Like Greene, Boyce shared some aspects of form and style with Handel: for example the chorus beginning 'O keep my soul and deliver me' from the anthem 'Turn thee unto me' (dating from c.1736) displays cumulative imitation based on juxtapositions of a running passage and a slower one, like 'For unto us a child is born' from Handel's *Messiah*. Again, the construction is similar but Handel's piece is larger, more colourful and, by comparison, supremely self-assured.

Although it is questionable whether or not Handel's oratorios can properly be considered as sacred music (see above, pp.48–50), they were certainly widely regarded as such in England by the beginning of the nineteenth century. The spread of musical literacy fuelled the growing appetite for oratorio, and the large choral works of composers such as Haydn and Mozart were performed in English translation by numerous choral societies as well as being sectionalized for use as church anthems. But the emergent romanticism that had begun to inform the works of the Viennese classical school and its adherents did not find unqualified favour in England. Works of this progressive nature were considered indecorous and thus not suitable for performance as sacred music. Consequently the works of Handel, particularly the oratorios, were elevated in public perception to the point where they epitomized the utmost respectability in church music. Therein lay the paradox of Handel's posthumous reputation in England: the composer who in the eighteenth century had done most to demythologize sacred music, was in the nineteenth century himself mythologized as the source of a seemly and separate sacred style.

Nineteenth-century English composers who wrote oratorios in response to festival commissions felt obliged to work in a fossilized pseudo-Handelian style in order to gain approval in respectable musical circles. Among these circles were the universities in which many English church composers were trained, and whose academic strictures encouraged the perpetuation of outdated styles in terms of 'rules' in harmony and counterpoint, to the exclusion of any flexibility or imaginative development. Degrees in music could be gained by the production of exercises in archaic styles, usually for choral forces, and these exercises were judged less in terms of originality and musical interest than in terms of observation of supposed 'rules'. A curious by-product of these academic strictures was the learned disapproval and editorial elimination of 'errors' in the works of composers such as Byrd and Purcell in cases where their individual characteristics of style did not conform to theoretical notions of harmony and counterpoint. The ability to write a good fugue in pastiche Baroque style was considered particularly estimable. But the idea of counterpoint, and especially fugue, as being the correct medium for sacred expression was not limited to English academic musicians. Continental composers of sacred music such as Mozart, Schubert and Bruckner felt the need for proficiency in counterpoint and sought tuition in it, often reserving fugue or fugato in their sacred compositions for the most climactic affirmations of faith.

It was the continuing prevalence of these musical conditions in England, rather than the incidence of Handel's music itself, that led to the apparent poverty of imagination in much English sacred music at the start of the nineteenth century. John Skelton Bumpus, writing in 1908, summed up this particular facet of musical composition as a 'large acquaintance with the works of Handel ... and ... excellent memories — these were substituted for invention'. Numerous oratorios and anthems in a pseudo-Handelian style were composed, performed and forgotten. The oratorios of Mendelssohn revitalized the outlook of massed choral singing in England but once again, the music was of a type that was hardly susceptible to further development but only to imitation, often in smaller-scale forms. The attempts by English composers to speak the same musical language as Mendelssohn turned out to be little more than insipid reflections of his style: like Handel's, fatally easy to contrive in a superficial way but wellnigh impossible to emulate on the same terms.[40]

Deliberate archaism

Particularly from the start of the nineteenth century, there was an increasing belief in a 'church style' in music: a style that did not have secular or indecorous associations and that was therefore considered appropriate for use in church. This special 'church style' eschewed modernism and was a reaction against the kinds of church music promoted in particular by Nonconformist and evangelical churches in the early years of the nineteenth century, which many considered frivolous and over-dramatic. Although this 'church style' appeared in a variety of guises, one attribute of it remained consistent: it was always the imitation of an archaic style, often a predominantly contrapuntal one, chosen for its supposed affinity with spiritual rather than temporal ideals. Mostly, too, the music was solemn, restrained and noble in demeanour rather than exuberant. This cultivation of a retrospective 'church style' in the nineteenth century was in some ways analogous to the deliberate recourse to polyphony undertaken from the late seventeenth century by composers such as William Croft and Henry Aldrich (see above, p.168). Tendencies like this, although significant in the history of English church music, were neither unique to it nor wholly predominant within it, yet it is probably these movements more than anything else which have led to a common overall misconception of English church music as almost completely conservative and iconoclastic rather than in any way progressive.

How far composers working in a supposed 'church style' succeeded in their aim of resurrecting the styles of the past is an open question. To twentieth-century perceptions their efforts sometimes seem incongruous and ill-conceived, for four main reasons. First, social and ecclesiastical conditions in the nineteenth century were inevitably different from those of earlier times, meaning that deliberate archaism in music could not attain universal affection and acceptance, but only respect. Second, composers' efforts in archaic styles were often coloured by modernisms that crept in; sometimes unwittingly, sometimes to lessen the severity of an austere style. Third, the 'church style' aimed at was in fact hypothetical: no one composer's style provided the model but rather a bland dilution of styles, whether Baroque or Renaissance, from which the individual features that characterized particular composers were expunged as lapses from a supposed ideal 'church style'. Fourth, this hypothetical style was sometimes imposed upon music that was entirely different in origin, function or period from the chosen 'church style', in the well-meaning but inaccurate belief that those with a knowledge of this 'church style' were in a position to effect 'improvements' on the supposedly inept efforts of other composers untrained in this way.

The adoption of aspects of Handel's style to form the model for an ideal supposed 'church style' has already been mentioned (see above, pp.168ff.). The promotion in England during the nineteenth century of the music of Johann Sebastian Bach (1685–1750) contributed towards the elevation of a Baroque musical style as ideal for sacred use. His music gained immensely in English esteem through the study and support of eminent musicians, particularly Felix Mendelssohn (1809–47), Samuel Wesley (1766–1837) and his son Samuel Sebastian Wesley (1810–76). The latter's collection of hymn tunes entitled *The European Psalmist* published in 1872 (see above, pp.57–58) owed a debt to Bach, not only in direct borrowings but also in many of the harmonizations, including those of his own hymn tunes such as 'Patmos' (no.569), offered as an alternative to Charles Henry Purday's somewhat arid 'Sandon' and John Bacchus Dykes's heart-rending masterpiece of its kind 'Lux benigna' to 'Lead, kindly light'. 'Patmos' has several features that mark it indelibly as a Victorian hymn tune, such as stepwise chromatic lines and conspicuous use of the tonic pedal and the appoggiatura. But it is more eventful, with a greater density of harmonic movement than either of the other tunes, although rhythmically it lacks the individuality of Dykes's unashamedly emotional effort. Several of Wesley's own tunes are characterized by this kind of melodic sturdiness and strong sense of direction combined with purposeful harmonic movement, both of which are essential elements in Bach's chorale workings. Good examples are Wesley's 'Gweedore'(A&MR 394) and 'Cornwall' (A&MR 195), which stand in antithesis to the feebler type of hymn tune, and indeed service and anthem, against which Wesley inveighed so strongly, deploring what he saw as their lack of suitability to carry texts for worship. Wesley's own services and anthems, while clearly products of the nineteenth century, owe less allegiance than those of many of his contemporaries to current foreign influences: rather, they show a mastery of Bach's technique absorbed into an individual style that stands without obvious immediate predecessors or successors, either English or foreign. Wesley sought to attain an appropriate 'church style' but his method was not merely to revert to Baroque models and imitate them: instead, he developed his own style which was enhanced rather than enveloped by borrowed elements.

The esteem accorded to Bach and Handel as masters of a supposed true 'church style' was reflected in the borrowing of their styles with the intention of adorning music whose style and purpose was entirely different from anything Bach or Handel ever composed. It was as if the use of these composers' names as informants of musical style endowed music with a kind of respectability which might otherwise be lacking. For example Alfred Bennett and William Marshall, in their time eminent church musicians, wrote as follows in the preface to their collection *Cathedral Chants,* published in London in 1829:

> The Editors of the present work (in harmonizing those Chants of which they did not possess original copies) have judged it best to adopt the style of harmony of the earlier English Composers for the Church, supported by the authority of HANDEL and SEBASTIAN BACH. They are satisfied that this plan will meet with the approbation of the real lovers of Cathedral Music ....

From this preface it seems that bold reference to Bach and Handel conferred a greater assurance of musical propriety and suitability for church use than did the unnamed 'earlier English Composers'. But the harmonizations of psalm chants in this volume by Bennett and Marshall are in an austere idiom which, though it is clearly an archaic borrowed style, is faceless: it is devoid of the individual characteristics that distinguish Bach, Handel or any other composer. This kind of borrowing is purely academic: it is far removed from the constructive absorption of a borrowed style exhibited in Wesley's music although the aim of achieving a supposed 'church style' is overtly similar.[41]

The belief in a separate and archaic 'church style' in music was given additional momentum in cultivated circles in the early nineteenth century by the Romantic revival, which promoted renewed interest in artistic aspects of the remote past (see above, pp.59–60). This revival, in turn, exerted a strong influence on the supporters of the Tractarian movement (see above, pp.60–61), whose aim of restoring dignity and beauty to worship found its musical ideal in plainsong and unaccompanied polyphony. As well as reviving earlier music of these kinds for use in church, the musical adherents of Tractarianism were concerned with encouraging further composition in an archaic borrowed style that went back to the Renaissance and beyond, in preference to some later techniques which could be seen as denials of the supposed simplicity, purity and impersonality of earlier music.

At the centre of the Tractarians' musical ideals stood the concept of the 'sublime', used to categorize plainsong and Renaissance sacred polyphony in particular: music which was supposedly untainted by secularism, modernity or frivolity. Music in the 'sublime' style was considered to attain the most elevated degree of purity and worthiness: the condition to which the Tractarians believed all church music should aspire. It was considered to be awe-inspiring, and to represent an evocation of the numinous. This concept of the 'sublime' in music was strongly advocated by William Crotch (1775–1847), Professor of Music at Oxford University, first Principal of the Royal Academy of Music and one of the most influential composers and musical theorists of his day. He saw parallels in music with the theory of painting put forward by Sir Joshua Reynolds: this led to his idea that the history of music could be divided into three periods represented in turn by the sublime, the beautiful and the ornamental. His detailed ideas were first published in 1831, but an illuminating summary of them entitled 'Dr Crotch on different styles in music' appeared in the first issue of *The Parish Choir,* an influential monthly journal dedicated to the spread and acceptance of Tractarian ideals. The following extracts from this summary encapsulate the aesthetic principle and sense of relative values that informed the revival of early sacred music and the borrowing of its conglomerate style:

> There are in music, as in other arts, certain *styles,* which are more or less valuable
> in proportion to the mental labour employed in their formation.

Music, like painting, may be divided into three styles — the sublime, the beautiful, and the ornamental, which are sometimes distinct, and sometimes combined.

The *sublime* is founded on principles of vastness and incomprehensibility .... this style, accordingly, never descends to anything small, delicate, light, pretty, playful, or comic. The grandest style in music is, therefore, the sacred style ... for it is least inclined to levity.

[This style has attributes of] solemnity .... vastness ... and uniformity, [for example] clearness of harmony ... in the full anthem, or the deep science of the organ fugue.

Beauty ... is the result of softness, smoothness, delicacy, smallness, gentle undulations .... In music, the melody is vocal, flowing, the measure symmetrical, the harmony simple and intelligible.

The *ornamental* style is the result of roughness, playful intricacy, and abrupt variations. In music, eccentric and difficult melody; rapid, broken and varied rhythms; wild and unexpected modulation.

The sublime, by its solemnity, takes off from the loveliness of beauty.

Crotch put these beliefs into practice by imitating what he considered to be the 'sublime' style in some of his own sacred compositions. He was one of the judges for the Gresham Prize, offered from 1832 by Maria Hackett, who did much to foster the improvement of conditions for church musicians. The prize was awarded for a service or anthem in 'the true sublime style', meaning the imitation of sixteenth-century sacred polyphony, but the result was a succession of scholarly and uninteresting pieces because the conditions of style were so limiting. Crotch's beliefs found much favour but this was not universal: some eminent church musicians, such as Henry John Gauntlett, deplored Crotch's insistence that 'expression' should have no place in church music. Yet Gauntlett was still seeking to establish a separate 'church style' based on archaic musical styles: in 1836 he advocated that composers for the church should write either in a style based on those of Gibbons, Purcell, Croft and Greene, with the possibility of fusion with the 'more dramatic manner' of Attwood and Vincent Novello, or in a style that unified those of Purcell, Bach and Beethoven. Like the supposed 'sublime' style, the styles proposed by Gauntlett were artificial and conservative, although perhaps superficially less easy to identify and achieve than the austere, rarefied counterpoint that was sometimes produced in aspiration to sublimity.

The effect on composers and editors of this glorification of the 'sublime' and the advocacy of a separate 'church style' were varied. The church music of Arthur Sullivan (1842–1900) presents one example. Several writers have drawn attention to the mediocrity of most of Sullivan's church music in comparison with the light operas which represent the pinnacle of his achievement, dismissing his church music as a chronicle of sanctimonious tedium punctuated by passages of deplorable vulgarity. But in a sense, Sullivan was caught on the horns of a musical dilemma. His early musical training was undertaken by Thomas Helmore (see above, pp.62–63), whom Sullivan later described as 'the greatest teacher of his youth'. Helmore was very strongly influenced by Crotch's theory of the 'sublime' in music: he used this expression a great deal in describing the church music that he considered the most appropriate. Under Helmore, Sullivan had to submit a small composition of his own, often a Sanctus or an anthem, every week. It is hardly surprising, therefore, that he was firmly inculcated with the notion of a separate 'church style', a style in which his natural gifts for expressive melody and harmony found almost no outlet. His attempts to suppress these attributes in the interests of a supposed 'church style' produced little that rose above dullness: in the moments when his abilities began to emerge, even modestly, the results seemed incongruous in their sacred context. His anthem 'O Love the Lord', composed in 1864, shows a degree of compactness and restraint in deference to a supposed 'church style', but with hints also of the partsong and even of the light opera ensemble. These combine to relieve monotony but the result is a kind of pseudo-religious hybrid that speaks volumes about Sullivan's lack of enduring success as a church composer.

Other composers of lesser talent and individuality than Sullivan were sometimes more successful at channelling their abilities into a separate 'church style' when the occasion demanded. William Henry Monk (1823–89), best known for his tune 'Eventide' for 'Abide with me' (EH 363, A&MR 27, MHB 948, SP 437) written for *Hymns Ancient and Modern* (1861) of which Monk was appointed the first music editor in 1857, was influenced in his early years as an organist and choirmaster by the Tractarian movement, taking a particular interest in the revival of plainsong. His contributions to the Tractarian journal *The Parish Choir* included three anthems specially composed in the 'sublime' style, with suspensions at cadences instead of dominant sevenths, and the use of the flattened seventh in imitation of modality. The harmonies associated with the 'sublime' style were thought by the Tractarians to be the only ones appropriate to a 'church style': they deplored the incursion of dominant sevenths and chromaticisms that were sometimes introduced into extemporized organ accompaniments or vocal harmonizations.

The church music of Frederick Arthur Gore Ouseley (1825–89) (see above, p.64) provides one of the more successful examples of the deliberate borrowing of aspects of Renaissance sacred polyphony as part of a separate 'church style' which aspired to the 'sublime'. Precociously musically gifted from childhood, Ouseley held several distinguished musical appointments and, as an ordained priest, worked first in one of the London churches in which Tractarian ecclesiastical and musical practices were at an early and vigorous stage of development. He devoted his life to church music, both in promoting the education and welfare of its practitioners and in composition, assiduously refining and developing his style along the lines of the 'sublime', with the aim of excluding from it any modern or supposedly secular influences. As a result, his church music tends to lack vitality and imagination but its technical accomplishment, consistency and fluency makes it successful within its own limited sphere. Ouseley's anthem 'Is it nothing to you?' offers a striking example of the deliberate borrowing of an archaic, austere polyphonic style by a nineteenth-century composer of English church music:

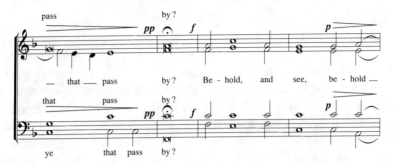

row like _____ un - to My sor - - - - row,

which is done un - to Me, which is

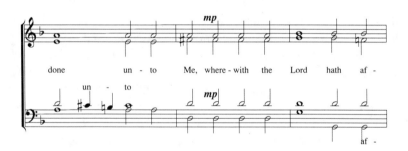

done un - to Me, where - with the Lord hath af -
un - to af -

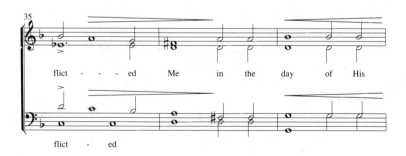

flict - - - ed Me in the day of His
flict - ed

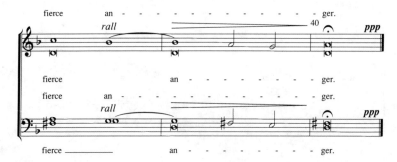

Perhaps the most easily identifiable archaic feature is the construction of the cadences: the use of suspensions and decoration (bars 5–6, 10–12), the circumspect treatment of the second inversion (bar 10), the preparation of the dominant seventh (bars 21–22) and the use of pedal points as cadential pivots (bars 22–25, 36–40). The slow harmonic pace, the limited range of key and the momentum arising from rhythmic and harmonic tension and relaxation are all characteristics of a variety of Renaissance styles of sacred polyphony. But in this case the whole is greater than the sum of the parts. The style is more than a bland 'lowest common denominator' of a con-glomeration of polyphonic styles. Ouseley's piece is remarkably reminiscent of the poignant setting of the same text, the Latin 'O vos omnes', by the Spanish composer Tomás Luis de Victoria (1548–1611). Victoria's setting, one of his group of responsories for Holy Week first published in 1585, uses a similarly transparent and mainly homophonic texture to great effect by the skilful manipulation of short, almost declamatory phrases and the close or wide spacing of the four voices. It is likely that Ouseley knew Victoria's set-ting, for as well as undertaking research into English polyphony he acquired a profound knowledge of the parallel Spanish school, writing about Spanish treatises on harmony and counterpoint and publishing a volume of motets by Spanish composers. This may well explain the degree of accomplishment of Ouseley's work in this borrowed 'church style'.[42]

The wish to attain a supposed 'church style' based predominantly on the styles of Renaissance sacred polyphony was not limited to composers. Editors and arrangers of church music sometimes regarded this kind of archaic bor-rowed style as an ideal, probably as a reaction against the incongruous mix-ture of styles to be found in cases where old borrowed material had been reharmonized in a modern style. Examples of the latter practice include Vin-cent Novello's plainsong hymns with piano accompaniments (see above, p.63) and Joseph Barnby's arrangement of *The Preces and Responses with Litany according to Tallis,* in which some of Tallis's harmonies have been adjusted to appeal to the tastes of a later age. The borrowing of an archaic 'church style' for editorial use with church music that had been rediscovered in melodic form only was perhaps most successfully carried out by Harry Ellis Wooldridge, music editor of *The Yattendon Hymnal,* published in 1899 (see above, pp.66–67). The plainsong harmonizations are in a scrupulously austere modal style described by the editors as 'Palestrinal'. While they may conform to the grammar of a supposed 'church style', they lack the flair, individuality and grandeur of Palestrina's music and stand as competent pastiche only. It is likely that the almost reverential regard for Palestrina's music as an example of the best 'church style' came about because, unlike some other composers of the Renaissance period, several aspects of his style are relatively easy to imitate. But, like the sacred works of Handel and Mendelssohn which were accorded exalted status and were imitated extensively in English church music, Palestrina's style is neither readily susceptible to further development nor easy to emulate on its own terms. A similar 'Palestrinal' style was used in the harmonization of other old melodies revived for *The Yattendon Hymnal,* such as those by Louis Bourgeois, (see above, pp.83–84).

Sometimes a borrowed 'church style' was editorially applied in circumstances where its use was hardly appropriate. Undoubtedly the use of such a style was thought to have connotations of decorum, respectability and learnedness, but this was not the only reason. Nineteenth-century musical historians and editors tended to take an evolutionary view of music in which each new development was perceived as an advance over that which had preceded it (see above, pp.59–60). They regarded Renaissance sacred polyphony as the earliest manifestation of a 'complete' harmonic system, yet entirely suitable for church use because of its supposed 'innocence' from secular musical influences. Where the characteristics of individual Renaissance composers' works failed to conform to this system, such features were regarded as unfortunate lapses from a single ideal polyphonic style. This was clearly the view held by Harry Ellis Wooldridge, whose justification for imposing editorial harmonies in this style on music from an earlier period runs as follows:

> As we ascend to the beginnings of the art we come to a time when harmony was so undeveloped as to be useless; and there is no choice but either to leave the tunes of this early date unaccompanied, or to explain them by the harmony at which we may be sure that the rude efforts of the time were aiming, because we know that they ultimately attained to it.

This somewhat specious argument, based on the supposition that music failing to conform to a single idealized concept must necessarily be defective

in some way, pervaded the attitudes of other editors of church music in the
nineteenth century and beyond. Richard Robert Chope, whose book of carols
published in 1875 was intended as a stimulus to the use of carols in church
in the manner of Christmas hymns (see above, pp.77–78), wrote as follows
about one of its contents, the tune known nowadays in an abridged version
(lacking the original repetition of the final two phrases) as 'Song 1' (EH 302,
384, A&MR 402, MHB 458, 892, SP 296, 485). Orlando Gibbons wrote this
tune for George Wither's metrical version of 'The first song of Moses' *(Ex-
odus* xv), but in Chope's book the music is set to a seasonal text beginning
'As on the night before this happy morn':

> This carol is from the 'Hymns and Songs of the Church' translated and com-
> posed by George Wither, and printed by his 'Assignes', A. D. 1623. 'Master
> Orlando Gibbons' supplied no music for the chorus [occurring in the seasonal
> text]. My friend, Mr. H[erbert] S[tephen] Irons [formerly organist of Southwell
> Minster], who has a true smack of good old Church music in him, has carefully
> remedied the defect.

The chorus added by Irons is not incongruous in style to the rest of the music,
but its presence makes this version unwieldy by upsetting the balance of the
verses. The interpolation of this extra music in a 'church style' to turn the
piece into a Christmas hymn shows the scant regard that was paid to the
artistry of Gibbons's own effort, complete in itself, for the supposed 'defect'
arose only in relation to the newly-applied seasonal text.

   Attitudes like this towards the editing of early music for modern use persisted in some quarters until well into the twentieth century. Sir Richard Run-
ciman Terry, who in 1932 edited Calvin's 1539 psalter with music, added
harmonizations so that the tunes could be used with modern English verses
as hymns for four-part choir. Acceptance and performance seem to have been
his main criteria rather than the pursuit of historical accuracy or authentici-
ty, although he points out that his harmonizations maintain the modal
character of the tunes. But in his edition of 1931 of fifteenth-century music,
some of which is sacred, the same four-part modal style is misapplied. In
A Medieval Carol Book, Terry takes the melodies of the carols, both sacred
and secular, eliminates many of their rhythmic complexities and clothes them
with bland modal four-part harmony. He did not regard this process as one
of adaptation; rather, as the revelation of what fifteenth-century composers
would have done had they had the benefit of the sixteenth-century repertory for guidance. Terry's harmony is mellifluous and overloaded in places
and he clearly encountered problems in reconciling this supposed universal
modal style with some of the more angular melodies. He considers that the

carols are 'unsuitable for performance as they stand in the manuscripts', having 'no aesthetic appeal to musicians of today'. He regards the melodies as the finished product, but justifies his own setting of them in terms of a later polyphonic style in the following way:

> The crude counterpoint which is woven around them is the first fumbling attempts in search of a technique which did not attain perfection until the sixteenth century.

This illustrates the continued use of an idealized archaic borrowed style in the belief that music that did not conform to such a style was somehow defective and therefore unacceptable. Singers and listeners would have been deluded if they had thought that Terry's versions were a reflection of what medieval carols actually sounded like, for this was a repertory that was not thoroughly brought to light until several decades later by John Stevens, initially in his volume for the *Musica Britannica* series. But Terry's work was valuable in pioneering the acceptance of early music, particularly church music, that was scarcely known among performers in the first half of the twentieth century.[43]

Popular styles in the nineteenth century

In contrast to the deliberate borrowing in some quarters of an archaic style of music for church use in the nineteenth century, most church music of the period continued to reflect styles current in music from other fields. The reaction in the early twentieth century against this almost unrelenting pursuit of popular styles in church music can be seen as a measure of the overwhelming predominance of these styles to the exclusion of all but the deliberate attempts of those who regarded church music as ideally separate from any kind of secular music. Perhaps as a latter-day part of this reaction, some writers in the twentieth century have deplored the work of the nineteenth century as representing the nadir of English church music. But in doing so they have acknowledged neither its legitimate background in contemporaneous secular music nor its fitness for nineteenth-century social and cultural circumstances, both of which led to its enormously successful acceptance and assimilation chiefly in the shape of the hymn tune in which choir and congregation alike could excel.

In the nineteenth century, several factors aided the promotion of church music in fashionable styles. One was the spread of musical literacy among all but the poorest social classes, another was the increasing realization by publishers that this greater musical awareness and ability, combined with cheaper methods of printing and disseminating sheet music, presented excellent opportunities for commercial enterprise. Domestic music-making flourished, fostering an eager market for music in the smaller forms: piano music, chamber music, solo songs and partsongs, all in current styles. The spread of musical literacy, combined with growing affluence and social and cultural change, led to greater concern with the standards of church music. In this area the established church was no match for the dissenting churches, in which well-organized singing of music with wide appeal drew large congregations, often at the expense of the established church. No longer content with the desultory and sometimes ill-disciplined efforts of untrained musicians, congregations in parish churches began to expect to hear music there that was comparable in both style and standard with what they could hear in the concert room or even at the opera. The installation of an organ and a robed choir under the tutelage of a professionally-trained organist, with services resembling those in cathedrals, was an ideal that was fulfilled by many churches in the nineteenth century. Composers and music publishers catered increasingly for parish choirs, making the best use possible of the limited expertise, resources and rehearsal time available to many such choirs.

The most conspicuous features of style borrowed from current secular music pertained chiefly to harmony, form and texture. Metre, rhythm and phrase-length were to a large extent predetermined by the metres of texts, and the tendency to cling to successions of short regular phrases and sequences makes some specimens of nineteenth-century church music seem mundane and at times predictable. But characteristic progressive devices reflecting currently-fashionable music included the increased deployment of melodic and harmonic chromaticism and the consequent wider variety of key within a single piece, also the greater incidence and versatility of sustained pedal-points and monotones to underpin melodies or act as pivots for modulation. In form, the use and development of motives and the imitation of larger structures, particularly those providing a well-defined key digression and climax followed by recapitulation, emerged increasingly. Composers paid greater attention to texture, in the use of both the vocal ensemble and the organ to produce effects that bordered on the orchestral. Much music was strongly influenced by the styles of Felix Mendelssohn (1809–47), Louis Spohr (1784–1859) and Charles Gounod (1818–93), all of whom wrote sacred music to English texts or furnished material that was eagerly adapted for English church use. But in some ways their musical ancestor in common was Franz Schubert (1797–1828), to whose affective use of chromaticism, especially in smaller forms, many of the idioms that characterize nineteenth-century church music can be traced.

The parallel growth in the nineteenth century of English church music and

secular music in a fashionable style is perhaps most evident in the relationship between the partsong and the small-scale anthem or hymn. Although
these smaller sacred forms undoubtedly borrowed many elements of style
from the partsong, the borrowing in this case was not exclusively in one
direction. Rather, there was cross-fertilization and linked development between the partsong and the sacred repertory. This can be seen particularly
in later partsongs of a 'serious' nature such as Sullivan's 'The long day closes'
(first published 1868), which builds on many of the characteristics of harmony, form and texture mentioned above. Used in a compact form as
displayed by this partsong, the impression they give is strongly hymnlike.
In this particular case it was probably Sullivan's intention to convey a religious
atmosphere, for the text is clearly meant to be construed as describing life
drifting into death, not merely wakefulness into sleep. A few years later
Sullivan composed *Five Sacred Partsongs* which obscure any distinction between sacred and secular styles, demonstrating the affinities between the partsong and the simple anthem in particular. But despite the possible implications
of the title, these are not church music: they are intended for performance
in a secular context.

The close relationship between the smaller forms of sacred music and the
partsong can be seen from the end of the eighteenth century, when the
currently-fashionable glee (see above, pp.136–38) provided a style for church
music that appealed to congregations and did not overstretch the abilities
of amateur performers. Several early nineteenth-century composers of glees
also wrote church music and there are often distinct parallels of style between works serving these two purposes: secular and sacred. The collection
edited by Samuel Arnold and John Wall Callcott entitled *The Psalms of David
for the Use of Parish Churches,* published in 1791, was designed for the use
of country choirs lacking the support of an organ or other instruments and
insufficiently skilled to sing 'imitations' and 'fugues'. It includes some simple four-part psalm settings by Callcott, typified by his music to Psalm 4 ('O
Lord, thou art my righteous judge, to my complaint give ear'), which is conventional, easy to sing and immediately appealing. It is extremely compact
without any ornamental or discursive writing, and the lightness and variety
of texture that Callcott manages to introduce into its tight harmonic
framework is a model of ingenuity. In these ways this psalm setting by
Callcott, like the others in the collection, has all the characteristics of the
simpler glee, in the composition of which Callcott was renowned. Arnold's
contributions to the same volume are somewhat more heavy handed and
denser but they aptly fulfil a similar purpose.

The increasing use of textural variety characterized the development of

the partsong and most forms of vocal church music, with exploitation of
devices such as unison and octave writing, smaller groups within the ensemble, and chords with a deliberately wide or narrow spread, depending upon
the effect required. Sometimes a passage of undistinguished or languorous
melody could be sustained purely by variety of harmony and texture.
Monotones given varied harmonic treatment for special effect were part of
the language of nineteenth-century composers from Beethoven to Liszt and
Brahms, with one of the best-known examples forming the opening of the
third ('Marche funèbre') movement of Chopin's second piano sonata, op.35
in B flat minor. A similar use of monotone or almost immobile melody occurs in many a partsong and hymn (in the latter, often at the opening), and
in an even briefer form is exemplified by the following psalm chant by A[lfred]
Bennett:

Even within this short piece there is considerable variety of texture, with
the relaxed chord spacing in the final section answering the tense, narrowly-
spaced writing approaching the midpoint. In the first section the note A forms
a pivot for the relatively remote modulation from F major to A major and
back, very much in the manner of Schubert. The melodic climax heralds the
return to F. The harmonized sections, which are little more than decorated
plagal cadences, exploit pedal-points and cadential second inversion chords
to draw out the cadences rather as Joseph Barnby does in what must surely
be regarded as a classic among Victorian partsongs, 'Sweet and low', published
in 1844.

The situation in which harmonic interest dominated that of the melody
was reversed by a further way in which pedal-points could be exploited. In
this way, a pedal-point (usually a tonic pedal) could be used to underpin a

mobile and usually rising melody line with static harmony that consisted of little more than successive redistributions of the notes in a single primary diatonic chord, often continuing into a plagal cadence. This was a device favoured by many nineteenth-century composers: in an expanded form it appears at the openings of Schubert's Moment musical op.94 no.3 in F minor, and of Brahms's *Wiegenlied* (Cradle song) op.49 no.4. But a particularly well-known and more compact example of this device and possibly one of the most influential as far as sacred choral music was concerned is the opening of the angels' trio for two sopranos and alto, 'Lift thine eyes', from the second part of Mendelssohn's *Elijah.* Many nineteenth-century hymn tunes rely partly on this device, particularly at their openings; borrowing and capitalizing on this feature of the musical language of the period. Examples include 'Unde et memores' (A&MR 397, MHB 586, 759), composed by William Henry Monk for publication in 1875 with William Bright's newly-composed text 'And now, O Father, mindful of the love', in some ways a better match than the tune by Gibbons to which this hymn is frequently sung. In Monk's tune a melody oscillating round a pedal note is a recurrent feature. Similar to it in both overall form and in the use of pedal-points is John Bacchus Dykes's 'Lux benigna' (EH 425, A&MR 298 ii, SP 554 ii) composed in 1865 for John Henry Newman's 'Lead, kindly light'. Here the characteristic rising melody line over the pedal-point is a striking feature, as it is in Richard Redhead's 'Petra' (A&MR 127, 210, MHB 498 as 'Redhead no. 76'), principally associated with Augustus Montague Toplady's text 'Rock of ages'. In the latter tune the middle section in particular shows this feature, although the harmonization often used nowadays seems to be the somewhat contorted result of an effort to eliminate this typically nineteenth-century manner of treating a rising melody based on a triad.

The three hymn tunes mentioned in connection with triadic melodies underpinned by pedal-points have another feature in common: that of overall form. Like many tunes of the period they exhibit compact versions of forms favoured by composers in fields outside the church. Thus, one of the most ubiquitous musical schemes, a tripartite form consisting of exposition, digression or development, and recapitulation, in the manner of many of Chopin's Nocturnes for piano (to take a single example at random), is condensed in 'Unde et memores', 'Lux benigna', 'Petra' and many more hymn tunes of the nineteenth century. The frequently-found placing of the musical climax in hymn tunes immediately before the recapitulation (whether of tonic key only, melodic material only or both of these) was a consequence of this compression of borrowed forms in which recapitulation had an increasingly important stabilizing function sometimes combined with further development.

A similar principle can be seen in anthems of the period. 'O Saviour of the world' by John Goss, composed in 1869, has a varied and extended recapitulation with emphasis on the subdominant to balance the dominant leanings in the development of its single theme. Thomas Attwood Walmisley, in 'From all that dwell below the skies', composed in 1835 very much in the partsong manner, heralds the key-recapitulation with a long dominant pedal but then prolongs the climax by a series of surprise modulations with the tonic as a pivot note before allowing the music its ultimate rest in the home key. Dramatic effects like this were a feature of longer anthems and 'set pieces' too. Some, like Joseph Barnby's anthem 'Abide with me', composed in the 1870s to Henry Francis Lyte's hymn text, aspired to the dramatic momentum of the operatic *gran scena,* in this case illustrating the passage of the individual soul through death to eternal life. Barnby's piece consists of a series of solos with throbbing organ accompaniment, long crescendos and textures that thicken progressively in an orchestral manner as climaxes approach. The organ interludes are vivid to the extent that they almost upstage the solo voices, but the main climax is reserved for the entry of the chorus at 'Heaven's morning breaks'. The vocal writing at this point is high and dense in texture, and rising sequences add to the climactic effect before the music calms down in a final reflection on the soul's achievement. The whole piece is so overtly theatrical and emotional that to twentieth-century perceptions it seems almost like a parody of Victorian exhibitionism encapsulated in church music. But on its own terms it is, like many products in the church music of its age, appropriate as a reflection of nineteenth-century attitudes and musical tastes of a majority of worshippers.

Similar principles, capitalizing on the appeal of popular secular music, governed much music of the gospel revival era which was influential in Great Britain from the 1870s to about 1920. The revival found much favour among those of the poorest social classes, for it offered the promise of eventual salvation from a mortal life blighted by desperate poverty and hopelessness. Accordingly the music of the gospel revival was simple, tuneful and easy to memorize. It had close affinities with the popular song of the day, but that of the music hall rather than the claustrophobic respectability of the drawing room. The leaders of the Salvation Army in particular recognized the potential of popular tunes as a means of transmitting their message of moral uplift. They furnished popular music-hall songs with new texts and promoted further musical material in a similar style. The borrowing in this case was reciprocal, for Salvation Army tunes were seized upon by music-hall artists for performance with texts that would certainly not have met with the approval of those whose mission was to elevate the moral standards of the populace.

In its own way the music of the gospel revival movement became, like much music-hall song, a kind of urban folk music. Most of it was regular and often repetitive, straightforward in a manner that matched the simplicity of the evangelistic message it purveyed. Especially in jubilant or militant hymns, refrains were frequently used. Composers and publishers of gospel music, such as the Americans William Howard Doane (1832–1915), Ira David Sankey (1840–1908) and Homer Alvan Rodeheaver (1880–1955), recognized the importance of music in their missions as a means of outreach towards people seeking religious expression with which they felt at ease and which gave them hope. The movement originated in the United States and some of the music is in borrowed styles, such as ragtime, that were currently popular there. American evangelists conducted revival meetings in Great Britain at which gospel hymns of this kind were introduced, meeting with widespread acceptance. Consequently it was hymns from a predominantly American background that survived in Great Britain as a distinctive 'gospel' repertory. Many such hymns have retained their popularity despite the apparently grudging acceptance of only a small number of them in *The English Hymnal,* or none at all in some of the more esoteric hymnals. A good example of a simple but striking gospel hymn in a popular late nineteenth-century style is 'Hold the fort' (EH 570), with words and music composed in 1870 by the American Philip Paul Bliss (1838–76). This tune depends heavily on the repetition using basic harmonies of a single melodic motto with a strong rhythm. The refrain offers modest departure from this scheme but its melody is even simpler than that of the verses, probably to facilitate rapid memorization. Despite its four-part harmonization in *The English Hymnal,* any hymnlike qualities of the piece as a whole are undermined by the inescapable impression that this music would be better served by a piano accompaniment of the type that by the end of the nineteenth century had become associated with ragtime. The borrowing of popular styles in this manner has been a consistent feature of gospel revival even after the decline of the movement that began in the 1870s, so that later popular idioms were and still are continually assimilated into an existing heritage of gospel music.[44]

The twentieth century

By the end of the nineteenth century, the overwhelming preference in English church music for the pursuit and imitation of current popular styles had precipitated adverse reaction in several quarters. Different aspects of the condition of nineteenth-century English church music produced a variety of musical responses aimed at rectifying what some saw as its inherent defects.

The exclusive pursuit of modern idioms that had characterized much nineteenth-century church music became less practicable as the twentieth century approached. One reason for this was that the concert hall and opera house had overtaken the church and court as the environment to which the most innovative composers owed their livings and for which they produced their most musically significant works. Another reason, linked to this, was that the ultimately most productive directions taken by music at the end of the nineteenth century were neither congenial to church choirs and congregations nor within reach of their musical abilities. From this point onwards, there was increasing divergence between church music and significant new music in practically every other field. Some change was inevitable if church music was to avoid becoming fossilized in the vestiges of a popular nineteenth-century style. The reaction to this situation produced borrowings, not only of actual material but in style also, that enriched the repertory of church music as the twentieth century progressed.

Although Charles Villiers Stanford had achieved eminence as composer and teacher by the 1880s, his attitude towards church music and his output in that area are more typical of the early twentieth century than the nineteenth. He had an eager intellectual grasp of the most progressive musical innovations of the late nineteenth century. Unusually, in addition to this, he exhibited a profound knowledge of early English music, particularly that of Purcell, as well as of Irish folk music that influenced his secular output to some extent. His training was that of many nineteenth-century aspiring English composers: a period at university combined with travel and study abroad, predominantly in Germany. Yet as far as church music was concerned Stanford did not believe in eclectic modernism but rather in the promotion of a specifically English style. To him, this style had to be be essentially something new, developed without seeking refuge in deliberate archaisms such as contrived modality. Accordingly, his church music shows an imaginative and rewarding use of voices and organ, with meticulous attention to textual detail, lively and concise melodies and inventive, energetic harmonies that do not lapse into triviality, languor or dullness. Stanford was at his best in services and anthems rather than hymns, for his operatic and symphonic experience showed him how to plan larger-scale church pieces effectively. These pieces are distinguished by a sense of balance, proportion and integration brought about by the careful use and redisposition of motivic material.

Stanford is often credited as the pioneer of an English musical renaissance.

In terms of the lasting popularity of his church music and of his influence on subsequent composers for the church this is true: he taught Charles Wood, Ralph Vaughan Williams and Herbert Howells, and influenced many others. But in terms of musical progress or innovation beyond the field of church music, Stanford has no place among the leaders. Despite his hope of establishing an English style of church music his work even in this area was essentially derivative and conservative, based on a tradition attributable most of all to Mendelssohn. This is not to dismiss or underrate Stanford, for his inventiveness and realization of hitherto unexplored possibilities of this borrowed style as it stood, rather than any expansion of its boundaries, were what distinguished him at a time when English church music was ready for a radical change of direction.

Stanford's successors capitalized on the most versatile aspects of his technique, sometimes following his example of incorporating material such as plainsong and letting the style of such material spill over into the original music surrounding it. The music of Charles Wood (1866-1926) offers some interesting examples: his canticles based on plainsong (see above, p.65) have accompaniments that reflect the suavity and undulating nature of the chants while at the same time owing some harmonic allegiance to the tradition drawn upon by Stanford. Wood's freely-composed music is varied in mood from the austerity of a service which he described as 'mainly in the Phrygian mode' to the uninhibited mystic splendour of 'Hail, gladdening light', in a later derivative style not unlike Stanford's, but with perhaps even greater skill and originality in the deployment of choral forces.

Recourse to deliberately archaic borrowed styles showed various degrees of compromise in the assimilation of more modern elements. At one extreme stood Harry Ellis Wooldridge (1845-1917), music editor of *The Yattendon Hymnal* (see above, pp.83-85), published in 1899. As well as making adaptations of borrowed material, Wooldridge also contributed seven tunes of his own in a borrowed archaic style. Its at times extreme austerity is almost devoid of character and seems to lack obvious affinity with the music of Palestrina or any other identifiable composer contemporary with him. Wooldridge's setting of 'Lead, kindly light' is a particularly colourless example, made even less satisfactory by the unedifying half close that ends every verse. That Wooldridge was, on occasions, able to produce an elegant and appealing melody is clear from his setting of 'Lord, thy word abideth', based on a rising sequence with extension at the final cadence to give an unconventional phrase length to the final line of this solidly regular text. This works well in the first verse, where melodic climax and rhythmic stress occur appropriately on 'joy' at 'Light and *joy* receiveth', but less well in subsequent ones, for example 'Message *of* salvation'. Some of Wooldridge's work survived in *The Oxford Hymn Book* (see above, p.83), published in 1908, but scarcely at all elsewhere.

Few composers were as uncompromising as Wooldridge in the deliberate imitation of an archaic style. In the majority of cases, elements that could be described as borrowed archaisms were assimilated into emergent personal styles. The most obvious of these elements were polyphonic texture, predominantly stepwise, undulating and irregularly-phrased melody in the manner of plainsong, modality marked particularly by use of the flattened seventh, and dissonances arising from the juxtaposition of chromatically-inflected notes ('false relations') within the confines of diatonic harmony. Among composers who made creative use of these aspects of earlier styles in their church music were Edmund Rubbra (1901–86) and Herbert Howells (1892–1983). In addition, many a lesser early twentieth-century composer for the church sought refuge in similar points of style, using modality to convey 'Englishness', polyphony as a mark of sacred propriety, and rhapsodic musical discourse as a substitute for genuine invention. Of the hymns in styles with borrowed archaic elements perhaps the most conspicuous is 'Mantegna' (SP 126), an ethereally wistful piece that is unmistakably the work of Ralph Vaughan Williams. Tunes by Rutland Boughton (1878–1960), Peter Warlock (1894–1930) and John Ireland (1879–1962) in *The Oxford Book of Carols* (nos.168, 169, 170), published in 1928, all exhibit certain archaisms, particularly the use of modality. The adoption of this aspect of an archaic style may have been intended to reflect the period of origin of the texts, the latest of which is from the early seventeenth century. But in each case the style is distinctively that of the composer rather than one in which archaisms are the prevailing feature. The same applies to certain hymns by Gustav Holst (1874–1934), such as 'Chilswell' (SP 498). Yet the more successful and enduring hymn tunes of composers like these are those in which archaic elements are less in evidence. Obvious examples include Vaughan Williams's 'Sine Nomine' (EH 641, MHB 832, SP 202), Ireland's 'Love unknown' (A&MR 102, MHB 144, SP 127) and Holst's 'Sheen' (EH 310, A&MR 417, MHB 30, SP 496). Perhaps ironically, the hymn tune by which Holst is best known is the one from his output that is most reminiscent of typical Victorian hymnody: 'Cranham' (EH 25, A&MR 67, MHB 137, SP 75), and as such forms an appropriate match for Christina Rossetti's text 'In the bleak midwinter'.

The adaptation of folksong melodies as hymns, combined with antipathy towards hymns of the Victorian era, led to the evolution in the early twentieth century of a category of tune that stood as the almost self-conscious antithesis to what were perceived as undesirable aspects of the Victorian hymn. This category is extremely broad and diverse, and cannot be fully explained as a borrowing of a folksong style, although for some new tunes a derived style of this kind has clearly formed the strongest influence. It would be more accurate to suggest that many tunes in this category shared with some folksong adaptations qualities that set them as far apart as possible from points of style that typified Victorian hymns. Thus, where the latter were perceived as exhibiting sluggish melodies and dull partwriting, their twentieth-century counterparts have agile, positive melodies; strident, businesslike bass lines and varied textures. Lingering chromatic harmonies were dispensed with in favour of austere, restless and occasionally angular harmonic movement, sometimes modally orientated, designed to enhance unison rather than four-part singing. Fluidity of rhythm and phrasing, an attribute shared with much folksong, was used to enhance word stress. This was part of a conscious effort to break free from the confines of conventional hymn metres: new texts in unconventional metres obviously called for new tunes, but it was considered that the lack of rhythmic variety in some nineteenth-century tunes provided an inadequate means of expression for the texts, even those from the Victorian era that were perfectly at ease with their four-square tunes. This over-reaction against Victorian hymnody meant that much that was good was shunned alongside that which was perceived as bad. It led to bracing, zestful music of a cast so objective that it was sometimes devoid of warmth and musical approachability, and some of the hymn tunes, in particular, have failed to supplant their Victorian equivalents in popular esteem.

Foremost in the composition and promotion of hymns and service music in this reactionary style were the brothers Martin (1875–1958) and Geoffrey (1879–1943) Shaw. Martin Shaw, jointly with Ralph Vaughan Williams, was music editor of *Songs of Praise* (first published 1926) and *The Oxford Book of Carols* (1928). Shaw's *Anglican Folk Mass,* published in 1917, uses repeated fragments of plainsong-related melody in free rhythm, with modal harmonies as background. This simple, repetitive structure was intended as a means of helping the congregation to join in the singing of the Communion service, an important departure from the earlier situation in which this function had belonged exclusively to the choir. Many of Martin Shaw's hymns, too, aimed at greater informality, with emphasis on unison singing. His antipathy towards Victorian hymnody in particular emerges in *The Principles of Church Music Composition* (1921), in which he states that in a hymn melody monotone is undesirable, and sequence is weak: principles that are untenable without some qualification even within the limited area of the hymn tune repertory. Martin Shaw's own hymn tunes are characterized by bold melodic lines covering wide ranges. He often uses modified ascending scalic figures as the basis of a tune so that the climax comes very near the end. 'Little Cornard' (A&MR 269, MHB 815, SP 64) and 'Marching' (A&MR 182, 495, MHB 616, SP 678) are good examples of this style. Similar in spirit but with a prominent modal flavour and the borrowed device of canon in the accompaniment bass, is 'Purpose' (MHB 812, SP 300); which, like many similar tunes, enjoyed some popularity as a school assembly song. Even Shaw's more docile tunes are typified by this kind of melodic restlessness: his 'Bromley Common' (SP 187 ii) consequently lacks the broad sweep of Dykes's 'Nicaea' to which it was intended as an alternative. Similar characteristics inform Geoffrey Shaw's tunes: in addition, he sometimes uses scalic bass lines as a feature of keyboard accompaniments. 'Glynthorpe' (SP 588) and 'Langham' (SP 326) typify Geoffrey Shaw's hymn style. Among other composers working in a similarly resolute hymn style, sometimes coloured by modality, were Guy Warrack (1900–86) and Cecil Armstrong Gibbs (1889–1960). Both had the facility to write music with popular appeal (Warrack for films, Gibbs for amateur music festivals) and this aspect of their styles is clear from their contributions to *Songs of Praise* (nos. 219, 81, 646 i, 661 ii).

The stance of *Songs of Praise* as a non-denominational book, combined with its freedom and freshness of approach, led to the adoption of some of its contents, together with further material based on similar ideals, by later hymnals including those for use by the Nonconformist churches. But the bulk of the hymn repertory in current use remained conservative, a situation reflected by the contents of the two collections that probably had the widest subsequent use: *The Methodist Hymn Book* (1933) and *Hymns Ancient and Modern Revised* (1950). The trend towards informality made possible largely by the influence of *Songs of Praise* received further impetus in the 1950s by experiments in using popular music idioms as the basis for service music, anthems, psalm settings, carols and hymns — categories which became increasingly diverse and interchangeable as methods of worship in many churches became less uniform. These experiments, aimed at producing worship music that had affinities with everyday popular music in an attempt to establish rapport with young people in particular, produced a great variety of material using means which, until the 1950s, would have been unimaginable as part of English church music. These borrowings of style, together with those from previous centuries, have added to the repertory rather than changing its outlook, and the increasing variety of music in use in many churches in the two decades immediately following 1950 reflects this: there was something available to suit almost every attitude and musical taste. The comfortable but ultimately sterile direction of nineteenth-century borrowed styles and the narrow perceptions causing a severe over-reaction against this in the early twentieth century were succeeded, in general, by a more balanced and conciliatory view of the many borrowed styles that in the early part of the second half of the twentieth century constituted the repertory of music for worship.[45]

Part IV

Select Bibliography

John Aplin, 'A Group of English Magnificats "Upon the Faburden"', *Soundings,* 7 (1978), 85–100

John Aplin, 'The Survival of Plainsong in Anglican Music', *Journal of the American Musicological Society,* 32 (1979), 247–75

John Aplin, '"The Fourth Kind of Faburden"; the Identity of an English Four-Part Style', *Music and Letters,* 61 (1980), 245–65

John Aplin, 'The Origin of John Day's "Certaine Notes" ', *Music and Letters,* 62 (1981), 295–99

John Aplin, 'Anglican Versions of two Sarum Invitatory Tones', *The Music Review,* 42 (1981), 182–92

Samuel Arnold (ed.), *Cathedral Music* (London, 1790)

Samuel Arnold (ed.), *A Collection of Hymn Tunes ... for ... Surry Chapel* (London, c.1797)

Samuel Arnold and John W. Callcott, *The Psalms of David for the Use of Parish Churches* (London, 1791)

Charles Avison, *An Essay on Musical Expression* (London, 1752)

Joseph Barnby (ed.), *The Cathedral Psalter Chants* (London, 1878)

Alfred Bennett and William Marshall (ed.), *Cathedral Chants* (London, 1829)

Louis F. Benson, *The English Hymn: its Development and Use in Worship* (Richmond, Virginia, 1915; repr. 1962)

Judith Blezzard (ed.), *The Tudor Church Music of the Lumley Books,* Recent Researches in the Music of the Renaissance, 65 (Madison, Wisconsin, 1985)

Judith Blezzard, 'Reconstructing Early English Vocal Music: History, Principle and Practice', *The Music Review,* 45 (1984), 85–95

Eric Blom, *Music in England* (London, 1942; revised 1947)

Friedrich Blume (ed.), *Protestant Church Music* (London, 1975)

Henry R. Bramley and John Stainer (ed.), *Christmas Carols New and Old* (London, 1871)

Robert Bridges and Harry Ellis Wooldridge (ed.), *The Yattendon Hymnal* (London, 1899)

Robert Bridges, 'English Chanting', *The Musical Antiquary,* 2 (1910-11), 125-41

Robert Bridges, *Collected Essays* (London, 1935)

The Bristol Tune Book (London, several edns, 1863-91; edn of c.1876)

David Brown (ed.), *Thomas Weelkes: Collected Anthems,* Musica Britannica, 23 (2nd edn, London, 1975)

Percy C. Buck (ed.), *John Taverner,* Tudor Church Music, 1 and 3 (London, 1923 and 1924)

Percy C. Buck (ed.), *Orlando Gibbons,* Tudor Church Music, 4 (London, 1925)

Percy C. Buck (ed.), *Robert White,* Tudor Church Music, 5 (London, 1926)

Percy C. Buck (ed.), *Thomas Tallis,* Tudor Church Music, 6 (London, 1928)

Percy C. Buck (ed.), *William Byrd: Masses, Cantiones and Motets,* Tudor Church Music, 9 (London, 1928)

Percy C. Buck (ed.), *Hugh Aston, John Marbeck, Osbert Parsley,* Tudor Church Music, 10 (London, 1929)

John S. Bumpus, *A History of English Cathedral Music 1549-1889* (London, 1908)

Christian K. J. von Bunsen, *Versuch eines allgemeinen evangelischen Gesang- und Gebetbuchs zum Kirchen- und Hausgebrauche* (Hamburg, 1833)

Walter E. Buszin, 'Luther on Music', *The Musical Quarterly,* 32 (1946), 80-97

John Caldwell (ed.), *Early Tudor Organ Music: I: Music for the Office,* Early English Church Music, 6 (London, 1966)

Raffaele Casimiri (ed.), *Giovanni Pierluigi da Palestrina: le opere complete* (Rome, 1939-)

George B. Chambers, *Folksong — Plainsong* (London, 1956; 2nd edn, 1972)

William Chappell, *Popular Music of the Olden Time* (London, 1859; repr. New York, 1965)

William Child, *The First Set of Psalmes ... after the Italian Way* (London, 1639; reissued 1656 by John Playford as *Choise Musick to the Psalmes ....*)

Richard R. Chope (ed.), *Carols for Use in Church during Christmas and Epiphany* (London, 1875)

The Congregational Hymnary (London, 1916)

C. Russell Crosby junior (ed.), *Hans Leo Hassler: Sämtliche Werke* (Wiesbaden, 1961-)

Ralph T. Daniel, 'Contrafacta and Polyglot Texts in the Early English Anthem', *Essays in Musicology: a Birthday Offering for Willi Apel,* ed. Hans Tischler (Bloomington, Indiana, 1968), 101-106

H. Walford Davies and Harvey Grace, *Music and Worship* (London, 1935)

H. Walford Davies and Henry G. Ley (ed.), *The Church Anthem Book* (London, 1933)

Percy Dearmer and Archibald Jacob, *Songs of Praise Discussed* (London, 1933)

Percy Dearmer and Ralph Vaughan Williams (ed.), *The English Hymnal* (London, 1906; revised 1933)

Percy Dearmer, Ralph Vaughan Williams and Martin Shaw (ed.), *Songs of Praise* (London, 1926; enlarged 1931)

Percy Dearmer, Ralph Vaughan Williams and Martin Shaw (ed.), *The Oxford Book of Carols* (London, 1928)

Christopher Dearnley, *English Church Music 1650-1750* (London, 1970)

Peter Dennison, *Pelham Humfrey* (London, 1986)

Alan E. F. Dickinson, *Vaughan Williams* (London, 1963)

Alan E. F. Dickinson, 'Vaughan Williams's Musical Editorship', *The Hymn Society Bulletin,* 4/85 (1959), 188-90

The Dictionary of National Biography (London, 1908-09; repr. 1973)

Paul Doe, *Tallis* (London, 1968; 2nd edn, 1976)

George H. Drummond and Edward Miller, *The Psalms of David* (London, 1790)

Edmondstoune Duncan, *The Story of the Carol* (New York, 1911)

Charles Dunkley (ed.), *The Official Report of the Church Congress (1899)* (London, 1899)

William Dyce, *Preface and Appendix to the Book of Common Prayer with Plain-tune* (London, 1844)

Leonard Ellinwood (ed.), revised by Paul Doe, *Thomas Tallis: English Sacred Music: I: Anthems; II: Service Music,* Early English Church Music, 12 and 13 (London, 1974)

Georg Feder and Jens Peter Larsen (ed.), *Joseph Haydn: Werke* (Munich, 1958-)

Edmund H. Fellowes, revised by Jack A. Westrup, *English Cathedral Music* (London, 1941; 5th edn, 1969)

Edmund H. Fellowes (ed.), *The Collected Works of William Byrd* (London, 1937-50)

Edmund H. Fellowes (ed.), revised by Philip Brett, *William Byrd: Songs of Sundry Natures,* The English Madrigalists, 15 (2nd edn, London, 1962)

Edmund H. Fellowes (ed.), revised by Thurston Dart, *The Collected Works of William Byrd: Cantiones Sacrae (1589),* 2 (London, 1966)

Edmund H. Fellowes (ed.), revised by Thurston Dart, *Thomas Tomkins: Songs of 3. 4. 5. & 6. Parts,* The English Madrigalists, 18 (London, 1922; 2nd edn. 1960)

Edmund H. Fellowes (ed.), revised by Thurston Dart, *John Wilbye: Second Set of Madrigals (1609),* The English Madrigalists, 7 (2nd edn, London, 1966)

Walter H. Frere (ed.), *The Use of Sarum* (Cambridge, 1898-1901)

Maurice Frost, *English and Scottish Psalm and Hymn Tunes c.1543-1677* (London, 1953)

Maurice Frost, *Historical Companion to Hymns Ancient and Modern* (London, 1962)

John A. Fuller Maitland and William Barclay Squire (ed.), *The Fitzwilliam Virginal Book* (London and Leipzig, 1894–99; revised 1963)

William Gardiner (ed.), *Sacred Melodies, from Haydn, Mozart and Beethoven ... Appropriated to the Use of the British Church* (London, 1812)

George Gardner and Sydney H. Nicholson (ed.), *A Manual of English Church Music* (London, 1923)

William J. Gatens, *Victorian Cathedral Music in Theory and Practice* (Cambridge, 1986)

Davies Gilbert (ed.), *Some Ancient Christmas Carols ...* (London, 1823; repr. 1972)

Anne G. Gilchrist, 'Sacred Parodies of Secular Folk Songs', *Journal of the English Folk Dance and Song Society,* 3 (1936), 157–82

Frederick J. Gillman, *The Evolution of the English Hymn* (London, 1927)

John and James Green, *A Book of Psalm-Tunes* (2nd edn, London, 1713)

Richard L. Greene, *A Selection of English Carols* (Oxford, 1962)

Richard L. Greene, *The Early English Carols* (2nd edn, Oxford, 1977)

The New Grove Dictionary of Music and Musicians (London, 1980)

Colin Hand, *John Taverner: his Life and Music* (London, 1978)

R. Alec Harman (ed.), *Thomas Morley: A Plaine and Easie Introduction to Practicall Musicke (1597)* (London, 1952; revised edn, 1963)

Basil Harwood (ed.), *The Oxford Hymn Book* (Oxford, 1908)

Thomas Helmore, *A Manual of Plainsong* (London, 1850)

Cecil Hill (ed.), *Sir William Leighton: The Teares or Lamentacions of a Sorrowfull Soule,* Early English Church Music, 11 (London, 1970)

Rowland Hill (ed.), *A Collection of Psalms and Hymns, chiefly intended for public worship* (4th edn. London, 1798)

Paul Hillier (ed.), *300 Years of English Partsongs* (London, 1983)

August H. Hoffmann and Ernst Richter (ed.), *Schlesische Volkslieder mit Melodien* (Leipzig, 1842)

Edward J. Hopkins (ed.), *The Temple Church Choral Service ...* (London, c.1867)

J. Eric Hunt, *Cranmer's first Litany, 1544, and Merbecke's Book of Common Prayer Noted* (London, 1939)

Peter le Huray, 'The English Anthem 1580–1640', *Proceedings of the Royal Musical Association,* 86 (1959–60), 1–13

Peter le Huray, *Music and the Reformation in England 1549–1660* (London, 1967; 2nd edn, Cambridge, 1978)

W. Henry Husk, *Songs of the Nativity* (London, 1868; repr. 1973)

Arthur Hutchings, *Church Music in the Nineteenth Century* (London, 1967)

Hymns Ancient and Modern Revised (London, 1950)

Reginald Jacques and David Willcocks (ed.), *Carols for Choirs* 1 (London, 1961)

Joseph Joachim and Friedrich Chrysander (ed.), *Les Oeuvres de Arcangelo Corelli* (Hamburg, 1871)

Journal of the Folk-Song Society, 1 (1899–1904), 2 (1905–06)

John Julian, *A Dictionary of Hymnology* (London, 1892; 2nd edn, 1907; repr. 1957)

Maud Karpeles, *Cecil Sharp's Collection of English Folk Songs* (London, 1974)

Michael Kennedy, *The Works of Ralph Vaughan Williams* (London, 1964)

Gerald H. Knight and William L. Reed (ed.), *The Treasury of English Church Music* (London, 1965)

Paul H. Lang, *George Frideric Handel* (London, 1966)

James T. Lightwood, *Hymn-tunes and their story* (London, 1905)

James T. Lightwood, *The Music of the Methodist Hymn-book* (London, 1935; 3rd revision 1955)

Walther Lipphardt (ed.), *Gesellige Zeit* 1 (Kassel, 1965)

Kenneth R. Long, *The Music of the English Church* (London, 1972)

Timo Mäkinen (ed.), *Piae Cantiones,* Documenta Musicae Fennicae, 10 (Helsinki, 1967)

Bernard L. Manning, *The Hymns of Wesley and Watts* (London, 1942)

Lowell Mason and George J. Webb (ed.), *The Boston Glee Book* (Boston, Massachusetts, 1844; repr. New York, 1977)

David Mateer (ed.), *Robert White,* Early English Church Music, 28, 29 and 32 (London, 1983–86)

The Methodist Hymn Book with Tunes (London, 1933)

John Milsom, 'Songs, Carols and *Contrafacta* in the Early History of the Tudor Anthem', *Proceedings of the Royal Musical Association,* 107 (1980–81), 34–45

John Milsom, 'A Newly-discovered Tallis Contrafactum', *The Musical Times,* 123 (1982), 429–31

Alexander F. Mitchell (ed.), *James, John and Robert Wedderburn: Ane Compendious Book of … Gude and Godlie Ballates (1567)* (Edinburgh and London, 1897)

John M. Neale and Thomas Helmore, *The Hymnal Noted* (London, 1851 and 1854)

Vincent Novello (ed.), *The Psalmist* (London, 1835)

Vincent Novello (ed.), *The Complete Collection of the Gregorian Hymns for the Whole Year* (London, c.1850)

John Page, *Harmonia Sacra* (London, 1800)

Roy Palmer (ed.), *Folk Songs Collected by Ralph Vaughan Williams* (London, 1983)

The Parish Choir or Church Music Book, [monthly journal] (London, 1846–51)

Edna Parks, *The Hymns and Hymn Tunes Found in the English Metrical Psalters* (New York, 1966)

Millar Patrick, *Four Centuries of Scottish Psalmody* (London, 1949)

Ronald Pearsall, *Victorian Popular Music* (Newton Abbot, 1973)

Charles H. Phillips, *The Singing Church* (London, 1945; revised 1979)

Thomas Pitt, *Church Music* (Worcester, 1788 and 1789)

Alfred W. Pollard and Gilbert R. Redgrave, *A Short Title Catalogue of Books ... printed ... 1475-1640* (London, 1926)

Elizabeth Poston (ed.), *The Penguin Book of Christmas Carols* (London, 1965)

Bernarr Rainbow, *The Choral Revival in the Anglican Church 1839-72* (London, 1970)

Richard Redhead, *Church Music: a Selection of Chants, Sanctuses and Responses* (London, 1840); Supplement *The Gregorian Chants for the Psalms* (London, 1841)

Richard Redhead, *Hymns and Canticles used at Morning and Evening Prayer, Pointed and Set to the Ancient Psalm Tones* (London, 1859)

Albert Riemenschneider (ed.), *Bach: 371 Harmonized Chorales and 69 Chorale Melodies* (New York and London, 1941)

Julius Rietz (ed.), *Felix Mendelssohn-Bartholdy: Werke: kritisch durchgesehene Ausgabe* (Leipzig, 1874-77)

Alec Robertson, *Music of the Catholic Church* (London, 1961)

Erik Routley, *The Music of Christian Hymnody* (London, 1957)

Erik Routley, *The English Carol* (London, 1958)

Erik Routley, *Church Music and Theology* (London, 1959)

Erik Routley, *Twentieth Century Church Music* (London, 1964)

Erik Routley, *The Musical Wesleys* (London, 1968)

Erik Routley, *A Short History of English Church Music* (London, 1977)

Percy A. Scholes, *The Puritans and Music in England and New England* (London, 1934)

Claude M. Simpson, *The British Broadside Ballad and its Music* (New Jersey, 1966)

Denis Stevens (ed.), *The Mulliner Book,* Musica Britannica, 1 (London, 1951; 2nd edn, 1962)

John Stevens, *Music and Poetry in the Early Tudor Court* (2nd edn, Cambridge, 1979)

John Stevens (ed.), *Medieval Carols,* Musica Britannica, 4 (2nd edn, London, 1958)

John Stevens (ed.), *Music at the Court of Henry VIII,* Musica Britannica, 18 (2nd edn, London, 1969)

Robert Stevenson, 'John Marbeck's *Noted Book* of 1550', *The Musical Quarterly,* 37 (1957), 220-33

Arthur Sullivan (ed.), *Church Hymns with Tunes* (London, 1874, repr. 1905)

Nicholas Temperley, 'Domestic Music in England, 1800–60', *Proceedings of the Royal Musical Association,* 85 (1958–59), 31–47

Nicholas Temperley, 'The Adventures of a Hymn Tune', *The Musical Times,* 112 (1971), 375–6, 488–9

Nicholas Temperley, 'Kindred and Affinity in Hymn Tunes', *The Musical Times,* 113 (1972), 905–09

Nicholas Temperley, 'John Playford and the Metrical Psalms', *Journal of the American Musicological Society,* 25 (1972), 331–78

Nicholas Temperley, *The Music of the English Parish Church* (Cambridge, 1979)

Nicholas Temperley, Review of William J. Gatens, *Victorian Cathedral Music in Theory and Practice* (Cambridge, 1986) in *Journal of the Royal Musical Association,* 113/1 (1988), 136–38

Richard R. Terry, 'John Merbecke', *Proceedings of the Musical Association,* 45 (1918–19), 75–96

Richard R. Terry (ed.), *A Medieval Carol Book* (London, 1931)

Richard R. Terry (ed.), *Calvin's First Psalter* (London, 1932)

Thomas Tomkins, *Musica Deo Sacra et Ecclesiae Anglicanae* (London, 1668)

John Troutbeck and J. Frederick Bridge (ed.), *The Westminster Abbey Chant Book* (3rd edn, London, 1894)

Ralph Vaughan Williams, *The First Fifty Years: a Brief Account of the English Hymnal from 1906 to 1956* (London, 1956)

Ralph Vaughan Williams and Martin Shaw (ed.), *Tunes Selected from Songs of Praise ... to be Sung to Familiar Hymns* (London, 1943)

John Ward, 'Music for A Handefull of Pleasant Delites', *Journal of the American Musicological Society,* 10 (1957), 151–80

John Ward, 'The Lute Music of Royal Appendix 58', *Journal of the American Musicological Society,* 13 (1960), 117–25

Samuel Webbe junior, *A Collection of Psalm Tunes .... compressed into two Lines for the Organ or Pianoforte* (London, c.1808)

James, John and Robert Wedderburn, *Ane Compendious Buik of Godlie Psalmes ... and Sindrie Ballatis ....* (Edinburgh, c.1578, repr. on microfilm)

Charles Wesley and John Frederick Lampe, *Hymns on the Great Festivals and Other Occasions* (2nd edn, London, 1753)

Samuel Sebastian Wesley, *Preface to A Morning and Evening Cathedral Service* (London, 1845)

Samuel Sebastian Wesley, *A Few Words on Cathedral Music ... with a Plan of Reform* (London and Leeds, 1849)

Samuel Sebastian Wesley, *The European Psalmist* (London, 1872)

William T. Whitley, *Congregational Hymn-singing* (London, 1933)

Archibald W. Wilson, *The Chorales: their Origin and Influence* (London, 1920)

Catherine Winkworth *The Chorale Book for England* (London, 1863)

Charles Wood and George R. Woodward (ed.), *The Cambridge Carol Book* (London, 1924)

George R. Woodward (ed.), *Songs of Syon* (London, 1904 and 1910)

George R. Woodward (ed.), *Piae Cantiones, a Collection of Church and School Song* ... (London, 1910)

George R. Woodward and Charles Wood (ed.), *The Cowley Carol Book* (London, 1902; complete edn, 1947)

Harry Ellis Wooldridge (ed.), *William Chappell: Old English Popular Music* (London, 1893)

Worcester Diocesan Conference 1904: Report of the Church Music Committee (Worcester, 1904)

James R. S. Wrightson, 'The Wanley Manuscripts: an Edition and Commentary' (Ph.D. dissertation, University of Cambridge, 1984)

David Wulstan, *Tudor Music* (London, 1985)

Paul Yeats-Edwards, *English Church Music: a Bibiliography* (London, 1975)

Percy M. Young, *The Choral Tradition* (London, 1962)

Franklin B. Zimmerman, *Henry Purcell 1659-1695: an Analytical Catalogue of his Music* (London, 1963)

Franklin B. Zimmerman (ed.), *The Works of Henry Purcell* (2nd edn, London, 1961-)

Notes

CHAPTER 1

1. For a detailed account of religious and musical practice under Edward VI and Elizabeth, see Peter le Huray, *Music and the Reformation in England 1549-1660* (London, 1967).

2. Paul Doe, *Tallis* (London, 1968; 2nd edn 1976), 55; *Thomas Tallis: English Sacred Music: II: Service Music,* ed. Leonard Ellinwood, revised by Paul Doe, Early English Church Music, 13 (London, 1974), 150-59; John Aplin, 'The Survival of Plainsong in Anglican Music', *Journal of the American Musicological Society,* 32 (1979), 247-75; Merbecke facsimiles in J. Eric Hunt, *Cranmer's First Litany, 1544, and Merbecke's Book of Common Prayer Noted, 1550* (London, 1939); Richard R. Terry, 'John Merbecke', *Proceedings of the Musical Association,* 45 (1918-19), 75-96; Robert Stevenson, 'John Marbeck's Noted Book of 1550', *The Musical Quarterly,* 37 (1957), 220-33; Edmund H. Fellowes, revised by Jack A. Westrup, *English Cathedral Music* (London, 1941; revised 1969), 47-48; William Dyce, *Preface and Appendix to the Book of Common Prayer with Plain-Tune* (London, 1844), Preface ff.3v-5; Te Deum and eighth psalm tone in *Early Tudor Organ Music: I: Music for the Office,* ed. John Caldwell, Early English Church Music, 6 (London, 1966), 151-53; other Sarum tones in Walter H. Frere (ed.), *The Use of Sarum* (Cambridge, 1898-1901), ii, pp.lxvi-lxxiv.

3. Nicholas Temperley, *The Music of the English Parish Church* (Cambridge, 1979), i, 9-10, 13, 15; Aplin, 'Plainsong'; John Aplin, 'A Group of English Magnificats "Upon the Faburden" ', *Soundings,* 7 (1978), 85-100; *The Mulliner Book,* ed. Denis Stevens, Musica Britannica, 1 (2nd edn, London, 1962) Redford's 'O Lux on the faburden' is no.28; *Thomas Tallis,* ed. Percy C. Buck, Tudor Church Music, 6 (London, 1928), 209; John Aplin, 'The Fourth Kind of Faburden: the Identity of an English Four-Part Style', *Music and Letters,* 61 (1980), 245-65; Aplin, 'Plainsong'; James R. S. Wrightson, 'The Wanley Manuscripts: an Edition and Commentary' (Ph.D. dissertation, University of Cambridge, 1984), the author is indebted to Dr Wrightson for additional information on the Wanley books; *The Tudor Church Music of the Lumley Books,* ed. Judith Blezzard, Recent Researches in the Music of the Renaissance, 65 (Madison, Wisconsin, 1985), 'Laudate pueri Dominum' is no.4 and the metrical Benedictus is no.16 in this edition.

4. le Huray, *Reformation,* 158-60, 163, 371-2, 384; Temperley, *Parish Church,* i, 24-26; Maurice Frost, *English and Scottish Psalm and Hymn Tunes c.1543-1677* (London, 1953), 57-58, 339-42; *Thomas Tallis: English Sacred Music: II: Service Music,* ed. Leonard Ellinwood, revised by Paul Doe, Early English Church Music, 13

(London, 1974), ix, 125–43; R. Alec Harman (ed.), *Thomas Morley: A Plaine and Easie Introduction to Practicall Musicke (1597)* (London, 1952; revised edn, 1963), 249–52.

5.   Walter E. Buszin, 'Luther on Music', *The Musical Quarterly,* 32 (1946), 80–97; Taverner's masses in *John Taverner,* ed. Percy C. Buck, Tudor Church Music, 1 (London, 1923), 70, 50; English adaptations in *John Taverner,* ed. Percy C. Buck, Tudor Church Music, 3 (London, 1924), 169, 143; le Huray *Reformation,* 175, 179; Colin Hand, *John Taverner: his Life and Music* (London, 1978), 82, 106–17; Ralph T. Daniel, 'Contrafacta and Polyglot Texts in the Early English Anthem', *Essays in Musicology: a Birthday Offering for Willi Apel,* ed. Hans Tischler (Bloomington, Indiana, 1968), 101–06.

6.   Daniel, 'Contrafacta'; *Robert White,* ed. David Mateer, Early English Church Music, 28, 29, 32 (London, 1983–86): 'Manus tuae fecerunt me' xxviii, 75, 'Domine, non est exaltatum' xxix, 85; 'O Lord, deliver me' is in Oxford, Christ Church MSS. 56–60 (c.1620); 'Praise the Lord, O my soul' is in London, Royal College of Music MSS. 1048–51 (early seventeenth century); *Robert White,* ed. Percy C. Buck, Tudor Church Music, 5 (London, 1926), 'Lord, who shall dwell in thy tabernacle' 192, 'O praise God in his holiness' 207 and 211; John Milsom, 'A Newly-discovered Tallis Contrafactum', *The Musical Times,* 123 (1982), 429–31; Doe, *Tallis,* 53–55; le Huray, *Reformation,* 194–95, 239–41; Buck, Tudor Church Music, 6: 'Salvator mundi' (first setting) 216; Leonard Ellinwood (ed.), revised by Paul Doe, *Thomas Tallis: English Sacred Music: I: Anthems,* Early English Church Music, 12 (London, 1974): 'With all our hearts and mouths' 88; *William Byrd: Masses, Cantiones and Motets,* Tudor Church Music, 9 (London, 1928), 'Civitas sancti tui' 190; Edmund H. Fellowes (ed.), revised by Thurston Dart, *The Collected Works of William Byrd: Cantiones Sacrae (1589),* 2 (London, 1966), 'Ne irascaris, Domine' 151; Edmund H. Fellowes (ed.), *The Collected Works of William Byrd,* (London, 1937–50), 'Bow thine ear' xi, 155.

7.   le Huray, *Reformation,* 370–71; Coverdale's tunes in Frost, *English and Scottish,* 293–339; Bach's version of 'Mit Fried' und Freud' ich fahr' dahin' in Albert Riemenschneider (ed.), *Bach: 371 Harmonized Chorales and 69 Chorale Melodies* (New York and London, 1941), nos. 49, 325; 'Erschienen ist der herrliche Tag' as a hymn tune, comments in Maurice Frost, *Historical Companion to Hymns Ancient and Modern* (London, 1962), 460, Percy Dearmer and Archibald Jacob, *Songs of Praise Discussed* (London, 1933), 103; Psalm 42 tune: Frost, *English and Scottish,* 92–93, Robert Bridges and Harry Ellis Wooldridge (ed.), *The Yattendon Hymnal,* (London, 1899), no. 27.

8.   Frost, *English and Scottish,* 69, 147–8, 394ff; le Huray, *Reformation,* 373–82; Percy Dearmer and Archibald Jacob, *Songs of Praise Discussed* (London, 1933), 237–8; six further sixteenth and seventeenth-century versions of the 'Old Hundredth'in Frost, *Historical Companion,* 233–36; 'Vater unser' in Frost, *English and Scottish,* 209–10; Temperley, *Parish Church,* i, 30-32, 54–65.

CHAPTER 2

9.   For a survey of the repertory at and after the Restoration see Christopher Dearnley, *English Church Music 1650-1750* (London, 1970); more versions of Tallis's Canon in Frost, *English and Scottish,* 389–92; Samuel Arnold (ed.), *Cathedral Music* (London, 1790): 'We have heard with our ears' i, 276; Raffaele Casimiri (ed.), *Giovanni*

Pierluigi da Palestrina: le opere complete (Rome, 1939-): 'Doctor bonus et amicus dei' iii, 100.

10. Temperley, *Parish Church*, i, 171-72; Frost, *Historical Companion*, 96-99, 145, 219.

11. Percy M. Young, *The Choral Tradition* (London, 1962) 106-7; Ronald Pearsall, *Victorian Popular Music* (Newton Abbot, 1973) 138-42; John S. Bumpus, *A History of English Cathedral Music 1549-1889* (London, 1908), 365-66; Thomas Pitt, *Church Music* (Worcester, 1788-9), i, Preface, ii, 29, 56; Temperley, *Parish Church,* i, 210, 215-16; George H. Drummond and Edward Miller, *The Psalms of David* (London, 1790), especially p.20; Samuel Webbe junior, *A Collection of Psalm Tunes* (London, c.1808), 8; Arthur Sullivan (ed.), *Church Hymns with Tunes* (London, 1905), no. 351; James T. Lightwood, *Hymn-Tunes and their Story* (London, 1905), 359-61.

12. William T. Whitley, *Congregational Hymn-Singing* (London, 1933), 178-80; Percy Dearmer and Archibald Jacob, *Songs of Praise Discussed* (London, 1933), 8; Frost, *Historical Companion*, 387.

CHAPTER 3

13. For further details of Tractarian practices and influences see Temperley, *Parish Church*, i, 248-62.

14. Bernarr Rainbow, *The Choral Revival in the Anglican Church 1839-72* (London, 1970), 41-58, 79-84; Richard Redhead, *The Gregorian Chants for the Psalms* Supplement (1841) to *Church Music: a Selection of Chants, Sanctuses and Responses* (London 1840), 3; Richard Redhead, *Hymns and Canticles used at Morning and Evening Prayer, Pointed and Set to the Ancient Psalm Tones* (London, 1859), 29; William Dyce, *Preface and Appendix to the Book of Common Prayer with Plain-Tune* (London, 1844); Thomas Helmore, *A Manual of Plainsong* (London, 1850).

15. Arthur Hutchings, *Church Music in the Nineteenth Century* (London, 1967) 60-62, 93; Erik Routley, *The Music of Christian Hymnody* (London, 1957), 155-57; Erik Routley, *A Short History of English Church Music* (London, 1977), 78-80; Temperley, *Parish Church*, i, 311-13, 264-65; Rainbow, *Choral Revival*, 91-94; Vincent Novello, *The Complete Collection of the Gregorian Hymns for the Whole Year* (London, c. 1850), 22-24; Louis F. Benson, *The English Hymn: its Development and Use in Worship* (Richmond, Virginia, 1915; repr. 1962), 503-504; Frost, *Historical Companion*, 155.

16. For further examples of nineteenth and twentieth-century arrangements of plainsong for English use see Temperley, *Parish Church*, ii, 13; for attitudes to plainsong see Charles H. Phillips, *The Singing Church* (London, 1945; revised 1979), 24, 44; *Worcester Diocesan Conference 1904: Report of the Church Music Committee* 21; Robert Bridges, *Collected Essays* (London, 1935), 36; Henry Walford Davies and Harvey Grace, *Music and Worship* (London, 1935), 175-80, 216; George Gardner and Sydney H. Nicholson (ed.), *A Manual of English Church Music* (London, 1923), 40-41; Bernard L. Manning, *The Hymns of Wesley and Watts* (London, 1942), 34; Letter from Colin Dunlop, Domestic Chaplain to the Bishop of Chichester, to the Dean of Liverpool, 18th May 1932, File marked 'Dean Dwelly: Correspondence re. Songs of Praise c.1933', Archive of the Anglican Cathedral, Liverpool.

17.   Rainbow, *Choral Revival,* 64–67; Gardner and Nicholson, *Manual,* 44–46; Henry Walford Davies and Henry G. Ley (ed.), *The Church Anthem Book* (London, 1933).

18.   Frost, *Historical Companion,* 270; Christian K. J. von Bunsen (ed.), *Versuch eines allgemeinen evangelischen Gesang- und Gebetbuchs zum Kirchen- und Hausgebrauche* (Hamburg, 1833), nos. 549, 589; Catherine Winkworth (ed.), *The Chorale Book for England* (London, 1863), Prefaces, nos.9, 93.

19.   *Piae Cantiones,* ed. Timo Mäkinen, Documenta Musicae Fennicae, 10 (Helsinki, 1967); George R. Woodward (ed.), *Piae Cantiones, a Collection of Church and School Song* ... (London, 1910), Preface; Erik Routley, *The English Carol* (London, 1958), 174–75, 193, 196; Henry R. Bramley and John Stainer (ed.), *Christmas Carols New and Old* (London, 1871); Elizabeth Poston (ed.), *The Penguin Book of Christmas Carols* (London, 1965), 9, 25; Percy Dearmer, Ralph Vaughan Williams and Martin Shaw (ed.), *The Oxford Book of Carols* (London, 1928), 180–82, 204–7, 271; Reginald Jacques and David Willcocks (ed.), *Carols for Choirs 1* (London, 1961), 42–51.

20.   Frost, *Historical Companion,* 448, 176; Review cited on final leaf of reprint of Richard R. Chope, *Carols for Use in Church during Christmas and Epiphany* (London, 1875); Jacques and Willcocks, *Carols for Choirs,* 136–41.

21.   Henry Walford Davies and Henry G. Ley (ed.), *The Church Anthem Book* (London, 1933): 'The strife is o'er' 445, 'Lo round the throne' 260, 'The day draws on' 427.

CHAPTER 4

22.   Letter (undated but before 1954) from Ralph Vaughan Williams to the Rev. Frederick W. Dwelly, Dean of Liverpool. Archive of the Anglican Cathedral, Liverpool.

23.   Alan E. F. Dickinson, *Vaughan Williams* (London, 1963), 128–29; Frost, *Historical Companion,* 240–41.

24.   For discussions, see Percy Dearmer and Archibald Jacob, *Songs of Praise Discussed* (London, 1933); Frost, *Historical Companion,* Erik Routley, *The Music of Christian Hymnody* (London, 1957); Ralph Vaughan Williams, *The First Fifty Years: a Brief Account of the English Hymnal from 1906 to 1956* (London, 1956); Temperley, *Parish Church,* i, especially 338–42.

CHAPTER 5

25.   Copy of letter (undated but 1929 or later) from Ralph Vaughan Williams to Percy Dearmer, file marked 'Vaughan Williams', Archive of the Anglican Cathedral, Liverpool; Ralph Vaughan Williams, *The First Fifty Years: a Brief Account of the English Hymnal from 1906 to 1956* (London, 1956), 4–5; Alec Robertson, *Music of the Catholic Church* (London, 1961), 94–96.

26.   Further on Lutheran secular borrowings: Archibald W. Wilson, *The Chorales: their Origin and Influence* (London, 1920), 40–52; Friedrich Blume, *Protestant Church Music* (London, 1975), 29–35, 509–23; *Hans Leo Hassler: Sämtliche Werke,* ed. C. Russell Crosby junior, 9 (Wiesbaden, 1968): 'Mein G'müt ist mir verwirret' 53; Heinrich Isaac 'Innsbruck, ich muss dich lassen' in numerous publications, example from Walther Lipphardt (ed.), *Gesellige Zeit 1* (Kassel, 1965), 96.

27. *Music at the Court of Henry VIII,* ed. John Stevens, Musica Britannica 18 (2nd edn, London, 1969): 'Blow thy horn, hunter' 29; *The Tudor Church Music of the Lumley Books,* ed. Judith Blezzard, Recent Researches in the Music of the Renaissance, 65 (Madison, Wisconsin, 1985): 'Domine Dominus noster' no.17; discussion of secular version in John Stevens, *Music and Poetry in the Early Tudor Court* (2nd edn, Cambridge, 1979), especially 401.

28. Claude M. Simpson, *The British Broadside Ballad and its Music* (New Jersey, 1966), especially 10-11, 36, 88, 141-2, 783-84; William Chappell, *Popular Music of the Olden Time* (London, 1859), i, 752; le Huray, *Reformation,* 383-84, 405; Temperley, *Parish Church,* i, 66-67; Alfred W. Pollard and Gilbert R. Redgrave, *A Short Title Catalogue of Books Printed in England, Scotland and Ireland and of English Books Printed Abroad, 1475-1640* (London, 1926), no.2996.7, microfilm reel 1772; Anne G. Gilchrist, 'Sacred Parodies of Secular Folk Songs', *Journal of the English Folk Dance and Song Society,* 3 (1936), 157-82; Harry E. Wooldridge (ed.), *William Chappell: Old English Popular Music* (London, 1893), i, 224; John A. Fuller Maitland and William Barclay Squire (ed.), *The Fitzwilliam Virginal Book* (London and Leipzig, 1894-99; repr. 1963).

29. John Milsom, 'Songs, Carols and *Contrafacta* in the Early History of the Tudor Anthem', *Proceedings of the Royal Musical Association,* 107 (1980-81), 34-45; *Thomas Tallis: English Sacred Music: I: Anthems,* ed. Leonard Ellinwood, revised by Paul Doe, Early English Church Music, 13 (London, 1974): 'Purge me, O Lord' 74, 'Fond youth is a bubble' 95; *The Mulliner Book,* ed. Denis Stevens, Musica Britannica, 1 (2nd edn, London, 1962): 'Fond youth is a bubble' 21, 'O happy Dames' 81; Paul Vining, Letter to *The Musical Times,* 114 (1973), 257-58; *John Wilbye: Second Set of Madrigals (1609),* ed. Edmund H. Fellowes, revised by Thurston Dart, The English Madrigalists, 7 (2nd edn, London, 1966), 201; *Sir William Leighton: The Teares or Lamentacions of a Sorrowfull Soule,* ed. Cecil Hill, Early English Church Music, 11 (London, 1970), 171; le Huray, *Reformation,* 388-89; *Thomas Tomkins: Songs of 3. 4. 5. and 6. Parts,* ed. Edmund H. Fellowes, revised by Thurston Dart, The English Madrigalists, 18 (2nd edn, London, 1960), 99; Thomas Tomkins, *Musica Deo sacra et Ecclesiae Anglicanae* (London, 1668), partbooks; David Wulstan, *Tudor Music* (London, 1985), 345-46.

CHAPTER 6

30. Temperley, *Parish Church,* i, 35, 102-3, 127, 136-38; Franklin B. Zimmerman, *Henry Purcell 1659-1695, an Analytical Catalogue of his Music* (London, 1963), 274, 341-42, 400, 632; Franklin B. Zimmerman (ed.), *The Works of Henry Purcell* (London, 1878-1965; 2nd edn, 1961), ii, xx 45, xxxi 92; Christopher Dearnley, *English Church Music 1650-1750* (London, 1970), 123-26, 139; *Les oeuvres de Arcangelo Corelli,* ed. Joseph Joachim and Friedrich Chrysander, Denkmäler der Tonkunst, 3 (Hamburg, 1871): Sonata in D minor, op.5 no.12, 'Folia' movement p.96; Samuel Webbe junior, *A Collection of Psalm Tunes* (London, c.1808), 7, 29.

31. Temperley, *Parish Church,* i, 210, 212, 231-32; ii, 11; Louis F. Benson, *The English Hymn: its Development and Use in Worship* (Richmond, Virginia, 1915; repr. 1962), 242-43, 294, 327-28; James T. Lightwood, *Hymn-Tunes and their Story* (London, 1905; 2nd edn, 1923), 140, 344, 347-49; Frost, *Historical Companion,* 156, 257, 258; Erik Routley, *The Music of Christian Hymnody* (London, 1957), 93, 112-14; William T. Whitley, *Congregational Hymn-Singing* (London, 1933), 142, 197; Jean Jacques

Rousseau, *Le devin du village* (Paris, c.1773); Charles Burney, *The Cunning Man* (London, c.1767); *The Dictionary of National Biography* (London, 1908-9, repr. 1973), ix, 862; Rowland Hill (ed.), *A Collection of Psalms and Hymns, Chiefly Intended for Public Worship* (4th edn, London, 1798), no.302; William Gardiner, *Sacred Melodies, from Haydn, Mozart and Beethoven* (London, 1812), i 39, 51; ii 129.

CHAPTER 7

32. Erik Routley, *The Music of Christian Hymnody* (London, 1957), 112-14; John Troutbeck and J. Frederick Bridge (ed.), *The Westminster Abbey Chant Book* (3rd edn, London, 1894), no.145; James T. Lightwood, *Hymn-Tunes and their Story* (London, 1905; 2nd edn, 1923), 362; Frost, *Historical Companion,* 377, 140; Edward J. Hopkins (ed.), *The Temple Church Choral Service* (London, c.1867), no.134; Temperley, *Parish Church,* i, 302.

33. Frost, *Historical Companion,* 284, 334-35, 162-63; Haydn's secular cantata: apparently not published but details given in Stanley Sadie (ed.), *The New Grove Dictionary of Music and Musicians* (London, 1980), viii, 364; Song in Georg Feder and Jens Peter Larsen (ed.), *Joseph Haydn: Werke* (Munich, 1958-), xxix/1, 89; Erik Routley, *The English Carol* (London, 1958), 151-52; Elizabeth Poston, *The Penguin Book of Christmas Carols* (London, 1965), 26; Julius Rietz (ed.), *Felix Mendelssohn-Bartholdy: Werke: kritisch durchgesehene Ausgabe* (Leipzig, 1874-77), xv, 7; German hymn tunes in Albert Riemenschneider (ed.), *Bach: 371 Harmonized Chorales and 69 Chorale Melodies* (London and New York, 1941), nos.4, 32.

34. Samuel Sebastian Wesley, *A Few Words on Cathedral Music and the Musical System of the Church, with a Plan of Reform* (London and Leeds, 1849), 37; John S. Bumpus, *A History of English Cathedral Music 1549-1889* (London, 1908), 360-61; John Page, *Harmonia Sacra* (London, 1800), iii, 34; Thomas Oliphant, 'Lady, see on every side', (London, c.1845); Henry Harington, 'Retirement', (London, c.1775); Nicholas Temperley, 'Domestic Music in England 1800-60', *Proceedings of the Royal Musical Association,* 85 (1958-59), 31-47; Rietz, *Mendelssohn,* xvi, 22; Sabilla Novello (translator), *Mendelssohn's Twenty-Four Four-Part Songs or Open-Air Music* (London, no date), 66; Temperley, *Parish Church,* i, 321; S. H. Ramsbotham, *On the Characteristics of a good Hymn Tune* (London, 1897), 6-8; Charles V. Stanford, 'Music in Cathedral and Church Choirs' in Charles Dunkley (ed.), *The Official Report of the Church Congress* (London, 1899), 420-24.

CHAPTER 8

35. Roy Palmer, *Folk Songs collected by Ralph Vaughan Williams* (London, 1983), viii-xxi; 'Ascalon' in *Congregational Hymnary* (London, 1916), 231; 'Jesu über alles' in August H. Hoffmann and Ernst Richter (ed.), *Schlesische Volkslieder mit Melodien* (Leipzig, 1842), no.287; William T. Whitley, *Congregational Hymn-Singing* (London, 1933), 180; Erik Routley, *The English Carol* (London, 1958), 160-61; Alan E. F. Dickinson, *Vaughan Williams* (London, 1963), 127-29; Michael Kennedy, *The Works of Ralph Vaughan Williams* (London, 1964), 65-75, 424-27, 507-9, 514-16, 647-81. The paperback edition of Michael Kennedy's book does not contain these details; *Journal of the Folk-Song Society:* folksong transcriptions from various collectors, especially those at i (1899-1904), 131, ii (1905-1906), 125, 159, 202, 203; John A. Fuller Maitland and William Barclay Squire (ed.), *The Fitzwilliam Virginal Book* (London and Leipzig, 1894-99, revised 1963), i nos.1 and 68, ii no.297; 'Agincourt' song as 'Deo gracias, Anglia' in *Medieval Carols,* ed. John Stevens, Musica Britannica, 4 (2nd edn, London, 1958), 6.

36. For details of further secular borrowings see Percy Dearmer and Archibald Jacob, *Songs of Praise Discussed* (London, 1933); Michael Kennedy, *The Works of Ralph Vaughan Williams* (London, 1964), 507-9, 514-16; Harry E. Wooldridge (ed.), *William Chappell: Old English Popular Music* (London, 1893), ii, 52; *Music at the Court of Henry VIII,* ed. John Stevens, Musica Britannica, 18 (2nd edn, London, 1969), 38; Claude M. Simpson, *The British Broadside Ballad and its Music* (New Jersey, 1966), 268-78; *Journal of the Folk-Song Society* i (1899-1904), 183.

37. Robert Bridges, *Collected Essays* (London, 1935), no.22 pp.65-66, no.23 p.71; Nicholas Temperley, *Parish Church,* i, 326-29; George Gardner and Sydney H. Nicholson (ed.), *A Manual of English Church Music* (London, 1923), 37-38, 44-46, 95; Henry Walford Davies and Harvey Grace, *Music and Worship* (London, 1935), 189-95; Bernard L. Manning, *The Hymns of Wesley and Watts* (London, 1942), 33-36; Charles H. Phillips, *The Singing Church* (London, 1945; revised 1979), especially p.230; Erik Routley, *Church Music and Theology* (London, 1959), 61-66; Ralph Vaughan Williams, *The First Fifty Years: a Brief Account of the English Hymnal* (London, 1956), 4-5.

CHAPTER 9

38. J. Eric Hunt, *Cranmer's First Litany, 1544, and Merbecke's Book of Common Prayer Noted, 1550* (London, 1939); Richard R. Terry, 'John Merbecke', *Proceedings of the Musical Association,* 45 (1918-19), 75-96; *Hugh Aston, John Marbeck, Osbert Parsley,* ed. Percy C. Buck, Tudor Church Music, 10 (London, 1929), 155-227: 'A Virgin and Mother' 213; *The Tudor Church Music of the Lumley Books,* ed. Judith Blezzard, Recent Researches in the Music of the Renaissance, 65 (Madison, Wisconsin, 1965): 'Celi enarrant' no.19, Tallis's Benedictus no.27; John Aplin, ' "The Fourth Kind of Faburden": the Identity of an English Four-Part Style', *Music and Letters,* 61 (1980), 245-65; John Milsom, 'Songs, Carols and *Contrafacta* in the Early History of the Tudor Anthem', *Proceedings of the Royal Musical Association,* 107 (1980-81), 34-45; Doe, *Tallis,* 50-52; *Thomas Tallis: English Sacred Music: II: Service Music,* ed. Leonard Ellinwood, revised by Paul Doe, Early English Church Music, 13 (London, 1974): Tallis's Benedictus 102; *William Byrd: Songs of Sundry Natures,* ed. Edmund H. Fellowes, revised by Philip Brett, The English Madrigalists, 15 (2nd edn, London, 1962): 'Christ rising again' 280; Thomas Morley verse anthem 'Out of the deep' ed. Peter le Huray, Tudor Church Music no. 71 (London, 1973); *Orlando Gibbons,* ed. Percy C. Buck, Tudor Church Music, 4 (London, 1925): 'This is the record of John' 298; *Thomas Weelkes: Collected Anthems,* ed. David Brown, Musica Britannica, 23 (2nd edn, London, 1975): 'Alleluia, I heard a voice' no. 1; *Thomas Tomkins: Songs of 3. 4. 5. and 6. Parts,* ed. Edmund H. Fellowes, revised by Thurston Dart, The English Madrigalists, 18 (London, 1922; 2nd edn, 1960): 'When David heard that Absalom was slain' 112.

39. le Huray, *Reformation,* chapter 10; Christopher Dearnley, *English Church Music 1650-1750* (London, 1970), 24-27, 42-47, 90; Peter Dennison, *Pelham Humfrey* (London, 1986), especially 6-7, 19-31.

40. Dearnley, *English Church Music,* 84-95, 248-59, 261-76; Frost, *Historical Companion,* 180-81, 262; Charles Wesley and John F. Lampe, *Hymns on the Great Festivals and Other Occasions* (2nd edn, London, 1753), 56; Fellowes, *English Cathedral Music,* 192-208; Maurice Greene 'My God, my God, look upon me', ed. Percy M. Young, Music of the Great Churches, Series 5/3 (New York, 1978); William Boyce 'Turn thee unto me', ed. Henry Walford Davies and Henry G. Ley, *The Church Anthem Book* (London, 1933), 491; Paul H. Lang, *George Frideric Handel* (London, 1966), 685-705; John S. Bumpus, *A History of English Cathedral Music 1549-1889* (London, 1908), 365; Temperley, 'Domestic Music'; Arthur Hutchings, *Church Music in the Nineteenth Century* (London, 1967), 13-16.

41.   Temperley, *Parish Church,* i, 309-10; Erik Routley, *The Music of Christian Hymnody* (London, 1957), 125-26; Fellowes, *English Cathedral Music,* 223-36; Samuel Sebastian Wesley, *A Morning and Evening Cathedral Service* (London, 1845), Preface, especially p.ii.

42.   Temperley, *Parish Church,* i, 244-49, 258-60; *The Parish Choir,* i/1 (February 1846), 24; John S. Bumpus, *A History of English Cathedral Music 1549-1889* (London, 1908), 367, 371; Erik Routley, *The Music of Christian Hymnody* (London, 1957), 124-25; Percy M. Young, *The Choral Tradition* (London, 1962), 236-37; Rainbow, *Choral Revival,* 62, 78; Arthur Hutchings, *Church Music in the Nineteenth Century* (London, 1967), 18, 109; Arthur Sullivan 'O love the Lord' in the 'Choir' Series, no.192 (London, c.1925), also *Congregational Hymnary* (London, 1916), anthem no.58; Fellowes; *English Cathedral Music,* 238-39; Frederick Ouseley 'Is it nothing to you?' in Henry Walford Davies and Henry G. Ley (ed.), *The Church Anthem Book* (London, 1933), no.38, also in Gerald H. Knight and William L. Reed (ed.), *The Treasury of English Church Music* iv (London, 1965), 127.

43.   *The Preces and Responses with Litany according to Tallis,* ed. Joseph Barnby (London, no date); Judith Blezzard, 'Reconstructing Early English Vocal Music: History, Principle and Practice', *The Music Review,* 45 (1984), 85-95; Richard R. Chope, *Carols for Use in Church during Christmas and Epiphany* (London, 1875), pp.xxix, 72; *Orlando Gibbons,* ed. Percy C. Buck, Tudor Church Music, 4 (London, 1925): 'Sorʒ 1' 317; Richard R. Terry (ed.), *Calvin's First Psalter* (London, 1932); Richard R. Te.,y (ed.), *A Medieval Carol Book* (London, 1931); *Medieval Carols,* ed. John Stevens, Musica Britannica, 4 (London, 1952; revised 1958).

44.   Temperley, 'Domestic Music'; Temperley, *Parish Church,* i, 296-314; Fellowes, *English Cathedral Music,* 242-43; Samuel Arnold and John W. Callcott, *The Psalms of David for the Use of Parish Churches* (London, 1791), 6-7; Lowell Mason and George J. Webb, *The Boston Glee Book* (Boston, Massachusetts, 1844; repr. New York, 1977), 39, 45, 86, 158; Erik Routley, *The Music of Christian Hymnody* (London, 1957), 124, 246-71, 130-33; Professor Arthur Hutchings, to whom the author is indebted for information, states in a letter that the tune 'Petra' is thought to have origins in unnamed Spanish plainchant; Ronald Pearsall, *Victorian Popular Music* (Newton Abbot, 1973), 47-48; Louis F. Benson, *The English Hymn: its Development and Use in Worship* (Richmond, Virginia, 1915, repr. 1962), 298; Paul Hillier (ed.), *300 Years of English Partsongs* (London, 1983): Sullivan 'The long day closes' no.30, Barnby 'Sweet and low' no.28; Gerald H. Knight and William L. Reed (ed.), *The Treasury of English Church Music* iv (London, 1965): Goss 'O Saviour of the world' 69; Henry Walford Davies and Henry G. Ley (eds.) *The Church Anthem Book* (London, 1933): Walmisley 'From all that dwell below the skies' no.21, also ed. Gerald H. Knight (Croydon, c.1957); *Congregational Hymnary* (London, 1916): Barnby 'Abide with me' anthem no.70, also published separately (London, c.1890).

45.   Arthur Hutchings, *Church Music in the Nineteenth Century* (London, 1967), 114; Friedrich Blume, *Protestant Church Music* (London, 1975), 729-32; Fellowes, *Cathedral Music*, 252-55; Charles H. Phillips, *The Singing Church* (London, 1945; revised 1979), 240-46; Erik Routley, *The Music of Christian Hymnody* (London, 1957), 134-37; Henry Walford Davies and Harvey Grace, *Music and Worship* (London, 1935), 191-95, 238; Temperley, *Parish Church*, i, 333-34, 339-41; Martin Shaw, *The Principles of Church Music Composition* cited in Erik Routley, *Church Music and Theology* (London, 1959), 66-67; Percy Dearmer and Archibald Jacob, *Songs of Praise Discussed* (London, 1933).

Index

Compiled by
Valerie M. Curtis

(n.b. page references to musical illustrations are
italicised)

1995-96 Supplement

to

HEALTH LAW:

CASES, MATERIALS AND PROBLEMS

Second Edition

by

BARRY R. FURROW
Professor of Law
Widener University

THOMAS GREANEY
Professor of Law
St. Louis University

SANDRA H. JOHNSON
Professor of Law and Associate Professor
of Law in Internal Medicine
St. Louis University

TIMOTHY S. JOST
Newton D. Baker, Baker & Hostetler Professor
of Law and Professor Health Services
Management and Policy
The Ohio State University

ROBERT L. SCHWARTZ
Professor of Law and Professor of Pediatrics
University of New Mexico

St. Paul, Minn.
WEST PUBLISHING CO.
1995

 TEXT IS PRINTED ON 10% POST CONSUMER RECYCLED PAPER

PREFACE TO THE 1995 SUPPLEMENT

This supplement is intended to serve several purposes. First, it provides substantial background materials on health care reform. While systemic federal reform may now be on hold, major reforms are being considered by a number of state legislatures, and, independent of the reforms being contemplated by government, the economic and corporate structure of the health care system is changing (and reforming itself, for better or worse) faster than it has at any point in the history of this country. We offer materials that describe the problems that face our nation's health care system, outline the major proposals designed to solve those problems at both the state and federal levels, and summarize alternative approaches to the organization of their health care systems taken by three other countries.

We also include a number of new cases, statutes, and regulations that have changed the legal analysis of health care issues over the four years since the second edition of the casebook was published in 1991, and we provide materials designed to describe new forms of health care organizations, including integrated delivery systems, that are now being developed. This supplement does not include a comprehensive revision of all of the casebook notes; that would have created a cumbersome teaching tool. Rather, we have attempted to identify the most important developments and to present these developments through edited primary material rather than through notes and comments. Because this casebook is designed around problems that can form the basis of classroom discussion, we have also included several new problems that address issues that have gained prominence since 1991.

This supplement will serve as a bridge to the third edition of the casebook, which is now in preparation and which will be available at the beginning of summer, 1996. We recognize that the discipline of health law has reached a maturity that requires a new structure, and we expect the third edition to provide it. We are also very pleased that Professor Thomas Greaney, one of the nation's leading health care antitrust scholars and an outstanding teacher who is working with the casebook authors on the third edition, has joined the rest of the authors of the casebook in preparing this supplement.

TABLE OF CONTENTS

HEALTH CARE REFORM: BACKGROUND MATERIALS

I. The Problems Driving Health Care Reform

The debate about health care reform that dominated the news during 1993 and 1994 has quieted down. Nonetheless, the problems that provoked that debate are still very much with us. It is worthwhile, therefore, for students of health law to examine those problems and to consider the most frequently proposed solutions to them.

Real reform of the health care system must address two major problems: the barriers that limit the access of many Americans to health care and the high and rapidly rising cost of health care. Reform must also, however, confront a host of related problems and issues.[1] We begin with a discussion of the access and cost issues.

A. Barriers to Access to Health Care Services

The problem of barriers to access is commonly portrayed as the problem of the uninsured. To understand the forces driving health care reform, however, it is important to realize that the uninsured population is not monolithic, and that the uninsured are not the only persons who face barriers limiting their access to health care. Nearly 40 million Americans are without health insurance at any one time. Over the 32 month period from February 1990 until September 1992, 60 million Americans, one quarter of the population, were uninsured for at least one month. Poor persons and minorities tend to be overrepresented among the uninsured. During the 1990-1992 period 49 percent of persons whose income was below the poverty level were without insurance coverage for at least one month, as were 48 percent of Hispanics and 36 percent of African Americans.[2]

Most of those who are uninsured are attached to the job market. At any one time 75% to 85% of those who are uninsured are either employed in jobs--generally low wage jobs--that do not provide health

---

[1] An excellent summary of the issues that must be addressed by health care reform is found in Robert J. Blendon, et al., Making the Critical Choices, 267 JAMA 2509 (1992).

[2] See U.S. Bureau of Census, Statistical Brief, Health Insurance Coverage--Who Had a Lapse Between 1990 and 1992? (1994).

1

insurance or are the dependents of persons so employed.[3] A majority of those who lose their insurance become uninsured because of a job loss, change of job, cancellation of job-related coverage by an insurance company or by an employer who can no longer afford the premiums, or other employment-related reasons.[4] While many of these persons regain insured status when they are reemployed or when their employer finds another insurer, they may thereafter be subject to "preexisting conditions" clauses that limit their coverage for health problems that existed at the time they were reinsured.[5] Many who are uninsured are unable to afford insurance because their health status makes insurance prohibitively expensive.[6]

Just because a person is uninsured does not mean, of course, that he or she is without access to health care. Many simply pay for their own health care out of pocket. Moreover, most hospitals must provide emergency health care whether or not they will be paid for it. An extensive series of studies, however, have shown that persons who are without insurance get less health care and get it later and when it is less effective.[7] Lack of health insurance is clearly related to premature death.[8]

---

[3] Emily Friedman, The Uninsured: From Dilemma to Crisis, 265 JAMA 2491 (1991).

[4] Families USA, How Americans Lose Health Insurance (1994).

[5] See Katherine Swartz, Dynamics of People Without Health Insurance: Don't Let the Numbers Fool You, 271 JAMA 64 (1994).

[6] See, discussing the current situation with respect to risk rating, Donald W. Light, The Practice and Ethics of Risk-Rated Health Insurance, 267 JAMA 2503 (1992); Deborah A. Stone, The Struggle for the Soul of Health Insurance, 18 J. Health Pol, Pol'y & L. 287 (1993).

[7] See, e.g., John Z. Ayanian, et al., The Relation Between Health Insurance Coverage and Clinical Outcomes Among Women with Breast Cancer, 329 New Eng. J. Med. 326 (1993); E. Richard Brown, Access to Health Insurance in the United States, 46 Med. Care Rev. 349 (1989); Jack Hadley, et al., Comparison of Uninsured and Privately Insured Hospital Patients: Condition on Admission, Resource Use, and Outcome, 265 JAMA 374 (1991).

[8] Peter Franks, et al., Health Insurance and Mortality: Evidence from a National Cohort, 270 JAMA 7373 (1993).

Moreover, lack of insurance is not the only factor that limits access to health care. Millions of insured persons have policies that include significant limitations. One third of conventional, employment-related insurance plans have lifetime maximums of under $1 million and 63 percent have preexisting conditions clauses with an average wait for coverage of over nine months.[9] High deductibles ($534 per year average for conventional family coverage) and coinsurance or copayment obligations, and exclusions of basic benefits like physicians visits or maternity benefits, are also common.[10] Indeed, over three quarters of the respondents to a recent survey who reported having had problems in paying their medical bills during the previous year in fact had insurance.[11]

Persons who live in remote rural areas often have to travel long distances to get medical care and have little access to specialists. Persons who live in inner city neighborhoods often have to endure long waits for medical care and must use emergency rooms for primary care. Even persons who are fully insured and have physical access to providers may be denied care by arbitrary utilization review decisions.[12]

These gaps in access to health care have obvious and serious effects on persons who must forego necessary medical care because of them. Perhaps more important politically, however, they provoke insecurity and anxiety among the increasingly affluent population vulnerable to insurance loss. Average citizens, and not just the poor, are threatened with financial ruin if they lose their jobs because of economic restructuring or are struck with an illness or injury the cost of which exceeds the maximum coverage afforded by their insurance. Their

---

[9] Jon Gabel, et al., The Health Insurance Picture in 1993: Some Rare Good News, Health Affairs, Spring 1993 at 327.

[10] Thomas Bodenheimer, Underinsurance in America, 327 New Eng. J. Med. 274 (1992).

[11] Robert J. Blendon, et al., Paying Medical Bills in the United States: Why Health Insurance Isn't Enough, 271 JAMA 949 (1994).

[12] William P. Peters & Mark C. Rogers, Variations in Approval by Insurance Companies of Coverage for Autologous Bone Marrow Transplantation for Breast Cancer, 330 New Eng. J. Med. 473 (1994).

children may well become uninsured upon reaching adulthood, and might contract an expensive illness or injury while uninsured.

The economic effects of insurance coverage limitations are also increasingly apparent. Up to one third of married men would move to another job if their health insurance were fully portable. Up to one quarter of one million welfare recipients would enter the labor force if they would not lose their Medicaid coverage by doing so.[13] Removing barriers to health care could potentially significantly increase economic productivity.

B. The Cost of Health Care

The high and rapidly rising cost of health care is the second problem that is driving interest in health care reform. According to one report, Americans spent $7739 per family for health care in 1993, 13.1% of family income, compared to $2590 or 9% of family income in 1980.[14] In 1991 the United States spent $2868 per capita, 13.2% of its gross domestic product for health care, compared to $1659 per capita or 8.5% of GDP in Germany; $1307 per capita or 6.8% of GDP in Japan; or $1043 or 6.6% of GDP in the United Kingdom.[15] Though the rise of health care costs has moderated over the last year, health care costs are still growing at a rate well in excess of general inflation.[16]

Beyond the general belief that the costs of the health care system are excessive, there is also a concern that money is being wasted within the system. First, there is evidence that administrative costs are too high; that too much money goes to shuffling paper instead of providing health

---

[13] See Alice Rivlin, et al., Financing, Estimation, and Economic Effects, Health Affairs, Spring 1993 at 30, 44-45; Philip F. Cooper & Alan C. Monheit, Does Employment-Related Health Insurance Inhibit Job Mobility? 30 Inquiry 400 (1993).

[14] Families USA, Skyrocketing Health Inflation, 1980-1993-2000: The Burden on Families and Businesses (1993).

[15] George J. Schieber, et al, Health Spending, Delivery, and Outcomes in OECD Countries, Health Affairs, Summer 1993 at 120.

[16] See, Health Care Spending: An Analytical Forum, Health Affairs, Winter 1994 at 7.

4

services.[17]   Second, many believe that some health care providers, in particular drug companies and physicians, receive excessive compensation or profits.[18]   Third, there is a general opinion that a great deal of money is wasted on unnecessary tests and technology or outright fraud.[19]

There are also particular concerns about costs being borne by particular payers. First, there is a concern that the high and rapidly rising cost of employment-related insurance is making American industry less competitive and diminishing profits. In fact, the amount of money that business spent on health care increased from 12.4% of the amount realized in profits after taxes in 1965 to 97.5% of the amount realized in profits after taxes in 1991.[20]   It is generally believed by economists, however, that the costs of employee health care benefits are ultimately borne by employees in diminished wages and have few long term effects on profits or competitiveness, though there may be short-term effects in periods of rapid increases.[21]   In fact health care cost increases have had a dramatic effect on wages: from 1970 to 1991 real wages and salaries per employee in the United States grew .4 percent, employer health

---

[17] See Steffie Woolhandler and David U. Himmelstein, The Deteriorating Administrative Efficiency of the U.S. Health Care System, 324 New Eng. J. Med. 1253 (1991); Steffie Woolhandler, et al., Administrative Costs in U.S. Hospitals, 329 New Eng. J. Med. 400 (1993).

[18] See, e.g., Doctors Under the Knife, Newsweek, April 5, 1993 at 28.

[19] See Jerry L. Mashaw and Theodore R. Marmor, Conceptualizing, Estimating, and Reforming Fraud, Waste, and Abuse in Healthcare Spending, 11 Yale J. Reg. 455 (1994).

[20] Cathy A. Cowan & Patricia A. McDonnell, Business, Households and Governments: Health Spending, 1991, 14 Health Care Fin. Rev. 227 (1993).

[21] See Mark V. Pauly, A Case for Employer-Enforced Individual Mandates, Health Aff., Spring (II) 1994 at 21; Alan B. Krueger & Uwe E. Rheinhardt, Economics of Employer versus Individual Mandates, Health Aff., Spring (II) 1994 at 34; Congressional Budget Office, Economic Implications of Rising Health Care Costs, 35-41 (1992).

expenditures per employee increased 234.1 percent.[22] Nevertheless, many believe that employers, rather than employees, are suffering because of the increase in health care costs.

It is much clearer that government has suffered from continual increases in health care costs. Growth in health care expenses has continually outpaced growth in general revenues at all levels of government for the decades.[23] From 1965 to 1991 the percentage of federal revenues spent on health care grew from 3.5 percent to 20.5 percent, state and local health spending grew from 8 percent to 21.4 percent of state and local revenues.[24] Growth of federal expenditures for health care has been a major factor driving the increase in the federal deficit. At the state level, Medicaid is consuming almost half of new revenue dollars, squeezing out state expenditures for higher education, transportation and other social welfare expenditures, and forcing states, which generally cannot engage in deficit financing, to raise taxes.[25]

While access and cost are the two major factors driving health care reform, a host of subsidiary problems also demand attention. First, there is a serious and growing imbalance between primary care providers and specialists. While some believe that an even mix of specialists and primary care providers would be ideal, currently only about a third of American medical doctors are primary care providers and only about 15% of new physicians are entering primary care.[26] Second, there is a widespread belief that fraud and abuse, particularly self-referrals, are common and costly, and that enforcement must be increased. Third, many believe that medical malpractice litigation is responsible for increased costs in the form of defensive medicine and diminished access because doctors are abandoning practices or specialties to avoid suits.

---

[22] Cowan & McDowell, supra note 20 at 238.

[23] Id. at 235.

[24] Id.

[25] The Kaiser Commission on the Future of Medicaid, The Medicaid Cost Explosion: Causes and Consequences, 33 (1993).

[26] Council on Graduate Medical Education, Third Report: Improving Access to Health Care through Physician Workforce Reform, 7-10 (1992).

Fourth, some believe that antitrust reform is necessary to either, depending on their perspective, encourage more competition or cooperation. These problems, as well as the primary problems of cost and barriers to access, are addressed by various reform proposals.

II. Solutions to the Problem

Though the problems of access and cost control are inevitably related, and integrated solutions to both problems must ultimately be found, it is useful analytically to consider the solutions separately. We begin with considering the problem of access and then turn to the problem of cost.

A. Solutions to the Access Problem

1. Government Financing of Health Care

Three primary solutions are currently being debated to the problem of access to health care. One would be to pay for health care out of tax revenues.[27] There are many ways this could be accomplished. Health care could be financed out of federal taxes, as is Medicare, or a mixture of state and federal taxes, as is Medicaid. The system could be financed by general revenues, as is Medicaid and much of Medicare Part B, or from earmarked payroll taxes, as is currently done with Medicare Part A. Additional revenues could be raised through the individual or corporate income tax; "sin taxes" on substances that contribute to increased health care costs, such as tobacco, or firearms; or new revenue sources such as a national sales tax or value-added tax.

Socialization of health care financing could be accompanied by socialization of the health care delivery system, as in the United Kingdom or Scandinavia. This is not necessary, however, and is extremely unlikely in the United States. A more realistic alternative would be to use public funds to pay private providers.

Public financing has the advantage of providing equitable, universal access to health care. Though geographical and class barriers

---

[27] See Jim McDermott, Evaluating Health System Reform, The Case for a Single-Payer Approach, 271 JAMA 782 (1994); P.D. Wellstone & E.R. Shaffer, The American Health Security Act--A Single Payer Proposal, 328 New Eng. J. Med. 1489 (1993).

to access to health care continue to exist in publicly financed health care systems, all persons have an equal entitlement to health care in such systems, and health care tends to be much more equitably available. Public financing would facilitate progressive funding of health care: those who have more would subsidize those who have less. It would provide a relatively efficient means of collecting revenues for health care in that the current tax system could be used rather than setting up a new system for collecting health care premiums. Finally, it would eliminate the marketing and underwriting costs inherent in private insurance, cutting administrative costs substantially.

Significant impediments make adoption of a public funding approach very unlikely, however. First, it would in all likelihood result in the elimination of the politically powerful private health insurance industry.[28] Second, it would require a significant increase in taxes, a prospect that is politically anathema to many legislators. Third, it runs contrary to the deeply held ideology of many Americans that government is constitutionally incapable of performing tasks more efficiently than the private sector, even though in this particular instance this ideology is demonstrably false.[29] Fourth, it could force health care to compete for public resources with other public programs, potentially imposing unpopular constraints on provision of health care. Fifth, it would raise difficult questions as to the extent to which individuals could opt out of the system or supplement its benefits. Should individuals be permitted to pay providers extra, for example, to receive preferential treatment where services are available on only a limited basis, or to receive higher quality services? Sixth, the increases in taxes necessary to take over public funding of the health care system would inevitably result in socially undesirable and economically inefficient responses as individuals and entities attempted to shield their income from additional taxation. For all of these reasons, universal public funding of health care was never seriously considered during the 1993-1994 health reform debate.

---

[28] The health insurance industry could be partially saved if the system were administered through private insurance programs, as is Medicare, but this would diminish potential savings in administrative costs and would only save the largest insurers.

[29] Ironically, the elderly, many of whom are quite conservative politically, are quite happy with Medicare, their own system of "socialized medicine."

2. Mandated Purchase of Insurance

The second solution is to require the purchase of health insurance. This could be done either through a mandate on employers, requiring them to purchase health insurance for their employees,[30] or a mandate on individuals, requiring them to purchase insurance for themselves and their families.[31] An insurance mandate would achieve universal coverage without increasing federal or state budgets or taxes. It would also cause less disruption in the current system. The vast majority of Americans (140 million Americans under age 65 including 89 million workers in 1991) are insured through an employer-sponsored health plan. This coverage could simply continue and be expanded. The private insurance industry could also remain largely unchanged. Finally, a private system could permit more diversity and innovation than would probably be possible under a universal public system.

An employer mandate would build directly on our current employment-based system. It would facilitate efficient collection of premiums. Large employers, or cooperatives consisting of small employers, could be empowered to bargain effectively with providers or insurers. But there are also politically powerful arguments against the employer mandate. Though it is probably the case, as noted above, that the cost of employee benefits, such as health insurance, is ultimately borne by workers in the form of reduced wages, in the short run it may be difficult for employers to pass on these costs, especially to workers whose wages are at or near the legal minimum wage. An employer mandate is likely, therefore, to impose additional financial burdens on some employers that may in turn result in business insolvencies or in lay-offs and reduced hiring. This potential effect can be ameliorated to some extent by excluding from the mandate small, low-wage, employers or by offering them subsidies, but this in turn is likely to result in gaming as employers restructure to qualify for such benefits. President Clinton's

---

[30] See, debating the wisdom of doing this, Nancy S. Jecker, Can an Employer-Based Health Insurance System be Just? 18 J. Health Pol., Pol'y & L. 657 (1993); David A. Rochefort, The Pragmatic Appeal of Employment-Based Health Care Reform. 18 J. Health Pol., Pol'y & L. 683 (1993) and the second Spring 1994 issue of Health Affairs, a symposium on employer versus individual mandates.

[31] See Michael J. Graetz, Mandating Employer Health Coverage: The Big Mistake, Tax Notes, Sept. 27, 1993 at 1765.

proposal of an employer mandate encountered vehement and effective political opposition from employer groups during 1993-1994.

An individual mandate, such as that proposed early in the 1993-1994 debate by Senators Chafee and Dole, would take the pressure off of employers. It would also make individuals more sensitive to the cost of health insurance, a factor currently concealed from them by the apparent "free" provision of health insurance by employers. Implementation of an individual mandate would be difficult, however. First, enforcing the obligation would be difficult. Experience with requirements that individuals purchase auto liability insurance, for example, provide little hope that enforcement of a universal individual mandate would be easy.

If individuals were simply expected to purchase insurance in an unregulated market, tremendous increases in administrative costs would result, because the costs of marketing and underwriting individual policies are much higher than those related to group policies. Unless risk-based discrimination on the part of insurers were tightly controlled, moreover, dramatic inequities would surface, with prohibitive costs being imposed on persons who were poor insurance risks. These problems could be avoided in large part through the establishment of purchasing alliances that could facilitate community rating and provide economies of scale in purchasing, but this solution would require extensive government intervention.

Subsidies would be necessary for persons who could not otherwise afford health insurance. Administering these subsidies, however, would be difficult as eligibility might change from month to month. Subsidies would also have to be phased out as income increased. If this phase-out was imposed too rapidly (as income rose from 100% to 200% of poverty level, for example), it would impose an extremely high tax on marginal income at these levels, discouraging persons from seeking employment. Finally, individual mandates might prove unpopular if they resulted in decreased provision of insurance as an employee benefit.

In the final analysis, moreover, an insurance premium that must be paid under penalty of law looks a great deal like a tax. It would in fact be a rather regressive tax, as the poor would pay no less than the rich, and might well pay more if premiums were experience-rated. Since the premium would simply replace premiums currently being paid voluntarily or under collective bargaining agreements, however, it might well be more palatable than a explicit new tax would be.

3. Use of Tax Incentives

The third strategy is based on incentives rather than mandates and encourages the private purchase of health insurance through tax incentives and market regulation.[32] Under this approach, refundable tax credits could be used to encourage the private purchase of health insurance. Favorable tax treatment could also be afforded to "Medisave" accounts, to encourage individual self-insurance for medical costs.

Employment-related health insurance provided by employers is currently excluded from taxable income. While this provides a $90 billion a year federal subsidy for the purchase of health insurance, it operates inequitably as the subsidy is not available to the unemployed, self-employed, or to employed persons who do not receive health insurance as a job benefit and is more valuable to wealthier persons in higher tax brackets than to lower income persons. The current system also encourages the concealment the true cost of insurance from employees as it encourages employers rather than employees to pay the direct cost of health insurance.

Tax credits, on the other hand, would be equally valuable regardless of the tax bracket of their recipient and could be increased in value to assist lower income persons or persons who faced higher health care costs. Most persons who received tax credits would be responsible individually for some share of the cost of their health insurance, encouraging them to be more price sensitive and less wasteful in their use of health care. Finally, because no one would be required to purchase health insurance, individual choice would be protected.

For this approach to work, it would need to be accompanied by insurance market reform. To achieve economies of scale in purchasing and avoid the exorbitant administrative costs that attend individual insurance policies, insurance purchasing alliances would need to be formed, or employers required to offer access to insurance coverage to their employees (though not to pay for it) or both. Reforms limiting the ability of insurers to exclude pre-existing conditions, adjust premiums for risk, or drop from coverage persons who become sick, would also be

----

[32] See, e.g., The Heritage Lectures: Is Tax Reform the Key to Health Care Reform? (Stuart M. Butler, ed., 1990); Stuart M. Butler, A Tax Reform Strategy to Deal with the Uninsured, 265 JAMA 2541 (1991); Mark V. Pauly, et al., Responsible National Health Insurance (1992).

important if insurance is to remain affordable and serviceable to insureds. Provisions such as these are usually included in incentive-based proposals.

The most basic problem with incentive-based proposals is that they do not, unless coupled with a mandate, create universal coverage. A number, probably a considerable number, of persons will inevitably pass up the offered incentives and remain uninsured. Some will do so because they choose to spend their money on other things rather than to purchase insurance which they could in fact afford. While this choice may well be rational, it is troublesome if the person subsequently becomes ill and is unable to pay for the required health care. Are we really prepared to allow such a person suffer or die as punishment for an unwise decision? More problematic are those persons who simply cannot afford to purchase health insurance and still pay for basic necessities such as food and housing. As the average family premium for health insurance is currently about $5200 a year, and non-group family policies can cost $10,000, a person earning a little over $8000 per year at a minimum wage job simply cannot afford health insurance. Indeed, unless the level of tax credits comes very close to approximating the full cost of health insurance, many poor persons will undoubtedly find the credits of little help.

The efficiency of this approach is also questionable. If tax credits come close to equaling insurance premiums, it would be much more efficient for government to simply pay for care directly rather than pay money to individuals to in turn purchase insurance, possibly in the very expensive individual insurance market. Other than subsidizing the insurance industry and preserving the virginity of the private market, it is unclear what justifies the tremendous transactions costs involved in this approach. Finally, relying on the Internal Revenue Service to determine whether medical expenses are necessary and appropriate and thus qualified for tax credit subsidization, as do some tax incentive proposals, is a daunting prospect. Nonetheless, tax incentive based proposals at this point seem to stand the greatest chance of adoption.

A subsidiary issue that must be addressed regardless of the basic approach taken to expanding access is the comprehensiveness of the benefits package.[33] As noted above, the access issue involves not

---

[33] See James F. Blumstein, Health Care Reform: The Policy Context, 29 Wake Forest L. Rev. 15 (1994).

simply whether or not a person is insured, but also the scope of coverage. If universal access were assured through a single payer system, but only for hospitalization for physical conditions, or only subject to high deductibles or coinsurance obligations, significant barriers to access to health care would remain. As comprehensiveness of coverage increases and cost-sharing obligations decrease, health care become more accessible. It also becomes more costly, however. A balance must be struck, therefore. One approach to this problem is to provide basic core benefits for all, which can be supplemented by those who can afford to do so. This approach requires, however, the ability to define basic benefits and a tolerance for some level of inequity.

A final access issue that to some extent stands alone is the problem of barriers to access facing special populations: rural populations, inner city residents, the institutionalized elderly, and others.[34] Whatever general approach is taken to expanding access, special steps may need to be taken to assure adequate service to these populations.

B. The Cost Problem

1. Regulation

The second major problem to be addressed by health care reform is the high and rapidly rising cost of health care. Here again three major approaches are advocated. First, cost increases could be controlled through regulation.[35] Regulation could take a number of forms. Fee schedules could be developed for various kinds of services, as now exist under Medicare for physician's services or hospital care. Caps could be placed on increases in prices of specific categories of goods or services (e.g. pharmaceuticals) or on insurance premiums. Expenditures for health care costs generally or on specific kinds of health care costs could be

---

[34] See, e.g., Eli Ginzberg, Improving Health Care for the Poor: Lessons From the 1980s, 271 JAMA 464 (1994).

[35] One of the leading champions for this approach is Robert Evans. See, Robert G. Evans, Tension, Compression and Shear: Directions, Stresses, and Outcomes of Health Care Cost Control, 15 J. Health Pol., Pol'y & L. 101 (1990).

budgeted.[36] Such budgets could either be negotiated or imposed by administrative or legislative order.[37]

Although regulation of prices is generally disfavored in the United States, it can be argued that health care costs are not adequately disciplined by the market, and that regulatory intervention is necessary. The primary advantage of regulation is that if it is applied comprehensively and with sufficient rigor it will control cost increases. Most other industrialized countries use some form of regulation to control costs, and most have done so fairly effectively.[38] The more global the control, the more likely it is to be effective: controls on price alone are likely to be undermined by volume increases; controls on inpatient hospital costs are likely to result in growth of outpatient costs; controls on public payments are likely to result in cost-shifting to private payers or discrimination against persons insured by public programs.

Regulation, like all other strategies, has its limitations. Where expenditures are held below those that would result from unregulated demand, shortages are likely to occur. Where there is a sufficiently large gap between public expectations for services and government-established budgets, as in Canada, shortages will be visible. Where budgets are held to unrealistically low levels, as in Britain, shortages may be severe. Where budgets are sufficiently generous and in accord with public expectations, as in Germany, shortages will not be perceptible.

Regulation is also likely to result in a different allocation of resources than would result from the market, discomfiting those providers or consumers who would benefit from the allocation that would result from the market. Finally, regulation is likely to encourage gaming

---

[36] See Richard B. Saltman, Single-Source Financing Systems: A Solution for the United States? 268 JAMA 774 (1992).

[37] Global budgets could also be imposed in tandem with managed competition, as was proposed in the Clinton Health Security Act, see Stuart H. Altman & Alan B. Cohen, Commentary: The Need for a Global Budget, 12 Health Aff. Supp. 1993 at 194; Henry J. Aaron & William B. Schwartz, Managed Competition: Little Cost Containment Without Budget Limits, 12 Health Aff. 1993 Supp. at 216.

[38] See Patrice R. Wolfe & Donald W. Moran, Global Budgeting in the OECD Countries, 14 Health Care Fin. Rev. Spring 1993 at 55.

behavior on the part of providers, particularly, again if regulation is only partial.

2. Managed Competition

The second strategy is managed competition.[39] Managed competition is based on the belief that competition is presently unable to control health care costs successfully because of pervasive failures in the market for health care services and insurance. Insurers do better competing for potential insureds who are good risks than competing based on premium prices. Providers, on the other hand, avoid competing on price because insured patients are largely insensitive to the price of any particular item or service. Patients who are insured (particularly those whose insurance is paid for by tax-subsidized employer contributions) have little direct incentive to forego any potentially beneficial medical service, and have little reliable information about the comparative quality of providers or the value of their services. The inevitable result of this situation is that the price and volume of services continues to escalate.[40]

Managed competition attempts to organize the market to make it work. Under managed competition, consumers are organized into purchasing alliances to give them market power in dealing with insurers.[41] Health insurers and managed care entities (usually designated collectively as "health plans") are required to sell a uniform product or

---

[39] See Alain C. Enthoven, Why Managed Care Has Failed to Contain Costs, Health Aff. Fall 1993 at 27; Paul Ellwood, et al., The Jackson Hole Initiatives for a Twenty-First Century American Health Care System, 1 Health Econ. 149 (1992). See, critiquing managed competition, Thomas Rice, et al., Holes in the Jackson Hole Approach to Health Care Reform, 270 JAMA 1357 (1993). The managed competition strategy was at the heart of the Clinton Health Security Act.

[40] For a stimulating critique of this account of the problems of the health care market see David M. Frankford, Privatizing Health Care: Economic Magic to Cure Legal Medicine, 66 S. Cal. L. Rev. 1 (1992).

[41] See Henry T. Greely, Policy Issues in Health Alliances: Of Efficiency, Monopsony, and Equity, 5 Health Matrix 37 (1995); Mark A. Hall, The Role of Insurance Purchasing Cooperatives in Health Care Reform, 3 Kan. J. of L. & Pub. Pol'y Winter 1993-94 at 95.

a small number of standardized products to permit price and quality comparisons. Explicit risk selection is outlawed and payments to insurers are standardized based on risk to obviate the need for risk selection. All providers are forced to sell their services through health plans, which have the sophistication to evaluate the quality of providers comparatively and the incentive to bargain with providers for low prices. Consumers are provided with comparative quality and price information to permit selection of health plans.

Managed competition could be structured in a variety of ways. Health insurance purchasing alliances could include all insureds, all insureds except for employees of firms large enough to themselves exercise substantial power in the market, or only insureds who are not employed or are employed by firms small enough to be at a substantial disadvantage in purchasing insurance.[42] To be effective, purchasing alliances must be large enough to achieve administrative economies of scale and significant power in bargaining with health plans. As more insureds are permitted to opt out of purchasing alliances, both of these strengths are compromised.

Another important structural issue is whether there will be one or several alliances in any particular area. If only one alliance is permitted it will not be subject to the discipline of a competitive market, and may become excessively regulatory and inefficient. If competing alliances are permitted, however, the advantages of economies of scale and market power may be lost, and risk selection becomes more of a problem.

The extent of regulatory power exercised by purchasing alliances must also be determined. The Clinton Health Security Act would have required alliances to determine eligibility of insureds for premium or cost-sharing subsidies, investigate complaints against plans and hear appeals from utilization review decisions. Critics of the plan were able to characterize the alliances as bureaucratic monstrosities.

While the Clinton plan would have given the purchasing alliances extensive regulatory power, it gave them little authority to bargain with health plans to negotiate premiums. Alternative models could allow

---

[42] See Greely, supra note 41; Hall, supra note 41; Walter A. Zelman, Who Should Govern the Purchasing Cooperatives? 12 Health Aff. 1993 Supp. at 49 (1993); Paul Starr, Design of Health Insurance Purchasing Cooperatives, 12 Health Aff. 1993 Supp. at 58.

purchasing alliances to bargain aggressively with health plans and only offer to their members the plans that offered the lowest prices.

There are few precedents for managed competition. The Federal Employees Health Benefits program and the California Public Employees Retirement System are the models most frequently referred to. They have enjoyed some success with holding down costs. No other nation has ever taken this approach, however. Getting a comprehensive national system of managed competition underway would be a daunting task. A particular problem would be the creation of health plans to compete in the market, which is likely to require considerable new capital since health plans are likely to be required to meet significant reserve requirements. Control over risk selection is also likely to be a major problem, as it is questionable whether the technology currently exists to adjust adequately for risk. Managed competition would be difficult to implement in rural areas or in other settings where few providers are available.[43] And managed competition would do little to control administrative costs.[44]

Finally, it is important to consider how managed competition would actually control costs. While managed competition relies on market forces to hold insurance premiums down, insurers must in turn, if they are to remain viable, find ways to hold down the cost of the medical care that they pay for. This may in part be done through health plans negotiating with professionals and institutions to drive down prices. But it is also likely that health plans would try to hold down costs through limiting the volume of services their providers deliver. Managed competition may in the end, therefore, have much the same effect on individual patients as regulation might: patients would be denied services that they might have received were health care financing unlimited.

3. Cost Sharing

The third strategy for controlling costs also relies on market forces, but attempts to introduce market pressures at the point of purchase

---

[43] See Jon Christianson & Ira Moscovice, Health Care Reform and Rural Health Networks, Health Aff. Fall 1993 at 58.

[44] See Carolyn M. Clancy, et al., Questions and Answers about Managed Competition, Health/PAC Bulletin, Spring 1993 at 30.

of services rather than at the point of purchase of insurance.[45] Proponents of this strategy argue that the real explanation for health care cost inflation is moral hazard. Health insurance is a commons that any individual insured can harvest without suffering him or herself the consequences of particular purchasing decisions. The collective consequences of this irresponsible individual conduct is spiraling health care inflation. The fact that employer payments for insurance premiums are not taxed exacerbates this problem by encouraging excessive insurance coverage, which in turn is used excessively by individuals to purchase health care goods and services.

If there were no insurance, proponents of this solution argue, there would be no problem of excessive health care costs. Each individual would decide whether or to spend money on a hip replacement or a new car when confronted with the choice. Antitrust enforcement would be necessary to make sure that the market was competitive, but consumers would do the rest. Because most consumers are risk adverse, however, insurance exists and is widely purchased. Moreover, because medical expenses may in particular situations outstrip the resources of all but the most wealthy, some form of insurance, private or public, is probably necessary if providers are to be paid.

Advocates of the point of service market approach, therefore, would permit insurance, but would encourage high levels of cost-sharing (deductibles, coinsurance, and copayments) to insure that, to the extent possible, consumers make trade-off choices at the point of purchase. This approach would also make insurance payments made by employers taxable as income to the employee to make insurance compete with other consumer goods on a level playing field, and would encourage Medisave accounts, a form of individual self-insurance. Advocates of this approach generally propose to accomplish these goals through manipulation of the tax system, offering credits, for example, to purchase high cost-sharing policies or giving favorable tax treatment to Medisave accounts.

---

[45] See, e.g. Ronald S. Bronow, The Physicians Who Care Plan: Preserving Quality and Equitability in American Medicine, 265 JAMA 2511 (1991).

Extensive research conducted by the Rand Corporation in the early 1980s demonstrates that cost-sharing in fact lowers costs.[46] It does so at a price, however.[47] First, it would disproportionately affect those who have less money and, therefore, fewer choices. This effect could be ameliorated to some extent through subsidies, but subsidies would in turn diminish the effectiveness of the strategy. Second, it disadvantages those with chronic diseases who need health care on a continual basis. Generally persons who require little health care would be better off, people who require a great deal of health care, worse off, with high cost sharing. Third, cost-sharing tends to discourage use of preventive care, necessitating the use of more expensive acute care at a later point. Fourth, if total cost-sharing obligations are held to a reasonable limit, limits will quickly be exceeded by the 10% of patients who are responsible for over 70% of health care costs. If total obligations are not limited, this group will simply go into bankruptcy, and society will have to bear the costs of their care.

Finally, we should learn from the Medicare program, which in fact has significant cost-sharing obligations. The result of this has been the creation of a huge market for Medicare supplement insurance, which insures Medicare beneficiaries against cost-sharing obligations. Because these policies are sold on an individual basis, they have high administrative costs. The Medicare experience indicates that people in fact do not want to make point-of-service choices, and unless forbidden by law to do so will purchase duplicate policies to avoid cost-sharing. The result of forcing point-of-service choices may be a less efficient, not a less costly health care system. At this point, however, the cost-sharing approach seems to enjoy the greatest political support in Congress.

In addition to these global approaches to the problem of health care costs, a number of specific cost problems are addressed by the health care plans. First, most legislative proposals would facilitate uniform and simplified billing procedures, including electronic billing, to decrease administrative costs. Second, most attempt to do something about malpractice, though this is done as much for political as for cost reasons.

---

[46] See Willard G. Manning, et al., Health Insurance and the Demand for Medical Care: Evidence from a Randomized Experiment, 77 Am.Econ.Rev. 251 (1987).

[47] M. Edith Rasell, Cost Sharing in Health Insurance--A Reexamination, 332 New Eng. J. Med. 1164 (1995).

Finally, most proposals recommend cracking down on fraud and abuse, which could have an effect on cost.

III. Reforms at the State Level

While the attention of the public has been focused in the last year on health care reform proposals at the federal level, reform efforts have been proceeding at a furious pace at the state level as well. During the 1993 state legislative session, all but two state legislatures considered health care reform legislation.[48] A few of the states have adopted comprehensive proposals to broaden access to health care insurance or to control health care costs. The programs adopted by these states will be discussed below. Most states have adopted much more modest reforms, intended to deal with specific problems or to marginally increase access or control costs.

Substantial barriers stand in the way of comprehensive reform; barriers that many states have found insurmountable to date. First, reform has been just as controversial at the state as at the federal level. Issues of who must pay for expanded access and whose incomes will be constrained by cost control have proved highly contentious. In particular, finding state revenues to finance expansion of access has proved difficult. An excellent account of the politics of enacting health care reform in eight of the states that have made the most progress in this arena is found in the Summer 1993 issue of Health Affairs.

Federal law has also stood in the way of state health care reform. The most serious impediment has been ERISA, the Employee Retirement Income Security Act of 1974. ERISA preempts any state law that relates to an employee benefit plan.[49] While federal law saves from preemption state laws regulating insurance,[50] it forbids states from "deeming" a self-insured employee benefit plan to be an insurance plan for purposes of regulation.[51] The immediate impact of ERISA on state

---

[48] John K. Iglehart, Health Care Reform: The States, 320 New Eng. J. Med. 75 (1994).

[49] 29 U.S.C. § 1144(a).

[50] 29 U.S.C. § 1144(b)(2)(A).

[51] 29 U.S.C. § 1144(b)(2)(B).

efforts to reform their health care systems is that they are barred from adopting comprehensive reforms. The courts have held that ERISA prohibits the states from imposing coverage mandates on self-insured employers,[52] and only the Hawaii employer mandate has been explicitly exempted from the prohibition by Congress.[53] As approximately 40% of employees covered by employment-related group insurance are in self-insured plans, ERISA sharply limits the ability of states to enact universal reforms. While New York State Conference of Blue Cross and Blue Shield Plans v. Travelers Insurance Company (infra at page   ), gives states somewhat more leeway in adopting laws that indirectly affect employer-benefit plans, the likelihood of federal litigation challenging such laws significantly chills state efforts to adopt comprehensive reforms.

States are further limited in their ability to expand access and cost-control by federal Medicaid laws and regulations. An obvious strategy for expanding access is to bring low income uninsured individuals under the Medicaid umbrella. States have shown a great deal of interest in controlling the cost of the Medicaid program, often one of the largest categories in the state budget, through managed care arrangements or through limiting benefits or payment rates.

Detailed provisions of the federal Medicaid statutes and regulations limit the ability of the states to pursue these strategies. The federal Medicaid law provides for a variety of waiver programs. Though the federal government has traditionally been reticent to grant waivers, it has been increasingly responsive under the Clinton presidency to innovative state waiver requests.[54] The Oregon and Tennessee programs, discussed below, are examples of significant recent waivers. Nevertheless, waivers merely alleviate federal constraints, they do not eliminate them, and the grant of waiver requests is dependent upon federal discretion.

---

[52] Standard Oil Co. v. Agsalud, 442 F.Supp. 695 (N.D.Cal. 1977), aff'd 633 F.2d 760 (9th Cir. 1980), aff'd mem. 454 U.S. 801, 102 S.Ct. 79 (1981).

[53] 29 U.S.C. § 1144(b)(5).

[54] See John Holahan, et al., Insuring the Poor Through Section 1115 Medicaid Waivers, 14 Health Affairs, Spring 1995, at 199.

Finally, state flexibility in achieving cost control is limited by the federal Medicare program, which covers nearly one fifth of total health care expenditures. The Medicare program is the largest single payer for health care, and sets its own rates. As these rates do not pay for the full cost of health care, the costs of caring for Medicare patients are shifted by health care professionals and institutions to other payers. Most states have no control over the amount Medicare pays and can do little to control cost-shifting that results. Only Maryland currently has authority to set Medicare rates under its comprehensive rate-setting system, other states can only partially address cost problems.

In spite of these barriers, virtually all of the states have taken some steps towards expanding access, controlling costs, or both. Forty-five of the states have now adopted laws to expand and improve coverage for employees of small businesses.[55] Both the National Association of Insurance Commissioners and the Health Insurance Association of America have proposed model laws for small group insurance reform.[56] States have adopted, for example, "guaranteed renewal" laws prohibiting insurers from cancelling or refusing to renew insurance because of claims experience or changes in health status; "portability" statutes restricting the length of the period during which pre-existing conditions can be excluded from coverage; or "guaranteed availability" laws requiring insurers to accept for at least a basic (minimal benefits) health plan, anyone who applies.

Standing alone these laws merely require the availability, not the affordability of coverage. Some states have gone further, therefore, restricting the ability of insurers to increase premiums for a particular group from year to year, restricting insurers to certain case characteristics (e.g. geographic, demographic and industry characteristics) and limiting the variance among the bands, requiring community rating (prohibiting insurers from considering the claims-experience of specific groups) or establishing a reinsurance market for private insurers. States have also tried to make writing insurance for small group markets more attractive by waiving mandates for coverage of specific services or providers that

---

[55] Anne R. Markus, et al., Small Group Reforms: A Snapshot of the States Experience (1995); GAO, Access to Health Insurance: State Efforts to Assist Small Businesses (1992).

[56] See Mark A. Hall, Reforming the Health Insurance Market for Small Businesses, 326 New Eng. J. Med. 565 (1992).

22

would otherwise apply or permitting insurers to offer a bare bones policy for small groups. A number of states have taken the further step of subsidizing the purchase of insurance by small businesses.

The goal of these reforms is simply to make private health insurance more affordable to small employer groups. None require the purchase of health insurance. Their effects have been modest. A 1993 study, for example, found that in 11 of the 16 states that offered "bare bones" policies, less than 300 persons purchased the policies.[57] A 1994 study of eleven states that had implemented small group reforms found that coverage of small employer groups had increased, but that premiums had also increased because of community rating, and that the number of insurers had decreased in some markets.[58] A third study found that small group market reforms had not had a significant effect on either insurance premiums or the number of small groups or total lives covered by insurance.[59]

A second strategy that states have pursued is to expand coverage at the margins for the uninsured population at the state's expense. Most states have traditionally had a state-funded indigent care programs for individuals not categorically eligible for Medicaid. Some states have expanded these programs.[60] Other states have established subsidized risk pools from which high-risk uninsurable persons can purchase insurance. Some states have taken full advantage of the options available under Medicaid for providing health care to children and pregnant women, while others have provided even more generous children's health insurance programs at state expense.

Instead of attempting to insure the medically indigent, some states take an alternative approach of subsidizing hospitals that provide uncompensated care. All states are required to provide "disproportionate

---

[57] Families USA, No Sale: The Failure of Barebones Insurance (1993).

[58] Survey by American Academy of Actuaries, reported in BNA Health Care Daily, March 30, 1994.

[59] Markus, supra note 55.

[60] See Intergovernmental Health Policy Project, George Washington University, A Review of State Indigent Care Programs: 1992.

share" payments under their Medicaid programs to hospitals that provide care in disproportionate numbers to Medicaid and indigent patients,[61] and some states go beyond these requirements to assist nongovernment hospitals that have large indigent patient populations.

On the cost-control side, most states have retained certificate of need programs, to limit the expansion of new health care facilities and services. A few states retain hospital rate-setting, though this strategy has been largely abandoned. A number of states have attempted to control the growth of their Medicaid expenditures through reliance on managed care, while a smaller number of states have attempted to introduce managed competition more widely into their health care system, as described below.

Though virtually all of the states have taken some tentative steps toward reforming their health care systems, a small, but growing number of states, have gone further and begun to reform their health care systems more comprehensively.

In the vanguard has been Hawaii, whose Prepaid Health Care Act first required employers to provide health insurance to their workers in 1974, with costs shared equally by employers and employees.[62] After several years of ERISA litigation, Hawaii was explicitly exempted from the ERISA preemption provisions by Congress in 1983, but the exemption only covers the law as it stood in 1974. The Prepaid Health Care Act assures coverage for nearly 90% of the population of Hawaii. Hawaii's extensive reliance on managed care and certificate of need programs have also permitted significant cost control, with Hawaii's health care costs equalling 8.1% of its gross domestic product compared to 14% nationally. Certain groups remained without insurance coverage, however, including part-time workers, seasonal workers, and the unemployed. In 1991 Hawaii adopted the State Health Insurance Program of Hawaii (SHIP) to create a state-subsidized basic health insurance program, focusing on primary and preventive care, to cover persons with incomes below 300% of poverty level, with premiums paid on a sliding scale basis.[63] In 1993, the Department of Health and

---

[61] 42 U.S.C. §§ 1396a(a)(13)(A), 1396r-4.

[62] Haw. Rev. Stat. ch. 393.

[63] Haw. Rev. Stat. ch. 431N. See Deane Neubauer, Hawaii: A Pioneer in Health System Reform, Health Aff. Summer 1993 at 31.

Human Services approved a waiver request for Hawaii to create a purchasing pool combining Medicaid and SHIP enrollees to purchase care from capitated managed care plans through a competitive bidding process.

The only other state to adopt a universal mandate has been Massachusetts, which adopted a play-or-pay program in 1988.[64] This system, together with expansion of the Medicaid program and health insurance programs for college students, the unemployed, disabled children and working adults, welfare recipients entering the work force, and a program for low-income residents was to have provided near universal coverage by 1992. The political and economic climate in Massachusetts, coupled with ERISA concerns, forced postponement of the mandate until 1995 and then to 1996, and as of this writing its ultimate implementation seems uncertain.

More recent comprehensive state health care reforms have avoided mandates in favor of combinations of managed competition market structures and subsidized programs for the low-income unemployed. The Florida statute establishes eleven "Community Health Purchasing Alliances" through which small businesses, individuals and the state (on behalf of its employees and Medicaid clients) can purchase health insurance, and imposes reforms on the small business insurance market.[65] The purchasing alliances will solicit from managed care plans and insurers proposals for standard and basic health benefit plans and provide information on cost, quality, enrollee satisfaction, and enrollee responsibilities for participating plans. Minnesota and Washington adopted comprehensive health care reform legislation during the 1993 and 1994 legislative sessions, but as this supplement goes to press Washington has repealed most of its health reform package and Minnesota seems poised to repeal or delay most of its reforms.

Oregon and Tennessee are among the states that have focused their health reform efforts on expanding their Medicaid programs to cover the uninsured poor. The Oregon approach has provoked more

---

[64] Mass. Ann. Laws. ch. 118F.

[65] Fla. Stat. Ann. § 408.70.

controversy than any other state health care reform plan.[66] In summer of 1991 Oregon adopted a plan through which it would expand coverage to its 120,000 citizens whose incomes fell below the poverty level but who were ineligible for Medicaid. It would do so by establishing a comprehensive list of conditions and treatments that could conceivably be covered by Medicaid (a list that now includes 688 services), prioritizing these through a process involving professional judgment and community input, and covering as many services as the legislature would fund (currently 565 of the services). Once the Medicaid program was reformed, a play or pay system would go into effect under which employers would have to provide coverage equivalent to that offered under Medicaid or pay into a state insurance pool fund to subsidize alternative insurance for the uninsured who did not qualify for the expanded Medicaid program.

To implement its program, Oregon was required to obtain a Medicaid waiver. The Bush Administration denied the Oregon request on Aug. 3, 1992, asserting that the proposed Oregon program would violate the Americans with Disabilities Act insofar as it denied coverage for some services to persons with certain disabilities. For example, the rationing program proposed by Oregon would have denied liver transplants for alcoholic cirrhosis or for extremely low-birth-weight babies under 23 weeks gestation. The Clinton Administration approved a revised waiver request on March 19, 1993 for the period from January 1, 1994 to January 1, 1998. The waiver was approved conditional upon Oregon meeting certain requirements that would lessen the impact of disability considerations on prioritizing treatments. While the Oregon Medicaid plan is currently being implemented, implementation of the play or pay system was postponed in 1993 and may not be implemented.

---

[66] A symposium on health care rationing, including several articles discussing the Oregon proposal, appeared at 140 U. Pa. L.Rev. 1505 - 1998 (1992). Other articles discussing the Oregon plan include Sara Rosenbaum, Mothers and Children Last, 18 Am. J. L. & Med. 97 (1992); Robert Schwartz, Medicaid Reform Through Setting Health Care Priorities, 35 St. Louis U. L.J. 837 (1991); W. John Thomas, The Oregon Medicaid Proposal: Ethical Paralysis, Tragic Democracy, and the Fate of a Utilitarian Health Care Program, 72 Oregon L. Rev. 49 (1993); and Symposium, The "Oregon Plan" 1 Health Matrix 135 - 273 (1991). A recent account of the progress of the Oregon plan is Daniel M. Fox & Howard M. Leichter, The Ups and Downs of Oregon's Rationing Plan, Health Aff. Summer 1993 at 66.

Oregon is only one of about 15 states that had either requested or obtained an federal 1115 waiver to reshape their Medicaid program as of the spring of 1995. Tennessee obtained a federal waiver in 1993 to expand its Medicaid program to cover 500,000 additional poor uninsured residents, and to place all of its Medicaid recipients into regional managed care plans. Arizona has operated its Medicaid program since its inception in 1982 under a waiver that permits all program services to be provided through managed care.

While the trend in state health care reform has been toward managed competition, a few states remain committed to rate regulation as a means of controlling costs and subsidizing access expansion. Maryland legislation requires insurers to offer a standard benefit package to employers of two to fifty workers.[67] Insurers are required to use an adjusted community rating system that strictly limits variation in rating, with the average community-rated premium is limited to 12% of the average annual wage in Maryland. If the rate is exceeded, the Health Care Access and Cost Commission may alter the standard benefits package. The law also allows the state insurance commissioner to require filing of new rates if loss or expense ratios fall below certain limits. The Maryland law also begins regulation of provider rates.

As of this writing in the middle of 1995, the situation of health care reform at the state level is very dynamic. While virtually all states have taken piecemeal steps toward reform, and many have debated or appointed study commissions to consider comprehensive reform, few have yet taken dramatic steps toward actually accomplishing reform. Reform is politically contentious and often costly. Much of the momentum toward reform that drove legislation in 1993 and 1994 was lost with the failure of health reform at the federal level and the political shift to the right at the federal and state level in the 1994 elections. A handful of states have, however, stepped out boldly. Their efforts may light the way toward reform at the national level.

IV. International Comparative Perspectives

As the debate regarding health care reform has gone forward in the United States, it has been suggested that we should look beyond our own country to find models for system reform. The United States is unique among industrialized nations in two respects: by virtually any

---

[67] Md. Ann. Code. Art. 48A, §§ 698-713.

measure it spends more on health care than any other nation in the world, and it is the only industrialized nation not to make health care available to all of its citizens. There should be lessons, therefore, in the experience of other nations regarding how to deliver health care less expensively and more comprehensively. In this section we examine briefly three alternative models for providing health care: England, Germany and Canada.

A. England

Medical care in England[68] is publicly funded and provided. Indeed, the British National Health Service (NHS), founded in 1946, represents the first and most ambitious attempt by a Western nation to provide health care for its citizens as a tax-funded entitlement rather than through a social insurance program. The NHS was extensively reorganized by the Conservative government in 1991. The ultimate goal of the 1991 NHS reorganization was to separate the purchasing and service provision functions of the NHS. It was an attempt to create internal markets in which competition could take place with the hope of increasing consumer satisfaction and lowering costs. These reforms, if successful, could ultimately make the NHS look more like an insurer and less like a provider of services.

The English health care system is centrally organized. The NHS is subject to the Secretary of State for Health. Its operations are headed by a NHS Management Executive Board, subject to a NHS Policy Board, which in turn is chaired and appointed by the Secretary of State for Health. In managing the NHS, the Secretary of State works through fourteen Regional Health Authorities (RHAs), which have responsibility for planning, resource allocation, monitoring service provision, and direct provision of a few services (such as blood transfusion services). Under the regions are District Health Authorities (DHAs), which prior to 1991 provided services to patients who lived in their districts. The DHAs are now responsible for purchasing services for their populations from their own hospitals, hospitals elsewhere in the NHS, private providers, or NHS hospital trusts (a new category of institutions created by the 1991 reforms that resemble our own non-profit hospitals). The vast majority of the funding of the NHS comes from general taxation (80%) with smaller

---

[68] Though the following discussion is specific to England, most of it applies throughout the United Kingdom.

28

shares coming from insurance contributions (15%) and patient charges (4%) (1990-91 figures).

General practitioners (GPs) are not employees of the NHS, but rather hold independent contracts with Family Health Services Authorities, which in turn are subject to the Regional Health Authorities. Although separation of primary and specialist care is characteristically European, England carries this principle even further than most of the other nations in this study. Every patient is England is attached to a GP, who acts as a gatekeeper for all specialist and hospital care. GPs are responsible for about 90% of the patient contacts of the NHS. Most English GPs work in group practices. Most GPs are paid under a complex formula including a basic practice allowance (adjusted for seniority and to provide incentives to practice in underserved areas), money to employ practice staff, a per patient capitation fee, and a fee-for-service component covering special services such as vaccination or contraception. Under the 1991 reforms, however, the government encourages GP practices (at their option) to manage capitated practice budgets that cover the costs of outpatient care, diagnostic tests, prescribing costs, and some inpatient care for their patients, as well as some practice costs. Under this system, GPs are allowed to use "profits" generated from these budgets to improve their practices, and thus ultimately--if "improved" practices attracted more patients--to increase their capitation payments.

Most specialists in England are employees of the NHS and work as "consultants" in its hospitals. They are paid based on schedules negotiated at the national level, supplemented by merit awards. The long course of specialist training in England assures that these doctors are assisted by a large number of junior doctors of different grades of experience. Heretofore consultants have effectively controlled important decisions in NHS hospitals, particularly with respect to resource allocation. In recent years, initiatives by the government have tried to strengthen the management role in the hospital. Recent reforms have supplemented this strategy with another, encouraging hospitals to opt out of NHS management structures to become self-governing, free to make their own "profits" or absorb their own losses, substituting the discipline of the market for the discipline of management.

The private sector in England is still small. It is growing, however, encouraged by the Conservative government. Nine percent of the population of the U.K. currently supplement their NHS coverage with private health insurance, and 17% of elective surgery in England is now provided in the private sector. The private sector plays a particularly important role in providing hospice and nursing home care.

England spends far less of its GNP on health care than do Germany, Canada, or the U.S. The growth of its health care expenditures has been effectively limited by its centrally controlled fixed budget, which has been held to very modest increases in recent years.[69]

B. Germany

The organization of health care delivery and financing in Germany presents a striking contrast to the English system. Though Germany boasts the oldest national health insurance program in the world (it was initiated by Bismark in 1883), both medical care delivery and financing in Germany take place largely in the private, or perhaps more accurately, quasi-public, sector. The ambulatory care sector in Germany is entirely private, nearly half of the hospital beds in Germany are private or voluntary, and health insurance, though compulsory for most workers, is administered by self-governing quasi-public entities.

Two themes encountered recurrently in health policy in Germany are federalism and "Selbstverwaltung" (self-governance). Germany is composed of eleven states (Länder), which take primary responsibility for many aspects of health policy. Physician licensure and discipline are regulated at the state level, as are most matters pertaining to hospitals. Indeed, about half of the hospital beds in Germany are controlled by the states or (more commonly) by local government, and issues of financing and regulation of hospitals are jealously preserved from federal control. The federal government's role is by and large limited to the adoption of laws that establish the framework within which the states operate, though it takes a more active role in setting policy for the health insurance system and regulating basic medical education.

---

[69] For further information on the British Health Care system, see Christopher Ham, Health Policy in Britain (3rd. ed. 1992). For a discussion of the 1991 reforms see A.J. Culyer & Andrew Meads, The United Kingdom: Effective, Efficient, Equitable? 17 J. Health Pol., Pol'y & L. 667 (1992); Patricia Day & Rudolf Klein, Britain's Health Care Experiment, Health Aff. Fall 1991 at 39; Alain C. Enthoven, Internal Market Reform of the British Health Service, Health Aff. Fall 1991 at 60.

Self-governance is an even more important theme. The German health care system is organized into quasi-public guild-like corporate structures. All doctors must be members of the physician chamber (Ärztekammer) of their state. The chambers are self-governing bodies, whose boards are elected by their members. They are responsible for professional, ethical, and disciplinary matters, as well as postgraduate and continuing education. Most physicians in ambulatory practice are also member of one of Germany's eighteen Kassenärztliche Vereinigungen, or organizations of insurance fund doctors, again headed by boards elected by their membership. These entities negotiate on behalf of the doctors with the insurance funds. Germany has over 1000 statutory sickness insurance funds (gesetzliche Krankenkassen or Ersatzkassen) which are established by law, but administered by boards elected by those who fund them: both employees and employers for the Krankenkassen and employees only for the Ersatzkassen. The entire system operates with relatively little regulatory interference or financial participation from the government.

Another characteristic of the German health system is the extent to which it relies on the ambulatory care sector for delivery of both primary and specialist care. As in most European countries, there is little overlap between office-based and hospital physicians. Unlike many other countries, however, a high percentage of office-based doctors, about half, are specialists. It is common for a primary care doctor to refer a patient to an office-based specialist rather than to a hospital for specialist care or even surgery. Group practice has grown less rapidly in Germany than in other countries, but laboratory partnerships permit office-based physicians direct access to expensive and sophisticated medical equipment.

Because statutory health insurance in Germany is tied to income and form of employment, its coverage is not universal, as in England. It covers about 91% of the population, however, including blue-collar workers, white-collar workers with incomes below a specified level (DM 64,800 for 1993), retired persons, the unemployed, and dependents of persons in these groups. The remaining 9% of the population includes persons who are privately insured or are public employees who have a special insurance program. Insurance premiums average 13.4% of wages, but range from 8.5 to 16.5%. A rather generous minimum benefit package is required of the mandatory sickness funds by law, including cash disability and maternity payments and coverage of most primary and hospital medical care, with modest copayments for hospital care and drugs. Sickness fund members can generally choose to see any primary

31

care physician who is a member of the insurance doctors association, but can normally, except in emergencies, only be admitted to hospital with the referral of an office-based doctor.

Fees for doctors in office-based insurance practice are established through a complex process. The sickness funds and insurance doctors associations negotiate both a relative value schedule for various kinds of physicians services and a total cap on expenditures. The insurance doctors organizations then allocate the total funds available among their member doctors on a fee-for-service basis, considering the number of services each doctor has delivered and the relative value of those services. Under this system, in which a doctor's share of the total pie depends in large part on the number of services he bills for, there is a temptation to bill for an excessive number of services. Thus the sickness funds and insurance doctor organizations have worked out a rather complex system of economic monitoring to catch doctors who attempt to game or defraud the system.

Hospital capital costs are reimbursed by the state government. Operating costs or user charges (including payments for physicians services received within the hospital) are reimbursed by the sickness funds through budgets set through negotiations between the sickness funds and hospitals. Doctors working within hospitals are generally employees whose salaries are negotiated collectively between their unions and the hospital organizations.

Health expenditures in Germany are rather high by European standards, measured by either share of GNP (8.5% in 1991), or by per capita health expenditures ($1659 per year in 1991). Physicians incomes are also extraordinarily high, at 4.4 times the income of the average worker compared to 3.9 times in the U.S. The growing cost of health care is a continuing concern, and was a major focus of 1993 health reform legislation, which imposed mandated global budgets on various services for the next three years, required the creation of a new prospective payment system for hospitals, and attempted to reduce disparities in contribution rates among the sickness funds.[70]

---

[70] Good recent English language accounts of the German health care system include GAO, 1993 German Health Reforms: New Cost Control Initiatives (1993) and J.-Matthias Graf v.d. Schulenburg, Germany: Solidarity at a Price, 17 J. Health Pol., Pol'y & L. 715 (1992).

C. Canada

Because of Canada's proximity and linguistic and cultural resemblance to the United States, its health care system has been more widely discussed in the American literature as an alternative model for the United States than that of any other country. Like England, Canada has a publicly financed system. Like Germany, its health care delivery system is largely private. Like the United States and Germany it has a federal political system--i.e. Canada in fact does not have one health care system, but a dozen provincial and territorial systems. Because the Canadian system delivers health care at a cost significantly lower than that in the United States with low administrative costs and high political acceptability, it has been widely praised by those who favor the United States moving to a health care system with greater government involvement. Those who oppose greater government involvement in health care, or those whose incomes would be threatened by a move toward a publicly financed system, have roundly criticized Canada, primarily because it relies to some extent on queues to ration some forms of health care.

Though the Canadian constitution assigns responsibility for health care to the provincial governments, the national government pays for a little over one third of health care expenditures. In exchange for receipt of national funding, provincial plans must agree to five principles:

- Universal coverage or all eligible residents;

- Comprehensive coverage for hospital and physician services;

- Reasonable access to care for patients, without cost-sharing obligations;

- Portable coverage, available anywhere within Canada; and

- Public administration--private insurance cannot be sold for covered services.

Most of the provinces supplement federally required coverage with coverage of additional services, often subject to cost-sharing requirements.

Hospitals in Canada each receive a fixed global budget each year from the province for operating expenditures. This forces hospitals to operate economically, but can lead to shortages and limits the government's ability otherwise to address misallocation of resources. The provincial governments also tightly control technology diffusion through control over capital and operating funds. Canadian hospitals tend to have more admissions and longer stays than American hospitals, but to have less high-technology equipment and to use services less intensively. Overall, their costs are significantly lower than the in the United States.

Most physicians are paid fee-for-service on the basis of a fee schedule negotiated between the provincial medical associations and the provincial governments. While fees for physician's services are lower in Canada than in the U.S., utilization is higher. Because Canadian physicians have only to deal with one payer and face relatively little malpractice litigation, their operating expenses are much lower than are those of U.S. physicians, thus their incomes are high by Canadian standards and higher than U.S. physician incomes in a few primary care specialties. In the last decade provinces have been moving toward global budgets and utilization review to control growth in the total cost of physician services.

Controls over hospital costs and technology diffusion has led to shortages in particular services and rationing through queuing. Anecdotes of shortages have been much publicized in the United States, where they have been invoked to demonstrate the failure of government financing of health care. Advocates of the Canadian system, however, note that these shortages are isolated and normally involve elective care, and that health care is on the whole much more accessible in Canada than in the U.S. In any event, the Canadian system remains far more popular with Canadians than is the U.S. system within the U.S., and, as one American pollster recently noted, there are more Canadians who believe that Elvis is still alive than there are who would prefer to trade their health care system for ours.[71]

---

[71] A good summary of the Canadian system is found in GAO, Canadian Health Insurance, Lessons for the United States (1991). Recent articles on the Canadian system include Murray G. Brown, Rationing Health Care in Canada, 2 Ann. Health L. 101 (1993); Raisa B. Deber, Canadian Medicare: Can it Work in the United States? Will it Survive in Canada? 19 AM. J. L. & Med. 75 (1993); Robert G. Evans, Canada: The Real Issues, 17 J. Health Pol., Pol'y & L. 739 (1992).

CHAPTER 1. REGULATING THE QUALITY OF HEALTH CARE

Insert in the second paragraph of note 2, page 15, the following:

Courts have generally deferred to a doctor's medical judgment as to the benefit of a particular treatment to a patient. Where the diagnostic or treatment modality is found to have no value, the physician may be negligent if a bad outcome results. In Riser v. American Medical International, Inc., 620 So.2d 372 (5th Cir. 1993), the doctor performed a femoral arteriogram on the patient, who suffered a stroke and died. The court found that the physician had breached the standard of care by subjecting the patient to a technology which he should reasonably have known would be of "no practical benefit to the patient".

Insert at page 53 the following:

IN RE WILLIAMS
573 N.E.2d 638 (Ohio 1991)

* * *

While the board need not, in every case, present expert testimony to support a charge against an accused physician, the charge must be supported by some reliable, probative and substantial evidence. It is here that the case against Dr. Williams fails, as it is very different from Arlen.

* * *

Arlen involved a physician who dispensed controlled substances in a manner which not only fell below the acceptable standard of medical practice, but also violated the applicable statute governing prescription and dispensing of these drugs. In contrast, Dr. Williams dispensed controlled substances in what was, at the time, a legally permitted manner, albeit one which was disfavored by many in the medical community. The only evidence in the record on this issue was the testimony of Dr. William's expert witnesses that his use of controlled substances in weight control programs did not fall below the acceptable standard of medical practice. While the board has broad discretion to resolve evidentiary conflicts, and determine the weight to be given expert testimony, it cannot convert its own disagreement with an expert's opinion into affirmative evidence of a contrary proposition where the issue is one of which medical experts are divided and there is no statute or rule governing the situation.

It should be noted, however, that where the General Assembly has prohibited a particular medical practice by statute, or where the board has done so through its rulemaking authority, the existence of a body of expert opinion supporting that practice would not excuse a violation.

* * *

...Were the board's decision to be affirmed on the facts in this record, it would mean that a doctor would have no access to meaningful review of the board's decision. The board, though a majority of its members have special knowledge, is not entitled to exercise such unbridled discretion.

NOTE

1.   If the medical board wants to avoid the requirement of expert testimony in Williams, how should it draft its rules on the use of narcotics? What advantages and disadvantages does the rule in Williams have as compared to a more specific rule?

2.   The question of whether expert testimony is required to support disciplinary action for violations of standards of practice remains controversial. Another question raised in regard to a requirement of expert testimony is whether lay members of the board can participate effectively if the board's disciplinary action is not supported by such evidence. See e.g., Devous v. Wyoming State Board of Medical Examiners, 845 P.2d 408 (Wyo. 1993); Levinson v. Connecticut Board of Chiropractic Examiners, 560 A.2d 403 (Conn. 1989), each requiring expert testimony for different purposes. See also, Andrew L. Hyams, Expert Psychiatric Evidence in Sexual Misconduct Cases Before State Medical Boards, 18 Am. J. Law & Medicine 171, 195-197 (1992).

Insert at page 73 the following:

The scope of practice of nurses and physician assistants, as well as that of other non-physician health care providers, continues to expand in response to cost-containment, managed care and the increasing professional stature of such providers. Expansion of scope of practice of nurses and physician assistants plays a significant role in some proposals for health care reform. See e.g., Linda H. Aiken and William M. Sage, Staffing National Health Care Reform: A Role for Advanced Practice Nurses, 26 Akron L.Rev. 187 (1992); Barbara J. Safreit, Health Care Dollars and Regulatory Sense: The Role of Advanced Practice Nursing, 9 Yale J. on Reg. 417 (1992); P. Eugene Jones and James F. Cawley, Physician Assistants and Health System Reform, 271 JAMA 1266 (Apr. 27, 1994). The increasing emphasis on primary care is just as likely, if not more likely, to benefit nurses and physician assistants as it is to benefit primary care physicians. See, Philip R. Alper, Primary Care in Transition, 272 JAMA 1523 (Nov. 16,1994).

Recently enacted statutes such as the following exemplify the direction of expansion of the scope of practice of nurses and physician assistants. Do such statutes cause you to alter your advice in the problem on page 73 of the text?

> A registered nurse who (1) has graduated from a program of study designed to prepare registered nurses for advanced practice as nurse practitioners, (2) is certified through a national professional nursing organization which certifies nurse practitioners and is included in the list of professional nursing organizations adopted by the board...and (3) has a written agreement with a physician based on standards established by the Minnesota nurses association and the Minnesota medical association that defines the delegated responsibilities related to the prescription of drugs and therapeutic devices, may prescribe and administer drugs and therapeutic devices within the scope of the written agreement and within practice as a nurse practitioner.

Minn. Stat. § 148.235(2).

> Delegation of authority to prescribe, dispense and administer drugs and medical devices. (a) A supervising physician may delegate to a physician assistant who is registered with the board of medical practice and certified by the National Commission on Certification of Physician Assistants and who is under the supervising physician's supervision, the authority to prescribe, dispense and

administer legend drugs and medical devices, subject to the requirements in this section and other requirements established by the commissioner of health in rules. ... (b) The agreement between the physician assistant and supervising physician and any alternate supervising physicians must include a statement by the supervising physician regarding delegation or nondelegation of the functions of prescribing, dispensing and administering of legend drugs and medical devices to the physician assistant. The statement must include a protocol indicating categories of drugs for which the supervising physician delegates prescriptive and dispensing authority. The delegation must be appropriate to the physician assistant's practice and within the scope of the physician assistant's training. The commissioner of health shall identify categories of drugs, if any, for which delegated prescribing and dispensing is inappropriate. Physician assistants who have been delegated the authority to prescribe, dispense and administer legend drugs and medical devices shall provide evidence of current certification by the National Commission on Certification of Physician Assistants when registering or re-registering as physician assistants. Supervising physicians shall retrospectively review, on a daily basis, the prescribing, dispensing and administering of legend drugs and medical devices by physician assistants, when this authority has been delegated to the physician assistant as part of the delegation agreement between the physician and the physician assistant.

Minn. Stat. § 147.34(1).

Insert at page 87 the following:

The Health Care Financing Administration has issued final regulations on the Medicare/Medicaid survey and certification process, including regulations relating to the intermediate sanctions required by OBRA 1987. 59 Fed. Reg. 56116-01 (Nov. 10, 1994).

Insert at page 102 the following:

In OBRA of 1987, Congress established requirements to govern the recognition of national private accreditation programs by the Department of Health and Human Services for the purpose of allowing facilities accredited through such programs to carry "deemed status" for compliance with Medicare certification. Under this provision, HHS has recognized accreditation by JCAHO and by the Community Health Accreditation Program as carrying deemed status for home health agencies. The final rule promulgated in regard to JCAHO illustrates the HHS approach to this issue. The summary of the rule, as described by HHS, follows:

Department of Health and Human Services
58 Fed. Reg. 35007-01 (June 30, 1993)

As a result of this notice, HHAs [home health agencies] accredited by JCAHO are deemed to meet the requirements for participation in the Medicare program and, therefore, may participate in the Medicaid program as a provider of home health services. We are currently considering the development of a separate rule that would permit the States to apply more stringent State-specific requirements for HHA participation in the Medicaid program. However, our recognition of JCAHO does not affect in any way a State's independent authority to license providers and inspect such providers to ensure compliance with its licensure standards.

* * *

[W]e would remove recognition of JCAHO accreditation if either of the following circumstances occur:

- JCAHO revises its standards so that the revised standards fail to provide reasonable assurance that JCAHO-accredited HHAs meet the Medicare conditions of participation. Conversely, we revise the Medicare HHA conditions of participation to such a degree that JCAHO's standards or accreditation policies would no longer provide reasonable assurance that JCAHO- accredited HHAs meet the conditions of participation; or

- Our validation or complaint surveys reveal widespread, systematic, or unresolvable problems with the JCAHO accreditation process, thereby providing evidence that there is not reasonable assurance that JCAHO-accredited HHAs meet the Medicare conditions of participation.

The proposed notice also made our recognition of JCAHO's accreditation program contingent on JCAHO's continued agreement to:

- Release JCAHO survey reports to us routinely and to the public upon request. If the reports reveal deficiencies which we believe warrant action by us, we may survey the HHAs identified as having deficiencies, withdraw recognition of the accreditation program if appropriate, and apply any other appropriate corrective measures or sanctions. The information to be released includes the accreditation findings, supporting documentation, the official accreditation survey reports of JCAHO surveyors, and other related information.

- Report to either the Office of Inspector General (OIG) (for Medicare) or to the State agency responsible for investigating fraud and abuse (for Medicaid), or to both, complaints received from persons working in the accredited HHA or any substantial complaints from others, anonymous or identified, concerning potential fraud and abuse violations, and any other indication of a Medicare or Medicaid program abuse encountered by JCAHO during a JCAHO inspection.

- Make JCAHO surveyors available to serve as witnesses if adverse action is taken by HCFA after JCAHO accreditation has been withdrawn.

Finally, we proposed to make our approval of JCAHO's accreditation program contingent on the following revisions to JCAHO's survey and accreditation process (JCAHO had already agreed to make these changes):

- Implementation of an annual, unannounced survey of those HHAs requesting JCAHO accreditation for Medicare deeming purposes.

- Adoption of the standardized functional assessment instrument used by HCFA and State agency surveyors and training of the JCAHO surveyors in its use.

- Adoption of a case-mix, stratified random sampling process and sample sizes of clinical records for review and home visits comparable to HCFA's.

- Maintenance of a timeframe and process for following up deficiencies found during an HHA survey comparable to HCFA's.

* * *

...The JCAHO Medicare Decision Rules, which establish JCAHO "deemed status" survey procedures, specify that the standard JCAHO Medicare survey will be expanded to a partial extended survey when the conditions of participation are found to be met, but the standard JCAHO Medicare survey indicates further evaluation is needed, usually in a specific area or service not fully addressed in the Medicare standard survey. The Decision Rules recommend that the JCAHO Medicare standard survey be fully extended when one or more of the conditions of participation are not met, or an immediate threat to patient or public health and safety exists within an organization.

* * *

As appropriate, however, we will perform announced and unannounced validation and complaint surveys of HHAs to assure that JCAHO-accredited HHAs that participate in Medicare meet the Medicare conditions of participation. As established in the proposed notice of February 3, 1992, we may withdraw recognition of JCAHO accreditation of HHAs at any time if we determine that JCAHO accreditation does not continue to provide reasonable assurance that Medicare conditions of participation are met.

NOTE

In view of the relationship between JCAHO and the Medicare standards and surveillance procedures reflected in this rule, would you support extension of deemed status for private accreditation in nursing homes? What strategy should a state in its licensure of home health agencies take in response to this acceptance of deemed status? What are the financial implications of the acceptance of deemed status for the Medicare and Medicaid survey and certification programs? For several articles on private accreditation, see Symposium, Private Accreditation in the Regulatory State, 57 Law and Contemporary Problems 1-242 (1994).

CHAPTER 2.   PROFESSIONAL LIABILITY

Insert in note 4, page 143, the following:

Experts in malpractice cases base their testimony on their knowledge, education and experience. They may also rely on outside studies in the research literature. On rare occasions, courts have allowed such research material into evidence in a malpractice suit. In Young v. Horton, 855 P.2d 502 (Mont. 1993), the court allowed into evidence four medical journal articles that had concluded that a majority of patients forget that they gave informed consent to their doctors prior to surgery. The medical expert then testified based both on his experience with informed consent and on the articles' conclusions.

The admissibility of "novel" scientific evidence is often a thorny issue in environmental and toxic tort cases, although rarely in malpractice cases. The Supreme Court, in Daubert v. Merrell Dow Pharmaceuticals, Inc., 113 S.Ct. 2786 (1993), rejected the *Frye* test of "general acceptability" as a threshold test of admissibility of novel scientific evidence. The court held that the Federal Rules of Evidence, particularly Rule 702, make the trial judge the gatekeeper of such evidence, with the responsibility to assess the reliability of an expert's testimony and its relevance. Expert testimony must have a valid scientific connection to the issues in the case, and be based on "scientifically valid principles".

Insert the following new note following note 2 on page 157:

3.   A medical intervention often requires the use of medical products: knee joints, bone graft material, pig heart valves. Breast implant prostheses are a common example of such a service-product intervention. Courts apply strict liability to the distributors of such products but are reluctant to extend strict liability to a health care provider using the product in a way incidental to the primary function of providing medical services. See, e.g., Cafazzo v. Central Medical Health Services, 635 A.2d 151 (Pa. Super. 1993)(mandibular prosthesis); Hoff v. Zimmer, 746 F.Supp 872 (W.D.Wis.1990)(hip prosthesis). But see Bel v. Poplar Bluff Physicians Group, 879 S.W.2d 618 (Mo.Ct.1994) (mandibular implant).

In Porter v. Rosenberg, 650 So.2d 79, 83(Fla.App.1995), the court considered a strict liability claim against the physician for a breast implant. The court rejected strict liability in the case but opened the door slightly to a judicial "essence of the transaction" test for future cases.

> ...we conclude that whether or not a plaintiff may bring an action against a physician, hospital, or other health care provider for strict liability depends upon the essence of the physician-patient relationship for the particular transaction. If the medical services could not have been rendered without utilizing the product, then strict liability does not apply. If the predominant purpose of the physician-patient relationship for that transaction is the provision of medical services based upon the physician's medical judgment, skill, or expertise, the malpractice statute applies and strict liability is inapplicable.

> The fact that the physician or health care provider is not solely or primarily in the business of distributing products is not the determinative factor for application of strict liability as long as distributing products is part of its business.[] Therefore, if distributing products is part of the health care provider's business and the sales or distribution aspect in the particular transaction between the health care provider and the patient predominates over the services aspect an action in strict liability may lie against the health care provider.[72]

The court rejected the action in this case on the grounds that the plaintiff had sued several other defendants from the manufacturers to distributors. "We perceive of no overriding public policy argument which would justify an obvious circumvention of the medical malpractice statute and an extension of strict liability to physicians under the circumstances presented here."

----

[72] Such examples might include a nutrition doctor selling diet products or a dentist selling electric toothbrushes. Some manufacturers may rely solely or mainly on utilizing health care professionals for distribution of their products and the health care professional may rely on selling the product as part of its business as additional profit separate from provision of other medical services.

Insert a new note 5 at page 171:

The AIDS epidemic has given rise to public fears of infection, and the health care setting has not escaped this anxiety. See the *Behringer* case, infra. Patients exposed to providers or blood materials in the health care setting have sued for the negligent infliction of emotional distress, based on their fear of contagion of the HIV virus. Courts have resisted such claims.

In K.A.C. v. Benson, 527 N.W.2d 553 (Minn.1995), the plaintiff sued a physician who had performed two gynecological examinations of her during a period when he suffered from AIDS and had open sores on his hands and forearms as a result of dermatitis. Shortly after the second examination, the Minnesota Department of Health contact 336 patients on whom Dr. Benson had performed one or more invasive procedures while gloved, but while suffering from exudative dermatitis. None of the patients tested HIV positive, but over 50 sued him and the Clinic where he worked. The plaintiff argued that she was in the 'zone of danger' for purposes of a claim of negligent infliction of emotional distress. The court wrote:

> This court has long recognized that a person within the zone of danger of physical impact who reasonably fears for his or her own safety during the time of exposure, and who consequently suffers severe emotional distress with resultant physical injury may recover emotional distress damages whether or not physical impact results.[] However, a remote possibility of personal peril is insufficient to place plaintiff within a zone of danger for purposes of a claim of negligent infliction of emotional distress. Consequently, we hold that a plaintiff who fails to allege actual exposure to HIV is not, as a matter of law, in personal physical danger of contracting HIV, and thus not within a zone of danger for purposes of establishing a claim for negligent infliction of emotional distress. Id at 559

The majority of jurisdictions considering this issue have agreed that the plaintiff allege actual exposure to HIV to recover emotional distress damages. See,e.g., Burk v. Sage Products, Inc., 747 F.Supp. 285 (E.D.Pa. 1990); Ordway v. County of Suffolk, 583 N.Y.S.2d 1014(Sup.Ct.1992); Carroll v. Sisters of St. Francis Health Serv., Inc., 868 S.W.2d 585 (Tenn.1993); Johnson v. West Virginia Univ. Hosp., 413 S.E.2d 889 (W.VA.1991).

Insert a new subsection 3, at p. 203, before section F:

3.   Causal Tests.

Proximate cause instructions continue to be given in most states, often confusing jurors, just as the doctrine has confused generations of law students. Courts worry that jurors will be misled, particularly where multiple sources of causation are involved, including acts or conditions of the plaintiffs. In Peterson v. Gray, 628 A.2d 244 (N.H. 1993), the plaintiff suffered from arthritis in her hand, and the defendant, a hand surgeon, performed a trapexiectomy that later required wrist fusion. The plaintiff's preexisting condition was clearly implicated in the harm that resulted. The court observed that "...if the jury determined that the plaintiff's arthritis was '*a* proximate cause' of her wrist fusion, then the defendant's actions could not possibly have been '*the* proximate cause'". Id at 246. At least one state, California, has rejected instructions on proximate cause as unduly confusing to the jury, adopting instead the "substantial factor" test. In Mitchell v. Gonzales, 819 P.2d 872 (Cal. 1991) the California Supreme Court in effect mandated a jury instruction that asks the jury to determine where the defendant's conduct was a "substantial factor" in bringing about harm, allowing a jury to find against the defendant even if their conduct was only a contributing factor. This "substantial factor" test has been around for 25 years, but the influence of California on tort law evolution is likely to push other states to replace the confusing proximate cause instructions with the "substantial factor" test.

Insert at page 226, at the end of section *a. The Control Test*, the following material:

Hospitals and managed care organizations have expanded utilization review and quality assurance activities, increasing their control over physicians as a result. Judicial application of the "control" test of agency law may further weaken the independent contractor defense that shields hospitals from liability. In Berel v. HCA Health Services of Texas, Inc., 881 S.W.2d 21(Tex.App), plaintiffs consulted Dr. Robinson in her professional capacity as a psychiatrist. She recommended that Kristy and Jake Berel, and Beverly Berel and her children Kelly and Brian, be hospitalized in Houston International Hospital for treatment of alleged emotional disturbances. The plaintiffs claimed that Dr. Robinson, as an agent of the hospital, was negligent in admitting them to the hospital on the basis of insufficient observation; recommending inpatient treatment; and negligently treating them. They further alleged that the hospital was negligent because it should have known of the malpractice committed by its agent, Dr. Robinson, and because it did not properly supervise and regulate her. The hospital moved for summary judgment, in part on the grounds that Dr. Robinson was an independent contractor, and that it had no right to control the details of her medical practice.

The court noted that independent contractor physicians normally transmit no liability to the hospital. But the court's analysis then continued:

> If, however, a hospital retains the right to control the details of the work to be performed by a contracting party, a master-servant relationship exists that will authorize the application of the doctrine of respondeat superior.[] It is the right of control, not actual control, that gives rise to a duty to see that the independent contractor performs his work in a safe manner. * * *

* * *

The plaintiffs rely on Dr. Robinson's deposition testimony. She testified that the hospital's staff included a "quality assurance person" who "reviewed charts to ... assure appropriate patient care." The plaintiffs' trial counsel asked Dr. Robinson additional questions regarding the quality assurance person: Q. If that quality assurance person felt like that there had been an over utilization or an under utilization, what would they do? A. As far as I can recall that person would discuss that with the doctor and also would--would write those recommendations up in a particular form as--as best of my recall and we present that to the particular doctor who's treating the patient and could also possibly--feeling that needed further information or clarification or whatever--talk with the medical director and also possibly the medical director of the--of the hospital and also possibly the utilization review

46

committee. Q. Could the utilization review committee and the medical director of the hospital override the admitting physician's orders? A. Yes. Q. Okay. Did the utilization review committee and the medical director have authority to discharge a patient that they thought was--had been admitted or did not need the services of Houston International Hospital? A. The medical director of the utilization review committee as far as my recall, there were appropriate procedures if they felt that the patient was not being administered appropriate treatment and needed--needed to--which would be if the patient did not need to be there, they could have overruled the admitting physician's order. Q. And have the patient discharged? A. If that was what was indicated that was needed.

We agree with the plaintiffs that Dr. Robinson's own testimony raises a fact question regarding whether the hospital maintained control over Dr. Robinson's treatment to a degree that would make the hospital liable for her negligent acts. We sustain this point of error.

Insert at the end of note 4, p. 247, the following paragraph:

Hospitals have the responsibility to ensure that a patient's informed consent is obtained in two limited areas: documentation of patient consent for the record, and experimental therapies. If a nurse fails to obtain a properly executed consent form and make it part of the patient record, the hospital may be liable for this failure as a violation of its own internal procedures. See, e.g., Butler v. South Fulton Medical Center, Inc., 452 S.E. 2d 768, 772 (Ga.App.1994). If a hospital participates in a study of an experimental procedure, it must ensure that the patient is properly informed of the risks of the procedure. See Kus v. Sherman Hospital, 644 N.E.2d 1214(1995)(hospital was part of a research study on intraocular lens implantation; the court held that "...a hospital, as well as a physician, may be held liable for a patient's defective consent in a case involving experimental intraocular lenses...")

CHAPTER 3. THE RELATIONSHIP OF PROVIDER AND PATIENT

Insert at the end of note 1, p. 292, the following paragraph:

Courts continue to follow *Tunkl*'s analysis, rejecting exculpatory agreements signed by patients. See, e.g., Cudnik v. Beaumont Hospital, 525 N.W.2d 891 (Mich.App.1994)(patient receiving radiation therapy for prostate cancer signed agreement; court held it to be "invalid and unenforceable as against public policy."); Ash v. New York Univ. Dental Center, 564 N.Y.S.2d. 308(1990). The only exception courts find acceptable is an exculpatory agreement for treatments involving experimental procedures as the patient's last hope for survival. See Colton v. New York Hospital, 414 N.Y.S.2d 866 (1979).

Insert the following paragraphs at the end of note 1, pages 315 - 316:

The courts impose on treating physicians a duty to inform patients or warn third parties when deadly illnesses such as AIDS or highly contagious ones such as hepatitis are involved. In Reisner v. Regents of the University of California, 37 Cal.Rptr. 2d 518 (Cal.App.1995), the patient of Dr. Fonklesrud, 12-year old Jennifer Lawson, received a transfusion contaminated with HIV antibodies during surgery. Dr. Fonkelsrud learned of the contamination, continued to treat Jennifer but never told her or her parents about the tainted blood. Three years later, she started to date Daniel Reisner and they had sexual relations. Two years later, the doctor finally told Jennifer she had AIDS and Jennifer told Daniel. Jennifer died a month later. Daniel then learned he was HIV positive.

The defendants argued they owed no duty to Daniel, who was an unidentified third party at the time Jennifer was infected with HIV. The court cited *Tarasoff* and other cases that had imposed a duty to warn either the patient or third parties about risks, holding that the defendants had a duty to warn a contagious patient to take steps to protect others.

One the physician warns the patient of the risk to others and advises the patient how to prevent the spread of the disease, the physician has fulfilled his duty -- and no more (but no less) is required....

...We need not decide in this case what the result would be if someone infected by Daniel sued the doctor who failed to warn Jennifer, and the fact that a duty is owed to Daniel does not mean it will be extended without limitation. However, the possibility of such an extension does not offend us, legally or morally. Viewed in the abstract...we believe that a doctor who knows he is dealing with the 20th Century version of Typhoid Mary ought to have a very strong incentive to tell his patient what she ought to do and not do and how she ought to comport herself in order to prevent the spread of her disease.

In DiMarco v. Lynch Homes--Chester County, 583 A.2d 422 (Pa.Sup.1990), the sexual partner of a patient sued her physicians, who had assured her that she would not contract hepatitis. The plaintiff Janet Viscichini, a blood technician, went to the Lynch Home to take a blood sample from one of the residents. During the procedure, her skin was accidentally punctured by the needle she had used to extract blood. When she learned that the patient had hepatitis, she sought treatment from Doctors Giunta and Alwine. They told her that if she remained symptom free for six weeks, she would not be infected by the hepatitis virus. She was not told to refrain from sexual relations for any period of time following her exposure to the disease, but she practiced sexual abstinence until eight weeks after the exposure. Since she had remained symptom-free during that time, she then resumed sexual relations with the plaintiff. She was later diagnosed as suffering from hepatitis B in September; in December, the plaintiff was similarly diagnosed.

The court cited Restatement (Second) Torts, s. 324A, which provided in part that one who provides services to another may be liable to a third person for harm resulting from his failure to exercise reasonable care, if the "the harm is suffered because of reliance of the other or the third person upon the undertaking." The court allowed the action, concluding that the class of persons at risk included any one who is physically intimate with the patient.

When a physician treats a patient who has been exposed to or who has contracted a communicable and/or contagious disease, it is imperative that the physician give his or her patient the proper advice about preventing the spread of the disease. ...Physicians are the first line of defense against the spread of communicable diseases, because physicians know what measures must be taken to prevent the infection of others.

Insert, at page 317, after Problem: The Stubborn Patient, the following materials:

BRADSHAW V. DANIEL
854 S.W.2d 865
Supreme Court of Tennessee, 1993

Anderson, J.

We granted this appeal to determine whether a physician has a legal duty to warn a non-patient of the risk of exposure to the source of his patient's non-contagious disease--Rocky Mountain Spotted Fever. The trial court denied the defendant physician's motion for summary judgment, but granted an interlocutory appeal on the issue of the physician's legal duty. The Court of Appeals limited the record and held that the facts were insufficient to show that the risk to the non-patient of contracting Rocky Mountain Spotted Fever was such that a legal duty arose on the part of the physician. We disagree and conclude, for the reasons stated herein, that the physician had a legal duty to warn the non-patient of the risk of exposure to the source of the patient's non-contagious disease.

BACKGROUND

On July 19, 1986, Elmer Johns went to the emergency room at Methodist Hospital South in Memphis, Tennessee, complaining of headaches, muscle aches, fever, and chills. He was admitted to the hospital under the care and treatment of the defendant, Dr. Chalmers B. Daniel, Jr. Dr. Daniel first saw Johns on July 22, 1986, at which time he ordered the drug Chloramphenicol, which is the drug of choice for a person in the latter stages of Rocky Mountain Spotted Fever. Johns' condition rapidly deteriorated, and he died the next day, July 23, 1986. An autopsy was performed, and the Center for Disease Control in Atlanta conclusively confirmed, in late September 1986, that the cause of death was Rocky Mountain Spotted fever. Although Dr. Daniel communicated with Elmer Johns' wife, Genevieve, during Johns' treatment, he never advised her of the risks of exposure to Rocky Mountain Spotted Fever, or that the disease could have been the cause of Johns' death.

A week after her husband's death, on August 1, 1986, Genevieve Johns came to the emergency room of Baptist Memorial Hospital in Memphis, Tennessee, with similar symptoms of chills, fever, mental disorientation, nausea, lung congestion, myalgia, and swelling of the hands. She was admitted to the hospital and treated for Rocky Mountain Spotted Fever, but she died three days later, on August 4, 1986, of that disease. It is undisputed that no patient- physician relationship existed between Genevieve Johns and Dr. Daniel.

The plaintiff, William Jerome Bradshaw, is Genevieve Johns' son. He filed this suit alleging that the defendant's negligence in failing to advise Genevieve Johns that her husband died of Rocky Mountain Spotted Fever, and in failing to warn her of the risk of exposure, proximately caused her death. The defendant filed a motion to dismiss for failure to state a cause of action on the grounds that the physician owed Genevieve Johns no legal duty because of the absence of a patient-physician relationship. The trial judge denied the motion.

Later, the defendant filed a motion for summary judgment on the same grounds, supported by the affidavit of Dr. Michael S. Gelfand. Dr. Gelfand testified that the medical standard of care did not require a physician treating a patient infected with, or suspected of being infected with, Rocky Mountain Spotted Fever to treat the family of the patient in contact with him, or to warn them of the risk of exposure to the disease or the risk of exposure to ticks or tick bites. The plaintiff responded with the affidavit of Dr. Burt Prater. Dr. Prater testified that because of the clustering effect of the disease, the medical standard of care required that a physician treating a patient with symptoms of Rocky Mountain Spotted Fever advise the family of the patient as to the incubation period, the symptoms of the disease, and the need for immediate medical attention upon manifestation of the symptoms. Dr. Prater further testified that the defendant, Dr. Daniel, negligently failed to diagnose Elmer Johns' fatal disease of Rocky Mountain Spotted Fever and failed to warn his wife, Genevieve Johns, of the incubation period of the disease, the symptoms, and the need to seek medical treatment upon manifestation of the symptoms. He also testified that the disease, if untreated, has a 40 percent mortality rate, but if treated promptly, has a 4 percent mortality rate. Based on the affidavits, the defendant's motion for summary judgment was denied.

The case was then transferred to another judge and tried before a jury, which returned a verdict of $50,000 against the defendant.

Thereafter, the plaintiff filed a motion for a new trial or additur on the grounds of inadequate damages, and the defendant filed a motion notwithstanding the verdict on the grounds, among others, that no legal duty existed. The plaintiff's motion for a new trial was granted, and the defendant's motion was overruled.

* * *

The Court of Appeals refused to consider the defendant's trial testimony in its determination of the substantive issue of legal duty. The intermediate court then granted the motion for summary judgment, concluding that the record did not contain sufficient facts to establish a risk to Genevieve Johns which would give rise to a legal duty. We granted the plaintiff's application for permission to appeal and now reverse for the reasons set out herein.

RECORD ON APPEAL

In this case, the trial judge ruled that the defendant's testimony at the first trial was properly includable in the record on appeal. The defendant, Dr. Daniel, testified at trial that he did not see his patient, Elmer Johns, for the first three days he was hospitalized, but communicated with another physician about him. On the fourth day of his hospitalization, Dr. Daniel examined him, recognized that Rocky Mountain Spotted Fever could be one of the causes of his symptoms, and prescribed a strong drug with significant side effects--which was the drug of choice for Rocky Mountain Spotted Fever victims. He also testified that although he was in communication with Genevieve Johns, he did not warn her that Rocky Mountain Spotted Fever could be causing her husband's symptoms, nor did he advise her of the incubation period, the need to be on the lookout for similar symptoms, and the need to seek immediate treatment if such symptoms occurred. Dr. Daniel conceded that there is a medical, but not a legal, duty to educate the family and provide information when a patient is diagnosed as having Rocky Mountain Spotted Fever. The Court of Appeals refused to consider this testimony, opining that since it was not transcribed at the time of the hearing on the motion, it was not before the trial judge when he ruled on the motion.

* * *

LEGAL DUTY

The defendant physician argues that he owed his patient's wife no legal duty because first, there was no physician-patient relationship, and second, Rocky Mountain Spotted Fever is not a contagious disease and, therefore, there is no duty to warn of the risk of exposure.

* * *

The defendant contends that the absence of a physician- patient relationship negates the existence of a duty in this case. While it is true that a physician-patient relationship is necessary to the maintenance of a medical malpractice action, it is not necessary for the maintenance of an action based on negligence, and this Court has specifically recognized that a physician may owe a duty to a non-patient third party for injuries caused by the physician's negligence, if the injuries suffered and the manner in which they occurred were reasonably foreseeable.[ ]

Here, we are asked to determine whether a physician has an affirmative duty to warn a patient's family member about the symptoms and risks of exposure to Rocky Mountain Spotted Fever, a non-contagious disease. Insofar as we are able to determine, there is no reported decision from this or any other jurisdiction involving circumstances exactly similar to those presented in this case.

We begin by observing that all persons have a duty to use reasonable care to refrain from conduct that will foreseeably cause injury to others.[ ]

In determining the existence of a duty, courts have distinguished between action and inaction. Professor Prosser has commented that "the reason for the distinction may be said to lie in the fact that by 'misfeasance' the defendant has created a new risk of harm to the plaintiff, while by 'nonfeasance' he has at least made his situation no worse, and has merely failed to benefit him by interfering in his affairs." [ ].

Because of this reluctance to countenance nonfeasance as a basis of liability, as a general rule, under the common law, one person owed no affirmative duty to warn those endangered by the conduct of another.[ ].

To mitigate the harshness of this rule, courts have carved out exceptions for cases in which the defendant stands in some special relationship to either the person who is the source of the danger, or to the person who is foreseeably at risk from the danger.[ ] Accordingly, while an actor is always bound to prevent his acts from creating an unreasonable risk to others, he is under the affirmative duty to act to prevent another from sustaining harm only when certain socially recognized relations exist which constitute the basis for such legal duty. [ ].

One of the most widely known cases applying that principle is *Tarasoff*, supra, in which the California Supreme Court held that when a psychotherapist determines or, pursuant to the standards of his profession, should determine that his patient presents a serious danger of violence to another, the therapist has an affirmative duty to use reasonable care to protect the intended victim against such danger, and the duty may require the physician to warn the intended victim of the danger.[ ] The special relationship of the patient to his psychotherapist supported imposition of the affirmative duty to act for the benefit of third persons.[ ]

Decisions of other jurisdictions have employed the same analysis and held that the relationship of a physician to his patient is sufficient to support the duty to exercise reasonable care to protect third persons against foreseeable risks emanating from a patient's physical illness. Specifically, other courts have recognized that physicians may be liable to persons infected by a patient, if the physician negligently fails to diagnose a contagious disease, or having diagnosed the illness, fails to warn family members or others who are foreseeably at risk of exposure to the disease.[ ]

* * *

Returning to the facts of this case, first, it is undisputed that there was a physician-patient relationship between Dr. Daniel and Elmer Johns. Second, here, as in the contagious disease context, it is also undisputed that Elmer Johns' wife, who was residing with him, was at risk of contracting the disease. This is so even though the disease is not contagious in the narrow sense that it can be transmitted from one person to another. Both Dr. Daniel and Dr. Prater, the plaintiff's expert, testified that family members of patients suffering from Rocky Mountain Spotted Fever are at risk of contracting the disease due to a phenomenon called clustering, which is related to the activity of infected ticks who transmit the disease to humans. Dr. Prater also testified that Dr. Daniel negligently failed to diagnose the disease and negligently failed to warn his patient's wife, Genevieve Johns, of her risk of exposure to the source of disease. Dr. Daniel's expert disputed these conclusions, but Dr. Daniel conceded there is a medical duty to inform the family when there is a diagnosis of the disease. Thus, this case is analogous to the Tarasoff line of cases adopting a duty to warn of danger and the contagious disease cases adopting a comparable duty to warn. Here, as in those cases, there was a foreseeable risk of harm to an identifiable third party, and the reasons supporting the recognition of the duty to warn are equally compelling here.

We, therefore, conclude that the existence of the physician- patient relationship is sufficient to impose upon a physician an affirmative duty to warn identifiable third persons in the patient's immediate family against foreseeable risks emanating from a patient's illness. Accordingly, we hold that under the factual circumstances of this case, viewing the evidence in a light most favorable to the plaintiff, the defendant physician had a duty to warn his patient's wife of the risk to her of contracting Rocky Mountain Spotted Fever, when he knew, or in the exercise of reasonable care, should have known, that his patient was suffering from the disease. Our holding here is necessarily limited to the conclusion that the defendant physician owed Genevieve Johns a legal duty. We express no opinion on the other elements which would be required to establish a cause of action for common-law negligence in this case.

Accordingly, the judgment of the Court of Appeals granting the defendant's motion for summary judgment is reversed, and this cause is remanded to the trial court for proceedings consistent with this opinion. The costs of this appeal are taxed against the defendant.

PROBLEM: THE TOUR BUS

A physician, Dr. Vivian Hayes, has been treating a patient, Steven Moore, who just returned from a bus tour of Germany. He has a illness caused by the bite of a small tick found on deer in the Black Forest of Germany. Dr. Hayes has successfully treated the illness. Moore took a bus tour of Germany and the Black Forest with a group put together by a travel agency, Rathskeller Travel, which declared bankruptcy shortly after the trip was over. What further obligations does Dr. Hayes have? Should she notify the state division of public health? The tour members were from fifty states. Should she call everyone on the roster of the tour, since only she has the ability to warn? What would you advise today, if *Bradshaw* were the law of your state?

BEHRINGER v. THE MEDICAL CENTER AT PRINCETON
249 N.J.Super. 597, 592 A.2d 1251
Superior Court of New Jersey, 1991.

* * *

I.

A.

[The plaintiff, a board-certified ENT surgeon, had a successful medical practice in the Princeton area, which he had developed over a decade, extending beyond ear, nose and throat surgery to include facial plastic surgery. He was an attending physician at the Medical Center and had performed surgery at the medical center since 1981. In June of 1987 he became ill. He was treated in the medical center emergency room, and a bronchoscopy was performed to determine if he had PCP, which was an indicator of AIDS. The information about his AIDS status spread rapidly, and plaintiff received many phone calls from friends and colleagues. His patients also began to cancel their appointments, and most of his office staff quit. The plaintiff continued his office practice until his death in 1989.]

[The court held that (1) the failure of the hospital and its laboratory director to take reasonable steps to maintain confidentiality of AIDS-infected surgeon's medical records was a breach of their duty to keep patient records confidential; (2) the relationship between the hospital and the surgeon with surgical privileges was sufficient to bring the surgeon within scope of New Jersey law against discrimination's protection;   (3) the hospital acted properly in initially suspending surgeon's surgical privileges, thereafter imposing a requirement of informed consent, and ultimately barring surgeon from performing surgery.]

B.

[The court first considered the medical center's handling of the plaintiff's condition, and his loss of staff privileges.]

The medical center's reaction to plaintiff's condition was swift and initially precise. Upon learning of plaintiff's diagnosis from the chief of nursing, the president of the medical center, defendant Dennis Doody (Doody), immediately directed the cancellation of plaintiff's pending surgical cases. This initial decision was made with little information or knowledge of potential transmission of the disease; thereafter, the chairman of the department of surgery, having privately researched the issue, reached a contrary result and urged that plaintiff could resume his surgical practice. The medical center procedure for suspending a physician's surgical privileges provides for summary suspension by a vote of the department chair, president of the medical center, president of the medical and dental staff, chairman of the board of trustees, and the physician in charge of the service. While Doody was defeated in a vote for summary suspension, the surgery remained cancelled, and the matter was ultimately brought before the board of trustees.

Doody's motivation in seeking the suspension of surgical privileges was described as one of concern for patients but also, and perhaps more important, concern for the medical center and its potential liability. Little was known about the dilemma now facing the medical center. In any event, plaintiff's surgical privileges were cancelled and would never, during plaintiff's life, be reinstated.

During the ensuing months, the medical center embarked on a torturous journey which shifted course as views were explored and, ultimately, a consensus reached between the medical and dental staff, hospital administration and the board of trustees.

On July 2, 1987, plaintiff privately informed the chairman of the department of surgery at the medical center of his medical condition. Plaintiff felt that the chairman of his department should know of his health status and informed the chair that plaintiff wished to continue to practice, including performing surgery.

[The executive committee of the medical and dental staff then held a series of meetings to discuss policies for HIV-positive staff. The committee concluded that a surgeon with AIDS should retain his privileges and not be required to disclose his status to patients. At a full meeting of the board of trustees, the board decided to require a special informed consent form for patients about to undergo surgery by HIV-positive surgeons, which explained the risks of transmission of the HIV virus.

The staff ultimately recommended that a physician or other provider with HIV positivity could continue to treat patients, but not procedures that pose "any risk of virus transmission to the patient." The requirement that an HIV-positive surgeon obtain a patient's informed consent, using the special form, was continued.]

* * *

Plaintiff's privileges, as a "potential risk," were ultimately suspended under this policy, and no action was taken by him challenging the policy or seeking recredentialling under the policy.

Following his diagnosis of AIDS, plaintiff never again performed surgery at the medical center.

C.

[The court next considered the efforts by the medical center to protect patient confidentiality after a finding of HIV positivity.]

D.

Plaintiff was diagnosed in June 1987 as having AIDS as a result of the positive HIV blood test and the diagnosis of PCP.

The expert testimony presented by both plaintiff and defendants, while differing significantly as to conclusion, was consistent as to the scientific underpinnings upon which their conclusions about HIV positively and AIDS were based.

*   *   *

In his analysis of the issues, Selwyn [the plaintiff's medical expert] utilized scientifically accepted information, statistics and health-care facility reactions to the treatment of hepatitis B virus and transmission between patient and HCW.

Hepatitis B, the virus that causes hepatitis, is a blood borne infectious disease transmitted through similar routes as HIV. Selwyn noted that the estimated rate of death among HCWs who contract hepatitis B, which develops into chronic disease in approximately six to ten percent of those cases, is higher than any estimates of HCWs occupationally infected with HIV.

In addition, he stated that for both hepatitis B and HIV, the risk of an HCW transmitting the virus to a patient is substantially less than the risk of a patient transmitting the virus to an HCW. Moreover, the risk of transmission of HIV from an HCW to a patient is even lower than the risk of an HCW transmitting hepatitis B to a patient. The recorded estimates of hepatitis B transmission from physicians to patients have all been based on anecdotal reports and are essentially reduced to situations where breaches in medical technique, such as a dentist's failure to wear gloves, were associated with increased likelihood of blood-to-blood contact. Where such breaches did occur and then precautions were instituted and studied, transmission of hepatitis B did not occur again. The medical center's epidemiologist agreed with Selwyn on this issue. The epidemiologist informed the medical and dental staff and Doody that change in technique would affect the risks of such transmissions.

Hepatitis B is less likely to be fatal but is more readily transmitted than HIV. Selwyn estimated that statistically the risk of death from exposure to a surgeon with HIV would be about the same as that from exposure to a surgeon with hepatitis B. Of critical importance, however, is that of the transmitted diseases, if the HIV infection develops into AIDS, fatality is certain.

While Selwyn noted the similarities between HIV and hepatitis B transmission, he indicated that there were no restrictions placed on hepatitis B-positive doctors performing invasive procedures; however, the record is absent any facts indicating any cases of hepatitis B-positive doctors performing any invasive procedure at the medical center. In this regard, Selwyn did note that such matters as surgeon's wound infection rates or a history of substance abuse would be critical to a patient's knowledge of the risks attendant to a surgical procedure, but no informed consent requirements have been imposed on physicians anywhere which require the physician to inform patients of such risks.

Selwyn observed that even assuming that an HIV-positive physician nicked a finger during surgery and a drop of the physician's blood fell into the patient, the risk of that patient contracting HIV is less than one-half of one percent. Selwyn explained that the actual risk of ultimate transmission is diluted by the probability of a series of events happening, all of which would be necessary before exposure occurs. Whether an injury occurs, whether it occurs within range of the patient's blood, whether the surgeon's blood makes its way out from beneath two layers of gloves, and whether there is then a transmission of the surgeon's blood into the patient's blood, are all independent events that geometrically reduce the chance of blood-to-blood contact. This reduces the less than one-half of one percent chance of infection associated with contact. Day conceded that the chance of all these events occurring in a procedure was .0025%. Selwyn added that the risk factor was affected by the nature of the surgery performed, e.g., orthopedic surgeons or gynecological surgeons operating in some areas by "feel" bear a higher risk of accident than do surgeons such as ENT specialists.

Selwyn's conclusion that the risk of transmission of HIV from an HIV-positive surgeon to a patient is remote was an accepted premise in 1987 at the time defendants learned plaintiff had AIDS.

. . .

[The defendant's expert, Dr. Day, testified as to a practitioner's concerns about AIDS, and the risks of needle-sticks.]

. . .

II.

Any examination of the legal issues in this matter requires an understanding of AIDS and HIV. [The court here discusses the nature of AIDS, the disease processes it sets in motion, and the magnitude of the public health risk.]

III.

[In section III of the court's opinion, the court discusses the medical center's duty of confidentiality in failing to restrict access to plaintiff's medical records. The court holds that "the failure of the medical center and [its director] to take reasonable steps to maintain the confidentiality of plaintiff's medical records, while plaintiff was a patient, was a breach of the medical center's duty and obligation to keep such records confidential."]

IV.

[The court discusses the plaintiff's action under New Jersey discrimination law.]

. . .

The ultimate resolution reached by the medical center restricting invasive procedures where there is "any risk to the patient," coupled with informed consent, implicates serious policy considerations which must be explored. It is axiomatic that physicians performing invasive procedures should not knowingly place a patient at risk because of the physician's physical condition.[] The policy adopted by the medical center barring "any procedures that pose any risk of virus transmission to the patient" appears to preclude, on its face, the necessity of an informed consent form; if there is "any risk," the procedure cannot be performed. The problem created by the "any risk" standard is best evidenced by the facts of this case.... [] This court, too, must be concerned that the medical center decision-makers, while no doubt acting in good faith in the decision-making process, are acting with the knowledge that their decisions may well affect their ultimate ability to practice their chosen profession. Nevertheless, there must be a way to free physicians, in the pursuit of their healing vocation, from possible contamination by self-interest or self- protection concerns which would inhibit their independent medical judgments for the well-being of their...patients. [] There are principles of law that guard against the concern for self-interest, by including in the decision-making process the most critical participant--the patient. The doctrine of informed consent, as an adjunct to the adopted medical center "any risk" policy, provides the necessary element of patient control which is lacking from the policy standing alone.

Before a physician may perform a surgical or invasive procedure upon a patient, he must obtain the patient's informed consent. [Informed consent] is essentially a negligence concept, predicated on the duty of a physician to disclose to a patient such information as will enable the

61

patient to make an evaluation of the nature of the treatment and of any attendant substantial risks, as well as of available options in the form of alternative therapies. [] The physician exposing the patient to a course of treatment has a duty to explain, in terms understandable to the patient, what the physician proposes to do. The purpose of this legal requirement is to protect each person's right to self-determination in matters of medical treatment.[] The physician's duty is to explain, in words the patient can understand, that medical information and those risks which are material. Medical information or a risk of a medical procedure is material when a reasonable patient would be likely to attach significance to it in deciding whether or not to submit to the treatment.

Taking into account what the physician knows or should know to be the patient's informational needs, the physician must make reasonable disclosure of the information and those risks which a reasonably prudent patient would consider material or significant in making the decision about what course of treatment, if any, to accept. Such information would generally include a description of the patient's physical condition, the purposes and advantages of the proposed surgery, the material risks of the proposed surgery, and the material risks if such surgery is not provided. In addition, the physician should discuss all available options or alternatives and their advantages and risks.[]

Plaintiff argues: 1) the risk of transmission of HIV from surgeon to patient is too remote to require informed consent, and 2) the law of informed consent does not require disclosure of the condition of the surgeon.

Both parties focus on the risk of transmission and results therefrom in applying the two standards raised in plaintiff's claim under the LAD. The *Jansen* standard states that the risk must be one which will create a "reasonable probability of substantial harm," and the *Largey* standard requires disclosure of a "material risk" or one to which a reasonable patient would likely attach significance in determining whether to proceed with the proposed procedure. It is the court's view that the risk of transmission is not the sole risk involved. The risk of a surgical accident, i.e., a needlestick or scalpel cut, during surgery performed by an HIV-positive surgeon, may subject a previously uninfected patient to months or even years of continual HIV testing. Both of these risks are sufficient to meet the *Jansen* standard of "probability of harm" and the *Largey* standard requiring disclosure.

Both Selwyn and Day agreed that the statistical risk of transmission from health-care worker to patient is small--less than one-half of one percent. At the time of trial, there were no reported cases of transmission.[] But the statistical analysis is flawed. [The court notes that sixteen cases so far have involved health care workers who seroconverted from occupational exposure to HIV.]

Physicians performing seriously invasive procedures, such as surgeons, have a potential to cut or puncture their skin with sharp surgical instruments, needles, or bone fragments. Studies indicate that a surgeon will cut a glove in approximately one out of every four cases, and probably sustain a significant skin cut in one out of every forty cases. Given these data, it has been calculated that the risk of contracting HIV in a single surgical operation on an HIV-infected patient is remote--in the range of 1/130,000 to 1/4,500. [footnotes omitted] It is impossible accurately to calculate the level of risk of HIV transmission from surgeon to patient. Surgeons who cut or puncture themselves do not necessarily expose the patient to their blood, and even if they do the volume is extremely small. A small inoculum of contaminated blood is unlikely to transmit the virus. This suggests that the risk of infection from surgeon to patient is much lower than in the opposite direction. Nonetheless, the fact that the surgeon is in significant contact with the patient's blood and organs, together with the high rate of torn gloves, makes it reasonable to assume that the risk runs in both directions, as is the case with the hepatitis B virus. The cumulative risk to surgical patients, arguably, is higher. While an HIV-infected patient is likely to have relatively few seriously invasive procedures, the infected surgeon, even if the virus drastically shortens his surgical career, can be expected to perform numerous operations. Assuming that the surgical patient's risk is exceedingly low (1/130,000), the risk that one of his patients will contract HIV becomes more realistic the more operations he performs--1/1,300 (assuming 100 operations) or 1/126 (assuming 500 operations). Patients, of course, cannot expect a wholly risk-free environment in a hospital. But there does come a point where the risk of a detrimental outcome becomes sufficiently real that it is prudent for the profession to establish guidelines. []

While the debate will rage long into the future as to the quantifiable risk of HIV transmission from doctor to patient, there is little disagreement that a risk of transmission, however small, does exist. This risk may be reduced by the use of universal precautions, such as double gloving and the use of goggles and other similar devices.

In quantifying the risk, one must consider not only statistical data, but the nature of the procedure being performed. Plaintiff was a surgeon who specialized in surgery performed in the ear and mouth cavities. As Day indicated, much of plaintiff's surgery involved contact with the mucous membrane--an area particularly susceptible to transmission of HIV should the surgeon incur a surgical accident involving the potential for exchange of blood.

In addition, the quantifiable risk of transmission is not dispositive of either the "materiality" or "risk of harm" issue. As Day testified, the risk of a surgical accident, such as a scalpel cut or needle stick, where there is exposure to the HIV-positive surgeon's blood will cause a patient to be exposed to the testing required by CDC recommendation no. 5, supra, notes 7 and 8. This includes HIV testing over an extended period with the attendant anxiety of waiting for test results, and the possible alterations to life style and child-bearing during the testing period, even if those results ultimately are negative. The risk of surgical accidents was quantified by Day and Selwyn as exceeding five percent, although, as set forth above, Gostin estimates glove cuts at 25% and significant skin cuts at 2 1/2 percent.[] In assessing the "materiality of risk," this court concludes that the risk of accident and implications thereof would be a legitimate concern to the surgical patient, warranting disclosure of this risk in the informed-consent setting. It is inconsistent with the underlying policy considerations expressed in *Largey* to suggest that the patient should be informed after the fact of the need for HIV testing and surveillance.

In balancing quantifiable risk with the necessity of informed consent, one must recognize the strong commitment of the New Jersey courts to the concept of a fully informed patient.[] Plaintiff argues that the use of the informed consent form is tantamount to a de facto termination of surgical privileges. Plaintiff further urges that patient reaction is likely to be based more on public hysteria than on a studied assessment of the actual risk involved. The answer to these arguments is two-fold. First, it is the duty of the surgeon utilizing the informed consent procedure to explain to the patient the real risk involved. If the patient's fear is without basis, it is likewise the duty of the surgeon to allay that fear. This court recognizes that the burden imposed on the surgeon may not be surmountable absent further education of both the public and the medical community about the realities of HIV and AIDS. Second, the difficulties created by the public reaction to AIDS cannot deprive the patient of making the ultimate decision where the ultimate risk is so significant. The last word has not been spoken on the issue of transmission of HIV and AIDS. Facts accepted at one point in time are no longer accurate as more is learned about this disease and its transmission. []

Plaintiff further argues that there is no requirement under the doctrine of informed consent that a surgeon's physical condition be revealed as a risk of the surgery itself. The informed consent cases are not so narrow as to support that argument. In Largey v. Rothman, supra, the court spoke of not only an evaluation of the nature of the treatment, but of "any attendant substantial risks."[73] [] As noted earlier, the risks can foreseeably include a needlestick or scalpel cut and, even with universal precautions can result in an exchange of the surgeon's blood.

Plaintiff urges that these issues should be dealt with on a case-by-case basis, wherein the hospital or medical staff monitors an HIV-positive surgeon and makes a determination as to the surgeon's ability to perform a particular invasive procedure. While this approach may be an appropriate starting point, it can not be dispositive of the issue. Plaintiff's position fails to account for "any risk" and, more important, fails to consider the patient's input into the decision-making process. The position plaintiff seeks to implement is replete with the "anachronistic paternalism" rejected in both Canterbury v. Spence, supra, and by the Supreme Court in Largey v. Rothman, supra.

---

[73] In addition to the concept of "risk" as a relevant factor in the area of informed consent, the "duty to warn" imposed on a physician provides additional support to conclude that an HIV-positive surgeon is required to inform a patient of his HIV positivity before performing an invasive procedure. The physician's "duty to warn" third parties of dangers created by the physician's patients is recognized in New Jersey. [] So too, physicians have a duty to report to the department of health infectious diseases, N.J.S.A. 26:4-15, including PCP, N.J.A.C. 8:57-1.2. It has been strongly urged that this "duty to warn" extends to third parties associated with AIDS victims.... If a physician has a duty to warn third parties of the HIV status of patients who may be, for example, sexual partners of the patient, it could legitimately be argued that the risk of transmission would similarly require the surgeon to warn his own patients.

Plaintiff's assertion that the risk of transmission is so low as to preclude the necessity of restriction on surgical practice or a requirement of informed consent prompts perhaps a different view of the issue. Dr. Gordon G. Keyes suggests: Instead of anguishing over the precise probability of an HIV-positive provider spreading AIDS to a patient, a more sensible approach weighs the risk posed by HIV-positive provider against the value of having these same providers performing invasive health-care services. [Keyes, "Health Care Professionals with AIDS: The Risk of Transmission Balanced Against the Interests of Professionals and Institutions," 16 Journal of College and University Law 589, 603 (1990). Keyes bases his analysis on the Restatement, Torts 2d, s 293(a)-(c) (1965), and its three-factor test. The factors include the social value which the law attaches to the interest which is to be advanced or protected by the conduct; the extent of the chance that this interest will be advanced or protected by the particular course of conduct; and the extent of the chance that such interest can be adequately advanced or protected by another and less dangerous course of conduct.]

Summarizing Keyes' broader policy considerations, the restrictions on HIV- positive physicians from providing services, where there is a chance of transmittal from injury and transfer of blood spillage into a surgical site, would have a limited effect on practitioners; the HIV-positive physicians could still practice medicine although precluded from performing invasive procedures. Lastly, the ethical relationship of doctor to patient would require such a restriction on invasive procedures. Health-care providers and institutions should consider ethical aspects of the doctor-patient relationship in examining the risk posed by health-care providers infected with HIV. The patient and doctor occupy unequal positions in the relationship. The doctor is trained to recognize, diagnose, and avoid contracting the patient's disease. The doctor stands in a position of trust--a fiduciary position--in relation to the patient. A small but palpable risk of transmitting a lethal disease to the patient gives the doctor an ethical responsibility to perform only procedures that pose no risk of transmission. The patient, on the other hand, has no corresponding ethical duty to the doctor. The patient is neither trained nor expected to ascertain the provider's health status. While secretive patients may transmit their diseases to unwary doctors, doctors are responsible for both their own health and the health of their patients. []

. . .

The obligation of a surgeon performing invasive procedures, such as plaintiff, to reveal his AIDS condition, is one which requires a weighing of plaintiff's rights against the patient's rights. New Jersey's strong policy supporting patient rights, weighed against plaintiff's individual right to perform an invasive procedure as a part of the practice of his profession, requires the conclusion that the patient's rights must prevail. At a minimum, the physician must withdraw from performing any invasive procedure which would pose a risk to the patient. Where the ultimate harm is death, even the presence of a low risk of transmission justifies the adoption of a policy which precludes invasive procedures when there is "any" risk of transmission. In the present case, the debate raged as to whether there was "any" risk of transmission, and the informed-consent procedure was left in place. If there is to be an ultimate arbiter of whether the patient is to be treated invasively by an AIDS-positive surgeon, the arbiter will be the fully-informed patient. The ultimate risk to the patient is so absolute--so devastating--that it is untenable to argue against informed consent combined with a restriction on procedures which present "any risk" to the patient.[74]

In assessing the medical center's obligation under the LAD, it is the court's view that the burden under *Jansen* has been met, and there was a "reasonable probability of substantial harm" if plaintiff continued to perform invasive procedures. Plaintiff is not entitled to recovery under this statute. The medical center acted properly in initially suspending plaintiff's surgical privileges, thereafter imposing a requirement of informed consent and ultimately barring him from performing surgery. These decisions were not made spontaneously or without thought. One need only review the minutes of meeting after meeting where the debate raged and the various competing interests--the medical and dental staff and board--expressed their views. The seeking of input from medical ethicists and attorneys knowledgeable in this area belies any suggestion of prejudgment or arbitrariness on the part of the medical center. The

---

[74] While the chances of a patient acquiring HIV from an infected provider are small, infected patients have transmitted HIV to a dentist and other health-care providers when small or inapparent quantities of blood are transferred during clinical procedures. Presumably, small blood transfers from the provider to patient likewise could cause transmission. One infected surgeon may perform many operations, increasing the opportunity for transmission. As small as the risk to any individual patient may be, the aggregate risk thus becomes significant enough that patient safety and prudent risk management dictate restricting infected providers from performing invasive procedures.

result, while harsh to plaintiff, represents a reasoned and informed response to the problem.

NOTES AND QUESTIONS

1.   Disclosure of a physician's HIV-positivity raises troubling legal issues.   Does the reasonable patient standard, which presumes a patient will not overreact to extremely remote risks, provide an escape clause? The contagious status of a physician will not drive patients away, even though AIDS is fatal at present, since no material risk is created, given the very low probability that the virus will be communicated from provider to patient. Is this a promising argument?

The American Medical Association (AMA) and the American Dental Association (ADA) have taken the position that HIV infected professionals should abstain from performing risky invasive procedures, or should disclose their sero-positive status to their patients. The burden is placed on the individual professional.   The calculation of the professional organizations appears to be that some patients will stick with the provider because they will take on the low risks of infection, valuing their relationship with the professional, or the professional's reputation for quality. But why should the professional disclose his status, if he knows it? He may see his practice diminish or disappear as patients spread the word. If a hospital or managed care organization finds out, they may restrict his practice and cut his income. It is more likely that they will restrict his privileges, or in the case of a managed care organization, remove him from panel membership. The infected provider therefore has little incentive to disclose and substantial incentives to remain silent.

2.   Should a contagious risk created by a health care provider, like that of HIV or hepatitis, be treated differently from risks of mistreatment by an incompetent provider? If the patient is to have a choice, then shouldn't informed consent require disclosures of all kinds of differential information relevant to choosing a physician?

3.   The emerging case law has focussed on the probability of infection and the severity of it, concluding, as the court did in *Beringer*, that even though little evidence supports provider to patient transmission of AIDs, the provider should disclose his or her HIV-positive status. See also Faya v. Almaraz, 620 A.2d 327 (Md. App. 1993), where the court

held that the jury should be allowed to evaluate the conduct of a surgeon with AIDS, to determine if he owed patients a duty of disclosure of his AIDS status. The court based its analysis of duty upon foreseeability of the risk, concluding that a finding of unreasonable risk depends on a balance of probability and serious of harm, against the availability of precautions. The court could not say as a matter of law that the doctor owed no duty to the plaintiff in light of this balance, and reinstated the plaintiffs' complaints.

4.   The studies to date have found no evidence of transmission from provider to patient, with the possible exception of the Bergalis case. See Jeffrey J. Sacks, AIDS in a Surgeon, 313 New Eng. J. Med. 1017 (1985) (study of 400 Florida patients of surgeon); Frances P. Armstrong et al, Investigation of a Health Care Worker with Symptomatic Immunodeficiency Virus Infection: An Epidemiologic Approach, 152 Military Medicine 414 (1987) (1004 patients of military surgeon); John D. Porter et al, Management of Patients Treated by Surgeon with HIV Infection, The Lancet, January 1990, at 113 (339 patients of British surgeon); Ban Mishu et al, A Surgeon with AIDS: Lack of Evidence of Transmission to Patients, 264 JAMA 467 (1990) (study of 2160 patients of Nashville surgeon).

————

NOTE: DISCLOSURE OF PHYSICIAN RISKS TO PATIENTS

Systems for evaluating and improving the quality of health care have evolved over the past two decades. Hospitals and managed care organizations have been actively engaged in programs to promote high quality and effective practice, through implementation of clinical algorithms, outcome studies, application of quality control principles from industry, and large scale analysis of practice patterns across plans. Outcome data is increasingly available. Physician profiling has become commonplace by insurers and providers to track provider behavior. See David W. Emmons et al., Data on Employee Physician Profiling, 26 J.Health and Hosp. Law 73 (1993); H. Gilbert Welch et al., Physician Profiling: An Analysis of Inpatient Practice Patterns in Florida and Oregon, 330 New Eng.J.Med. 607 (1994); Jerome P. Kassirer, The Use and Abuse of Practice Profiles, 330 New Eng.J.Med. 634 (1994). See also John H. Eichhorn et al., Standards for Patient Monitoring During Anesthesia at Harvard Medical School, 256 JAMA 1017 (1986).

The rapid acceleration of information gathering by health care institutions may lead to disclosure of comparative success rates and outcome data where available, both of hospitals and individual physicians. Managed care organizations competing for subscribers will use it in their advertising; hospitals will use it to attract patients; and consumers will look for it for details on their own doctors. Two states, Pennsylvania and New York, have already begun to release physician-specific data.

Informed consent doctrine, driven by these trends, may require a physician to disclose success rates, his or her "batting average". One court has suggested that the physician should disclose both the general statistical success rate for a given procedure, and his or her particular experience with that procedure. See Hales v. Pittman, 576 P.2d 493 (Ariz. 1978) (discussing the battery count of the plaintiff's complaint).

See generally William Fifer, The Evolution of Quality Assurance Systems in Health Care -- A Personal Retrospective, 4 The Medical Staff Counselor 11 (1990); Paul D. Rheingold, The Admissibility of Evidence in Malpractice Cases: The Performance Records of Practitioners, 58 Brook. L. Rev. 75, 80 (1992); Aaron D. Twerksi and Neil B. Cohen, Comparing Medical Providers: A First Look at the New Era of Medical Statistics, 58 Brook. L. Rev. 5, 12-13 (1992); Note, Provider-Specific Quality-of-Care Data: A Proposal for Limited Mandatory Disclosure, 58 Brook. L. Rev. 85 (1992).

Suppose that a surgeon in his late fifties is aware that his skill level -- his vision, his fine motor skills -- is diminishing. His success rate is dropping, which means that his patient survival statistics are worsening. The odds of an iatrogenic injury with this surgeon have increased from 1 in 1,000 to 1 in 750. His record is still excellent. Should he disclose to his patients that he is beginning to suffer the inevitable results of aging? Or just that his success rate is a certain percentage? Institutional peer review is likely to restrict the surgeon's practice to those procedures he is competent to perform, with regular proctoring to guarantee good results, when he falls below a reasonable norm. We might also expect a physician with integrity to recognize his limits and begin to cut back on procedures. The role of the institution and peers in controlling these practices is central to reducing risks, backstopped by the ever present threat of a tort suit for damages. Hospital medical staff law has focused on provider competency in articulating the limits of negligent staff selection. Hospitals screen their medical staff to reduce the level of risk of injury to their patient population, refusing to credential high risk physicians, defining risk by a competency/quality definition.

The disclosure of a contagious status that exposes a patient to a risk of death is arguably different from performance-based risks. A competent physician may expose a patient to the HIV virus, while the risks discussed above are created by performance failures. The distinction is however not compelling. From the patient's perspective, the source of the risk is less important that the risk itself, whether death or impairment. From a patient's perspective, if the low risk of transmission of the HIV-virus must be disclosed, then surely so must alcoholism in a surgeon. A provider's performance can be affected by fatigue, depression, anger, and other psychological states with potentially lethal results for the patient. We don't presently require disclosure of the various forces that affect providers, and it is hard to imagine how this could be done. If a court is to avoid singling out AIDs as presenting unique risks to a patient, then vastly expanded disclosure obligations may well be next.

While the theory and application of informed consent doctrine by the courts seems to justify disclosure of HIV positive status, the efficacy of the doctrine in actually inducing providers to so act is unclear at best. HIV status does not pose unique risks: the risk of either contagion or death is inherent in a range of provider-created risks. A better way to frame the risks for the courts is to think of such status risks as better regulated by both threshold screening of providers for staff privileges, by institutional policies to promote safer health care delivery, and by use of tort law to set a standard of unreasonable risk creation.

Methods of achieving such threshold screening to protect patients against high-risk providers include staff privilege limitations, the threat of a negligence suit against a provider who is truly a "typhoid surgeon", and professional self-restraint by physicians who become aware that they are high-risk providers. Informed consent doctrine seems ill-suited to carry such additional baggage -- it is unfair to providers, moves doctrine into an area of risk disclosure that lacks a clear stopping point or bright line, and is simply not justified by a risk analysis.

See generally Leonard H. Glantz et al., Risky Business: Setting Public Health Policy for HIV-infected Health Care Professionals, 70 The Milbank Quart. 43, 72-73 (1992); Norman Daniels, HIV-Infected Health Care Professionals: Public Threat or Public Sacrifice?, 70 Milbank

Quart. 3(1992); Mark Barnes et al., The HIV-infected Health Care Professional: Employment Policies and Public Health, 18 Law, Med. & Health Care 311, 324 (1990): contra, Dorsett D. Smith, Physicians and the Acquired Immunodeficiency Syndrome, 264 JAMA 452 (1990).

PROBLEMS: IMPAIRED PHYSICIANS

Mercy Hospital employs Dr. Frank Tehr, a surgeon who in the past has sexually assaulted female patients. Suppose that he sees a thousand patients a year, half of them women, and has only assaulted two women over five years, making the risk for the individual female patient 2/2500, or .0008, or .08%. Should every female patient be informed of the low risk of sexual assault? What else might the hospital do?

Boosier City Memorial Hospital has a staff surgeon, Dr. Williams, who is a chronic alcoholic. He is an excellent surgeon when he is not impaired by drinking, but because he is a chronic alcoholic it is hard to predict when he may be impaired. Should Dr. Williams be required to disclose to patients that he is an alcoholic, so they can choose whether to continue with him?

See Hidding v. Williams, 578 So. 2d 1192 (La. Ct. App. 1991)(plaintiff sued on an informed consent theory, alleging in part that the physician had failed to disclose that he was a chronic alcoholic; held, such a failure to inform violated Louisiana informed consent requirements); contra, Ornelas v. Fry, 727 P.2d 819 (Ariz. Ct. App. 1986) (court refused to allow evidence as to alcoholism of anesthesiologist as a separate claim of negligence, absent a showing that the physician was impaired at the time of the procedure.)

––––––––

Insert at page 345, before section C, the following material:

Patients with diseases such as cancer usually face a reduced life expectancy even with the best medical treatment. Such patients would presumably like to know as much as possible about their life expectancy for a variety of reasons -- estate planning, goodbyes to family and friends, fortifying themselves to face death for personal and religious reasons. Must the doctor inform the patient of his life expectancy based on statistical tables?

ARATO V. AVEDON
5 Cal.4th 1172, 858 P.2d 598, 23 Cal.Rptr.2d 131
Supreme Court of California, 1993

Arabian, Justice.

A physician's duty to disclose to a patient information material to the decision whether to undergo treatment is the central constituent of the legal doctrine known as "informed consent." In this case, we review the ruling of a divided Court of Appeal that, in recommending a course of chemotherapy and radiation treatment to a patient suffering from a virulent form of cancer, the treating physicians breached their duty to obtain the patient's informed consent by failing to disclose his statistical life expectancy.

* * *

I.

A.

Miklos Arato was a successful 42-year-old electrical contractor and part-time real estate developer when, early in 1980, his internist diagnosed a failing kidney. On July 21, 1980, in the course of surgery to remove the kidney, the operating surgeon detected a tumor on the "tail" or distal portion of Mr. Arato's pancreas. After Mrs. Arato gave her consent, portions of the pancreas were resected, or removed, along with the spleen and the diseased kidney. A follow-up pathological examination of the resected pancreatic tissue confirmed a malignancy. Concerned that the cancer could recur and might have infiltrated adjacent organs, Mr. Arato's surgeon referred him to a group of oncology practitioners for follow-up treatment.

During his initial visit to the oncologists, Mr. Arato filled out a multipage questionnaire routinely given new patients. Among the some 150 questions asked was whether patients "wish[ed] to be told the truth about [their] condition" or whether they wanted the physician to "bear the burden" for them. Mr. Arato checked the box indicating that he wished to be told the truth.

The oncologists discussed with Mr. and Mrs. Arato the advisability of a course of chemotherapy known as "F.A.M.," a treatment employing a combination of drugs which, when used in conjunction with radiation therapy, had shown promise in treating pancreatic cancer in experimental trials. The nature of the discussions between Mr. and Mrs. Arato and the treating physicians, and in particular the scope of the disclosures made to the patient by his doctors, was the subject of conflicting testimony at trial. By their own admission, however, neither the operating surgeon nor the treating oncologists specifically disclosed to the patient or his wife the high statistical mortality rate associated with pancreatic cancer.

Mr. Arato's oncologists determined that a course of F.A.M. chemotherapy was indicated for several reasons. According to their testimony, the high statistical mortality of pancreatic cancer is in part a function of what is by far the most common diagnostic scenario--the discovery of the malignancy well after it has metastasized to distant sites, spreading throughout the patient's body. As noted, in Mr. Arato's case, the tumor was comparatively localized, having been discovered in the tail of the pancreas by chance in the course of surgery to remove the diseased kidney.

Related to the "silent" character of pancreatic cancer is the fact that detection in such an advanced state usually means that the tumor cannot as a practical matter be removed, contributing to the high mortality rate. In Mr. Arato's case, however, the operating surgeon determined that it was possible to excise cleanly the tumorous portion of the pancreas and to leave a margin of about one-half centimeter around the surgical site, a margin that appeared clinically to be clear of cancer cells. Third, the mortality rate is somewhat lower, according to defense testimony, for pancreatic tumors located in the distal part of the organ than for those found in the main body. Finally, then-recent experimental studies on the use of F.A.M. chemotherapy in conjunction with therapeutic radiation treatments had shown promising response rates--on the order of several months of extended life--among pancreatic cancer patients.

Mr. Arato's treating physicians justified not disclosing statistical life expectancy data to their patient on disparate grounds. According to the testimony of his surgeon, Mr. Arato had exhibited great anxiety over his condition, so much so that his surgeon determined that it would have been medically inappropriate to disclose specific mortality rates. The

74

patient's oncologists had a somewhat different explanation. As Dr. Melvin Avedon, his chief oncologist, put it, he believed that cancer patients in Mr. Arato's position "wanted to be told the truth, but did not want a cold shower." Along with the other treating physicians, Dr. Avedon testified that in his opinion the direct and specific disclosure of extremely high mortality rates for malignancies such as pancreatic cancer might effectively deprive a patient of any hope of cure, a medically inadvisable state. Moreover, all of the treating physicians testified that statistical life expectancy data had little predictive value when applied to a particular patient with individualized symptoms, medical history, character traits and other variables.

According to the physicians' testimony, Mr. and Mrs. Arato were told at the outset of the treatment that most victims of pancreatic cancer die of the disease, that Mr. Arato was at "serious" or "great" risk of a recurrence and that, should the cancer return, his condition would be judged incurable. This information was given to the patient and his wife in the context of a series of verbal and behavioral cues designed to invite the patient or family member to follow up with more direct and difficult questions. Such follow-up questions, on the order of "how long do I have to live?," would have signaled to his doctors, according to Dr. Avedon's testimony, the patient's desire and ability to confront the fact of imminent mortality. In the judgment of his chief oncologist, Mr. Arato, although keenly interested in the clinical significance of the most minute symptom, studiously avoided confronting these ultimate issues; according to his doctors, neither Mr. Arato nor his wife ever asked for information concerning his life expectancy in more than 70 visits over a period of a year. Believing that they had disclosed information sufficient to enable him to make an informed decision whether to undergo chemotherapy, Mr. Arato's doctors concluded that their patient had as much information regarding his condition and prognosis as he wished.

Dr. Avedon also testified that he told Mr. Arato that the effectiveness of F.A.M. therapy was unproven in cases such as his, described its principal adverse side effects, and noted that one of the patient's options was not to undergo the treatment. In the event, Mr. Arato consented to the proposed course of chemotherapy and radiation, treatments that are prolonged, difficult and painful for cancer patients. Unfortunately, the treatment proved ineffective in arresting the spread of the malignancy. Although clinical tests showed him to be free of cancer in the several months following the beginning of the F.A.M. treatments, beginning in late March and into April of 1981, the clinical signs took an adverse turn.[75] By late April, the doctors were convinced by the results of additional tests that the cancer had returned and was spreading. They advised the patient of their suspicions and discontinued chemotherapy. On July 25, 1981, a year and four days following surgery, Mr. Arato succumbed to the effects of pancreatic cancer.

B.

Not long after his death, Mr. Arato's wife and two children brought this suit against the physicians who had treated their husband and father in his last days, including the surgeon who performed the pancreas resection and the oncologists who had recommended and administered the chemotherapy/radiation treatment. As presented to the jury, the gist of the lawsuit was the claim that in discussing with their patient the advisability of undergoing a course of chemotherapy and radiation, Mr. Arato's doctors had failed to disclose adequately the shortcomings of the proposed treatment in light of the diagnosis, and thus had failed to obtain the patient's informed consent. Specifically, plaintiffs contended that the doctors were aware that, because early detection is difficult and rare, pancreatic cancer is an especially virulent malignancy, one in which only 5 to 10 percent of those afflicted live for as long as five years, and that given the practically incurable nature of the disease, there was little chance Mr. Arato would live more than a short while, even if the proposed treatment proved effective.

Such mortality information, the complaint alleged--especially the statistical morbidity rate of pancreatic cancer--was material to Mr. Arato's decision whether to undergo postoperative treatment; had he known the bleak truth concerning his life expectancy, he would not have undergone the rigors of an unproven therapy, but would have chosen to live out his

---

[75] Around this time--on March 12, 1981, according to the record--an article appeared in the Los Angeles Times stating that only 1 percent of males and 2 percent of females diagnosed as having pancreatic cancer live for five years. According to his wife's testimony, Mr. Arato read the Times article and brought it to the attention of his oncologists. One of his oncologists confirmed such a discussion but denied that he told Mr. Arato that the statistics did not apply to his case, as Mrs. Arato testified. Mr. Arato continued to undergo chemotherapy treatment after reading the article and evidently made no changes in his estate planning or business and real estate affairs.

last days at peace with his wife and children, and arranging his business affairs. Instead, the complaint asserted, in the false hope that radiation and chemotherapy treatments could effect a cure--a hope born of the negligent failure of his physicians to disclose the probability of an early death--Mr. Arato failed to order his affairs in contemplation of his death, an omission that, according to the complaint, led eventually to the failure of his contracting business and to substantial real estate and tax losses following his death.

As the trial neared its conclusion and the court prepared to charge the jury, plaintiffs requested that several special instructions be given relating to the nature and scope of the physician's duty of disclosure. Two proffered instructions in particular are pertinent to this appeal. In the first, plaintiffs asked the trial court to instruct the jury that "A physician has a fiduciary duty to a patient to make a full and fair disclosure to the patient of all facts which materially affect the patient's rights and interests." The second instruction sought by plaintiffs stated that "The scope of the physician's duty to disclose is measured by the amount of knowledge a patient needs in order to make an informed choice. All information material to the patient's decision should be given."

The trial judge declined to give the jury either of the two instructions sought by plaintiffs. Instead, the court read to the jury a modified version of BAJI No. 6.11, the so-called "reality of consent" instruction drawn from our opinion in Cobbs v. Grant []. As can be seen by a comparison of the two instructions, the texts of which are set out in the margin,[76] the instruction actually given the jury by the trial court

----

[76] BAJI No. 6.11 (7th ed. 1986 bound vol.) reads: "Except as hereinafter explained, it is the duty of the physician to disclose to the patient all material information to enable the patient to make an informed decision regarding the proposed operation or treatment. [P] Material information is information which the physician knows or should know would be regarded as significant by a reasonable person in the patient's position when deciding to accept or reject a recommended medical procedure. To be material a fact must also be one which is not commonly appreciated. [P] There is no duty to make disclosure of risks when the patient requests that he or she not be so informed or where the procedure is simple and the danger remote and commonly understood to be remote. [P] Likewise, there is no duty to discuss minor risks inherent in common procedures, when such procedures very seldom result in serious ill effects. [P]

However, when a procedure inherently involves a known risk of death or serious bodily harm it is the physician's duty to disclose to the patient the possibility of such outcome and to explain in lay terms the complications that might possibly occur. The physician or surgeon must also disclose such additional information as a skilled practitioner of good standing would provide under the same or similar circumstances. [P] A physician has no duty of disclosure beyond that required of physicians of good standing in the same or similar locality when he or she relied upon facts which would demonstrate to a reasonable person that the disclosure would so seriously upset the patient that the patient would not have been able to rationally weigh the risks of refusing to undergo the recommended [treatment] [operation]. [P] Even though the patient has consented to a proposed treatment or operation, the failure of the physician to inform the patient as stated in this instruction before obtaining such consent is negligence and renders the physician subject to liability for any injury [proximately] [legally] resulting from the [treatment] [operation] if a reasonably prudent person in the patient's position would not have consented to the [treatment] [operation] if he or she had been adequately informed of all the significant perils." The trial judge read to the jury the following instruction: "Except as hereinafter explained, it is the duty of the physician to disclose to the patient all material information to enable the patient to make an informed decision regarding proposed treatment. [P] Material information is information which the physician knows or should know would be regarded as significant by a reasonable person in the patient's position when deciding to accept or reject a recommended medical procedure. To be material a fact must also be one which is not commonly appreciated. [P] A physician has no duty of disclosure beyond that required of physician of good standing in the same or similar locality when he or she relied upon facts which would demonstrate to a reasonable person that the disclosure would so seriously upset the patient that the patient would not have been able to rationally weigh the risks of refusing to undergo the recommended treatment. [P] Even though the patient has consented to a proposed treatment or operation, the failure of the physician to inform the patient as stated in this instruction before obtaining such consent is negligence and renders the physician subject to liability for any damage legally resulting from the failure to disclose or for any injury legally resulting from the treatment if a reasonably prudent person in the patient's position would not have consented to the treatment if he or she had been adequately informed of the likelihood of his [sic] premature death."

substantially recapitulated the wording of BAJI No. 6.11, except for the omission of two brief paragraphs dealing with exceptions to the duty of disclosure and a third paragraph that appears on its face not to have been relevant to the case as it developed at trial.

After concluding its deliberations, the jury returned two special verdicts--on a form approved by plaintiffs' counsel--finding that none of the defendants was negligent in the "medical management" of Mr. Arato, and that defendants "disclosed to Mr. Arato all relevant information which would have enabled him to make an informed decision regarding the proposed treatment to be rendered him." Plaintiffs appealed from the judgment entered on the defense verdict, contending that the trial court erred in refusing to give the jury the special instructions requested by them. As noted, a divided Court of Appeal reversed the judgment of the trial court, and ordered a new trial. We granted defendants' ensuing petition for review and now reverse the judgment of the Court of Appeal.

C.

In the Court of Appeal's view, Mr. Arato's doctors had breached the duty to disclose to their patient information material to the decision whether to undergo the radiation and drug therapy. According to the Court of Appeal, because there are so many different cancers, the lethality of which varies dramatically, telling a patient that cancer might recur and would then be incurable, without providing at least some general information concerning the virulence of the particular cancer at issue as reflected in mortality tables, was "meaningless." In addition, the Court of Appeal reasoned that his physicians were under a duty to disclose numerical life expectancy information to Mr. Arato so that he and his wife might take timely measures to minimize or avoid the risks of financial loss resulting from his death.

The Court of Appeal also concluded that the instructions concerning the physicians' duty of disclosure given the jury by the trial judge were defective in two respects. First, one paragraph of BAJI No. 6.11 improperly emphasized a physician's defense to a failure-to-disclose claim as well as the importance of community medical standards in measuring the adequacy of the disclosures. These defects would have

. . .

been mitigated by giving the jury plaintiffs' requested instructions, the court reasoned.

* * *

In addition, the Court of Appeal concluded that the instruction, given at the request of the defendants, to the effect that the primary duty of a physician is "to do what is best for his patient," operated to mislead the jury into believing that a physician's duty of disclosure may be limited by his or her own opinion as to what is in the patient's best interests. The Court of Appeal also concluded that the jury was misled as to the governing legal standard by the fact that the specific disclosure instructions modeled on BAJI No. 6.11 were preceded by other, lengthy instructions from BAJI (BAJI Nos. 6.00, 6.01, 6.02, 6.03, 6.30 [7th ed. 1986 bound vol.]) dealing with the general standard of care for medical professionals in negligence actions--an ordering that, the court reasoned, compounded the skewed impression already conveyed to the jury regarding the significance of community medical standards in informed consent cases.

Finally, the Court of Appeal concluded that the trial court had erred in permitting defendants to introduce the testimony of expert medical witnesses. Although conceding that expert testimony is appropriate where the physician's defense rests on the so-called "therapeutic exception" (e.g., that the patient was emotionally incapable of making a rational decision concerning a proposed treatment), the court reasoned that the expert defense testimony permitted by the trial court went well beyond that narrow exception to the duty of disclosure, misleading the jury in their deliberations regarding the significance of community medical practice and prejudicing plaintiffs' case.

II.

A.

The fount of the doctrine of informed consent in California is our decision of some 20 years ago in Cobbs v. Grant, [] an opinion by a unanimous court that built on several out-of-state decisions significantly broadening the scope and character of the physician's duty of disclosure in obtaining the patient's consent to treatment. In Cobbs v. Grant, we not only anchored much of the doctrine of informed consent in a theory of negligence liability, but also laid down four "postulates" as the foundation on which the physician's duty of disclosure rests.

"The first [of these postulates,]" we wrote, "is that patients are generally persons unlearned in the medical sciences and therefore, except in rare cases, courts may safely assume the knowledge of patient and physician are not in parity. The second is that a person of adult years and in sound mind has the right, in the exercise of control over his own body, to determine whether or not to submit to lawful medical treatment." [].

"The third [postulate,]" we continued, "is that the patient's consent to treatment, to be effective, must be an informed consent. And the fourth is that the patient, being unlearned in medical sciences, has an abject dependence upon and trust in his physician for the information upon which he relies during the decisional process, thus raising an obligation in the physician that transcends arms-length transactions." [] From these ethical imperatives, we derived the obligation of a treating physician "of reasonable disclosure of the available choices with respect to proposed therapy and of the dangers inherently and potentially involved in each." []

Since Cobbs v. Grant [] was decided, we have revisited the doctrine of informed consent. In Truman v. Thomas [], we held that the physician's duty of due care embraced disclosure of the material risks resulting from the patient's refusal to consent to a recommended treatment--in that case, a routine annual pap smear. In concluding that the trial court had erred reversibly in refusing to instruct the jury on the physician's duty of disclosure, we said that the doctrine of informed consent recognized in Cobbs v. Grant, [] was imposed "so that patients might meaningfully exercise their right to make decisions about their own bodies." []

Our opinion also stressed the paramount role of the trier of fact in informed consent cases. We recognized, for example, that questions such as whether the danger posed by a failure to disclose a particular risk is remote, whether the risk was or was not commonly known, and whether circumstances unique to a given case supported a duty of disclosure were matters for the jury to decide. We accordingly declined to hold that as a matter of law the physician owed no duty to make a given disclosure to the patient. That question, we concluded, was one for the jury to decide. []

We recently returned to the scope of a physician's duty of disclosure in Moore v. Regents of University of California []. Although the chief focus of Moore was whether the nonconsensual use of human cells in medical research supported a patient's action seeking to impose on health professionals liability for conversion, our opinion reaffirmed the "well-established principles" enunciated in Cobbs v. Grant []. It was on that foundation that we held "a physician must disclose personal interests unrelated to the patient's health, whether research or economic, that may affect the physician's personal judgment...." (Ibid.)

B.

Together with companion decisions in other jurisdictions, [*Cobbs*] is one of the epochal opinions in the legal recognition of the medical patient's protectible interest in autonomous decisionmaking. After more than a generation of experience with the judicially broadened duty of physician disclosure, the accumulated medicolegal comment on the subject of informed consent is both large and discordant. Those critics writing under the banner of "patient autonomy" insist that the practical administration of the doctrine has been thwarted by a failure of judicial nerve and an unremitting hostility to its underlying spirit by the medical profession. Others, equally earnest, assert that the doctrine misapprehends the realities of patient care and enshrines moral ideals in the place of workable rules.

Despite the critical standoff between these extremes of "patient sovereignty" and "medical paternalism," indications are that the Cobbs-era decisions helped effect a revolution in attitudes among patients and physicians alike regarding the desirability of frank and open disclosure of relevant medical information. The principal question we must address is whether our holding in Cobbs v. Grant, [] as embodied in BAJI No. 6.11, accurately conveys to juries the legal standard under which they assess the evidence in determining the adequacy of the disclosures made by physician to patient in a particular case or whether, as the Court of Appeal here appeared to conclude, the standard instruction should be revised to mandate specific disclosures such as patient life expectancy as revealed by mortality statistics.

In our view, one of the merits of the somewhat abstract formulation of BAJI No. 6.11 is its recognition of the importance of the overall medical context that juries ought to take into account in deciding whether a challenged disclosure was reasonably sufficient to convey to the patient information material to an informed treatment decision. The contexts and clinical settings in which physician and patient interact and exchange information material to therapeutic decisions are so multifarious, the informational needs and degree of dependency of individual patients so various, and the professional relationship itself such an intimate and irreducibly judgment-laden one, that we believe it is unwise to require as a matter of law that a particular species of information be disclosed....[]

Our opinion in Cobbs v. Grant [] recognized these "common practicalities" of medical treatment which, we said, make the ideal of "full disclosure" a "facile expression[ ]." [] Eschewing both a "mini-course in medical science" and a duty to discuss "the relatively minor risks inherent in common procedures," we identified the touchstone of the physician's duty of disclosure in the patient's need for "adequate information to enable an intelligent choice," a peculiarly fact-bound assessment which juries are especially well-suited to make. []

This sensitivity to context seems all the more appropriate in the case of life expectancy projections for cancer patients based on statistical samples. Without exception, the testimony of every physician-witness at trial confirmed what is evident even to a nonprofessional: statistical morbidity values derived from the experience of population groups are inherently unreliable and offer little assurance regarding the fate of the individual patient; indeed, to assume that such data are conclusive in themselves smacks of a refusal to explore treatment alternatives and the medical abdication of the patient's well-being. Certainly the jury here heard evidence of articulable grounds for the conclusion that the particular features of Mr. Arato's case distinguished it from the typical population of pancreatic cancer sufferers and their dismal statistical probabilities--a fact plaintiffs impliedly acknowledged at trial in conceding that the oncologic referral of Mr. Arato and ensuing chemotherapy were not in themselves medically negligent.

In declining to endorse the mandatory disclosure of life expectancy probabilities, we do not mean to signal a retreat from the patient-based standard of disclosure explicitly adopted in Cobbs v. Grant. [] We reaffirm the view taken in *Cobbs* that, because the "weighing of these risks [i.e., those inherent in a proposed procedure] against the individual subjective fears and hopes of the patient is not an expert skill," the test "for determining whether a potential peril must be divulged is its materiality to the patient's decision." [] In reaffirming the appropriateness of that standard, we can conceive of no trier of fact more suitable than lay jurors to pronounce judgment on those uniquely human and necessarily situational ingredients that contribute to a specific doctor-patient exchange of information relevant to treatment decisions; certainly this is not territory in which appellate courts can usefully issue "bright line" guides.

Rather than mandate the disclosure of specific information as a matter of law, the better rule is to instruct the jury that a physician is under a legal duty to disclose to the patient all material information--that is, "information which the physician knows or should know would be regarded as significant by a reasonable person in the patient's position when deciding to accept or reject a recommended medical procedure"--needed to make an informed decision regarding a proposed treatment. That, of course, is the formulation embodied in BAJI No. 6.11 and the instruction given in this case. Having been properly instructed, the jury returned a defense verdict--on a form approved by plaintiffs' counsel--specifically finding that defendants had "disclosed to Mr. Arato all relevant information which would have enabled him to make an informed decision regarding the proposed treatment to be rendered him."

We decline to intrude further, either on the subtleties of the physician-patient relationship or in the resolution of claims that the physician's duty of disclosure was breached, by requiring the disclosure of information that may or may not be indicated in a given treatment context. Instead, we leave the ultimate judgment as to the factual adequacy of a challenged disclosure to the venerable American jury, operating under legal instructions such as those given here and subject to the persuasive force of trial advocacy.

Here, the evidence was more than sufficient to support the jury's finding that defendants had reasonably disclosed to Mr. Arato information material to his decision whether to undergo the proposed chemotherapy/radiation treatment. There was testimony that Mr. and Mrs. Arato were informed that cancer of the pancreas is usually fatal; of the substantial risk of recurrence, an event that would mean his illness was incurable; of the unproven nature of the F.A.M. treatments and their principal side effects; and of the option of forgoing such treatments. Mr. Arato's doctors also testified that they could not with confidence predict how long the patient might live, notwithstanding statistical mortality tables.

In addition, the jury heard testimony regarding the patient's apparent avoidance of issues bearing upon mortality; Mrs. Arato's testimony that his physicians had assured her husband that he was "clear" of cancer; and the couple's common expectation that he had been "cured," only to learn, suddenly and unexpectedly, that the case was hopeless and life measurable in weeks. The informed consent instructions given the jury to assess this evidence were an accurate statement of the law, and the Court of Appeal in effect invaded the province of the trier of fact in overturning a fairly litigated verdict.[77]

C.

In addition to their claim that his physicians were required to disclose statistical life expectancy data to Mr. Arato to enable him to reach an informed treatment decision, plaintiffs also contend that defendants should have disclosed such data because it was material to the patient's nonmedical interests, that is, Mr. Arato's business and investment affairs and the potential adverse impact of his death upon them. In support of this proposition, plaintiffs rely on the following statement in Bowman v. McPheeters []: "As fiduciaries it was the duty of defendants [physicians] to make a full and fair disclosure to plaintiff of all facts which materially affected his rights and interests." Plaintiffs contend that since Mr. Arato's contracting and real estate affairs would suffer if he failed to make timely changes in estate planning in

---

[77] Despite their claim that life expectancy information is material to a patient's treatment decision and therefore should have been disclosed to Mr. Arato, plaintiffs did not seek an instruction to that specific effect. As noted, the version of BAJI No. 6.11 that was given by the trial court instructed the jury that the duty of disclosure encompassed "information which the physician knows or should know would be regarded as significant by a reasonable person in the patient's position when deciding to accept or reject a recommended medical procedure," a formulation adequate on its face to permit a jury to decide that, as plaintiffs' contend, life expectancy information should have been disclosed to Mr. Arato. Nowhere do plaintiffs even attempt to demonstrate that their proposed special instructions ... would have conveyed the principle of materiality better than the instruction actually given. Rather than focus on this fatal defect in plaintiffs' theory of error and resulting prejudice, the Court of Appeal discussed the general question of the scope of a physician's duty of disclosure.

contemplation of imminent death, and since these matters are among "his rights and interests," his physicians were under a legal duty to disclose all material facts that might affect them, including statistical life expectancy information. We reject the claim as one founded on a premise that is not recognized in California.

The short answer to plaintiffs' claim is our statement in *Moore* [] that a "physician is not the patient's financial adviser."[] From its inception, the rationale behind the disclosure requirement implementing the doctrine of informed consent has been to protect the patient's freedom to "exercise ... control over [one's] own body" by directing the course of medical treatment.[] We recently noted that "the principle of self-determination ... embraces all aspects of medical decisionmaking by the competent adult...."[] Although an aspect of personal autonomy, the conditions for the exercise of the patient's right of self-decision presuppose a therapeutic focus, a supposition reflected in the text of BAJI No. 6.11 itself. The fact that a physician has "fiducial" obligations ...which ...prohibit misrepresenting the nature of the patient's medical condition, does not mean that he or she is under a duty, the scope of which is undefined, to disclose every contingency that might affect the patient's nonmedical "rights and interests." Because plaintiffs' open-ended proposed instruction--that the physician's duty embraces the "disclosure ... of all facts which materially affect the patient's rights and interests"--failed to reflect the therapeutic limitation inherent in the doctrine of informed consent, it would have been error for the trial judge to give it to the jury.

Finally, plaintiffs make much of the fact that in his initial visit to Dr. Avedon's office, Mr. Arato indicated in a lengthy form he was requested to complete that he "wish[ed] to be told the truth about [his] condition." In effect, they contend that as a result of Mr. Arato's affirmative answer, defendants had an absolute duty to make specific life expectancy disclosures to him. Whether the patient has filled out a questionnaire indicating that he or she wishes to be told the "truth" about his or her condition or not, however, a physician is under a legal duty to obtain the patient's informed consent to any recommended treatment. Although a patient may validly waive the right to be informed, we do not see how a request to be told the "truth" in itself heightens the duty of disclosure imposed on physicians as a matter of law.

III.

86

[The final issue involved the role of experts in testifying about the "therapeutic exception" to the physician's duty of disclosure. Plaintiff's and defense experts disagreed as to the merits of disclosing life expectancy data to patients unless it was specifically requested. The court came down in favor of a professional standard corollary to the reasonable patient approach.]

* * *

In reckoning the scope of disclosure, the physician will for the most part be guided by the patient's decisional needs--or..."the test for determining whether a potential peril must be divulged is its materiality to the patient's decision."[] A physician, however, evaluates the patient's decisional needs against a background of professional understanding that includes a knowledge of what information beyond the significant risks associated with a given treatment would be regarded by the medical community as appropriate for disclosure under the circumstances.

It is thus evident that under the formulation we adopted in Cobbs v. Grant,[] situations will sometimes arise in which the trier of fact is unable to decide the ultimate issue of the adequacy of a particular disclosure without an understanding of the standard of practice within the relevant medical community. For that reason, in an appropriate case, the testimony of medical experts qualified to offer an opinion regarding what, if any, disclosures--in addition to those relating to the risk of death or serious injury and significant potential complications posed by consenting to or declining a proposed treatment--would be made to the patient by a skilled practitioner in the relevant medical community under the circumstances is relevant and admissible.

We underline the limited and essentially subsidiary role of expert testimony in informed consent litigation.... [T]here may be a limited number of occasions in the trial of informed consent claims where the adequacy of disclosure in a given case may turn on the standard of practice within the relevant medical community. In such instances, expert testimony will usually be appropriate.

Because statistical life expectancy data is information that lies outside the significant risks associated with a given treatment, the disclosure of which is mandated by Cobbs v. Grant, [] it falls within the scope of the "additional information ... a skilled practitioner ... would

87

provide" language of *Cobbs*.[] And since the question of whether a physician should disclose such information turns on the standard of practice within the medical community, the trial court did not err in permitting expert testimony directed at that issue.

* * *

Conclusion

The judgment of the Court of Appeal is reversed and the cause is remanded with directions to affirm the judgment of the trial court.

NOTES AND QUESTIONS

1.   The California Supreme Court says it is simply applying the *Cobbs* analysis to the facts of the *Arato* case. It refuses to impose as a matter of law any requirement that a physician disclose to the patient his life expectancy. Why? Is it a desire to leave the lay jury some "wriggle" room, empowering it as the trier of fact? Or a desire to give physicians the flexibility to avoid difficult disclosures? Is life expectancy data so inherently untrustworthy that patients should not be told?

2.   Does *Arato* in effect expand the defense of "therapeutic privilege", giving professional standards undue weight in both the instructions and the expert testimony? If a patient has a cancer that is often lethal in a short time, how much more terrifying is specific knowledge as to life expectancy?

3.   To what extent should a health care provider's informational power expand its obligations to protect a patient's financial interests? A middle-aged patient, facing imminent death, might pursue several alternatives to protect assets for his or her family: he or she might declare personal bankruptcy to wipe out debts; might undertake estate planning to protect assets for the family; might restructure a small business to bring in new administrators. *Arato* seems to blame the plaintiff for not asking, letting the physicians off the hook. Should we let them off so easily? Physicians historically had to discuss treatment costs with patients. In the early days of fee-for-service medicine, patients had to choose between expensive treatments and their other needs, since insurance was not readily available. Today, patients seeking organ

transplantation or experimental therapies need to know about their insurance coverage or the availability of Medicaid or other government sources. The health care provider clearly has some role in helping a patient sort out payment sources and costs.

4.   Courts have generally refused to find a hospital or physician negligent for failing to advise patients that they were eligible for government funding. See, e.g., Mraz v. Taft, 619 N.E.2d 483 (Ohio App. 8 Dist. 1993)(neither hospital nor nursing home had any duty to advise husband that he qualified for Medicaid). Nor is a physician liable for the financial consequences of a misdiagnosis, for example a patient's cancellation of a life insurance policy upon being erroneously informed that he did not have cancer. See Estate of Blacher v. Garlett, 857 P.2d 566, 568 (Co.C.A., Div.III,1993).

———

CHAPTER 4. REFORMING THE TORT SYSTEM FOR MEDICAL INJURIES

Insert at page 454, just above new section C:

ENTERPRISE LIABILITY

President Clinton's original health reform proposal in 1993 made enterprise liability the cornerstone of malpractice reform. See Health Security Act, s. 1775, 103rd Cong., 1st Sess., Nov. 22, 1993, s. 1400 (hereafter "Health Security Act"). The original proposal called for the Health Plans to bear all liability for medical malpractice. After opposition arose from organized medicine, however, the proposal was downgraded to a demonstration project in the Act. Enterprise liability continues, however, to be a favorite of tort reformers. Current tort reform efforts in Congress have focused on product liability rules, especially punitive damage awards, while malpractice reform has slipped out of the spotlight. At the moment, it is unclear that any major legislation will emerge from Congress addressing professional liability issues.

Enterprise liability, also referred to as "organizational liability" by the American Law Institute, changes the locus of liability for patient injuries without other significant alterations to the rules of proof and damages. The idea is not new; developments in vicarious liability and corporate negligence have moved the locus of much medical liability from independent contractor physicians to the hospital. See generally George Priest, The Invention of Enterprise Liability: A Critical History of the Intellectual Foundations of Modern Tort Law, 14 J.Leg.Stud. 461 (1985). This proposal, as articulated by the American Law Institute, would make a hospital liable for physician negligence that injures patients within the hospital:

> ...we would exculpate doctors from personal liability for negligence (and thus eliminate their need to purchase insurance against such liability), on the condition that the hospital assume such liability and provide the insurance, a change that would leave untouched the patient's present entitlement to recover for injuries caused by the doctor's negligence.

The American Law Institute, Reporters' Study, Enterprise Responsibility for Personal Injury, Vol.II: Approaches to Legal and Institutional Change (April 15, 1991) 115 (hereafter ALI Study).

Such channeling of liability to the hospital is justified by several arguments. First, insurers would have an improved ability to price insurance, since difficulties in pricing for individual physicians in high-risk specialties will be eliminated; in most other areas of tort law, from environmental to products risks, business enterprises bear the cost of insuring against liability. Second, by eliminating the insurance problems inherent in the fragmented malpractice market, specialties such as obstetrics would no longer face onerous burdens, nor will physicians have to face premiums that fluctuate excessively from year to year. Third, physicians would be freed from the psychological stress inflicted by being named defendants in malpractice suits. Fourth, administrative and litigation costs would be reduced by having only one defendant, rather than the multiplicity of providers named in the typical malpractice suit. Fifth, and most important, patterns of poor medical practice would be deterred by placing liability on institutions rather than individuals, since organizations have superior data collecting abilities and management tools for managing risks. See generally Lewis A. Kornhauser, An Economic Analysis of the Choice Between Enterprise and Personal Liability for Accidents, 70 Cal.L.Rev. 1345(1982); Sykes, The Economics of Vicarious Liability, 93 Yale L.J. 1231(1984).

The critique of such enterprise liability begins with its impact on the autonomy of physicians. Physicians fear that such liability will force them from the status of autonomous practitioners into the status of employees for large health care institutions, with attendant loss of power. The position of the American Medical Association's House of Delegates is summed up by Richard Corlin, MD: "One proposal Clinton's made that is absolutely nonnegotiable is enterprise liability, which means if you work for an HMO and get sued, you could get fired. This will lead to a firestorm like nothing they've ever seen. If they want a doctor strike, this is the best way to do it." American Medical News 7 (May 17, 1993). The ALI proposal acknowledges that enterprise liability will treat physicians as staff physicians in managed care settings. But such forces are already in operation, as evidenced by the rapid growth of managed care organizations, the purchase of group medical practices by hospitals, and other forces that have reduced the autonomy of physicians. The issue for health care reform in the next decade will be how to implement such a liability approach in a changing health care environment where care is as likely to be delivered through loose networks of providers as through hospitals. The benefits of deterrence and risk management may be elusive if enterprise liability is applied to broad regional health authorities or other networks that lack the centralizing powers of individual hospitals.

Enterprise liability may also increase compensation costs due to the increased volume of claims filed. The California study in the 1970s estimated that a no-fault system in California could increase malpractice premiums 300% higher than the tort system's insurance costs. California Medical and Hospital Associations, Report on the Medical Insurance Feasibility Study (1977). A critique of the Harvard New York study likewise concluded that the costs of a no-fault system could be greater than the present tort system, when the costs of many more claims and system administrative costs are combined. See Maxwell Mehlman, Saying "No" to No-Fault: What the Harvard Malpractice Study Means for Medical Malpractice Reform (New York State Bar Association 1990).

From the insurance industry perspective, these proposals are worrisome, since there seems to be far more malpractice in the world than is ever detected or litigated. A no-fault system may set off an avalanche of litigation, depending upon the design of the system, methods of discussing misadventures to the injured patient, and other structural issues, as yet unresolved. Patients are also more likely to sue their HMO or Health Alliance than their personal physician.

If a compensation system rewards many more claimants, particularly small ones, in a more evenhanded and rapid fashion than does the current tort system, it will be an improvement even if it is not cheaper. See generally Paul C. Weiler et al., A Measure of Malpractice: Medical Injury, Malpractice Litigation, and Patient Compensation (1993) for an excellent economic discussion of the costs of a no-fault system to replace medical malpractice litigation. Weiler et al estimates that a no-fault scheme would cost somewhat more than liability under the current system, but they argue that "...a reasonably comprehensive patient compensation scheme--which would fully reimburse all actual longer-term financial losses that patients suffer as a result of iatrogenic injury--would be a small and readily affordable item in the budget of the health care system that generates these injuries..." Id at 109.

See also Kenneth S. Abraham and Paul C. Weiler, Enterprise Liability and the Evolution of the American Health-Care System, 108 Harv.

L.Rev. 381(1994); Barry R. Furrow, Enterprise Liability, 39 St. Louis L. Rev. 79(1995); Paul C. Weiler, The Case for No-Fault Medical Liability, 52 Md.L.Rev 908 (1993); Paul C. Weiler, <u>Medical Malpractice on Trial</u> (1991).

The following charts illustrate some of the permutations of enterprise liability. It is not a unitary concept; it varies with the fact-finding administrative structure, the nature of liability imposed, the measure of damages, and the mode of implementation.

Approach	Status Quo: Erratic Evolution	Organizational Liability Fault-Based	
		Provider as Big HMO	Neo-no-fault
Features	Fault-based liability determination; Jury as trier of fact, settlement in shadow of jury. Causal link required to specific physician; Damages include wages, medical expenses, pain & suffering (subject only to state statutory limits, such as caps)	Liability "channelled" to enterprise: hospital, HMO, rather than left on each provider; Can be achieved by legislation or by unilateral action, such as hospital excess coverage policy.	Institutional tender of offer of settle claim for an injury, on fixed schedule, in exchange for patient giving up right to sue.
Advantages	Evolutionary response to changes in environment of providers, as evidenced by doctrinal expansions of liability, damages, causal tests. Moral judgment as to individual physician error	Firm is better choice for managing risk, doing statistical analyses of risks, and providing feedback and incentives for risk reduction; Relieves physicians of defendant status; Lower administrative costs.	Reduces administrative costs by reducing litigation; Compensates more injuries, including small ones; Provides incentives for provider to monitor patient injury, due to direct financial impact.
Drawbacks	Fails to identify and compensate small injuries; Angers and terrifies physicians; Places deterrent focus on wrong pressure point.	Possibility of firm seeking to adversely select against higher risk patients; Firm might overreact, reducing physician autonomy by "overmanaging" their care, as HMO physicians sometimes have complained.	Incentive to tender likely to focus on litigious patients with serious injuries; Provider likely to cover up or avoid small claims, for which suits are not now filed, to minimize costs; One-sided, coercive of patients. Quid pro quo suspect, given possibility that injuries will be concealed.
Source	Fifty state court systems, plus federal system, with overlay of legislative reforms at the margins.	American Law Institute, Enterprise Responsibility for Personal Injury. Paul Weiler, et al. A Measure of Malpractice 122 et seq	Jeffrey O'Connell's writings of contract no-fault; Moore-Gephardt HR.3400; Weiler et al. Measure at 151.

Approach	Fault AMA	Workers Comp	No-Fault ACEs
		Administrative Models	
Features	State administrative agency, lawyer provided by state to patient; Claims reviewed, presented to Medical Board for decision. Fault-based criteria, no attempt to focus liability on enterprise, but rather on the individual physician.	Strict liability on enterprises for patient injuries Payment for tangible physical losses; collateral sources offset Causal test for payment, rather than fault.	List of Accelerated Compensable Events (ACEs); Bad outcomes on list automatically compensated for certain expenses and losses, foreclosed from litigation; Litigation or arbitration for uncovered outcomes; Prompt payment from insurer for claims on list.
Advantages	Smaller claims will be compensated, since state lawyer on salary, not dependent on contingency fee; Accuracy of fact-finding improved by elimination of jury, replacement by expert reviewers. Frivolous claims screened out early.	All the advantages of organizational liability, in centralizing risk management; Payment of many more claims, including ignored small ones, while limiting larger claims; Makes doctors happy by eliminating jury trials and proof of fault.	No-fault: a list of bad outcomes; easy determination in many cases; Quick payout, enhancing compensation of smaller claims. Reduced administrative costs.
Drawbacks	Focus on individual provider, weakens incentives for quality improvement; Layers of administrative structure may screen out high percentage of close cases, and undercompensate larger injuries; Expensive, politically unattractive administrative structure.	If new administrative agency required, same political objections as to AMA proposal, i.e. cost, new bureaucracy; Loss of moral force of tort suit; Definition of origin of claim; How does patient find out?	Costs in generating and constantly reforming the lists of compensable events; Disputes in the close cases end up in courts or arbitration.
Source	A.M.A. proposal	Weiler, *Measure* at 149.	Havighurst and Tancredi, "Medical Adversity Insurance--A No-Fault Approach to Medical Malpractice and Quality Assurance", 51 Milbank Mem Fund Q. 125 (Spring 1973).

Approach	"Pure" No-fault Systems Social Insurance	Performance Systems
Features	Compensation for medical injuries subsumed under general social insurance, like Social Security disability.	Medical injury compensation folded into provider reimbursement; Enterprise covers all subscriber care, including added medical costs from medical injury; No inquiry into fault or cause; Provider payment based on good and bad aggregate outcomes.
Advantages	Administratively efficient; Eliminates overlapping compensation systems and costly inquiry about cause or fault; Increases compensation of smaller injuries.	Good incentives for reducing costs of medical risks; Compensation of all claims, although at lower levels than tort suit; Administratively easy to process claims, since, like first party insurance, coverage is part of the subscriber's benefits.
Drawbacks	No deterrent effect for risk creating providers; Discontinuity between risk and deterrence may raise level of medical injuries; Requires effective backup regulatory or quality assurance systems.	Risks of adverse selection by firm to avoid riskier, more expensive subscribers; Calculation of reimbursement much more complicated, assuming ability to set a baseline for each subscriber, with payment for bad outcomes; Possible abuses by organizations of physician profiles to eliminate below average doctors based on faulty data, since costs much higher with compensation included.
Source	New Zealand until 1992.	Models for some features include staff model HMOs; contingency fees in litigation; performance bonuses in some businesses; B. Furrow, "Paying for Performance", forthcoming.

CHAPTER 5. ORGANIZING HEALTH CARE DELIVERY

Insert at page 457, after the Introduction, the following:

NOTE ON THE CHANGING STRUCTURE OF THE MODERN HEALTH CARE ENTERPRISE

Not very long ago, health care services were delivered primarily by doctors working in solo practice or as part of small groups usually practicing the same specialty and by non-profit hospitals operating independently or as part of a not terribly complex system that shared a few administrative or operational services. This began to change in the late 1970's and 1980's as hospitals adopted more complex organizational structures and entered into joint ventures and alliances with others. However, in the last several years we have witnessed an unprecedented wave of innovation and change in the way health care providers conduct business. Prompted by developments in health care financing and the possibility of health care reform, physicians, hospitals, and other providers have begun to reorganize their business enterprises and contractual relationships. In particular, they have developed so-called "integrated delivery systems" and other methods of increasing inter-provider linkages in order to meet the needs of managed care purchasers, such as HMOs, PPOs and self-insured employers. As described below, a whole new generation of organizations has begun to evolve to accomplish the objective of integrating the formerly autonomous business activities of providers.

PHYSICIAN PAYMENT REVIEW COMMISSION, ANNUAL REPORT TO CONGRESS (1995)

PROVIDER-DRIVEN INTEGRATION

The U.S. Health care system has been moving steadily away from delivery of health care through independent practitioners and toward more integrated approaches. As late as 1987, more than half of U.S. physicians were self-employed in solo or two-partner practice. By 1993, this figure had fallen to 37 percent.

While some of this reorganization of health care had been done directly by insurers, for example, through ownership of facilities and exclusive contracting with physicians, in other cases providers developed integrated arrangements on their own. Multispecialty group practices have long served to bring physicians together under common medical and financial management. More recently, physicians, hospitals, and other providers have begun to form new types of organizations at a fairly rapid pace. These new organizations range from relatively loose associations of physicians, through physician-hospital joint ventures, up to fully integrated insurer-provider HMOs.

* * *

INTEGRATING ORGANIZATIONS

Defining the new integrating organizations is not an easy task. Health care organizations are in flux as markets move toward more intensive management of care. A definition that describes the typical organization today might be obsolete two years from now as the typical style of practice changes. Consequently there are no agreed-upon standard definitions, and these definitions should be taken as approximate only.

* * *

INDEPENDENT PRACTICE ASSOCIATION

The independent practice association (IPA) is typically a physician-organized entity that contracts with payers on behalf of its member physicians. The typical IPA negotiates contracts with insurers and pays physicians on a fee-for-service basis with a withhold. Physicians may maintain significant business outside the IPA, join multiple IPAs, retain ownership of their own practices, and typically continue in their traditional style of practice. Physicians usually invest a modest fee (a few thousand dollars) to join the IPA. IPAs may also undertake a variety of additional roles, including utilization review, and practice management functions such as billing and group purchasing, resulting in greater centralization and standardization of medical practice.

* * *

PHYSICIAN-HOSPITAL ORGANIZATION

The physician-hospital organization [PHO] contracts with payers on behalf of the hospital and its affiliated physicians. The organization is responsible for negotiating health plan contracts, and in some cases, conducting utilization review, credentialing, and quality assurance. The

98

PHO may centralize some aspects of administrative services or encourage use of shared facilities for coordination of clinical care.

The typical PHO is a hospital-sponsored organization that centers around a single hospital and its medical staff. PHOs may also form as joint ventures between hospitals and existing physician organizations such as a large multispecialty medical group or an IPA. PHOs are further divided into open PHOs, which are open to all members of the hospital's staff, and closed PHOs, where the PHO chooses some physicians and excludes others.

As with the IPA, the typical PHO accounts for only a modest share of the physician's (or the hospital's) business. Physicians retain their own practices, and their relationship to payers other than those with whom the PHO negotiates is unchanged. As with IPAs, the PHO can move toward greater centralized control over practice management and medical practice.

* * *

GROUP PRACTICE

A medical group practice is defined as "the provision of health care services by three or more physicians who are formally organized as a legal entity in which business and clinical facilities, records, and personnel are shared. Income from medical services provided by the group are treated as receipts of the group and are distributed according to some prearranged plan."

The group practice is a well-established form of organization and one of the few organizational types for which good data are available. In 1991, physicians were split almost equally among three practice settings: group practice, solo or two-physician practice, or other patient care such as hospital-based practice.

* * *

GROUP PRACTICE WITHOUT WALLS

A group practice without walls (GPWW) refers to physicians in physically independent facilities who form a single legal entity to centralize the business aspects of their organization. In the typical case, the GPWW is organized by a strong, centralized clinic that adds individual physicians or small groups in satellite offices. In some cases, the GPWW is financially identical to a traditional group practice: It owns the assets of the individual practices and physicians share ownership of the GPWW, making it a unified business organization for the decentralized delivery of care. In other cases, physicians retain ownership of their own practices but enter into agreements for administrative and marketing functions. The GPWW may itself own certain ancillary services such as laboratory services.

MANAGEMENT SERVICES ORGANIZATION

The management services organization provides administrative and practice management services to physicians. An MSO may typically be owned by a hospital, hospitals, or investors. Large group practices may also establish MSOs as a way of capitalizing on their organizational skill by selling management services to otherwise unorganized physician groups.

MSOs can provide a very wide variety of services. Smaller and not-for-profit MSOs may limit operations to selling physicians various administrative support services, such as billing, group purchasing, and various aspects of office administration. In other cases, hospital-owned MSOs are the vehicle through which hospitals purchase physician practices outright, leaving the physician either as an employee of the hospital or as an independent contractor with the physical assets of the practice owned by the hospital. Large, for-profit MSOs typically purchase the assets of physician practices outright, install office managers and other personnel, hire the physician through a professional services contract, and negotiate contracts with managed-care plans, all in exchange for a share of gross receipts typically based on the physicians' current practice expenses.

* * *

HOSPITAL-OWNED MEDICAL PRACTICE

In addition to the purchase of a medical practice through an MSO, hospitals can directly purchase medical practices, typically as part of their outpatient department.

* * *

Finally, a number of functionally similar organizations are built around hospitals and physicians linked in exclusive arrangements. In these integrated delivery systems (IDSs), a hospital or hospitals and large multispecialty group practices form an organization for the delivery of care, with all physician revenues coming through the organization.[78] These include foundation model, staff model, and equity model IDSs.

The main difference among these organizations is in the legal formalities of who works for whom and in the professional autonomy of the affiliated physicians. In a typical foundation model system, the hospital establishes a not-for-profit foundation that purchases the assets of an existing physician group, signing an exclusive professional services contract with the physician corporation. Payers pay the foundation, which then pays the physicians' professional corporation.[79] In a staff model system, physicians work directly for the system without the intervening not-for-profit foundation and professional corporation. In an equity model system, physicians own a part of the system and share significantly in its financial success or failure.

In some markets, large group practices appear to be a significant alternative to these types of physician-hospital systems. In testimony before the Commission, [one witness] identified the capitated multispecialty group practice as the "center of gravity" of integrating activities in Southern California. In that marketplace, some large multispecialty groups are accepting capitation contracts from payers, then purchasing hospital services and coordinating the delivery of care, achieving system-type organization without a formal alliance with the hospital.

---

[78] While some researchers would call these integrated delivery systems a form of PHO, most reserve the term PHO for those organizations where only a small fraction of the physicians' revenues come through the organization.

[79] The presence of the foundation model system is due in part to state laws prohibiting the corporate practice of medicine, and the need for arms-length financial agreements between for-profit and not-for-profit entities.

As the preceding excerpt from the Physician Payment Review Commission suggests, providers have a wide variety of organizational models to choose among for promoting greater integration. The selection of any given arrangement seems to depend on a number of diverse and market-specific factors such as the degree of managed care penetration in the area; the nature and extent of rivalry among providers; the "politics" and "culture" of the provider community; and the business judgments of those in leadership positions.

In most markets, provider integration is still in its formative stages. Surveys indicate that as of 1994 only 9 percent of physicians had contracts with an MSO and 7 percent had joined a PHO in the last two years. Physician Payment Review Commission, 1995 Annual Report, 243-63 (1995). However, most observers believe that most hospitals and physicians will join some form of integrating organization within the near future. In addition, it is commonly noted that some of the new integrating organizations such as PHOs and MSOs are really transitional vehicles that will serve to "acclimatize" hospitals and physicians to the new environment created by managed care. By this view, after becoming accustomed to cooperating with each other, most providers will ultimately wind up in more fully integrated organizations that entail employment relationships and asset purchases. (For a different viewpoint, contending that much of the current trend will be undone and providers will revert to contractual arrangements, see Jeff Goldsmith, The Illusive Logic of Integration, Healthcare Forum 26 (Sept/Oct. 1994)).

For the lawyer advising clients considering these alternatives, structuring these evolving arrangements poses an enormous challenge. As discussed infra in this chapter and elsewhere in this Supplement, the selection and design of any health care organization typically raises problems that run the gamut of legal issues covered in this casebook: e.g.:

tax exempt status;

staff privileges;

physician recruitment and physician contracts;

corporate practice of medicine;

labor and employment issues;

fraud and abuse/self-referral issues;

antitrust; and

liability

With respect to each issue studied in this and ensuing chapters, it is useful to keep in mind the alternative integrated delivery structures being created and to evaluate what steps might be advisable to minimize legal risks.

There is a growing literature discussing the various organizational models for integration and analyzing the legal issues posed by each form. See, e.g., Carl H. Hitchner, et al., Integrated Delivery Systems: A Survey of Organizational Models, 29 Wake Forest L. Rev. 273 (1994); Integrated Delivery Systems Manual (Alan Fine, ed. 1993); Managed Care Law Manual (Health Law Center, 1994); 1 Furrow, et al., Health Law, § 5-49. See also, Steven Shortell et al., The New World of Managed Care: Creating Organized Delivery Systems, 13 Health Affs. 46 (Spring, 1994); Kenneth L. Levine, The Tax Status of Vertically Integrated Health Care Delivery Systems, 26 J.Health & Hosp. L. 257 (1993).

Insert at page 467, just above the Notes and Questions, the following:

NOTE: INTERNAL REVENUE TAX-EXEMPT HOSPITAL AUDIT GUIDELINES

Current Internal Revenue Service audit guidelines for the examination of tax-exempt hospitals evidence a more aggressive posture toward enforcement of the standards of tax exemption. The audit guidelines direct increased review of the satisfaction by the hospital of the community benefit standard (including an examination of the relationship between the number of Medicaid beneficiaries the facility serves compared to the number of Medicaid beneficiaries in the area). The guidelines also detail standards for the examination of physician compensation arrangements and joint ventures for violations of the private inurement proscription. Under the current audit guidelines, the Service coordinates its activities with those of the Department of Health and Human Services in the enforcement of the Emergency Medical Treatment and Labor Act, directing the examiners to review reports and records maintained by the hospital in relation to EMTALA. The Service also coordinates its activities with those of the Office of Inspector General in enforcing the fraud and abuse requirements. The audit guidelines are included in the Internal Revenue Manual, 7(10)69, HB 333.

Insert at page 474, just above Section B, the following:

GEISINGER HEALTH PLAN
v.
COMMISSIONER OF INTERNAL REVENUE
985 F.2d 1210 (3d Cir. 1993)

Lewis, Circuit Judge.

...This case requires us to decide whether a health maintenance organization (an "HMO") which serves a predominantly rural population, enrolls some Medicare subscribers, and which intends to subsidize some needy subscribers but, at present, serves only its paying subscribers, qualifies for exemption from federal income taxation under 26 U.S.C. § 501(c)(3). We hold that it does not.

* * *

. . .GHP was formed as a nonprofit corporation in 1984 and, by March 31, 1988, had enrolled 4,396 individuals and 448 groups (accounting for another 66,441 individual subscribers).

The Geisinger System consists of GHP and eight other nonprofit entities. All are involved in some way in promoting health care in 27 counties in northeastern and northcentral Pennsylvania. They include: the Geisinger Foundation (the "Foundation"); Geisinger Medical Center ("GMC"); the Geisinger Clinic (the "Clinic"); Geisinger Wyoming Valley Medical Center ("GWV"); Marworth; Geisinger System Services ("GSS") and two professional liability trusts. Each of these entities is exempt from federal income taxation under one or more sections of the Internal Revenue Code (the "Code").

In order to provide cost-effective delivery of health care to areas it had identified as medically underserved, GMC experimented with a pilot prepaid health plan between 1972 and 1985. The results were sufficiently favorable that the Geisinger System formed GHP to provide its own prepaid health plan. GHP's service area encompasses 17 predominantly rural counties within the area served by the Geisinger System. As of November 30, 1987, according to a finding of a bureau of the federal Department of Health and Human Services, 23 percent of GHP's subscribers resided in medically underserved areas while 65 percent resided in counties containing medically underserved areas.

GHP has two types of subscribers. First, it is open to all adult individuals who reside in its service area and satisfactorily complete a routine questionnaire regarding their medical history. From its inception through June 30, 1987, GHP accepted all but 11 percent of its individual applicants. Second, it enrolls group subscribers. Any individual who resides in GHP's service area and belongs to a group of at least 100 eligible enrollees may enroll as a group subscriber without completing a health questionnaire.

* * *

GHP describes itself as "providing health services." In reality, it contracts with other entities in the Geisinger System (at least one of which will contract with physicians from outside the Geisinger System) to provide services to GHP's subscribers. It also contracts with entities such as pharmacies to provide medical and hospital services to its subscribers in exchange for compensation. Under the terms of these contracts, GHP reimburses the hospitals and clinics by paying a negotiated per diem charge for inpatient services and a discounted percentage of billed charges for outpatient services. For the fiscal year ended June 30, 1987, the Clinic and GWV provided 80 percent of all hospital services to GHP subscribers. The remaining 20 percent were provided by other hospitals.

All physician services are provided to GHP subscribers pursuant to a contract between GHP and the Clinic. The contract requires the Clinic to open its emergency rooms to all GHP subscribers, regardless of ability to pay, just as the Clinic's emergency rooms are open to all members of the public, regardless of ability to pay. The Clinic will contract with unaffiliated physicians to provide required services, but for the year ended June 30, 1987, more than 84 percent of the physician services which the Clinic provided to GHP's subscribers were performed by physicians who were employees of the Clinic. GHP compensates the Clinic for the physicians' services by paying a fixed amount per subscriber.

* * *

GHP has adopted a subsidized dues program which has not yet been implemented. The program would establish a fund comprised of charitable donations and operating funds to subsidize GHP subscribers who are unable to pay their premiums. The fund would, in GHP's view, "add to the security of [subscribers], any of whom may at some time suffer financial misfortune due to loss of employment, physical or mental disability or other causes beyond their control and which impute no dishonor to the [subscriber]." Although the program makes reference to subsidizing people who are already subscribers, GHP's submissions indicate that it also intends to admit people who require subsidization at the time they apply.

Despite GHP's initial projection that it would fund the program by raising $125,000 in contributions over its first three years of operation, it has been unable to do so, it claims, because potential donors cannot be assured that contributions will be deductible on their federal income tax returns until GHP receives recognition of tax-exempt status under section 501(c)(3). GHP has likewise been unable to support the program with operating funds because it operated at a loss from its inception through the time the record in this case closed.

GHP enrolls some subscribers who are covered by Medicare and Medicaid. As of March 31, 1988, it had enrolled 1,064 Medicare recipients at a reduced rate on a wraparound basis, meaning that it will cover what Medicare does not. It also has enrolled a small number of Medicaid recipients in a few exceptional situations. Generally, however, GHP cannot offer coverage to Medicaid recipients until and unless it contracts with the Pennsylvania Department of Welfare, which administers Pennsylvania's Medicaid program. GHP has negotiated with the Department to obtain such a contract, but efforts to reach agreement have thus far been unsuccessful.

Shortly after its incorporation, GHP applied to the IRS for recognition of exemption. The Commissioner ruled that GHP was not exempt because (1) it was not operated exclusively for exempt purposes under section 501(c)(3); and (2) it could not vicariously qualify for exemption as an "integral part" of the Geisinger System. [GHP filed suit in Tax Court, which reversed the IRS denial of tax exempt status.]

* * *

106

GHP argues that it qualifies for exemption because it serves the charitable purpose of promoting health in the communities it serves. There are no published revenue rulings and only one previously litigated case addressing whether an HMO may qualify for exemption under section 501(c)(3). The sole case on this issue is a Tax Court case, Sound Health Association v. Commissioner, 71 T.C. 158 (1978), acq. 1981-2 C.B. 2.

* * *

In Sound Health, the Tax Court applied the law pertaining to nonprofit hospitals as charitable entities in measuring an HMO's claim for exemption. Although this case does not involve a hospital, neither the IRS nor GHP argue that this distinction rendered inappropriate the Tax Court's reliance upon Sound Health in examining GHP's request for exemption. To the contrary, in fact, the IRS concedes that GHP's stated purpose, like a hospital's stated purpose, is to promote health; it simply argues that Sound Health and the hospital precedents require more than mere promotion of health in order to qualify for tax exemption. The IRS argues that the relevant precedents require at least some "indicia of charity" in the form of serving the public and providing some services free of charge.

While we are not bound by any approach taken by the Tax Court, we find no reason to conclude that the Tax Court erred in applying hospital precedent to its analysis of GHP's exempt status. Accordingly, in light of the parties' and the Tax Court's reliance on the law regarding the tax-exempt status of nonprofit hospitals in formulating the test to be applied to HMOs seeking exemption under section 501(c)(3), we will measure GHP's tax-exempt status against that standard. In doing so, we recognize that courts are to give weight to IRS revenue rulings but may disregard them if they conflict with the statute they purport to interpret or its legislative history, or if they are otherwise unreasonable. [ ]

* * *

[N]o clear test has emerged to apply to nonprofit hospitals seeking tax exemptions. Instead, a nonprofit hospital will qualify for tax-exempt status if it primarily benefits the community. One way to qualify is to provide emergency room services without regard to patients' ability to pay; another is to provide free care to indigents. A hospital may also benefit the community by serving those who pay their bills through public programs such as Medicaid or Medicare. For the most part, however, hospitals must meet a flexible "community benefit" test based upon a variety of indicia.

* * *

The Sound Health HMO resembled GHP in many ways. Its articles of incorporation listed a number of charitable purposes relating to the promotion of health. Like GHP's subscribers, its subscribers paid for services based upon a community rating system, and a subsidized dues program assisted those who could not afford subscribership. Subscribers also had to satisfy eligibility requirements similar to GHP's.

Unlike GHP, however, the Sound Health HMO provided health care services itself rather than simply arranging for others to provide them to its subscribers. [FN] It also employed doctors, health care providers and medical personnel who were not affiliated with the HMO to provide health care to its subscribers. Significantly, the Sound Health HMO provided services to both subscribers and members of the general public through an outpatient clinic which it operated and at which it treated all emergency patients, subscribers or not, and regardless of ability to pay. It also adjusted rates for and provided some free care to patients who were not subscribers. It offered public educational programs regarding health.

* * *

The Sound Health court went to great lengths to find a benefit to the community rather than simply a benefit to the HMO's subscribers. It rejected the argument that the HMO at issue benefitted only its subscribers, finding: The most important feature of the Association's [subscribership] form of organization is that the class of persons eligible for [subscribership], and hence eligible to benefit from the Association's activities, is practically unlimited. The class of possible [subscribers] of the Association is, for all practical purposes, the class of members of the community itself. The major barrier to [subscribership] is lack of money, but a subsidized dues program demonstrates that even this barrier is not intended to be absolute.... It is safe to say that the class of persons potentially benefitted by the Association is not so small that its relief is of no benefit to the community.

As we have observed, however, the court listed several factors in addition to open subscribership as indications that the Sound Health HMO was operated for charitable purposes. Chief among these were the HMO's operation of an emergency room open to all persons, subscribers or not, and regardless of ability to pay; rendering some free care to both subscribers and those who did not subscribe; conducting research; and offering an educational program. GHP refers to these as "marketing techniques," but, as the Sound Health court noted, the HMO benefitted the community by engaging in these activities.

* * *

In administrative proceedings in this case, the IRS contended that GHP had to meet a strict, fourteen-factor test based upon the facts of Sound Health in order to qualify for tax-exempt status. Upon review, we cannot agree that any strict, multi-factor test is appropriate when determining whether an HMO qualifies for tax-exempt status under section 501(c)(3). Rather, the determination must be based upon the totality of the circumstances, with an eye toward discerning whether the HMO in question benefits the community in addition to its subscribers.

Viewed in this light, GHP standing alone does not merit tax-exempt status under section 501(c)(3). GHP cannot say that it provides any health care services itself. Nor does it ensure that people who are not GHP subscribers have access to health care or information about health care. According to the record, it neither conducts research nor offers educational programs, much less educational programs open to the public. It benefits no one but its subscribers.

GHP argues that the Sound Health requirement that an HMO seeking exemption must provide an emergency room open to all is rendered obsolete by Rev.Rul. 83-157. This may indeed be the case. Under the logic of Rev.Rul. 83-157, GHP need not provide an emergency room if doing so would unnecessarily duplicate services offered elsewhere in the area. Because the Clinic and other Geisinger System facilities provide emergency care to GHP's subscribers, requiring GHP to operate an emergency room may be unnecessarily duplicative and wasteful.

This conclusion would not, however, automatically bestow upon GHP an entitlement to tax-exempt status. The test remains one of community benefit, and GHP cannot demonstrate that it benefits anyone but its subscribers.

It is true that GHP is open to anyone who can afford to pay and that, like the HMO in Sound Health, GHP apparently intends to lower, or even to remove, this potential economic barrier to subscribing through its subsidized dues program. As we explain below, however, the mere presence of the subsidized dues program does not necessarily invite a conclusion that GHP benefits the community.

First, the Sound Health court ventured too far when it reasoned that the presence of a subsidized dues program meant that the HMO in question served a large enough class that it benefitted the community.

* * *

The mere fact that a person need not pay to belong does not necessarily mean that GHP, which provides services only to those who do belong, serves a public purpose which primarily benefits the community. The community benefitted is, in fact, limited to those who belong to GHP since the requirement of subscribership remains a condition precedent to any service. Absent any additional indicia of a charitable purpose, this self-imposed precondition suggests that GHP is primarily benefiting itself (and, perhaps, secondarily benefiting the community) by promoting subscribership throughout the areas it serves.

* * *

Second, the Sound Health court need not have gone as far as it did. The presence of a subsidized dues program was not the only factor it considered when deciding that the HMO in question qualified for tax-exempt status. For example, the HMO in Sound Health "in effect, [ran] a substantial outpatient clinic as an important ingredient of its medical care services." It also provided free care even to persons who did not subscribe and offered educational programs to the public.

Finally, even considering the subsidized dues program, the amount of benefit GHP intends to confer on people other than paying subscribers is minuscule. GHP anticipates subsidizing approximately 35 people. We cannot say that GHP operates primarily to benefit the community at large rather than its subscribers by arranging for health care for only 35 people, who would not otherwise belong, as compared to more than 70,000

110

paying subscribers. GHP argues that the HMO in Sound Health had provided only $158.50 in subsidies when it was granted tax-exempt status. This is true, but, as previously noted, the HMO in that case also benefitted the community in other ways, most notably by providing free or reduced-cost care to people who were not subscribers. An HMO must primarily benefit the community, not its subscribers plus a few people, in order to qualify for tax-exempt status under section 501(c)(3).

FN. GHP is, in fact, a different type of HMO than the HMO in Sound Health. HMOs had traditionally owned or provided hospital services themselves for a set, prepaid fee. In the late 1970's and early 1980's, however, Individual Practice Association (IPA) HMOs proliferated. "Unlike the traditional group practice or staff model HMOs, IPA-type HMOs do not directly own or provide hospital services. Rather, they arrange for the provision of hospital services by contracting with existing hospitals on a fee for service, capitation, per diem, or other basis." Mancino, Income Tax Exemption of the Contemporary Nonprofit Hospital, 32 St. Louis U.L.J. 1015, 1034 (1988). GHP appears to fall within the IPA-HMO category. Also in the 1980's, nonprofit hospitals themselves began to form, purchase and contract with alternative delivery systems such as HMOs to vertically integrate and to maintain control over patient admissions. Mancino, 32 St. Louis U.L.J. at 1035. The Geisinger System's formation of GHP fits perfectly into this pattern.

NOTE

What does GHP need to do to gain § 501(c)(3) status under this case? Could it simply expand its subsidy program? Could subsidized memberships be considered the equivalent of charity care for hospitals, satisfying an unmet need for primary care?

The Third Circuit subsequently considered and rejected Geisinger Health Plan's claim that it should be granted tax exempt status as an "integral part" of the Geisinger System:

GEISINGER HEALTH PLAN
v.
COMMISSIONER OF INTERNAL REVENUE
30 F.3d 494 (3d Cir. 1995)

Lewis, Circuit Judge.

* * *

The Geisinger System consists of GHP and eight other entities, all involved in some way in promoting health care in 27 counties in northeastern and northcentral Pennsylvania. They are: the Geisinger Foundation (the "Foundation"), Geisinger Medical Center ("GMC"), Geisinger Clinic (the "Clinic"), Geisinger Wyoming Valley Medical Center ("GWV"), Marworth, Geisinger System Services ("GSS") and two professional liability trusts. All of these other entities are recognized as exempt from federal income taxation under one or more sections of the Internal Revenue Code.

The Foundation controls all these entities, as well as three for-profit corporations. It has the power to appoint the corporate members of GHP, GMC, GWV, GSS, the Clinic, and Marworth, and those members elect the boards of directors of those entities. The Foundation also raises funds for the Geisinger System. * * *

GMC operates a 569-bed regional medical center * * * It accepts patients without regard to ability to pay, including Medicare, Medicaid and charity patients. It operates a full-time emergency room open to all, regardless of ability to pay. It also serves as a teaching hospital.

GWV is a 230-bed hospital located in Wilkes-Barre, Pennsylvania. It accepts patients regardless of ability to pay, and it operates a full-time emergency room open to all, regardless of ability to pay.

The Clinic provides medical services to patients at 43 locations throughout the System's service area. It also conducts extensive medical research in conjunction with GMC and physicians who perform medical services for GMC, GWV and other entities in the Geisinger System * * * It accepts patients without regard to their ability to pay.

Marworth operates two alcohol detoxification and rehabilitation centers and offers educational programs to prevent alcohol and substance abuse.

GSS employs management and other personnel who provide services to entities in the Geisinger System.

* * * [T]he Geisinger System apparently decided to create GHP after GMC experimented with a pilot prepaid health plan between 1972

and 1985. The experience was positive, and the Geisinger System formed GHP to provide its own prepaid health plan.

It organized GHP as a separate entity within the System (as opposed to operating it from within the Clinic, GMC or GWV) for three reasons. First, HMOs in Pennsylvania are subject to extensive regulation by the Commonwealth's Departments of Health and Insurance. [ ] Operating GHP separately enables other entities in the System to avoid having to comply with the burdensome requirements associated with that regulation. Second, those administering the System believe it preferable for GHP's organization and management to remain separate from those of the System's other entities because it serves a wider geographic area than any of those other entities. Finally, under Pennsylvania law at least one-third of GHP's directors must be subscribers. [ ] Establishing GHP as a separate entity avoids disrupting the governance of the other Geisinger System entities to comply with this requirement. For example, establishing an HMO within GMC would have required GMC to canvass its board of directors to ensure that one-third of them subscribed to the HMO. If they did not, GMC would have had to amend its by-laws or other governing documents to add directorships so that one-third of the directors were subscribers. Incorporating GHP separately eliminates the need for such reorganization.

* * *

GHP's interaction with other Geisinger System entities is varied. Its most significant contact is with the Clinic, from which it purchases the physician services its subscribers require by paying a fixed amount per member per month, as set forth in a Medical Services Agreement. Eighty-four percent of physician services are provided by doctors who are employees of the Clinic; the remaining 16 percent are provided by doctors who are not affiliated with the Clinic but who have contracted with the Clinic to provide services to GHP subscribers. GHP has similarly entered into contracts with GMC and GWV, as well as 20 non-related hospitals. When GHP subscribers require hospital care, these hospitals provide it pursuant to the terms of their contracts, for either a negotiated per diem charge or a discounted percentage of billed charges. GHP has also contracted with GSS to purchase office space, supplies and administrative services.

* * *

GHP argues that [the "integral part" doctrine requires the court] to examine whether the Clinic or GMC could retain tax-exempt status if it were to absorb GHP. It thus compares the attributes of a hypothetically merged Clinic/GHP or GMC/GHP entity to the attributes of the HMO held to be exempt in [Sound Health]. Concluding that the merged entity would display more indicia of entitlement to exemption than the Sound Health HMO, GHP urges that it is exempt because of the characteristics of the hypothetical merged entity. Despite its superficial appeal, we reject this argument and hold that the integral part doctrine does not mean that GHP would be exempt solely because either GMC or the Clinic could absorb it while retaining its tax-exempt status. While this is a necessary condition to applying the doctrine, it is not the only condition. GHP is separately incorporated for reasons it found administratively and politically advantageous. While it may certainly benefit from that separate incorporation, it must also cope with the consequences flowing from it. [ ]

* * *

. . . [A] subsidiary which is not entitled to exempt status on its own may only receive such status as an integral part of its § 501(c)(3) qualified parent if (i) it is not carrying on a trade or business which would be an unrelated trade or business (that is, unrelated to exempt activities) if regularly carried on by the parent, and (ii) its relationship to its parent somehow enhances the subsidiary's own exempt character to the point that, when the boost provided by the parent is added to the contribution made by the subsidiary itself, the subsidiary would be entitled to § 501(c)(3) status. [Editor's note: The court states in a footnote that its discussion would extend to "some other form of affiliation" and is not intended to refer only to a single parent, single subsidiary structure.]

* * *

[Editor's note: The court describes organizations which have been granted exempt status by the Service through application of the integral part doctrine, including a law journal which, though sold to the "public," was operated by and within a law school and staffed by law students as part of the educational program of the school.]

Here, we do not think that GHP receives any "boost" from its association with the Geisinger System * * * [T]he contribution that GHP makes to community health is not increased at all by the fact that GHP is a subsidiary of the System rather than being an independent organization which sends its subscribers to a variety of hospitals and clinics.

As our examination of the manner in which GHP interacts with other entities in the System makes clear, its association with those entities does nothing to increase the portion of the community for which GHP promotes health -- it serves no more people as a part of the System than it would serve otherwise. It may contribute to the System by providing more patients than the System might otherwise have served, thus arguably allowing the System to promote health among a broader segment of the community than could be served without it, but its provision of patients to the System does not enhance its own promotion of health; the patients it provides -- its subscribers -- are the same patients it serves without its association with the System. To the extent it promotes health among non-GHP-subscriber patients of the System, it does so only because GHP subscribers' payments to the System help finance the provision of health care to others. An entity's mere financing of the exempt purposes of a related organization does not constitute furtherance of that organization's purpose so as to justify exemption.

* * *

NOTES

1.   The court refers to "unrelated trade or business" as a part of the test for the integral part doctrine. The issue of the taxation of unrelated business income earned by a tax-exempt entity is treated at pages 474-482 of the case book.

2.   Structuring complex health care delivery systems often requires trade-offs between the advantages and disadvantages of particular organizational forms. What were the trade-offs faced by the Geisinger System in its choice of organizational form for GHP?

3.   It is possible that the Geisinger System, including GHP, could qualify for tax-exempt status as an integrated delivery system under the current standards applied by the Service. (See discussion below.) If Congress were to enact legislation to "rationalize" the exempt status of hospitals, HMOs and integrated delivery systems, such as the Geisinger System, what would you advise them to do?

NOTE: TAX EXEMPT STATUS OF INTEGRATED DELIVERY SYSTEMS

The development of integrated delivery systems (IDSs) has been the most significant change in health care delivery systems in the early 1990s. An IDS may take many forms, but in all its forms an IDS represents a vertical integration of health care services, usually including hospital and other institutional services, office-based primary medical care and a managed care component. An IDS also may represent a consolidation of health care providers; for example, a number of hospitals in a city or region may join together, with varying degrees of central control of decisionmaking.

A variety of legal issues, beyond tax exemption, arise in the organization of an IDS. For example, the physician-hospital arrangement, particularly if organized as an entity jointly owned by physicians and a non-physician entity such as a hospital or foundation or holding company, raises issues of the corporate practice of medicine. The inclusion of a managed care function, where the system or particular entities within a system take on a risk, for example, through capitation, may trigger state insurance regulation. Licensure and accreditation procedures may differ with the placement of certain functions, such as home health services, within another organization rather than structuring them as stand-alone independent entities. Compensation and purchases within the system may raise self-referral and fraud and abuse issues. Each of these issues, as well as the demands of tax-exempt status if that is desired, will have an effect on the structure chosen for the system.

The tax treatment of IDSs has evolved rapidly under the pressure of many applications for § 501(c)(3) status over the past few years. The IRS has granted § 501(c)(3) status to many IDSs organized in a variety of ways. See e.g., Rockford Memorial Health Services Corporation Exemption Ruling, 1994 WL 510148 (April 4, 1994). In granting exempt status to an IDS, the Service examines satisfaction of the community benefit standard, private inurement, the terms of any purchases of medical practices and the system's governance structure, limiting physician representation on the board to no more than 20%. The Service also continues to incorporate fraud and abuse concerns within their review of exempt status. Integrated Delivery Systems Pose Administrative Challenges, CCH Tax Day: Federal 94-105-008 (Apr. 15, 1994). Concerning integrated delivery systems, see discussion in this supplement supra and Symposium in 29 Wake Forest Law Review 1-339

(1994), which includes articles on corporate structure, tax exemption and other issues.

Increased integration between hospitals and physicians through the formation of physician-hospital organizations (PHOs) and management service organizations (MSOs) has also raised exemption issues. The Service thus far has used its traditional standards for examination of joint ventures that involve both for-profit and not-for-profit entities. So, for example, the Service examines an exempt hospital's participation in a PHO to assure that the ability of the hospital to achieve its exempt purposes is not jeopardized by exposing the hospital to an unacceptable financial risk or by so limiting the hospital's decisionmaking authority in the organization that it may not be able to achieve its exempt purposes. (See e.g., PLR 9024085 in the casebook at pages 477, 479-480 for an application of these standards.) The Service currently assumes that PHOs are not exempt themselves due to the degree of physician control typical of their governance structure. The Service is examining MSO-physician contracts under the proscription against private inurement to assure that physicians pay fair market value for MSO services. (See discussion of private inurement at pages 505-511 in the casebook and GCM 39862 below.) Integrated Delivery Systems Warned on Tax Exemption, 94 Tax Notes Today 250-7 (Dec. 22, 1994). For further description of PHOs and MSOs, see discussion supra this supplement.

Insert at page 505, just above Section C, the following:

NOTE: THE EFFECT OF MANAGED CARE ON PHYSICIAN PRIVILEGES, CONTRACTS AND EMPLOYMENT

An article in the American Medical News calls it "an ugly new reality for a shiny new time," in reporting on the striking increase in physician terminations. Howard Larkin, You're Fired, 38 Am. Med. News 17 (Feb. 13, 1995). Increasing insecurity for physicians -- from termination of hospital contracts, layoffs from employment with physician partnerships and group practices and "deselection" from managed care provider lists -- has been a by-product, or goal, of change in health care delivery and finance systems (depending on your point of view).

Traditional staff privileges arrangements provided physicians with a high degree of security and substantial power within the hospital. As described in note 4 at page 490 and note 5 at page 505 in the casebook, the shift from privileges to contract represents a shift in power from physicians to health care organizations, a change that has been stimulated by managed care, in which management of physician decisionmaking is essential. Hospital-physician relationships continue to change with an apparent increase in the incorporation of practice profiles within the privileges process (see note 6 at page 491 of the casebook) and in the use of contracts for physician services. Courts have continued to be amenable to cost-explicit considerations and generally have upheld no-cause, no-procedure termination clauses, such as those described in Mateo-Woodburn at page 498 in the casebook, including contract termination clauses which specifically provide for automatic and simultaneous revocation of privileges. See e.g., St. Mary's Hospital of Athens v. Radiology Professional Corporation, 421 S.E.2d 731 (Ga.App. 1992)

Hospital staff privileges are still quite important to most physicians, but participation in managed care programs (whether that be a health maintenance organization, a preferred provider organization or some other organization) has become critical in markets where the vast majority of patients are insured in a managed care rather than fee-for-service program. The issues of physician-organization relationships presented in this chapter extend beyond hospitals, of course, and increasingly reach the relationship of physicians with managed care organizations and other delivery and financing systems. In particular, issues relating to admission of a physician to a managed care program and to termination from such a program (called "deselection" by some) have begun to appear in the case law.

Case law on hospital privileges and hospital-physician contracts (as well as law concerning employment-at-will and restrictive covenants, discussed at pages 511 et seq. in the casebook) forms the current doctrinal framework for analysis of common law claims in disputes arising from denial of an application for or termination from participation in a managed care program. One of the many issues raised by the changes in the health care system stimulated by managed care is how the public interest is best served -- in terms of quality, cost and access to care. Should the law governing managed care replicate some form of the staff privileges procedural system or should it adopt the stance the majority of courts have taken in enforcing physician contracts, including no-cause, no-procedure terminations, as written and agreed upon by the parties. By and large, cases concerning contractual relations between physicians and managed care plans have thus far enforced contract terms as written. One court, however, has indicated that managed care plans would be required, under the common law, to meet minimum procedural requirements in making adverse decisions against providers:

DELTA DENTAL PLAN
v.
BANASKY
27 Cal.App.4th 1598, 33 Cal.Rptr.2d 381 (1994)

Klein, Presiding Justice.

The essential question presented is whether Delta's determination as to what constitutes the usual, customary and reasonable fees for certain dental procedures by its participating dentists is final and binding, or whether Delta's internal decision is subject to judicial review by way of administrative mandamus. [ ]

* * *

a. Overview of Delta's internal review mechanism.

Under the Membership Procedures [the provider-plan contract], the procedures summarized below apply to Delta's modification of a participating dentist's list of usual fees. [According to the court, these procedures also apply to other "membership actions," including admission of a provider to membership, termination of membership, probation of a dentist member, refusal of a participating dentist agreement and/or list of usual fees, and termination of a participating dentist agreement.]

* * *

Delta may initiate a membership action by mailing written notice of the nature, effective date and factual basis for the membership action, at least 15 days before the effective date thereof. The notice shall advise the dentist that Delta shall review and consider any written evidence presented to refute the basis for the membership action.

Within 45 days of receiving such evidence, Delta's president is required to render a written decision to be mailed to the dentist. The decision shall overrule or modify the membership action only if the dentist has refuted the factual basis for the membership action with acceptable documentary evidence.

The dentist may appeal said decision to the Committee by filing notice of appeal within 10 days, along with a written statement of reasons why the dentist disagrees with Delta's decision. The dentist may request the Committee to conduct a hearing. Delta is required to forward to the Committee its written evidence in support of the membership action, the written evidence previously submitted by the dentist, the decision, the notice of appeal, and the dentist's written contentions. The Committee decides by majority vote whether to hold a hearing.

The Committee consists of three corporate members or dentist members appointed by the chairman of the board. In the event the Committee decides not to hold a hearing, the Committee must issue a written decision within 45 days of the date of the notice of appeal. If the Committee proceeds with a hearing, it considers the written evidence previously submitted as well as any additional evidence offered at the hearing, and issues a written decision within five days of the close of the hearing. In either case, the decision of the Committee "shall be final and binding upon Delta and the [dentist] and there shall be no further right to administrative review or appeal." [ ]

The issue becomes whether the Committee's decision is subject to judicial scrutiny, notwithstanding this provision in the Membership Procedures to the contrary.

b. Delta is required to accord the dentists fair procedure.

"California courts have long recognized a common law right to fair procedure protecting individuals from arbitrary exclusion or expulsion from private organizations which control important economic interests." [ ] Fair procedure comes into play where private organizations are "tinged with public stature or purpose" or attain a "quasi-public significance," as contrasted with purely private associations which have no larger "purpose or stature than pleasant, friendly and congenial social relationships." [ ] Further, the right to fair procedure with respect to membership actions is not limited to matters of exclusion or expulsion. [ ]

Delta controls an important economic interest as the largest dental health plan in California, covering over 8 million individuals. Therefore, continued membership on Delta's panel of participating dentists and Delta's modification of a participating dentist's list of usual, customary and reasonable fees implicates the right to fair procedure.

* * *

Here, Delta is required by law to accord its participating dentists fair procedure. What constitutes fair procedure is not fixed or judicially prescribed, but the basic ingredients include notice and a hearing, even if the rules of the association make no provision therefor. [ ] Because Delta's Committee's decision must be pursuant to a hearing, which contemplates the receiving of evidence and the vesting of discretion in a trier of fact, Delta's decision is subject to judicial review [pursuant to California's mandamus statute].

* * *

NOTES

1.   How does the court's opinion in Banasky compare to the California decision of Mateo-Woodburn at page 498 of the text? Are they compatible?

2.   The American Medical Association lobbied hard in 1994-1995 in state legislatures and in the U.S. Congress for a legislative package that would, among other things, guarantee physicians some degree of security in their contractual relationships with managed care organizations by allowing terminations for cause only and by requiring pre-termination procedures. The campaign failed in state legislatures, but apparently will be pursued on the federal level. American Medical Association Physician Health Plans and Networks Act of 1994, Chicago (1994). What are the interests at stake in such proposals?

3.   Physician credentialing in managed care, including the standards used by such organizations for evaluation of physicians, has been a significant issue for the private accreditation programs that evaluate managed care. See, e.g., Madeline Schneikart, Credentialing in Managed Care, 20 Physician Executive 31 (Sept. 1994), reporting on credentialing standards established for accredited managed care plans by the JCAHO and the National Committee for Quality Assurance; Howard Larkin, All Aboard? Managed Care Plans Increasingly Require Physicians to be Board Certified, 38 Am. Med. News 17 (Mar. 13, 1995).

4.   In managed care plans that are part of a self-insured employee benefits plan, ERISA may preempt both common law breach of contract claims by terminated physicians and state legislation that attempts to

prescribe the relationship between physicians and managed care organizations See e.g., Zuniga v. Blue Cross and Blue Shield of Michigan, 1995 WL 251112 (6th Cir.); BPS Clinical Laboratories v. Blue Cross and Blue Shield of Michigan, 522 N.W.2d 902 (Mich.App. 1994). But see, Stuart Circle Hospital Corp. v. Aetna Health Management, 995 F.2d 500 (4th Cir. 1993). See chapters 6 and 7 in the casebook.

5.   Antitrust claims have formed a significant portion of the litigation by physicians against managed care organizations. See chapter 8 in the casebook and supplemental materials infra.

6.   Federal and state employment discrimination statutes, such as Title VII, the Age Discrimination in Employment Act and the Americans with Disabilities Act, can reach physician claims against managed care plans and organizations, even where the physician-plan or physician-organization relationship does not meet a layperson's definition of an employment relationship. See note 9 at page 492 in the casebook.

Insert at page 511, just above the Notes and Questions, the following:

The Internal Revenue Service issued a General Counsel Memorandum (GCM 39862) late in 1991 that revoked three earlier Private Letter Rulings concerning physician-hospital joint ventures in which the hospital sold its future net income from certain outpatient departments to an entity in which members of the hospitals' medical staff held ownership interests. Contrary to the earlier Private Letter Rulings, the Service in GCM 39862 found that such joint ventures would jeopardize the § 501(c)(3) status of the hospital. The analysis of GCM 39862 is generally viewed as going beyond the specific joint venture considered and as having implications for all physician-hospital joint ventures. It also provides an insight into the Service's current view toward § 501(c)(3) status for hospitals.

**General Counsel Memorandum
39862 (Dec. 2, 1991)**

ANALYSIS

Background

The [net income stream] joint venture arrangements...are just one variety of an increasingly common type of competitive behavior engaged in by hospitals in response to significant changes in their operating environment. Many medical and surgical procedures once requiring inpatient care, still the exclusive province of hospitals, now are performed on an outpatient basis, where every private physician is a potential competitor. The marked shift in governmental policy from regulatory cost controls to competition has fundamentally changed the way all hospitals, for-profit and not, do business.

A driving force behind the new hospital operating environment was the federal Medicare Program's 1983 shift from cost-based reimbursement for covered inpatient hospital services to fixed, per- case, prospective payments. This change to a diagnosis-related prospective payment system ("PPS") dramatically altered hospital financial incentives. PPS severed the link between longer hospital stays with more services provided each patient and higher reimbursement. It substituted strong incentives to control the costs of each individual inpatient's care while attracting a greater number of admissions. Medicare policies are highly influential; the program accounts for nearly 40% of the average hospital's revenues.

The need to increase admission volume was accompanied by a perceived need to influence physician treatment decisions which, by and large, were unaffected by the change to PPS. Hospitals realized that, in addition to attracting more patients, they needed to control utilization of ancillary hospital services, discharge Medicare beneficiaries as quickly as is medically appropriate, and operate more efficiently. Traditionally, physicians treating their private patients at a hospital had enjoyed nearly complete independence of professional judgement. Since they are paid separately by Medicare and other third party payers on the basis of billed charges, they still have an incentive to render more services to each patient over a longer period in order to enhance their own earnings. Once hospital and physician economic incentives diverged, hospitals began seeking ways to stimulate loyalty among members of their medical staffs and to encourage or reward physician behaviors deemed desirable.

* * *

As in the present cases, there often are multiple reasons why hospitals are willing to engage in joint ventures and other sophisticated financial arrangements with physicians. In seeking Service approvals for transactions, hospitals frequently cite the need to raise capital and to give physicians a stake in the success of a new enterprise or service.

* * *

I. SALE OF THE REVENUE STREAM FROM A HOSPITAL
ACTIVITY ALLOWS NET PROFITS TO INURE TO THE BENEFIT
OF PHYSICIAN-INVESTORS.

* * *

That previously stated position [that physician members of the
hospital's medical staff are subject to the prohibition against inurement]
clearly fits the facts in the present cases. While most physicians on the
medical staffs of the subject hospitals presumably are not employees and
do not provide any compensable services directly to the hospitals, they
do have a close professional working relationship with the hospitals. The
physicians have applied for and been granted privileges to admit and treat
their private patients at the hospital. They are bound by the medical staff
bylaws, which may be viewed as a constructive contract between them
and the hospital. Individually, and as a group, they largely control the
flow of patients to and from the hospital and patients' utilization of
hospital services while there. Some may serve other roles at the hospital,
such as that of part-time employee, department head, Board member, etc.
Moreover, once the arrangements at issue commenced, each
physician-investor became a joint venture partner of the hospital or an
affiliate.

Even though medical staff physicians are subject to the inurement
proscription, that does not mean there can be no economic dealings
between them and the hospitals. The inurement proscription does not
prevent the payment of reasonable compensation for goods or services.
It is aimed at preventing dividend-like distributions of charitable assets
or expenditures to benefit a private interest. This Office has stated
"inurement is likely to arise where the financial benefit represents a
transfer of the organization's financial resources to an individual solely
by virtue of the individual's relationship with the organization, and
without regard to the accomplishment of exempt purposes." . . . GCM
38459, EE-68-79 (July 31, 1980).

* * *

The proper starting point for our analysis of the net revenue
stream arrangements is to ask what the hospital gets in return for the
benefit conferred on the physician-investors. Put another way, we ask

124

whether and how engaging in the transaction furthers the hospital's exempt purposes. Here, there appears to be little accomplished that directly furthers the hospitals' charitable purposes of promoting health. No expansion of health care resources results; no new provider is created. No improvement in treatment modalities or reduction in cost is foreseeable. We have to look very carefully for any reason why a hospital would want to engage in this sort of arrangement.

* * *

Assuming, arguendo, that [a hospital] did have a pressing need for an advance of cash, we could examine this type of transaction strictly as a financing mechanism. It certainly is permissible for a section 501(c)(3) hospital to borrow funds against future earnings; in fact, they often use tax exempt bonds to borrow at favorable interest rates. Nevertheless, we do not believe it would be proper under most circumstances for a charitable organization to borrow funds under an agreement, even with an outside commercial lender, where the organization would pay as interest a stated percentage of its earnings. While doing so might not constitute inurement if an outside lender were involved (but see discussion of private benefit, below), it would if the lender were, as here, an insider. In any event, we do not believe these transactions were undertaken to raise needed cash.

Whether admitted or not, we believe the hospitals engaged in these ventures largely as a means to retain and reward members of their medical staffs; to attract their admissions and referrals; and to pre-empt the physicians from investing in or creating a competing provider....Giving (or selling) medical staff physicians a proprietary interest in the net profits of a hospital under these circumstances creates a result that is indistinguishable from paying dividends on stock. Profit distributions are made to persons having a personal and private interest in the activities of the organization and are made out of the net earnings of the organization. Thus, the arrangements confer a benefit which violates the inurement proscription of section 501(c)(3).

* * *

II. SALE OF THE REVENUE STREAM FROM A HOSPITAL ACTIVITY BENEFITS PRIVATE INTERESTS MORE THAN INCIDENTALLY.

Another key principle in the law of tax exempt organizations is that an entity is not organized and operated exclusively for exempt purposes unless it serves a public rather than a private interest. Thus, in order to be exempt, an organization must establish that it is not organized or operated for the benefit of private interests such as designated individuals, the creator or his family, shareholders of the organization, or persons controlled, directly or indirectly, by such private interests. Treas. Reg. section 1.501(c)(3)-1(d)(1). However, this private benefit prohibition applies to all kinds of persons and groups, not just to those "insiders" subject to the more strict inurement proscription.

* * *

In our view, some private benefit is present in all typical hospital-physician relationships. Physicians generally use hospital facilities at no cost to themselves to provide services to private patients for which they earn a fee. The private benefit accruing to the physicians generally can be considered incidental to the overwhelming public benefit resulting from having the combined resources of the hospital and its professional staff available to serve the public. Though the private benefit is compounded in the case of certain specialists, such as heart transplant surgeons, who depend heavily on highly specialized hospital facilities, that fact alone will not make the private benefit more than incidental.

In contrast, the private benefits conferred on the physician-investors by the instant revenue stream joint ventures are direct and substantial, not incidental. If for any reason these benefits should be found not to constitute inurement, they nonetheless exceed the bounds of prohibited private benefit. Whether viewed as giving the physicians a substantial share in the profits of the hospital or simply as allowing them an extremely profitable investment, the arrangements confer a significant benefit on them. Against this, we must balance the public benefit achieved by the hospitals in entering into the arrangements. The public benefit expected to result from these transactions -- enhanced hospital financial health or greater efficiency achieved through improved utilization of their facilities -- bears only the most tenuous relationship to the hospitals' charitable purposes of promoting the health of their communities. Obtaining referrals or avoiding new competition may improve the competitive position of an individual hospital, but that is not necessarily the same as benefitting its community.

* * *

As noted in the discussion of inurement, an alternative way of analyzing a net revenue stream sale is as a financing technique. It seems likely that private interests would be served more than incidentally if a hospital obtained an advance from a commercial lender, and, instead of paying a commercially reasonable rate of interest, it assigned to the lender a 100% interest in its profits from a specified department or activity for a term of years. Even assuming, arguendo, that the advance would be used to further exempt purposes, the relevant portion of the hospital would be operated, at least to some extent, to serve the private interest of the lender. Operation in such a manner could be inconsistent with exemption.

* * *

The Service no longer contends that participation as a general partner in a partnership is per se inconsistent with exemption. However, when such activities involve private, taxable parties, they must be scrutinized for private inurement or more than incidental private benefit. The Service weighs all the facts and circumstances in each case, applying a "careful scrutiny" standard of review.

* * *

...In our view, there are a fixed number of individuals in a community legitimately needing hospital services at any one time. Paying doctors to steer patients to one particular hospital merely to improve its efficiency seems distant from a mission of providing needed care. We question whether the Service should ever recognize enhancing a hospital's market share vis-a-vis other providers, in and of itself, as furthering a charitable purpose. In many cases, doing so might hamper another charitable hospital's ability to promote the health of the same community.

* * *

Finally, we believe these arrangements create a substantial conflict between the charitable purposes of a hospital and its fiduciary duty or natural desire to further the pecuniary interests of the physician-investors. Charitable hospitals regularly proclaim that what distinguishes them from their investor-owned counterparts is their willingness to subjugate concern for the bottom line to concern for mission. This will no longer be the case, at least for the facilities subject to the joint ventures.

* * *

[The Service's analysis of the Medicare anti-kickback statute is deleted.]

NOTES

1.   Does GCM 39862 alter the analysis of GCM 39498? If so, how? Should the Service treat rural hospitals differently then suburban hospitals in relation to physician recruitment? Is the Service placing tax-exempt hospitals at a significant disadvantage in competing for physicians?

2.   Does GCM 39862 alter the analysis of the joint venture in Private Letter Ruling 9024085 (at page 477)? If so, how? Are there any non-financial, quality-related reasons for a hospital to attract a certain level of volume to a particular service?

Insert at page 514, just above the Notes and Questions, the following:

WATERS v. CHURCHILL
114 S.Ct. 1878 (1994)

[Plaintiff Churchill was discharged from her employment and claimed that her dismissal resulted from her criticism of the hospital administration's policy of "cross-training" which required that nurses shift among the various units of the facility depending on the volume of work available. Churchill had criticized the policy as resulting in the service of inadequately trained nurses in particular units at certain times. The defendant hospital administrator claimed that she investigated Churchill's behavior by interviewing co-workers and interviewing Churchill herself. The hospital found Churchill to be a disruptive employee and discharged her. Churchill filed suit claiming that, as a public employee, her dismissal penalized speech protected under the First Amendment.]

O'Connor, J.:

There is no dispute in this case about when speech by a government employee is protected by the First Amendment: To be protected, the speech must be on a matter of public concern, and the employee's interest in expressing herself on this matter must not be outweighed by any injury the speech could cause to "the interest of the State, as an employer, in promoting the efficiency of the public services it performs through its employees." []

128

* * *

The dispute is over how the factual basis for applying the test --
what the speech was, in what tone it was delivered, what the listener's
reactions were -- is to be determined. Should the court apply the
Connick test to the speech as the government employer found it to be, or
should it ask the jury to determine the facts for itself? The Court of
Appeals held that the employer's factual conclusions were irrelevant, and
that the jury should engage in its own factfinding. [Hospital
administration] argue[s] that the employer's factual conclusions should be
dispositive. [Churchill] take[s] a middle course: They suggest that the
court should accept the employer's factual conclusions, but only if those
conclusions were arrived at reasonably, something they say did not
happen here.

* * *

The government's interest in achieving its goals as effectively and
efficiently as possible is elevated from a relatively subordinate interest
when it acts as sovereign to a significant one when it acts as employer.
The government cannot restrict the speech of the public at large just in
the name of efficiency. But where the government is employing someone
for the very purpose of effectively achieving its goals, such restrictions
may well be appropriate.

* * *

The problem with the Court of Appeals' approach -- under which
the facts to which the Connick test is applied are determined by the
judicial factfinder -- is that it would force the government employer to
come to its factual conclusions through procedures that substantially
mirror the evidentiary rules used in court. The government manager
would have to ask not what conclusions she, as an experienced
professional, can draw from the circumstances, but rather what
conclusions a jury would later draw. If she relies on hearsay, or on what
she knows about the accused employee's character, she must be aware
that this evidence might not be usable in court. If she knows one party
is, in her personal experience, more credible than another, she must
realize that the jury will not share that personal experience. If she thinks
the alleged offense is so egregious that it is proper to discipline the
accused employee even though the evidence is ambiguous, she must
consider that a jury might decide the other way.

* * *

It is necessary that the decisionmaker reach its conclusion about what was said in good faith, rather than as a pretext; but it does not follow that good faith is sufficient. . . .We think employer decisionmaking will not be unduly burdened by having courts look to the facts as the employer reasonably found them to be. It may be unreasonable, for example, for the employer to come to a conclusion based on no evidence at all. Likewise, it may be unreasonable for an employer to act based on extremely weak evidence when strong evidence is clearly available -- if, for instance, an employee is accused of writing an improper letter to the editor, and instead of just reading the letter, the employer decides what it said based on unreliable hearsay.

* * *

We have never held that it is a violation of the Constitution for a government employer to discharge an employee based on substantively incorrect information. Where an employee has a property interest in her job, the only protection we have found the Constitution gives her is a right to adequate procedure. And an at-will government employee -- such as Churchill apparently was, generally has no claim based on the Constitution at all.

Of course, an employee may be able to challenge the substantive accuracy of the employer's factual conclusions under state contract law, or under some state statute or common-law cause of action. In some situations, the employee may even have a federal statutory claim. Likewise, the state or federal governments may, if they choose, provide similar protection to people fired because of their speech. But this protection is not mandated by the Constitution.

* * *

Even if Churchill's criticism of cross- training reported by [co-workers] was speech on a matter of public concern -- something we need not decide -- the potential disruptiveness of the speech as reported was enough to outweigh whatever First Amendment value it might have had. According to [a co-worker] Churchill's speech may have substantially dampened [others'] interest in working in obstetrics. Discouraging people from coming to work for a department certainly qualifies as disruption. Moreover, [a co-worker] perceived Churchill's statements about Waters to be "unkind and inappropriate," and told management that she knew they could not continue to "tolerate that kind of negativism" from Churchill.

* * *

Nonetheless, we agree with the Court of Appeals that the District Court erred in granting summary judgment in petitioners' favor. Though [the hospital] would have been justified in firing Churchill for the statements outlined above, there remains the question whether Churchill was actually fired because of those statements, or because of something else.

Churchill has produced enough evidence to create a material issue of disputed fact about petitioners' actual motivation. Churchill had criticized the cross- training policy in the past; management had exhibited some sensitivity about the criticisms; Churchill pointed to some other conduct by hospital management that, if viewed in the light most favorable to her, would show that they were hostile to her because of her criticisms. A reasonable factfinder might therefore, on this record, conclude that petitioners actually fired Churchill not because of the disruptive things she said to [her co-worker], but because of nondisruptive statements about cross- training that they thought she may have made in the same conversation, or because of other statements she may have made earlier. If this is so, then the court will have to determine whether those statements were protected speech, a different matter than the one before us now.

NOTES

1.   Does Justice O'Connor appropriately balance the public's, the discharged employee's and the government's interests?

2.   The Court refers to potential state common law actions. Would Churchill have a claim for wrongful discharge under McQuary? Should doctors and nurses working under at-will arrangements receive broader legal protection for complaints and actions related to protests over quality of patient care? Should they be treated differently than other workers?

Insert, at page 518 the following:

NLRB
v.
HEALTH & RETIREMENT CORP.
114 S.Ct. 1778 (1994)

Kennedy, J:

Congress defined a supervisor as: "Any individual having authority, in the interest of the employer, to hire, transfer, suspend, lay off, recall, promote, discharge, assign, reward, or discipline other employees, or responsibly to direct them, or to adjust their grievances, or effectively to recommend such action, if in connection with the foregoing the exercise of such authority is not of a merely routine or clerical nature, but requires the use of independent judgment." 61 Stat. 138, codified at 29 U. S. C. § 152(11).

* * *

As the Board has stated the statute requires the resolution of three questions; and each must be answered in the affirmative if an employee is to be deemed a supervisor. First, does the employee have authority to engage in one of the 12 listed activities? Second, does the exercise of that authority require "the use of independent judgment"? Third, does the employee hold the authority "in the interest of the employers"? This case concerns only the third question, and our decision turns upon the proper interpretation of the statutory phrase "in the interest of the employer."

In cases involving nurses, the Board admits that it has interpreted the statutory phrase in a unique manner. The Board has held that "a nurse's direction of less skilled employees, in the exercise of professional judgment incidental to the treatment of patients, is not authority exercised in the interest of the employer." [T]he Board believes that its special interpretation of "in the interest of the employer" in cases involving nurses is necessary because professional employees (including registered nurses) are not excluded from coverage under the Act.

* * *

At Heartland, the Director of Nursing has overall responsibility for the nursing department. There is also an Assistant Director of

Nursing, 9 to 11 staff nurses (including both registered nurses and the four licensed practical nurses involved in this case), and 50 to 55 nurses' aides. The staff nurses are the senior ranking employees on duty after 5 p.m. during the week and at all times on weekends -- approximately 75% of the time. The staff nurses have responsibility to ensure adequate staffing; to make daily work assignments; to monitor the aides' work to ensure proper performance; to counsel and discipline aides; to resolve aides' problems and grievances; to evaluate aides' performances; and to report to management.

* * *

The interpretation of the "in the interest of the employer" language mandated by our precedents and by the ordinary meaning of the phrase does not render the phrase meaningless in the statutory definition. The language ensures, for example, that union stewards who adjust grievances are not considered supervisory employees and deprived of the Act's protections. But the language cannot support the Board's argument that supervision of the care of patients is not in the interest of the employer. The welfare of the patient, after all, is no less the object and concern of the employer than it is of the nurses. And the statutory dichotomy the Board has created is no more justified in the health care field than it would be in any other business where supervisory duties are a necessary incident to the production of goods or the provision of services.

* * *

NOTES

1.   The four dissenters argued that the Court's rejection of the Board's interpretation of supervision in the interest of the employer results in the exclusion of all professionals from the protection of the Act. Are they correct? Or does this case simply recognize that registered nurses and licensed practical nurses usually provide a supervisory function over unlicensed nurses' aides in nursing homes? For opposing views of the reach of the Court's decision, see Laura Bruck, Can Nurses Be Fired for Complaining?, 43 Nursing Homes 38 (July-August 1994).

2.   Many hospitals have shifted their nurse staffing patterns to a pattern called "patient-centered care" or "patient-focused care." In this

staffing pattern, the patient load per R.N. increases significantly, but the number of nurses' aides, nursing assistants or technicians are increased to assist the nurse. How would this case apply to R.N.s employed by a hospital using patient-centered nursing care?

3.   What is the practical impact of this case if it does not imply that every nurse is a supervisor but merely states that the National Labor Relations Board must review the specific circumstances of an individual nurse's duties in order to judge whether nurses are acting as supervisors?

4.   Protests and demonstrations by nurses against the reduction of nurse staffing in hospitals have increased in the last two years. The first national demonstration of nurses took place in Washington D.C. in March, 1995, when nearly 30,000 nurses demonstrated against cost cutting on the basis of reductions in nurse staffing. Lacy McCrary, Nurses to Protest in D.C., Saying Job Cuts Erode Care, Philadelphia Inquirer (March 31, 1995). One purpose of the demonstration was to advocate amendment of the NLRA to overturn the Supreme Court's decision in this case. Health Care Employees: Nurses Rally in Washington to Protest Hospital Practices of Restructuring, 1995 BNA Daily Labor Report, 63 d19 (April 3, 1995). Job actions, such as "sick-ins" have also occurred. See e.g., Sabin Russell, San Francisco Nurses Call in Sick to Protest Stalled Talks, San Francisco Chronicle (May 28, 1994).

5.   As stated in the notes in the casebook, the NLRA requires a ten-day notice prior to a strike of hospital employees. For a report on a national company that provides temporary replacement nurses during labor disputes see, Dena Bunis, Nurses On Call Company Finds Replacements for Hospitals Involved in Labor Disputes, Star Tribune (April 11, 1995).

Insert as Note 8 on page 564, the following:

8. See New York State Conference of Blue Cross and Blue Shield Plans v. Travelers Insurance Company, reproduced below.

Insert at page 577 following the statute:

The Omnibus Budget Reconciliation Act of 1993 attempted to further tighten up limitations on asset transfers. It extends from 30 to 36 months the look-back period during which asset transfers will be scrutinized when a person applies for Medicaid, and extends this period further to 60 months for certain transfers to trusts. 42 U.S.C. § 1396p(c)(1)(A) & (B). If a transfer is discovered during this look-back period, the individual who made the transfer (or for whose benefit it was made) continues to be ineligible for Medicaid payment for nursing facility or home health care for a period of time determined by dividing the total cumulative value of transferred assets by the average monthly cost of private patient care in a nursing home. 42 U.S.C. § 1396p(c)(1)(E). The period of ineligibility is not limited to 30 months as was previously the case. Moreover, the period is determined based on the cumulative value of transfers, not on the basis of each individual transfer, as was arguably appropriate previously. The law further specifies that actions taken with respect to assets held in common or by joint tenancy are transfers to the extent that they reduce the control or ownership of the applicant over those assets. 42 U.S.C. § 1396p(c)(3)

OBRA 1993 works significant changes with respect to the effect of trusts on Medicaid eligibility. If a revocable trust is established including the assets of the applicant or his or her spouse, all of the corpus of the trust is regarded as an asset available to the individual and all payments by the trust to the individual are considered as his or her income. 42 U.S.C. § 1396p(D)(3)(A)(i) & (ii). All other payments by the trust are considered to be assets disposed of by the individual. 42 U.S.C. § 1396p(d)(3)(A)(iii). If an irrevocable trust has been established that includes the assets of the applicant or his or her spouse, any corpus available to the individual under any circumstances is considered to be assets and any available income is considered to be income for eligibility purposes. 42 U.S.C. § 1396p(3)(B)(i). All of the rest of the corpus is considered as a transferred asset as of the date the trust was established or became unavailable to the applicant, for up to 5 years prior to the application for Medicaid. 42 U.S.C. § 1396p(3)(B)(ii).

States may, at their option, extend the asset transfer prohibitions to noninstitutionalized applicants for home or community based care. 42 U.S.C. § 1396p(c)(1)(C)(ii). The asset transfer provisions do not apply retroactively to transfers made or trusts established before October 1, 1993. Finally, the legislation also requires that states attempt to recover from the estate of Medicaid recipients aged 55 and older the cost of expenditures for long term care. 42 U.S.C. § 1396p(b)(1). States may grant hardship waivers, however, from both the asset transfer and estate recovery requirements of the legislation. 42 U.S.C. § 1396p(b)(3), (c)(2)(D), (d)(5).

CHAPTER 6. ACCESS TO HEALTH CARE

Insert at page 623, just above the Notes and Questions, the following:

BABER
v.
HOSPITAL CORPORATION OF AMERICA
977 F.2d 872 (1992)

Williams, Circuit Judge:

* * *

In the present case, the material facts regarding EMTALA liability are undisputed. Brenda Baber, accompanied by her brother, Barry, sought treatment at RGH's [Raleigh General Hospital] emergency department at 10:40 p.m. on August 5, 1987. When she entered the hospital, Ms. Baber was nauseated, agitated, and thought she might be pregnant. She was also tremulous and did not appear to have orderly thought patterns. She had stopped taking her anti-psychosis medications, Haldol and Cogentin, and had been drinking heavily. Dr. Kline, the attending physician, described her behavior and condition in the RGH Encounter Record as follows: Patient refuses to remain on stretcher and cannot be restrained verbally despite repeated requests by staff and by me. Brother has not assisted either verbally or physically in keeping patient from pacing throughout the Emergency Room. Restraints would place patient and staff at risk by increasing her agitation.

In response to Ms. Baber's initial complaints, Dr. Kline examined her central nervous system, lungs, cardiovascular system, and abdomen. He also ordered several laboratory tests, including a pregnancy test.

While awaiting the results of her laboratory tests, Ms. Baber began pacing about the emergency department. In an effort to calm Ms. Baber, Dr. Kline gave her five milligrams of Haldol. When this failed to relieve Ms. Baber's hyperactivity and agitation, he administered 100 milligrams of Thorazine. He also gave Ms. Baber 100 milligrams of Thiamine and two ounces of magnesium citrate because of her earlier alcohol consumption. The medication did not immediately control her agitation. Mr. Baber described his sister as becoming restless, "worse and more disoriented after she was given the medication," and wandering around the emergency department.

While roaming in the emergency department around midnight, Ms. Baber, without warning, convulsed and fell, striking her head upon a table and lacerating her scalp. The seizure lasted three minutes, but she quickly regained consciousness and emergency department personnel carried her by stretcher to the suturing room. Once in the suturing room, Dr. Kline examined her again. He obtained a blood gas study which did not reveal any oxygen deprivation or acidosis. Ms. Baber was verbal and could move her head, eyes, and limbs without discomfort. With attendants restraining her limbs, Dr. Kline closed the one-inch laceration with a couple of sutures. Although she became calmer and drowsy after the wound was sutured, Ms. Baber was easily arousable and easily disturbed. Ms. Baber experienced some anxiety, disorientation, restlessness, and some speech problems, which Dr. Kline concluded were caused by her pre-existing psychiatric problems of psychosis with paranoia and alcohol withdrawal.

Dr. Kline discussed Ms. Baber's condition with Dr. Whelan, the psychiatrist who had treated Ms. Baber for two years. Dr. Whelan believed she suffered from undifferentiated schizophrenia and noted that her mental illness was associated with periods of extreme alcohol abuse. Dr. Whelan concluded that Ms. Baber's hyperactive and uncontrollable behavior during her evening at RGH was compatible with her behavior during a relapse of her serious psychotic and chronic mental illness. Both Dr. Whelan and Dr. Kline were concerned about the seizure she had while at RGH's emergency department because it was the first one she had experienced. They believed the seizure might be linked to Ms. Baber's psychosis. They also agreed Ms. Baber needed further treatment for what they believed to be her recurring psychiatric problems and decided to transfer her to the psychiatric unit at BARH [Beckley Appalachian Regional Hospital] because RGH did not have a psychiatric ward, and both doctors believed it would be beneficial for her to be treated in a familiar setting. The decision to transfer Ms. Baber was further supported by the doctors' belief that any tests to diagnose the cause of her initial seizure, such as a computerized tomography scan (CT scan), could be performed at BARH once her psychiatric condition was under control. The transfer to BARH was discussed with Mr. Baber who neither expressly consented nor objected. His only request was that his sister be x-rayed because of the blow to her head when she fell.

Although Mr. Baber stated that he did not see Dr. Kline perform any type of examination on his sister between the suturing of her scalp and her transport to BARH by ambulance, Dr. Kline testified in his deposition that for approximately an hour subsequent to the convulsion he watched Ms. Baber from across the room for focal neurological signs. Dr. Kline also stated she was stable, easily arousable, not struggling at random, and, in his medical judgment, she had shown improvement by the time of transfer.

Because Dr. Kline did not conclude Ms. Baber had a serious head injury, he believed that she could be transferred safely to BARH where she would be under the observation of the BARH psychiatric staff personnel. At 1:35 a.m. on August 6, Ms. Baber was admitted directly to the psychiatric department of BARH upon Dr. Whelan's orders. She was not processed through BARH's emergency department. Although Ms. Baber was restrained and regularly checked every fifteen minutes by the nursing staff while at BARH, no physician gave her an extensive neurological examination upon her arrival. Mr. Baber unsuccessfully repeated his request for an x-ray.

At the 3:45 a.m. check, the nurse found Ms. Baber having a grand mal seizure. At Dr. Whelan's direction, the psychiatric unit staff transported her to BARH's emergency department. Upon arrival in the emergency department, her pupils were unresponsive, and hospital personnel began CPR. The emergency department physician ordered a CT scan, which was performed around 6:30 a.m. The CT report revealed a fractured skull and a right subdural hematoma. BARH personnel immediately transferred Ms. Baber back to RGH because that hospital had a neurosurgeon on staff, and BARH did not have the facility or staff to treat serious neurological problems. When RGH received Ms. Baber for treatment around 7 a.m., she was comatose. She died later that day, apparently as a result of an intracerebrovascular rupture.

* * *

Mr. Baber also alleges that RGH, acting through its agent, Dr. Kline, violated several provisions of EMTALA. These allegations can be summarized into two general complaints: (1) RGH failed to provide an appropriate medical screening to discover that Ms. Baber had an emergency medical condition as required by 42 U.S.C.A. § 1395dd(a); and (2) RGH transferred Ms. Baber before her emergency medical condition had been stabilized, and the appropriate paperwork was not completed to transfer a non-stable patient as required by 42 U.S.C.A. §§ 1395dd(b) & (c). Because we find that RGH did not violate any of these

EMTALA provisions, we affirm the district court's grant of summary judgment to RGH.

Mr. Baber first claims that RGH failed to provide his sister with an "appropriate medical screening". He makes two arguments. First, he contends that a medical screening is only "appropriate" if it satisfies a national standard of care. In other words, Mr. Baber urges that we construe EMTALA as a national medical malpractice statute, albeit limited to whether the medical screening was appropriate to identify an emergency medical condition. We conclude instead that EMTALA only requires hospitals to apply their standard screening procedure for identification of an emergency medical condition uniformly to all patients and that Mr. Baber has failed to proffer sufficient evidence showing that RGH did not do so. Second, Mr. Baber contends that EMTALA requires hospitals to provide some medical screening. We agree, but conclude that he has failed to show no screening was provided to his sister.

* * *

...While [the Act] requires a hospital's emergency department to provide an "appropriate medical screening examination," it does not define that term other than to state its purpose is to identify an "emergency medical condition."

* * *

[T]he goal of "an appropriate medical screening examination" is to determine whether a patient with acute or severe symptoms has a life threatening or serious medical condition. The plain language of the statute requires a hospital to develop a screening procedure [6] designed

---

6 While a hospital emergency room may develop one general procedure for screening all patients, it may also tailor its screening procedure to the patient's complaints or exhibited symptoms. For example, it may have one screening procedure for patients suffering a heart attack and another for women in labor. Under our interpretation of EMTALA, such varying screening procedures would not pose liability under EMTALA as long as all patients complaining of the same problem or exhibiting the same symptoms receive identical screening procedures. We also recognize that the hospital's screening procedure is not limited to personal observation and assessment but may include available ancillary services through departments such as radiology and laboratory.

to identify such critical conditions that exist in symptomatic patients and to apply that screening procedure uniformly to all patients with similar complaints.

[W]hile EMTALA requires a hospital emergency department to apply its standard screening examination uniformly, it does not guarantee that the emergency personnel will correctly diagnose a patient's condition as a result of this screening. [7]

The statutory language clearly indicates that EMTALA does not impose on hospitals a national standard of care in screening patients. The screening requirement only requires a hospital to provide a screening examination that is "appropriate" and "within the capability of the hospital's emergency department," including "routinely available" ancillary services. 42 U.S.C.A. § 1395dd(a). This section establishes a standard which will of necessity be individualized for each hospital, since hospital emergency departments have varying capabilities. Had Congress intended to require hospitals to provide a screening examination which comported with generally accepted medical standards, it could have clearly specified a national standard. Nor do we believe Congress intended to create a negligence standard based on each hospital's capability....

* * *

_____

7 Some commentators have criticized defining "appropriate" in terms of the hospital's medical screening standard because hospitals could theoretically avoid liability by providing very cursory and substandard screenings to all patients, which might enable the doctor to ignore an emergency medical condition. See, e.g., Karen I. Treiger, Note, Preventing Patient Dumping: Sharpening the COBRA's Fangs, 61 N.Y.U.L.Rev. 1186 (1986). Even though we do not believe it is likely that a hospital would endanger all of its patients by establishing such a cursory standard, theoretically it is possible. Our holding, however, does not foreclose the possibility that a future court faced with such a situation may decide that the hospital's standard was so low that it amounted to no "appropriate medical screening." We do not decide that question in this case because Ms. Baber's screening was not so substandard as to amount to no screening at all.

The Sixth Circuit has also held that an appropriate medical screening means "a screening that the hospital would have offered to any paying patient" or at least "not known by the provider to be insufficient or below their own standards."[8]

* * *

Applying our interpretation of section (a) of EMTALA, we must next determine whether there is any genuine issue of material fact regarding whether RGH gave Ms. Baber a medical screening examination that differed from its standard screening procedure. Because Mr. Baber has offered no evidence of disparate treatment, we find that the district court did not err in granting summary judgment.

* * *

Dr. Kline testified that he performed a medical screening on Ms. Baber in accordance with standard procedures for examining patients with head injuries. He explained that generally, a patient is not scheduled for advanced tests such as a CT scan or x-rays unless the patient's signs and symptoms so warrant. While Ms. Baber did exhibit some of the signs and symptoms of patients who have severe head injuries, in Dr. Kline's medical judgment these signs were the result of her pre-existing psychiatric condition, not the result of her fall. He, therefore, determined that Ms. Baber's head injury was not serious and did not indicate the need at that time for a CT scan or x-rays. In his medical judgment, Ms. Baber's condition would be monitored adequately by the usual nursing checks performed every fifteen minutes by the psychiatric unit staff at BARH. Although Dr. Kline's assessment and judgment may have been

---

8 The one distinction between the tests used by the Sixth and D.C. Circuits is that the D.C. Circuit would impose liability for any disparate treatment, regardless of the hospital's motive, [Gatewood v. Washington Healthcare Corp., 933 F.2d 1037, 1041 (D.C. Cir. 1991)], while the Sixth Circuit will only impose liability if the hospital had a bad motive in providing the disparate treatment, Cleland, 917 F.2d at 272. For the Sixth Circuit, such bad motives for the disparate treatment might include the patient's indigence, drunkenness, political affiliations, or medical condition, such as AIDS. 917 F.2d at 272. In this case, we are not required to decide which view is correct since Mr. Baber did not make any allegation of disparate treatment.

erroneous and not within acceptable standards of medical care in West Virginia, he did perform a screening examination that was not so substandard as to amount to no examination. No testimony indicated that his procedure deviated from that which RGH would have provided to any other patient in Ms. Baber's condition.

. . . Dr. Chibber [plaintiff's expert] did not state that his requirements for good and appropriate medical care corresponded with or deviated from RGH's standard medical screening examination. Absent such a showing, his affidavit did not address the essential issue of whether Ms. Baber received disparate treatment.

* * *

Mr. Baber admitted that he did not maintain a constant vigil over his sister while she waited to be transferred and that he was not always in a position to observe Dr. Kline's actions. Mr. Baber could not testify as to what Dr. Kline did or did not do when Mr. Baber was not present; his testimony was only that he did not see Dr. Kline examine his sister after suturing her wound. Such testimony is no more than mere speculation and is not sufficient to create a genuine issue of material fact.

* * *

Moreover, Mr. Baber is not a doctor and is not qualified to evaluate whether Dr. Kline's actions constitute a medical screening examination.

* * *

Mr. Baber also asserts that RGH inappropriately transferred his sister to BARH * * * EMTALA's transfer requirements do not apply unless the hospital actually determines that the patient suffers from an emergency medical condition. Accordingly, to recover for violations of EMTALA's transfer provisions, the plaintiff must present evidence that (1) the patient had an emergency medical condition; (2) the hospital actually knew of that condition; (3) the patient was not stabilized before being transferred; and (4) prior to transfer of an unstable patient, the transferring hospital did not obtain the proper consent or follow the appropriate certification and transfer procedures.

Mr. Baber argues that requiring a plaintiff to prove the hospital had actual knowledge of the patient's emergency medical condition would allow hospitals to circumvent the purpose of EMTALA by simply requiring their personnel to state in all hospital records that the patient did not suffer from an emergency medical condition. Because of this concern, Mr. Baber urges us to adopt a standard that would impose liability upon a hospital if it failed to provide stabilizing treatment prior to a transfer when the hospital knew or should have known that the patient suffered from an emergency medical condition.

* * *

[T]he plain language of the statute dictates a standard requiring actual knowledge of the emergency medical condition by the hospital staff.

* * *

. . . Dr. Kline stated in his affidavit that Ms. Baber's condition was stable prior to transfer and that he did not believe she was suffering from an emergency medical condition. While Mr. Baber testified that he believed his sister suffered from an emergency medical condition at transfer, he did not present any evidence beyond his own belief that she actually had an emergency medical condition or that anyone at RGH knew that she suffered from an emergency medical condition. In addition, we note that Mr. Baber's testimony is not competent to prove his sister actually had an emergency medical condition since he is not qualified to diagnose a serious internal brain injury.

* * *

HOWE
v.
HULL
874 F.Supp. 779 (N.D. Ohio 1994)

Potter, Senior Judge.

[Ruling on defendants' motions for summary judgment.]

On April 17, 1992, Charon and plaintiff Howe were travelling through Ohio, on their way to vacation in Wisconsin. Charon was HIV positive. That morning Charon took a floxin tablet for the first time. Floxin is a prescription antibiotic drug. Within two hours of taking the drug, Charon began experiencing fever, headache, nausea, joint pain, and redness of the skin.

Due to Charon's condition, Charon and plaintiff checked into a motel and, after consulting with Charon's treating physician in Maine, sought medical care at the emergency room of Fremont Memorial Hospital. Charon was examined by the emergency room physician on duty, Dr. Mark Reardon.

* * *

Dr. Reardon determined that Charon "definitely needed to be admitted" to Memorial Hospital. Since Charon was from out of town, procedure required that Charon be admitted to the on-call physician, Dr. Hull. Dr. Reardon spoke with Dr. Hull on the telephone and informed Dr. Hull that he wanted to admit Charon, who was HIV-positive and suffering from a non-AIDS related severe drug reaction.

While Dr. Reardon and Dr. Hull discussed Charon's situation, the primary area of their discussion appears to have been whether Charon's condition had advanced from HIV to full-blown AIDS. Dr. Hull inquired neither into Charon's physical condition nor vital signs, nor did he ask Dr. Reardon about the [diagnosis]. During this conversation, it is undisputed that Dr. Hull told Dr. Reardon that "if you get an AIDS patient in the hospital, you will never get him out," and directed that plaintiff be sent to the "AIDS program" at MCO. When Dr. Hull arrived at the hospital after Dr. Reardon's shift but prior to Charon's transfer, he did not attempt to examine or meet with Charon.

* * *

Charon was transferred to the Medical College of Ohio some time after 8:45 P.M. on April 17. After his conversation with Dr. Hull and prior to the transfer, Dr. Reardon told Charon and plaintiff that "I'm sure you've dealt with this before ..." Howe asked, "What's that, discrimination?" Dr. Reardon replied, "You have to understand, this is a small community, and the admitting doctor does not feel comfortable admitting [Charon]."

145

* * *

Defendant Memorial Hospital has moved for summary judgment on plaintiff's EMTALA claim, arguing that, as a matter of law, Charon was stable at the time of transfer. Plaintiff disputes this interpretation of the facts. Defendant is correct that once an emergency room patient is stabilized, a hospital's responsibilities under the EMTALA end. * * *

It is important to note that, even if Memorial Hospital did transfer Charon solely because of his HIV status, there will be no liability under the EMTALA if he was stabilized prior to the transfer. . . .

Under the EMTALA, "stabilized" means that to a reasonable degree of medical probability, no material deterioration of the [patient's] condition is likely to result from or occur during the transfer. [ ] Defendant has presented evidence that Charon's condition was in fact stable. Dr. Reardon and several of defendant's experts testified to this fact, and one of plaintiff's experts was unable to say that, to a reasonable degree of medical probability, a material deterioration of Charon's condition was likely to occur. Plaintiff has, however, presented sufficient evidence to create an issue of material fact in this regard.

Dr. Waxman testified that he did not agree that there was no material deterioration of Charon's condition during the transfer, and that there was a "50/50 chance" that a material deterioration in Charon's condition would occur at the time of transfer. Dr. Waxman further testified that Charon's vital signs were dangerous, that he would have been uncomfortable transferring Charon, and that Charon was in near-shock condition. From this testimony, a reasonable jury could find that defendant had not stabilized Charon prior to transfer.

. . . In this case, defendant's asserted reason for the transfer was that Charon had TEN [toxic epidermal necrolysis], a condition beyond the treatment capabilities of Memorial Hospital. Plaintiff has alleged that Charon was not diagnosed with TEN, and because Charon had HIV defendant Memorial Hospital transferred him without first providing him with treatment that was within defendant's capacity. In short, plaintiff claims defendant "dumped" Charon on MCO because defendant Memorial Hospital did not wish to treat an AIDS patient.

Applying the facts in the case at bar in the light most favorable to and drawing all reasonable inferences in favor of the plaintiff, the

Court cannot conclude that defendant Memorial Hospital is entitled to summary judgment on plaintiff's EMTALA claim. Many of the facts are disputed, and a reasonable jury could find that Memorial Hospital provided Charon with a lesser degree of care because of his HIV status.

Much of this case turns on what in fact Dr. Reardon's initial diagnosis of Charon's condition was. Dr. Reardon testified that the diagnosis was TEN, and this is supported by the entry Dr. Reardon made in the medical records. However, Dr. Reardon also testified that Charon "possibly" had an early case of TEN, even though he had never seen one and had only read about TEN at medical school. Plaintiff's expert, however, testified that TEN was not the "likely or even probable" diagnosis. Dr. Reardon also never told Dr. Lynn, the admitting physician at MCO, about the TEN diagnosis. Given Dr. Reardon's conflicting testimony, the expert's analysis of Charon's medical records, and the fact that Dr. Reardon never told Lynn that Charon had an incredibly rare affliction which was the alleged reason for the patient transfer, a jury could reasonably conclude that the TEN diagnosis was a fabrication or ad hoc justification for Charon's transfer. Since the evidence is contradictory as to Charon's actual diagnosis, most of Memorial Hospital's subsequent summary judgment arguments based upon this premise fail. Dr. Hull's statement about AIDS patients could cause a reasonable jury to believe that the sole reason for transfer was Charon's HIV status. Plaintiff also presented evidence that Charon was not given the appropriate medical treatment by defendant. Further, if the jury found that Charon's actual diagnosis was simply a non-AIDS-related severe allergic drug reaction, that jury could reasonably conclude that Memorial Hospital transferred Charon, while he was unstable, without providing him with necessary medical care that was within their capability to provide.

* * *

[The court's opinion concerning plaintiff's claims under the Americans with Disabilities Act and the Rehabilitation Act is reproduced below.]

NOTES

1.   The Sixth Circuit, in considering EMTALA, declared the word "appropriate" to be "one of the most wonderful weasel words in the dictionary, and a great aid to the resolution of disputed issues in the drafting of legislation." Cleland v. Bronson Health Care Group, 917 F.2d 266 (6th Cir. 1990). That may be so, but it certainly has generated

substantial litigation. Why, do you think, Congress did not choose to be more specific? The Department of Health and Human Services has issued regulations under the Act. 59 Fed. Reg. 32086 (1994).

2.   Baber is typical of the courts' interpretation of the screening requirement. In contrast to the standard the courts have applied to the adequacy of the screening examination, the standard applied to the question of whether the patient was discharged or transferred in an unstable condition is an objective professional standard, as in Howe. How should discovery be structured by plaintiff to meet these two standards?

3.   Two early EMTALA cases (referenced in note 3 at page 626 of the casebook) held that plaintiff had a cause of action under the statute only if he or she could prove that the motive for the transfer was financial. Subsequent to these early cases, however, the courts have almost uniformly concluded that proof of indigency is not required under EMTALA. See, e.g., Collins v. DePaul Hospital, 963 F.2d 303 (10th Cir. 1992). Although proof of motive is not required as an element of an EMTALA claim, how might proof of the hospital's motive for transfer assist plaintiff in making her or his case?

Insert at page 631, just above the Problem, the following:

HOWE
v.
HULL
874 F.Supp. 779 (N.D. Ohio 1994)

[The court's opinion concerning plaintiff's EMTALA claim is reproduced above.]

* * *

The ADA prohibits discrimination by places of public accommodation:

> No individual shall be discriminated against on the basis of disability in the full and equal enjoyment of the goods, services, facilities, privileges, advantages, or accommodations of any place of public accommodation by any person who owns, leases (or

leases to), or operates a place of public accommodation. 42 U.S.C. s 12182(a).

* * *

[The court concludes that Dr. Hull may be held individually liable under the ADA for his actions in this case as the operator of the hospital, a public accommodation, because he was in a position of authority, had the power and discretion to perform discriminatory acts, and the discriminatory acts were a result of his own discretion, as opposed to implementation of institutional policy.]

Defendant Memorial Hospital and defendant Hull also move for summary judgment on plaintiff's ADA claim as well as plaintiff's FRA [Section 504 of the Rehabilitation Act] claim, on the basis that the evidence does not establish that Charon was denied treatment solely on the basis of his HIV status, and that plaintiff was not "otherwise qualified" for treatment due to the TEN diagnosis.

Before examining the merits of defendants' contentions, the Court must look at and compare the applicable parameters of the ADA and FRA. There are three basic criteria plaintiff must meet in order to establish a prima facie case of discrimination under the ADA:

a) the plaintiff has a disability;
b) the defendants discriminated against the plaintiff; and
c) the discrimination was based on the disability. [ ]

The discrimination can take the form of the denial of the opportunity to receive medical treatment, segregation unnecessary for the provision of effective medical treatment, unnecessary screening or eligibility requirements for treatment, or provision of unequal medical benefits based upon the disability. [ ] A defendant can avoid liability by establishing that it was unable to provide the medical care that a patient required. [ ]

Similarly, to establish a prima facie case under the FRA the plaintiff must show

a) the plaintiff has a disability;
b) plaintiff was otherwise qualified to participate in the program;

149

c) defendants discriminated against plaintiff solely on the basis of the disability; and

d) the program received federal funding. [ ]

As this Court has already stated, a reasonable jury could conclude that the TEN diagnosis was a pretext and that Charon was denied treatment solely because of his disability. Further, there is no evidence to support the conclusion that Memorial Hospital was unable to treat a severe allergic drug reaction. In fact, the evidence indicates that Dr. Reardon initially planned to admit Charon for treatment. Therefore, Charon was "otherwise qualified" for treatment within the meaning of the FRA. Defendants' arguments in this regard are not persuasive.

The Court notes that defendant Memorial Hospital argues that the "solely on the basis of ..." standard that appears in the FRA should be imported into the ADA as well. This argument is without merit.

The FRA states that "no otherwise qualified individual with a disability ... shall, solely by reason of his or her disability ... be subjected to discrimination...." [ ] The equivalent portion of the ADA reads "No individual shall be discriminated against on the basis of disability...." [ ] It is abundantly clear that the exclusion of the "solely by reason of ... disability" language was a purposeful act by Congress and not a drafting error or oversight * * * [ ]

The inquiry under the ADA, then, is whether the defendant, despite the articulated reasons for the transfer, improperly considered Charon's HIV status. More explicitly, was Charon transferred for the treatment of a non-AIDS related drug reaction because defendant unjustifiably did not wish to care for an HIV-positive patient? Viewing the evidence in the light most favorable to the plaintiff, the Court finds plaintiff has presented sufficient evidence to preclude a grant of summary judgment on these claims. Defendant Memorial Hospital's motion for summary judgment on the plaintiff's ADA and FRA claims will be denied.

* * *

NOTES

1.   Will the ADA or the Rehabilitation Act prove friendlier to plaintiffs challenging denials of medical treatment? See also, Johnson v.

Thompson, 971 F.2d 1487 (10th Cir. 1992), in which the parents of infants born with spina bifida claimed that their children were selected for non-treatment, in an experiment, without their knowledgeable consent and in a discriminatory fashion based on the infants' physical handicap and on the families' socio-economic status. The parents lost their § 504 claim.

2. In the trial conducted after the court's denial of defendants' summary judgment motions, the jury returned a verdict in favor of the plaintiff on the § 504 claim, awarding plaintiff's estate $62,000 in compensatory damages and punitive damages of $150,000 against Dr. Hull and $300,000 against the hospital. The jury found in favor of the defendants on the plaintiff's EMTALA claim and on his state claim for emotional distress. The ADA claim was tried to the bench, and the judge found that defendants' actions violated the Act. The court permanently enjoined defendants from violating the Act and ordered the hospital to "prominently post" signs in the waiting rooms, stating: "This health care provider is prohibited by law from discriminating on the basis of HIV or AIDS. If you believe that this health care provider has discriminated on the basis of AIDS or HIV, you may wish to consult with an attorney." The court noted that Dr. Reardon had recorded Dr. Hull's statements about AIDS patients in the official emergency room record and also recorded that Charon's allergic reaction was not related to AIDS or HIV infection in any way.

3.   In its findings, the court stated:

The ADA is not a medical malpractice statute. The test, whether the referring provider would similarly refer an individual without a disability, implies a contemporaneous analysis of the referring provider's subjective belief at the time of the referral. Thus, a provider who believes that a disabled individual requires treatment beyond the provider's capability for a medical condition that is unrelated to the disability, may refer that individual to another provider if the provider would likewise refer an individual without a disability in the same fashion. [FN2]

FN2. Clearly, where the disability and the medical condition for which treatment is sought are unrelated, the health care provider may not properly consider the disability in referring the patient elsewhere. The more

151

complicated question, however, concerns a medical condition that is complicated by the disability. Given the disposition of this case, the Court need not reach, and specifically declines to address, whether a health care provider may proper consider an individual's disability when that disability complicates the medical condition for which the individual is seeking treatment.

The Supreme Court in Bowen (discussed at page 630 in the casebook) was able to sidestep this difficult issue by relying upon the absence of parental consent to treatment. The district court in the Baby K case considered the § 504 and ADA claims of an anencephalic infant who required repeated resuscitation due to the physical condition of anencephaly. The hospital physicians had claimed that it was medically inappropriate to repeatedly resuscitate an infant in that condition. The district court held that the infant could state a claim for denial of medical treatment under § 504 and the ADA. 832 F.Supp. 1022 (E.D.Va. 1993). The Fourth Circuit Court of Appeals did not review the district court's holding as to ADA and § 504, but did affirm the Court's holding that the infant could state a claim under EMTALA. This case is reproduced in this supplement, infra.

4.   In the typical managed care insurance plan, the approval of the patient's primary care physician is required prior to hospitalization. In Woolfolk v. Duncan, 872 F.Supp. 1381 (E.D.Pa. 1995), the district court considered Rehabilitation Act and ADA claims that the physician refused authorization for hospitalization because the patient had HIV infection. The court denied summary judgment, holding, inter alia, that the patient, as a subscriber to the plan, was otherwise qualified for medical services (as required for the Rehabilitation Act claim) and that the issue of whether the plan would be vicariously liable for the physician's alleged discriminatory treatment decision was a question of fact for the jury.

CHAPTER 7.   HEALTH CARE COST CONTROL

Insert at page 698, just above Section III, the following:

While the rate-setting scheme at issue in the case that follows was more directly intended to expand access than to control costs, the strategy of hospital rate-setting has more commonly been used to control costs. The case, therefore, is an important breakthrough for states interested in regulatory approaches to the problems of cost as well as access.

NEW YORK STATE CONFERENCE OF
BLUE CROSS & BLUE SHIELD PLANS
v.
TRAVELERS INSURANCE COMPANY
Supreme Court of the United States
1995 WL 238409 (1995)

Justice Souter delivered the opinion of the Court.

A New York statute requires hospitals to collect surcharges from patients covered by a commercial insurer but not from patients insured by a Blue Cross/Blue Shield plan, and it subjects certain health maintenance organizations (HMOs) to surcharges that vary with the number of Medicaid recipients each enrolls.[] This case calls for us to decide whether the Employee Retirement Income Security Act of 1974 (ERISA), 29 U.S.C. § 1001 et seq., pre-empts the state provisions for surcharges on bills of patients whose commercial insurance coverage is purchased by employee health-care plans governed by ERISA, and for surcharges on HMOs insofar as their membership fees are paid by an ERISA plan. We hold that the provisions for surcharges do not "relate to" employee benefit plans within the meaning of ERISA's pre-emption provision, § 514(a), 29 U.S.C. § 1144(a), and accordingly suffer no pre-emption.

I.A.   New York's Prospective Hospital Reimbursement Methodology (NYPHRM) regulates hospital rates for all in-patient care, except for services provided to Medicare beneficiaries.[] The scheme calls for patients to be charged not for the cost of their individual treatment, but for the average cost of treating the patient's medical problem, as classified under one or another of 794 Diagnostic Related Groups (DRGs). The charges allowable in accordance with DRG classifications are adjusted for a specific hospital to reflect its particular operating costs, capital investments, bad debts, costs of charity care and the like.

Patients with Blue Cross/Blue Shield coverage, Medicaid patients, and HMO participants are billed at a hospital's DRG rate.[] Others, however, are not. Patients served by commercial insurers providing in-patient hospital coverage on an expense-incurred basis, by self-insured funds directly reimbursing hospitals, and by certain workers' compensation, volunteer firefighters' benefit, ambulance workers' benefit, and no-fault motor vehicle insurance funds, must be billed at the DRG rate plus a 13% surcharge to be retained by the hospital.[] For the year ending March 31, 1993, moreover, hospitals were required to bill commercially insured patients for a further 11% surcharge to be turned over to the State, with the result that these patients were charged 24% more than the DRG rate.[]

New York law also imposes a surcharge on HMOs, which varies depending on the number of eligible Medicaid recipients an HMO has enrolled, but which may run as high as 9% of the aggregate monthly charges paid by an HMO for its members' in-patient hospital care.[] This assessment is not an increase in the rates to be paid by an HMO to hospitals, but a direct payment by the HMO to the State's general fund.

B.   ERISA's comprehensive regulation of employee welfare and pension benefit plans extends to those that provide "medical, surgical, or hospital care or benefits" for plan participants or their beneficiaries "through the purchase of insurance or otherwise."[] The federal statute does not go about protecting plan participants and their beneficiaries by requiring employers to provide any given set of minimum benefits, but instead controls the administration of benefit plans,[] as by imposing reporting and disclosure mandates,[] participation and vesting requirements,[] funding standards,[] and fiduciary responsibilities for plan administrators.[] It envisions administrative oversight, imposes criminal sanctions, and establishes a comprehensive civil enforcement scheme.[] It also pre-empts some state law.[]

Section 514(a) provides that ERISA "shall supersede any and all State laws insofar as they * * * relate to any employee benefit plan" covered by the statute, 29 U.S.C. § 1144(a), although pre-emption stops short of "any law of any State which regulates insurance." 29 U.S.C. § 1144(b)(2)(A). (This exception for insurance regulation is itself limited, however, by the provision that an employee welfare benefit plan may not "be deemed to be an insurance company or other insurer ... or to be engaged in the business of insurance...." 29 U.S.C. § 1144(b)(2)(B).) * * *

C.   On the claimed authority of ERISA's general preemption provision, several commercial insurers, acting as fiduciaries of ERISA plans they administer, joined with their trade associations to bring actions against state officials in United States District Court seeking to invalidate the 13%, 11%, and 9% surcharge statutes. * * * The District Court consolidated the actions and granted summary judgment to the plaintiffs.[] The court found that although the surcharges "do not directly increase a plan's costs or [a]ffect the level of benefits to be offered" there could be "little doubt that the [s]urcharges at issue will have a significant effect on the commercial insurers and HMOs which do or could provide coverage for ERISA plans and thus lead, at least indirectly, to an increase in plan costs."[] It found that the "entire justification for the [s]urcharges is premised on that exact result--that the [s]urcharges will increase the cost of obtaining medical insurance through any source other than the Blues to a sufficient extent that customers will switch their coverage to d ensure the economic viability of the Blues." Ibid. (footnote omitted). The District Court concluded that this effect on choices by ERISA plans was enough to trigger pre-emption under § 514(a) and that the surcharges were not saved by § 514(b) as regulating insurance.[] The District Court accordingly enjoined enforcement of "those surcharges against any commercial insurers or HMOs in connection with their coverage of ... ERISA plans."[]

The Court of Appeals for the Second Circuit affirmed * * *.

* * * The court's conclusion, in sum, was that "the three surcharges 'relate to' ERISA because they impose a significant economic burden on commercial insurers and HMOs" and therefore "have an impermissible impact on ERISA plan structure and administration."[] In the light of its conclusion that the surcharge statues were not otherwise saved by any applicable exception, the court held them pre-empted. * * *

II.   Our past cases have recognized that the Supremacy Clause, U.S. Const., Art. VI, may entail pre-emption of state law either by express provision, by implication, or by a conflict between federal and state law.[] And yet, despite the variety of these opportunities for federal preeminence, we have never assumed lightly that Congress has derogated state regulation, but instead have addressed claims of pre-emption with the starting presumption that Congress does not intend to supplant state law.[] Indeed, in cases like this one, where federal law is said to bar state action in fields of traditional state regulation,[] we have worked on the "assumption that the historic police powers of the States were not to be superseded by the Federal Act unless that was the clear and manifest purpose of Congress."[]

* * * The governing text of ERISA is clearly expansive. * * * If "relate to" were taken to extend to the furthest stretch of its indeterminacy, then for all practical purposes pre-emption would never run its course, for "[r]eally, universally, relations stop nowhere," H. James, Roderick Hudson xli (1980). But that, of course, would be to read Congress's words of limitation as mere sham, and to read the presumption against pre-emption out of the law whenever Congress speaks to the matter with generality. That said, we have to recognize that our prior attempt to construe the phrase "relate to" does not give us much help drawing the line here.

In Shaw, we explained that "[a] law 'relates to' an employee benefit plan, in the normal sense of the phrase, if it has a connection with or reference to such a plan."[] The latter alternative, at least, can be ruled out. The surcharges are imposed upon patients and HMOs, regardless of whether the commercial coverage or membership, respectively, is ultimately secured by an ERISA plan, private purchase, or otherwise, with the consequence that the surcharge statutes cannot be said to make "reference to" ERISA plans in any manner."[] But this still leaves us to question whether the surcharge laws have a "connection with" the ERISA plans, and here an uncritical literalism is no more help than in trying to construe "relate to." * * * We simply must go beyond the unhelpful text and the frustrating difficulty of defining its key term, and look instead to the objectives of the ERISA statute as a guide to the scope of the state law that Congress understood would survive.

A.   As we have said before, § 514 indicates Congress's intent to establish the regulation of employee welfare benefit plans "as exclusively a federal concern."[] We have found that in passing § 514(a), Congress intended

> "to ensure that plans and plan sponsors would be subject to a uniform body of benefits law; the goal was to minimize the administrative and financial burden of complying with conflicting

directives among States or between States and the Federal Government ..., [and to prevent] the potential for conflict in substantive law ... requiring the tailoring of plans and employer conduct to the peculiarities of the law of each jurisdiction."[]

* * *

Accordingly in Shaw, for example, we had no trouble finding that New York's "Human Rights Law, which prohibit[ed] employers from structuring their employee benefit plans in a manner that discriminate[d] on the basis of pregnancy, and [New York's] Disability Benefits Law, which require[d] employers to pay employees specific benefits, clearly 'relate[d] to' benefit plans."[] These mandates affecting coverage could have been honored only by varying the subjects of a plan's benefits whenever New York law might have applied, or by requiring every plan to provide all beneficiaries with a benefit demanded by New York law if New York law could have been said to require it for any one beneficiary. * * * Along the same lines, New Jersey could not prohibit plans from setting workers' compensation payments off against employees' retirement benefits or pensions, because doing so would prevent plans from using a method of calculating benefits permitted by federal law.[] In each of these cases, ERISA pre-empted state laws that mandated employee benefit structures or their administration. * * *

B.   Both the purpose and the effects of the New York surcharge statutes distinguish them from the examples just given. The charge differentials have been justified on the ground that the Blues pay the hospitals promptly and efficiently and, more importantly, provide coverage for many subscribers whom the commercial insurers would reject as unacceptable risks. The Blues' practice, called open enrollment, has consistently been cited as the principal reason for charge differentials, whether the differentials resulted from voluntary negotiation between hospitals and payers as was the case prior to the NYPHRM system, or were created by the surcharges as is the case now.[] Since the surcharges are presumably passed on at least in part to those who purchase commercial insurance or HMO membership, their effects follow from their purpose. Although there is no evidence that the surcharges will drive every health insurance consumer to the Blues, they do make the Blues more attractive (or less unattractive) as insurance alternatives and thus have an indirect economic effect on choices made by insurance buyers, including ERISA plans.

An indirect economic influence, however, does not bind plan administrators to any particular choice and thus function as a regulation of an ERISA plan itself; commercial insurers and HMOs may still offer more attractive packages than the Blues. Nor does the indirect influence of the surcharges preclude uniform administrative practice or the provision of a uniform interstate benefit package if a plan wishes to provide one. It simply bears on the costs of benefits and the relative costs of competing insurance to provide them. * * *

There is, indeed, nothing remarkable about surcharges on hospital bills, or their effects on overall cost to the plans and the relative attractiveness of certain insurers. Rate variations among hospital providers are accepted examples of cost variation, since hospitals have traditionally "attempted to compensate for their financial shortfalls by adjusting their price ... schedules for patients with commercial health insurance." * * *

If the common character of rate differentials even in the absence of state action renders it unlikely that ERISA pre-emption was meant to bar such indirect economic influences under state law, the existence of other common state action with indirect economic effects on a plan's costs leaves the intent to pre-empt even less likely. Quality standards, for example, set by the State in one subject area of hospital services but not another would affect the relative cost of providing those services over others and, so, of providing different packages of health insurance benefits. * * *

* * *

Indeed, to read the pre-emption provision as displacing all state laws affecting costs and charges on the theory that they indirectly relate to ERISA plans that purchase insurance policies or HMO memberships that would cover such services, would effectively read the limiting language in § 514(a) out of the statute, a conclusion that would violate basic principles of statutory interpretation and could not be squared with our prior pronouncement that "[p]reemption does not occur ... if the state law has only a tenuous, remote, or peripheral connection with covered plans, as is the case with many laws of general applicability." * * * While Congress's extension of pre-emption to all "state laws relating to benefit plans" was meant to sweep more broadly than "state laws dealing with the subject matters covered by ERISA[,] reporting, disclosure, fiduciary responsibility, and the like,"[] nothing in the language of the

158

Act or the context of its passage indicates that Congress chose to displace general health care regulation, which historically has been a matter of local concern, see [] 1 B. Furrow, T. Greaney, S. Johnson, T. Jost, & R. Schwartz, Health Law §§ 1-6, 1-23 (1995).

In sum, cost-uniformity was almost certainly not an object of pre-emption, just as laws with only an indirect economic effect on the relative costs of various health insurance packages in a given State are a far cry from those "conflicting directives" from which Congress meant to insulate ERISA plans.[] Such state laws leave plan administrators right where they would be in any case, with the responsibility to choose the best overall coverage for the money. We therefore conclude that such state laws do not bear the requisite "connection with" ERISA plans to trigger pre-emption.

* * *

D.   It remains only to speak further on a point already raised, that any conclusion other than the one we draw would bar any state regulation of hospital costs. The basic DRG system (even without any surcharge), like any other interference with the hospital services market, would fall on a theory that all laws with indirect economic effects on ERISA plans are pre-empted under § 514(a). This would be an unsettling result and all the more startling because several States, including New York, regulated hospital charges to one degree or another at the time ERISA was passed, * * *   And yet there is not so much as a hint in ERISA's legislative history or anywhere else that Congress intended to squelch these state efforts.

Even more revealing is the National Health Planning and Resources Development Act of 1974 (NHPRDA)[] which was adopted by the same Congress that passed ERISA, and only months later [and provided federal grants for state rate regulation demonstration projects. ed.] * * *

* * *

* * * To interpret ERISA's pre-emption provision as broadly as respondent suggests, would have rendered the entire NHPRDA utterly nugatory, since it would have left States without the authority to do just what Congress was expressly trying to induce them to do by enacting the NHPRDA. * * *

III.   That said, we do not hold today that ERISA pre-empts only direct regulation of ERISA plans, nor could we do that with fidelity to the views expressed in our prior opinions on the matter.[] We acknowledge that a state law might produce such acute, albeit indirect, economic effects, by intent or otherwise, as to force an ERISA plan to adopt a certain scheme of substantive coverage or effectively restrict its choice of insurers, and that such a state law might indeed be pre-empted under § 514. But as we have shown, New York's surcharges do not fall into either category; they affect only indirectly the relative prices of insurance policies, a result no different from myriad state laws in areas traditionally subject to local regulation, which Congress could not possibly have intended to eliminate.

The judgment of the Court of Appeals is therefore reversed and the case remanded for further proceedings consistent with this opinion.

Insert at page 758, just above the Notes and Questions, the following:

THE HANLESTER NETWORK v. SHALALA
Ninth Circuit Court of Appeals, 1995
1995 WL 148280

Tanner, District Judge.

Plaintiffs/appellants appeal the district court's grant of summary judgment in favor of the Secretary, and denial of plaintiffs/appellants motion for summary judgment.

The issues presented are whether appellants violated the provisions of the Medicare-Medicaid anti-kickback statue by (1) offering or paying remuneration to physician limited partners to induce the referral of program-related business to limited partnership laboratories, or (2) soliciting or receiving remuneration "in return for" referrals by virtue of their management agreement with Smithkline BioScience Laboratories (SKBL), and whether the Secretary of the Department of Health and Human Services (Secretary) erred in excluding appellants from Medicare and Medicaid participation for various periods due to alleged violations of the Medicare/Medicaid anti-kickback statute, 42 U.S.C. § 1320a-7b(b).

In order to resolve these issues, we must determine (1) whether the Secretary properly interpreted the Medicare/Medicaid anti-kickback statute in the context of health care joint ventures, (2) whether the statute is unconstitutionally vague as applied to the facts of this case, and (3) whether appellants knowingly and willfully committed the acts which are alleged to violate the anti-kickback statute. * * * We affirm in part and reverse in part.

FACTS

In 1987, The Hanlester Network (Hanlester), a California general partnership, was formed. The original general partners in Hanlester were the Hanlester Corporation, James A. Padova, M.D., Inc., a California medical corporation, Gene Tasha, and Ned Welsh.[9] The Hanlester Corporation owned the majority interest in the Hanlester Network prior to 1989.

* * *

On April 9, 1987, Hanlester and SKBL entered into a master laboratory service agreement. In that agreement, SKBL agreed to provide laboratory management services to all joint venture laboratories in which Hanlester had an ownership interest.[10] Hanlester had exclusive authority to make all management decisions for Placer, PPCL, and Omni.

Between March 1987 and March 1988, Hanlester issued private placement memoranda offering limited partnership shares in PPCL, Placer, and Omni. The purpose of the private placement memoranda was to offer limited partnership shares in joint venture laboratories. Hanlester marketed limited partnership shares, and offered investors partnership shares in Omni, Placer, and PPCL for a minimum three shares at $500 each. On July 27, 1987, SKBL entered into a laboratory management agreement with PPCL. The agreement required PPCL to provide the

---

[9] Appellants in this case (Respondents below) are: The Hanlester Network (Hanlester); the Keorle Corporation (Keorle); Pacific Physicians Clinical Laboratory (PPCL); Omni Physicians Clinical Laboratory, Ltd. (Omni); Placer Physicians Clinical Laboratory, Ltd. (Placer); Kevin Lewand, Gene Tasha, Melvin L. Huntsinger, M.D., and Ned Welsh.

[10] Hanlester had an interest in Respondents Omni, Placer and PPCL.

services of a licensed Medical Director, and to pay SKBL a monthly management fee of $15,000 or 80% of all net cash receipts, whichever was greater. Hanlester and SKBL entered into a laboratory support services agreement in which Hanlester would set up and service client accounts for PPCL.

Subsequently, SKBL executed laboratory management agreements with the other Hanlester laboratories under which SKBL agreed to supervise their administrative and operational activities; provide and compensate all staff to operate them; provide and maintain all lab equipment not already provided by the labs; and to conduct all billing and collection activities for them. In accordance with these agreements, 85 to 90% of tests physicians ordered from the Hanlester labs were performed at SKBL facilities in California.

Hanlester was notified by the Investigator General (I.G.) of the Department of Health and Human Services (DHHS) in December 1989 that he had determined that the Hanlester respondents * * * had violated § 1128B(b)(2) of the Social Security Act (the Act) by offering and paying remuneration to physician-investors to induce them to refer laboratory tests to the three Hanlester laboratories. The Hanlester appellants were also told they had violated § 1128B(b)(1) of the Act by soliciting and receiving payments from SKBL in return for referrals of lab tests, and that it would be proposed that all of the appellants be excluded from the Medicare and state health care programs under § 1128(b)(7) for varying periods of time. The Hanlester appellants requested a hearing on the proposed exclusions before an Administrative Law Judge (ALJ). * * * The ALJ concluded that appellants Hanlester, PPCL, Placer, and Omni violated § 1128B(b)(2) through the actions of their agent, Patricia Hitchcock, while Lewand, Tasha, Welsh, Huntsinger and Keorle had not. The ALJ also concluded that none of the appellants knowingly and willfully solicited or received any remuneration for referring program-related business in violation of § 1128B(b)(1) of the Act. The ALJ declined to impose permissive exclusions from Medicare or Medicaid based on the violations. The I.G. then appealed to an Appellate Panel of the Departmental Appeals Board (DAB), * * *. On September 18, 1991 the DAB reversed all findings excepted to by the I.G.,* * * *.

In its March 1992 Decision on Remand, the ALJ found that all nine appellants had violated § 1128B(b)(2) of the Social Security Act by knowingly and willfully offering or paying remuneration to physicians to induce them to refer program-related business. The ALJ also found that all appellants except Welsh and Huntsinger violated § 1128B(b)(1) by knowingly and willfully soliciting or receiving remuneration in return for referring program-related business. The ALJ further concluded that permissive exclusions under § 1128(b)(7) were necessary for some, but not all appellants.

In the DAB's July 1992 Final Decision, the DAB affirmed the ALJ's findings and conclusions with respect to the violations by appellants, but vacated his decision not to impose exclusions on all appellants. Hanlester appealed to the district court * * *. The district court granted the Secretary's motion for summary judgment, and denied appellants' motion for summary judgment. Appellants timely appealed.

* * *

II. Analysis

This is the first instance in which physician self-referral joint ventures have been challenged under the Act, and in which the Act has been applied to arrangements other than kickbacks, bribes, or rebates, as a basis for excluding persons from participation in Medicare/Medicaid programs.

Nothing in the language of the statute itself prohibits joint venture arrangements. We must, therefore, look to the legislative history, the Act's purpose and context to determine whether such arrangements violate the statute.

The Statute Congress, concerned with escalating fraud and abuse in the Medicare-Medicaid system, amended the misdemeanor anti-kickback statute in 1977 to strengthen the government's ability to prosecute and punish fraud in the system. Language was added prohibiting (1) the solicitation or receipt of "any remuneration (including any kickback, bribe, or rebate) directly or indirectly, overtly or covertly, in cash or in kind," in return for referrals, and (2) the offer or payment of such remuneration to "induce" referrals.[] Congress also upgraded the violation to a felony.

In 1987, Congress * * * authorized the exclusion from Medicare or Medicaid program participation of individuals or entities found by the

163

Secretary to have committed an act proscribed by § 1128B(b) of the Act.[]

* * *

Proof of Agreement

We first address the threshold question of whether proof of an agreement is required to establish a violation of either subsection of the anti-kickback statute.

The courts have not held that proof of an agreement to refer program-related business is a prerequisite to establishing a violation of § 1128B.

The cases which appellants rely on involve interpretations of former bribery statute 18 U.S.C. § 201. They do not support appellants' contention that the "in return for" language in § 1128B(b)(1) is contract-type language which contemplates a quid pro quo, which in turn implies a promise, contract, or agreement.

* * *

There is no basis in the statute, case law or legislative history to require an agreement to refer program-related business.

Vagueness
[The court held the statute was not unconstitutionally vague]

* * *

Offer or Payment to Induce Referrals

The Secretary claims that appellants knowingly and willfully engaged in conduct which violated the anti-kickback laws. We address the subsection (b)(2) violation first.

In order to find a violation of 42 U.S.C. § 1320a-7b(b)(2), we must conclude that appellants knowingly and willfully offered or paid remuneration to induce referrals of program-related business.

Remuneration

Congress introduced the broad term "remuneration" in the 1977 amendment of the statute to clarify the types of financial arrangements and conduct to be classified as illegal under Medicare and Medicaid. * * * The phrase "any remuneration" was intended to broaden the reach of the law which previously referred only to kickbacks, bribes, and rebates.

Inducement

Appellants argue that the term "induce" is synonymous with "to encourage", and that encouragement is not prohibited by the statute. Appellants are correct that mere encouragement would not violate the statute. However, the term "induce" is not defined simply by reference to influence or encouragement.

The term "induce" has been defined as follows: to bring on or about, to affect, cause, to influence to an act or course of conduct, lead by persuasion or reasoning, incite by motives, prevail on.[]

The Secretary determined that the phrase "to induce" in § 1128B(b)(2) of the Act connotes "an intent to exercise influence over the reason or judgment of another in an effort to cause the referral of program-related business". We agree with this interpretation. We now look to the conduct of the parties to determine whether the statute was violated.

Hanlester Appellants

The I.G. argued that appellants unlawfully induced referrals in the way in which they marketed the limited partnerships.[11]

At the time appellants entered into the management agreements, these types of arrangements were fairly common. Health care joint ventures such as that entered into by appellants were not per se unlawful. The evidence shows that Hanlester desired to comply with the law and structured its business operation in a manner which it believed to be lawful. There is ample evidence that appellants intended to encourage limited partners to refer business to the joint venture laboratories. The

---

[11] The marketing strategy was to enlist physician investors who were in a position to refer substantial quantities of tests to joint venture labs.

appellants offered physicians the opportunity to profit indirectly from referrals when they could not profit directly. Potential partners were told that the success of the limited partnerships depended on referrals from the limited partners. While substantial cash distributions were made to limited partners by the joint venture labs, dividends were paid to limited partners based on each individual's ownership share of profits, and not on the volume of their referrals. Payments were made to limited partners whether or not they referred business to the joint venture labs.

The fact that a large number of referrals resulted in the potential for a high return on investment, or that the practical effect of low referral rates was failure for the labs, is insufficient to prove that appellants offered or paid remuneration to induce referrals. The conduct of Patricia Hitchcock, however, is another matter.

Hanlester told prospective limited partners of the joint venture labs that the private placement memoranda issued for the limited partnerships were the only sales material which could be used in connection with the sale of shares. In spite of this, Ms. Hitchcock implied that eligibility to purchase shares depended on an agreement to refer program-related business; told prospective limited partners that the number of shares they would be permitted to purchase in PPCL, Omni, and Placer would depend on the volume of business that they referred to the labs; and stated that partners who did not refer business would be pressured to leave the partnerships. Hitchcock also told potential investors that the partners' return on their investment would be virtually guaranteed. Hitchcock's representations to limited partners constitutes offers of payment to induce referrals of program-related business.

The ALJ found that Patricia Hitchcock, acting as an agent of the Hanlester Network and the joint venture laboratories, violated section 1128B(b)(2), and held the Hanlester Network, PPCL, Omni, and Placer liable for her acts on the theory of respondeat superior.

In order to prove that appellants violated the anti-kickback statute, the government must also prove that appellants' conduct was knowing and willful. 42 U.S.C. § 1320a-7b.

The Scienter Requirement
* * *

166

* * * The Supreme Court has defined "Willfully" as "a voluntary, intentional violation of a known legal duty".[]   Most recently, the Supreme Court has ruled that to establish willfulness, the Government must prove that defendants knew their conduct was unlawful. Ratzlaf v. United States, 114 S. Ct. 655, 657 (1994). * * *

We construe "knowingly and willfully" in § 1128B(b)(2) of the anti-kickback statute as requiring appellants to (1) know that § 1128B prohibits offering or paying remuneration to induce referrals, and (2) engage in prohibited conduct with the specific intent to disobey the law.

Liability of the Hanlester Network and Joint Venture Labs
Patricia Hitchcock's representations to limited partners exceeded the parameters of the private placement memorandum issued by the Hanlester Network. Her actions reflect both knowledge that he conduct was unlawful, and a specific intent to disobey the law. Her conduct was knowing and wilful.

Because Hitchcock was acting as an agent for Hanlester and the joint venture labs, these corporate entities may be held vicariously liable for her actions.[] Moreover, the fact that Hitchcock acted contrary to the corporations' stated policy does not absolve them of liability.[] "Merely stating or publishing instructions and policies without diligently enforcing them is not enough to place the acts of an employee who violates them outside the scope of his employment."[]   The ALJ determined that Hanlester and the joint venture labs permitted Hitchcock to engage in conduct violative of § 1128B within the scope of her employment. Thus, the Secretary's finding that Respondents Hanlester, Placer, Omni and PPCL "knowingly and willfully" violated § 1128B(b)(2) through the conduct of their agent, Ms. Hitchcock, is supported by substantial evidence in the record.

Vicarious liability, however, does not extend to the partners individually.[]

* * *

The I.G. did not prove that any of the individual appellants conditioned the purchase of shares on an agreement to order tests; or that they conditioned the number of shares sold on the amount of business that the physicians agreed to refer; or authorized the ouster of partners who failed to refer business.   Therefore, these appellants are not

167

personally liable for the unlawful conduct of Hanlester, PPCL, Omni, and Placer, which resulted from Ms. Hitchcock's unlawful acts. To the extent that the Secretary now contends that appellants' conduct was unlawful, any illegality was not intentional.

We now consider whether appellants violated § 1128B(b(1).

Solicitation or Receipt of Remuneration in Return for Referrals

* * *

The Secretary characterized the joint venture labs as "sham" operations which served as mere conduits for the payment of monies to physicians in return for the referral of tests from the labs to SKBL.

* * *

The master laboratory services agreement between Hanlester and SKBL specified that PPCL, Omni, and Placer were required to provide facilities and equipment necessary for the operation of the clinical labs, and to repair and maintain lab space and pay utility charges. SKBL had a duty to staff, operate, and supervise the labs, and to conduct all billing and collection activities on their behalf. SKBL was to receive a fee of 76 percent of the laboratories' net revenues. The appellants received 24 percent of net revenues.

There is no question that appellants received substantial economic benefit from their relationship with SKBL. In addition to a net profit, appellants received benefits in the form of (1) SKBL's assumption of the operating risks and management responsibilities for the laboratories and appellants' corresponding relief from those duties, (2) SKBL's payment of anticipated receipts in advance, and (3) the use of SKBL's name and reputation as an enticement for enlisting potential limited partners.

The management services agreement between SKBL and appellants reflects a relatively common practice in the clinical laboratory field. There is no evidence that appellants intended to conceal payments from SKBL to physicians in return for referrals.

The Hanlester appellants believed their conduct to be lawful. The evidence shows that no payments were made to appellants, and that payments actually flowed from PPCL, Omni, and Placer to SKBL in the form of fees for its management services.

The I.G. did not prove that any of the appellants intentionally solicited or received remuneration from SKBL in return for referrals. Therefore, the Secretary's finding that appellants "knowingly and willfully" solicited and received remuneration in return for referrals is not supported by substantial evidence.

Permissive Program Exclusions

The Secretary's authority to impose a civil remedy against parties who violate § 1128B(b) derives from § 1128(b)(7), which applies to "any individual or entity" whom the Secretary determines has committed an act described in § 1128B.

The remedial purpose of § 1128(b) is to enable the Secretary to protect federally-funded health care programs and their beneficiaries and recipients from future conduct which is or might be harmful.[]

There is no evidence that Hanlester, PPCL, Omni, or Placer caused harm to the Medicare or Medicaid programs. Because liability is strictly vicarious, emanating totally from the conduct of Ms. Hitchcock, any untrustworthiness on the part of the Hanlester appellants which existed while Hitchcock represented them ceased to exist once Hitchcock left the employ of Hanlester. Exclusion of these appellants is therefore unnecessary to meet the remedial purposes of the Act.

Individual Appellants

Since we find that Lewand, Tasha, Huntsinger, Keorle and Welsh did not violate either subsection of § 1128B, no remedial purpose would be served by excluding these appellants. Based on the foregoing, we AFFIRM the Secretary's conclusion that appellants Hanlester, Omni, Placer and PPCL violated subsection (b)(2) of § 1128B. We reverse the Secretary's conclusion that any of appellants violated subsection (b)(1) of § 1128B, and reverse the imposition of permissive exclusions on appellants.

NOTES

The specific application of the bribe and kickback law in Hanlester is now largely moot because the Stark legislation (see below) prohibits the sort of self-referrals at issue in Hanlester under most circumstances. Its holding applies more broadly, however, to a host of other arrangements. What is left of the bribe and kickback prohibition after Hanlester? Can you reconcile the Hanlester decision with Greber?

Insert at page 761 the following:

THE STARK II SELF-REFERRAL AMENDMENTS

The coverage of the Stark self-referral legislation was significantly expanded by the 1993 Omnibus Budget Reconciliation to cover services paid for by Medicaid as well as by Medicare and to Act to cover, (in addition to clinical laboratory services) "designated health services" including physical therapy services; occupational therapy services; radiology, including MRI, CT and ultrasound services; radiation therapy services; durable medical equipment and supplies; parenteral and enteral nutrients, equipment, and supplies; prosthetics, orthotics, and prosthetic devices; home health services and supplies; outpatient prescription drugs; and inpatient and outpatient hospital services.

As amended, the self-referral ban prohibits physicians from making referrals to entities and entities from billing for services where the physician or an immediate family member of the physician has an ownership or investment interest or a compensation arrangement with the entity. 42 U.S.C.A. § 1395nn(a)(1) & (2). No payment can be made by Medicare or Medicaid for such services. Any amounts billed in violation of the section must be refunded. Any person knowingly billing or failing to make a refund in violation of the prohibition is subject to a civil fine of $15,000 per item billed and to exclusion. 42 U.S.C.A. § 1395nn(g).

The self-referral statute covers much of the same conduct as the bribe and kickback prohibition, but has its own exceptions that are worded somewhat differently. How does your analysis of problems 3, 6 and 7 at pages 750 - 752 change under the self-referral provisions reproduced below?

42 U.S.C. §1395nn

(e) Exceptions relating to other compensation arrangements
The following shall not be considered to be a compensation arrangement described in subsection (a)(2)(B) of this section:
(1) Rental of office space; rental of equipment

(A) Office space

Payments made by a lessee to a lessor for the use of premises if--

(i) the lease is set out in writing, signed by the parties, and specifies the premises covered by the lease,

(ii) the space rented or leased does not exceed that which is reasonable and necessary for the legitimate business purposes of the lease or rental and is used exclusively by the lessee when being used by the lessee, * * *

(iii) the lease provides for a term of rental or lease for at least 1 year,

(iv) the rental charges over the term of the lease are set in advance, are consistent with fair market value, and are not determined in a manner that takes into account the volume or value of any referrals or other business generated between the parties,

(v) the lease would be commercially reasonable even if no referrals were made between the parties, and

(vi) the lease meets such other requirements as the Secretary may impose by regulation as needed to protect against program or patient abuse.

(3) Personal Service Arrangements

[Certain personal service contracts are permitted if they meet certain conditions, including the condition that compensation not be related to the volume or value of referrals.]

* * *

(B) Physician incentive plan exception

(i) In general

In the case of a physician incentive plan (as defined in clause (ii)) between a physician and an entity, the compensation may be determined in a manner (through a withhold, capitation, bonus, or otherwise) that takes into account directly or indirectly the volume or value of any referrals or other business generated between the parties, if the plan meets the following requirements:

(I) No specific payment is made directly or indirectly under the plan to a physician or a physician group as an inducement to reduce or limit medically necessary services provided with respect to a specific individual enrolled with the entity.

171

(II) In the case of a plan that places a physician or a physician group at substantial financial risk as determined by the Secretary pursuant to section 1395mm(i)(8)(A)(ii) of this title [which establishes the requirements for Medicare HMOs], the plan complies with any requirements the Secretary may impose pursuant to such section.

(III) Upon request by the Secretary, the entity provides the Secretary with access to descriptive information regarding the plan, in order to permit the Secretary to determine whether the plan is in compliance with the requirements of this clause.

(ii) Physician incentive plan defined

For purposes of this subparagraph, the term "physician incentive plan" means any compensation arrangement between an entity and a physician or physician group that may directly or indirectly have the effect of reducing or limiting services provided with respect to individuals enrolled with the entity.

* * *

(5) Physician recruitment

In the case of remuneration which is provided by a hospital to a physician to induce the physician to relocate to the geographic area served by the hospital in order to be a member of the medical staff of the hospital, if--

(A) the physician is not required to refer patients to the hospital,

(B) the amount of the remuneration under the arrangement is not determined in a manner that takes into account (directly or indirectly) the volume or value of any referrals by the referring physician, and

(C) the arrangement meets such other requirements as the Secretary may impose by regulation as needed to protect against program or patient abuse.

The Stark self-referral prohibitions also include significant exceptions applicable to group practices. Consider the application of these exceptions, set out below, to the following problem.

Drs. Chung, Snyder, Williams, Mendez, Patel, and Jones have heretofore each operated independent solo practices. All have offices within a three square mile area, but none share offices with each other. Several years ago they formed a joint venture to provide a variety of laboratory services to their patients. Their attorney has now informed them that their joint venture violates the prohibitions of the Stark legislation. He has suggested that they consider forming a group practice to operate the laboratory. What steps must they take to form a group practice that will permit they to operate a laboratory together under the relevant language of revised 42 U.S.C. § 1395nn?

(b) General exceptions to both ownership and compensation arrangement prohibitions

[The self-referral prohibitions] of this section shall not apply in the following cases:

(1) Physicians' services

In the case of physicians' services * * * provided personally by (or under the personal supervision of) another physician in the same group practice (as defined in subsection (h)(4) of this section) as the referring physician.

(2) In-office ancillary services

In the case of services (other than durable medical equipment (excluding infusion pumps) and parenteral and enteral nutrients, equipment, and supplies)--

(A) that are furnished--

(i) personally by the referring physician, personally by a physician who is a member of the same group practice as the referring physician, or personally by individuals who are directly supervised by the physician or by another physician in the group practice, and

(ii)(I) in a building in which the referring physician (or another physician who is a member of the same group practice) furnishes physicians' services unrelated to the furnishing of designated health services, or

(II) in the case of a referring physician who is a member of a group practice, in another building which is used by the group practice--

(aa) for the provision of some or all of the group's clinical laboratory services, or

(bb) for the centralized provision of the group's designated health services (other than clinical laboratory services),

173

unless the Secretary determines other terms and conditions under which the provision of such services does not present a risk of program or patient abuse, and

(B) that are billed by the physician performing or supervising the services, by a group practice of which such physician is a member under a billing number assigned to the group practice, or by an entity that is wholly owned by such physician or such group practice,
* * *

* * *

(h)(4)
(A) Definition of group practice

The term "group practice" means a group of 2 or more physicians legally organized as a partnership, professional corporation, foundation, not-for-profit corporation, faculty practice plan, or similar association--

(i) in which each physician who is a member of the group provides substantially the full range of services which the physician routinely provides, including medical care, consultation, diagnosis, or treatment, through the joint use of shared office space, facilities, equipment and personnel,

(ii) for which substantially all of the services of the physicians who are members of the group are provided through the group and are billed under a billing number assigned to the group and amounts so received are treated as receipts of the group,

(iii) in which the overhead expenses of and the income from the practice are distributed in accordance with methods previously determined,

(iv) except as provided in subparagraph (B)(i), in which no physician who is a member of the group directly or indirectly receives compensation based on the volume or value of referrals by the physician,

(v) in which members of the group personally conduct no less than 75 percent of the physician-patient encounters of the group practice, and

(vi) which meets such other standards as the Secretary may impose by regulation.

(B) Special rules
(i) Profits and productivity bonuses

174

A physician in a group practice may be paid a share of overall profits of the group, or a productivity bonus based on services personally performed or services incident to such personally performed services, so long as the share or bonus is not determined in any manner which is directly related to the volume or value of referrals by such physician.

Insert at the beginning of the Notes and Questions on page 764 the following:

Final regulations have been published replacing the proposed regulations at 42 C.F.R. § 1001.952.

CHAPTER 8. ANTITRUST

Insert at page 789, just above Section I, the following:

NOTE ON ANTITRUST AND HEALTH REFORM AND THE DEPARTMENT OF JUSTICE/FTC POLICY STATEMENTS

Antitrust enforcement in the health care industry has been at the center of the debate over health reform in recent years. On the one hand, some in the provider community have argued that antitrust law is too complex and uncertain and that efforts by providers to efficiently reorganize their business affairs through mergers and joint ventures will be thwarted by strict enforcement. See e.g., James W. Todd, Physicians as Professionals, Not Pawns, 12 Health Affs. 145 (Fall, 1993); Frederic J. Entin, et al., Hospital Collaboration: The Need for an Appropriate Antitrust Policy, 29 Wake Forest L. Rev. 107 (1994). Others contend that antitrust is a critical ingredient of any public policy that relies on competitive market forces and is necessary to prevent the harms to consumers associated with provider cartels and market power. See e.g. James F. Blumstein, Health Care Reform and Competing Visions of Medical Care: Antitrust and State Provider Cooperation Legislation, 79 Cornell L. Rev. 1459 (1994); Thomas L. Greaney, When Politics and Law Collide: Why Health Care Reform Does Not Need Antitrust "Reform," 39 St. Louis. U. L.J. 135 (1994); see generally, Physician Payment Review Commission, Annual Report to Congress 283-301 (1995)(concluding there is insufficient evidence to justify antitrust exemption for physician-sponsored networks). Although a number of states have responded by passing laws that provide limited immunity for certain collaborative activities where providers obtain approval from state regulators, it is not clear whether such laws will confer state action immunity from federal antitrust law, and in any event, providers do not seem to be availing themselves of these options. See Blumstein, supra; Sara S. Vance, Immunity for State-Sanctioned Provider Collaboration after Ticor, 62 Antitrust L.J. 409 (1994).

In response to the claim that antitrust uncertainty is deterring cost-saving collaboration, and in an effort to ward off calls for legislative exemption from antitrust law for providers, in September, 1994 the United States Department of Justice and the Federal Trade Commission jointly issued Statements of Enforcement Policy and Analytical Principles Relating to Health Care and Antitrust, 4 Trade Reg Rep. (CCH) para.

13152, 20769 (September 30, 1994). These Statements, which revise and supplement statements promulgated one year earlier, reflect the general principles employed by the federal agencies in deciding whether to challenge mergers, joint ventures and other collaborative activities among health care providers. Seven of the nine statements announce "safety zones" which the agencies will not challenge except under unspecified "extraordinary circumstances." The Statements also include a description of the analytical methodology employed by the agencies in dealing with a variety of joint activities and contain a number of specific examples of how these principles apply to specific circumstances.

Summary of Department of Justice/FTC Policy Statements

1.   Hospital Mergers

Safety Zone. Mergers of general hospitals where one hospital has fewer than 100 beds, has fewer than 40 patients a day, and is more than five years old will not be challenged, absent extraordinary circumstances.

For hospital mergers falling outside the safety zone, the agencies will apply the analytical principles set forth in their 1992 Horizontal Merger Guidelines, 57 Fed. Reg. 42,552 (1992).

2.   High Tech Joint Ventures

Safety Zone. Joint ventures among hospitals to purchase, operate and market high-technology or other expensive medical equipment that involve only the number of hospitals necessary to support the equipment will not be challenged, absent extraordinary circumstances. If more than the minimum number of hospitals are included in the venture, but the additional hospitals could not support the equipment on their own or through a competing joint venture, the agencies will not challenge the venture.

For ventures that fall outside the safety zone, the Statement outlines the key analytic determinations that must be made. First, the product and geographic markets for the venture must be defined. This entails identifying all other providers that could offer services that patients or physicians would consider good substitutes. For example, the market for an MRI joint venture would include all other MRIs in the area that are reasonable alternatives for the same patients but would not include providers with only traditional x-ray equipment. Second, the

177

venture's competitive effects must be evaluated by determining whether (1) it would eliminate existing or potentially viable competing providers and (2) whether there were only a few other competing providers of that service or cooperation in the joint venture market might spill over to lessen competition in other markets in which the parties competed. If competitive problems are identified, the agencies will look further at the competitive characteristics of the market, entry conditions, and the effect of government regulation to determine if there are any anticompetitive effects. Third, for those markets in which competitive problems have been identified, the agencies will evaluate whether significant cost savings or quality-enhancing efficiencies outweigh competitive risks. Finally, the agencies will ascertain whether any anticompetitive collateral agreements exist that would harm competition and that are not necessary to achieve the venture's procompetitive benefits.

3. Joint Ventures Involving Specialized Clinical or Other

Expensive Health Care Services

Safety Zone. None included because the agencies believe that they must acquire more expertise in evaluating the cost of, demand for, and potential benefits from such joint ventures before they can articulate a meaningful safety zone.

The Statement explains how the agencies will analyze hospital joint ventures to provide specialized clinical or other expensive health care services. Under a "rule-of-reason" analysis similar to that set forth in Statement 2, the agencies will define all relevant markets, weigh any anticompetitive effects against any procompetitive efficiencies generated by the venture, and examine whether collateral restraints, if any, are in fact necessary to achieve the efficiencies sought by the venture.

4. Information Sharing

Safety Zone. The Agencies will not challenge, absent extraordinary circumstances, a medical society collecting outcome data from its members about a particular procedure and then providing that information to purchasers or the development of suggested standards for clinical patient care by physicians. This safety zone does not protect physician conduct that coerces others to comply with recommendations and does not cover the collective provision of fee-related information to purchasers.

178

5.   Information Collection

Safety Zone.   Health care providers' collective provision of current or historical, but not prospective, fee-related information to health care purchasers will not be challenged as long as the activity meets the following conditions designed to ensure that providers cannot coordinate prices or engage in other conduct that harms consumers: (1) Collection of the information must be managed by a third party.   (2) Any information that is shared among the providers generally must be more than three months old.   (3) The shared information must be based on information from at least five providers; no one provider's data can represent more than 25 percent of the statistic; and the data must be aggregated so recipients cannot identify the prices charged by an individual provider.

The Statement identifies certain circumstances that are not covered by the safety zone and are viewed with extreme suspicion, e.g., information by competing providers that involves joint negotiation of, or agreement on, price or other competitively-sensitive terms, or involves any coercive collective conduct.

6.   Price Surveys

Safety Zone.   The agencies will not challenge, absent extraordinary circumstances, participation by competing providers in written surveys of prices for health care services, or wages, salaries, or benefits of health care personnel, if the following conditions designed to ensure the data is not used to coordinate prices or costs are satisfied: (1) The survey must be managed by a legitimate third-party; (2) The data must be more than three months old; and (3) at least five providers must report the data on which each statistic is based (no individual provider's data can represent more than 25 percent of the statistic, and the survey results must be sufficiently aggregated to make it impossible to determine the prices or compensation for any particular provider).

7.   Purchasing Arrangements

Safety Zone.   The agencies will not challenge, absent extraordinary circumstances, joint purchasing arrangements among health care providers, as long as they meet conditions designed to ensure that they do not become vehicles for monopsonistic purchasing or for price fixing. To fall within the safety zone, the purchases made by the health care providers must account for less than 35 percent of the total market for the purchased items; and for joint purchasing arrangements including direct competitors, the cost of the purchased items must account for less than 35 percent of the total market for the purchased items, and the cost of the purchased items must account for less than 20 percent of the total revenues of each purchaser.

Concerns about joint purchasing arrangements that fall outside the safety zone may be mitigated if members are not required to use the arrangement for all their purchases of a product or service where negotiations are conducted by a third party, and where communications between the purchasing group and each participant are kept confidential. However, the Statement also cautions that where competitors are excluded from an arrangement and are unable to compete effectively without access to the arrangement and competition is harmed, antitrust concerns will exist.

8.   Physician Network Joint Ventures

<u>Safety zone</u>.   (1) <u>Exclusive physician network joint ventures</u> (ventures that restrict the ability of physicians to affiliate with other such ventures or to contract individually with health insurance plans): If comprised of not more than 20 percent of the physicians in any specialty in a geographic market who have active hospital staff privileges and who share substantial financial risk, such ventures will not be challenged absent extraordinary circumstances. If there are fewer than five of one type of specialist in the market, the venture may include one of them on a non-exclusive basis.

(2) <u>Non-exclusive physician network joint ventures</u> (ventures that do not involve limitations on the ability of participating physicians to affiliate with other ventures or to contract individually with health plans): If comprised of no more than 30 percent of the physicians in each specialty in a geographic market who have active staff privileges and who share substantial financial risk, such ventures will not be challenged absent extraordinary circumstances. Where there are fewer than four of one type of specialist in the entire market, the venture may include one of them.

Ventures falling outside the safety zone still may pass muster under the antitrust laws under various circumstances. In these cases, the

180

ventures will be analyzed by weighing their competitive risks and benefits under the rule of reason.

9.   Multiprovider Networks

Safety Zone.   None.   Because multiprovider networks are relatively new to the health care industry, the agencies believe that they do not yet have sufficient experience evaluating them to issue a formal statement of antitrust enforcement policy or to set out a safety zone.

The Statement discusses the general principles the agencies will apply to networks among competing providers and among providers offering complementary services such as PHOs, MSOs and other integrated delivery systems. If such networks involve agreements that allocate markets, fix prices or similarly restrict competition among competitive providers, the agencies will examine whether the members are "sufficiently integrated" to allow the agencies to weigh the anticompetitive effects and competitive benefits of the agreements. Absent sufficient integration such conduct will be regarded as per se unlawful. The key to demonstrating sufficient integration is establishing that providers share substantial risk. The Statement provides that this requirement is satisfied where providers agree to provide services at a capitated rate or where the venture creates substantial financial incentives for its members to achieve cost containment goals such as through substantial "fee withholds" contingent on achieving cost containment goals.

If the networks are sufficiently integrated, the agencies will define the markets where the networks operate and have substantial impact, and then examine the competitive effects of the networks in each of these markets. That examination will take into account any cost savings or other efficiencies that will be attributable to such networks. The Statement indicates that competitive concerns will arise as to horizontal aspects of multiprovider networks where in any relevant market the network has a substantial market share so that it could increase prices. Multiprovider networks may raise concerns in numerous markets including the network market, the market for physician services (or each medical specialty services market), and other services such as those provided by acute care hospitals. Competitive concerns may be mitigated where third party payers may readily switch to other providers or networks in response to a price increase. Exclusive arrangements between networks and providers may exacerbate concerns depending on

181

the market shares involved, the duration of the agreement, disincentives to withdrawals, and other factors.

The Statement also indicates that multiprovider networks can raise vertical issues as well. Where a network has explicit or de facto exclusive arrangements with providers, the agencies will evaluate whether it can thereby limit the ability of other networks or plans to compete in the market. For example, a PHO contracting exclusively with a large percentage of a group of specialists may unreasonably restrict competition unless purchasers could form a satisfactory competing network. The Statement also indicates that exclusion of providers by a multiprovider network will present competitive concerns only where providers are unable to compete without access to the network and if competition is thereby harmed. Finally, even where competitive risks are present, the agencies will balance procompetitive benefits (particularly those involving cost savings associated with assumption of financial risk as well as others) against prospective harms.

Insert at page 868, just above the Note, the following:

NOTE: ANTITRUST AND INTEGRATED DELIVERY SYSTEMS

With the recent explosion in new integrating organizations and network formation among health care providers, state and federal antitrust enforcement agencies have been extremely active in examining a variety of networks, alliances and integrated delivery systems. In addition to issuing their joint Policy Statements (supra, this Supplement), the Department of Justice and FTC have issued a large number of advisory opinions concerning physician networks. The great majority of these opinions have expressed no intention to challenge the proposal, including a number of situations in which the parties exceeded the "safety zone" thresholds. See, e.g., Letter from Anne K. Bingaman, Assistant Attorney General, Antitrust Division to John R. Cummins (October 27, 1994)(approving nonexclusive physician network comprised of 37% of physicians in relevant market and of percentages "significantly higher" than 30% in some specialties); but cf. Letter from Mark J. Horoschak, Assistant Director, Bureau of Competition, Federal Trade Commission to Paul W. McVay (July 5, 1994)(declining to approve physician controlled PPO in which fee withhold arrangement did not constitute significant risk-sharing).

Of considerable interest will be the treatment afforded to evolving integrated delivery systems (or "multiprovider networks") under the antitrust laws. Although Statement 9 of the Department of Justice/FTC Policy Statements addresses the vertical and horizontal issues posed by networks linking hospitals and physicians (see supra this Supplement), no cases have been filed and no advisory opinions have been issued as yet involving such systems. However, in a widely-noted private antitrust case, Blue Cross and Blue Shield of Wisconsin recently won a $16 million jury verdict (later reduced to $5.7 million before trebling) in a challenge to the activities of a vertically-integrated system. In that case, plaintiff alleged that the Marshfield Clinic and its HMO had willfully acquired a monopoly and restrained trade through its direct employment and affiliation with a large percentage of the physicians in ten rural Wisconsin counties. See Blue Cross Prevails on Monopolization, §1 Charges Against Marshfield Clinic, HMO, 68 Antitrust & Trade Reg. Rep. 1707 (April 6, 1995). In addition, the State of Missouri has challenged and settled by consent decree the acquisition of physician practices by a hospital constituting over 50 percent of the physicians practicing in several relevant markets. See Hospital Resolves Antitrust Concerns over Integration of Physician Practices, 68 Antitrust & Trade Reg. Rep. 24 (January 12, 1995). On the issues raised in applying antitrust law to the activities of integrated delivery systems, see Thomas L. Greaney, Managed Competition, Integrated Delivery Systems and Antitrust, 79 Cornell L. Rev. 1507 (1994).

Insert on page 878, just above the Notes and Questions, the following:

U.S. HEALTHCARE, INC. v. HEALTHSOURCE, INC.
986 F.2d 589 (1st Cir. 1993)

Boudin, Circuit Judge.

U.S. Healthcare and two related companies (collectively "U.S. Healthcare") brought this antitrust case in the district court against Healthsource, Inc., its founder and one of its subsidiaries. Both sides are engaged in providing medical services through health maintenance organizations ("HMOs") in New Hampshire. In its suit U.S. Healthcare challenged an exclusive dealing clause in the contracts between the Healthsource HMO and doctors who provide primary care for it in New

Hampshire. After a trial in district court, the magistrate judge found no violation, and U.S. Healthcare appealed. We affirm.

I. BACKGROUND

Healthsource New Hampshire is an HMO founded in 1985 by Dr. Norman Payson and a group of doctors in Concord, N.H. Its parent company, Healthsource, Inc., is headed by Dr. Payson and it manages or has interests in HMOs in a number of states. We refer to both the parent company and its New Hampshire HMO as "Healthsource."

* * *

Healthsource's HMO operations in New Hampshire were a success. At the time of suit, Healthsource was the only non-staff HMO in the state with 47,000 patients (some in nearby areas of Massachusetts), representing about 5 percent of New Hampshire's population. Stringent controls gave it low costs, including a low hospital utilization rate; and it sought and obtained favorable rates from hospitals and specialists. Giving doctors a further stake in Healthsource's success and incentive to contain costs, Dr. Payson apparently encouraged doctors to become stockholders as well, and at least 400 did so. By 1989 Dr. Payson was proposing to make Healthsource a publicly traded company, in part to permit greater liquidity for its doctor shareholders.

U.S. Healthcare is also in the business of operating HMOs. U.S. Healthcare, Inc., the parent of the other two plaintiff companies--U.S. Healthcare, Inc. (Massachusetts) and U.S. Healthcare of New Hampshire, Inc.--may be the largest publicly held provider of HMO services in the country, serving over one million patients and having total 1990 revenues of well over a billion dollars. Prior to 1990, its Massachusetts subsidiary had done some recruiting of New Hampshire doctors to act as primary care providers for border-area residents served by its Massachusetts HMO. In 1989, U.S. Healthcare had a substantial interest in expanding into New Hampshire.

Dr. Payson was aware in the fall of 1989 that HMOs operating in other states were thinking about offering their services in New Hampshire. He was also concerned that, when Healthsource went public, many of its doctor-shareholders would sell their stock, decreasing their interest in Healthsource and their incentive to control its costs.

184

After considering alternative incentives, Dr. Payson and the HMO's chief operating officer conceived the exclusivity clause that has prompted this litigation. Shortly after the Healthsource public offering in November 1989, Healthsource notified its panel doctors that they would receive greater compensation if they agreed not to serve any other HMO.

The new contract term, effective January 26, 1990, provided for an increase in the standard monthly capitation paid to each primary care physician, for each Healthsource HMO patient cared for by that doctor, if the doctor agreed to the following optional paragraph in the basic doctor-Healthsource agreement:

> 11.01 Exclusive Services of Physicians. Physician agrees during the term of this Agreement not to serve as a participating physician for any other HMO plan; this shall not, however, preclude Physician from providing professional courtesy coverage arrangements for brief periods of time or emergency services to members of other HMO plans.

A doctor who adopted the option remained free to serve non-HMO patients under ordinary indemnity insurance policies, under Blue Cross/Blue Shield plans, or under preferred provider arrangements. A doctor who accepted the option could also return to non-exclusive status by giving notice.[12]

Although Healthsource capitation amounts varied, a doctor who accepted the exclusivity option generally increased his or her capitation payments by a little more than $1 per patient per month; the magistrate judge put the amount at $1.16 and said that it represented an average increase of about 14 percent as compared with non-exclusive status. The dollar benefit of exclusivity for an individual doctor obviously varies with the number of HMO patients handled by the doctor. Many of the doctors had less than 100 Healthsource patients while about 50 of them had 200 or more. About 250 doctors, or 87 percent of Healthsource's primary care physicians, opted for exclusivity.

---

[12] The original notice period was 180 days. This was reduced to 30 days in March or April 1991. It appears, at least in practice, that a doctor could switch to non-exclusive status more rapidly by returning some of the extra compensation previously paid.

* * *

In this court, U.S. Healthcare attacks the exclusivity clause primarily as a per se or near per se violation of section 1; accordingly we begin by examining the case through the per se or "quick look" lenses urged by U.S. Healthcare. We then consider the claim recast in the more conventional framework of *Tampa Electric Co. v. Nashville Coal Co.*, 365 U.S. 320, 81 S.Ct. 623, 5 L.Ed.2d 580 (1961), the Supreme Court's latest word on exclusivity contracts, appraising them under section 1's rule of reason. Finally, we address U.S. Healthcare's claims of section 2 violation and its attacks on the market-definition findings of the magistrate judge.

The Per Se and "Quick Look" Claims

U.S. Healthcare's challenge to the exclusivity clause, calling it first a per se violation and later a monopolization offense, invokes a signal aspect of antitrust analysis: the same competitive practice may be reviewed under several different rubrics and a plaintiff may prevail by establishing a claim under any one of them. Thus, while an exclusivity arrangement is often considered under section 1's rule of reason, it might in theory play a role in a per se violation of section 1. But each rubric has its own conditions and requirements of proof.

* * *

U.S. Healthcare's main argument for per se treatment is to describe the exclusivity clause as a group boycott. To understand why the claim ultimately fails one must begin by recognizing that per se condemnation is not visited on every arrangement that might, as a matter of language, be called a group boycott or concerted refusal to deal. Rather, today that designation is principally reserved for cases in which competitors agree with each other not to deal with a supplier or distributor if it continues to serve a competitor whom they seek to injure.

We doubt that the modern Supreme Court would use the boycott label to describe, or the rubric to condemn, a joint venture among competitors in which participation was allowed to some but not all, although such a restriction might well fall after a more complete analysis under the rule of reason. What is even more clear is that a purely vertical arrangement, by which (for example) a supplier or dealer makes

186

an agreement exclusively to supply or serve a manufacturer, is not a group boycott. Were the law otherwise, every distributor or retailer who agreed with a manufacturer to handle only one brand of television or bicycle would be engaged in a group boycott of other manufacturers.

There are multiple reasons why the law permits (or, more accurately, does not condemn per se) vertical exclusivity; it is enough to say here that the incentives for and effects of such arrangements are usually more benign than a horizontal arrangement among competitors that none of them will supply a company that deals with one of their competitors. No one would think twice about a doctor agreeing to work full time for a staff HMO, an extreme case of vertical exclusivity. Imagine, by contrast, the motives and effects of a horizontal agreement by all of the doctors in a town not to work at a hospital that serves a staff HMO which competes with the doctors.

In this case, the exclusivity arrangements challenged by U.S. Healthcare are vertical in form, that is, they comprise individual promises to Healthsource made by each doctor selecting the option not to offer his or her services to another HMO. The closest that U.S. Healthcare gets to a possible horizontal case is this: it suggests that the exclusivity clause in question, although vertical in form, is in substance an implicit horizontal agreement by the doctors involved.   U.S. Healthcare appears to argue that stockholder- doctors dominate Healthsource and, in order to protect their individual interests (as stockholders in Healthsource), they agreed (in their capacity as doctors) not to deal with any other HMO that might compete with Healthsource. We agree that such a horizontal arrangement, if devoid of joint venture efficiencies, might warrant per se condemnation.

The difficulty is that there is no evidence of such a horizontal agreement in this case. Although U.S. Healthcare notes that doctor-stockholders predominate on the Healthsource board that adopted the option, there is nothing to show that the clause was devised or encouraged by the panel doctors. On the contrary, the record indicates that Dr. Payson and Healthsource's chief operating officer developed the option to serve Healthsource's own interests.   Formally vertical arrangements used to disguise horizontal ones are not unknown, but U.S. Healthcare has supplied us with no evidence of such a masquerade in this case.

* * *

Rule of Reason

Exclusive dealing arrangements, like information exchanges or standard settings, come in a variety of forms and serve a range of objectives. Many of the purposes are benign, such as assurance of supply or outlets, enhanced ability to plan, reduced transaction costs, creation of dealer loyalty, and the like. But there is one common danger for competition: an exclusive arrangement may "foreclose" so much of the available supply or outlet capacity that existing competitors or new entrants may be limited or excluded and, under certain circumstances, this may reinforce market power and raise prices for consumers.

Although the Supreme Court once said that a "substantial" percentage foreclosure of suppliers or outlets would violate section 1, the Court's *Tampa* decision effectively replaced any such quantitative test by an open-ended inquiry into competitive impact. What is required under *Tampa* is to determine "the probable effect of the [exclusive] contract on the relevant area of effective competition, taking into account.... [various factors including] the probable immediate and future effects which pre-emption of that share of the market might have on effective competition therein." 365 U.S. at 329, 81 S.Ct. 623, 5 L.Ed.2d 580.

* * *

U.S. Healthcare simply asserts that competitive impact has already been discussed and that the exclusivity clause has completely foreclosed U.S. Healthcare and any other non- staff HMO from operation in New Hampshire.

This is not a persuasive treatment of a difficult issue or, rather, a host of issues. First, the extent to which the clause operated economically to restrict doctors is a serious question. True, most doctors signed up for it; but who would not take the extra compensation when no competing non-staff HMO was yet operating? The extent of the financial incentive to remain in an exclusive status is unclear, since it varies with patient load, and the least loaded (and thus least constrained by the clause) doctors would normally be the best candidates for a competing HMO. Healthsource suggests that by relatively modest amounts, U.S. Healthcare could offset the exclusivity bonus for a substantial number of Healthsource doctors. U.S. Healthcare's reply brief offers no response.

Second, along with the economic inducement is the issue of duration. Normally an exclusivity clause terminable on 30 days' notice would be close to a de minimis constraint (*Tampa* involved a 20-year contract, and one year is sometimes taken as the trigger for close scrutiny). On the other hand, it may be that the original 180-day clause did frustrate U.S. Healthcare's initial efforts to enlist panel doctors, without whom it would be hard to sign up employers. Perhaps even a 30-day clause would have this effect, especially if a reimbursement penalty were visited on doctors switching back to non-exclusive status. Once again, U.S. Healthcare's brief offers conclusions and a few record references, but neither the precise operation of the clause nor its effects on individual doctors are clearly settled.

Third, even assuming that the financial incentive and duration of the exclusivity clause did remove many of the Healthsource doctors from the reach of new HMOs, it is unclear how much this foreclosure impairs the ability of new HMOs to operate. Certainly the number of primary care physicians tied to Healthsource was significant--one figure suggested is 25 percent or more of all such primary care physicians in New Hampshire--but this still leaves a much larger number not tied to Healthsource. It may be, as U.S. Healthcare urges, that many of the remaining "available" doctors cannot fairly be counted (e.g., those employed full time elsewhere, or reaching retirement, or unwilling to serve HMOs at all). But the dimensions of this limitation were disputed and, by the same token, new doctors are constantly entering the market with an immediate need for patients.

U.S. Healthcare lays great stress upon claims, supported by some meeting notes of Healthsource staff members, that the latter was aware of new HMO entry and conscious that new HMOs like U.S. Healthcare could be adversely affected by the exclusivity clause.[13] Healthsource in turn says that these were notes made in the absence of policy-making officers and that its real motivation for the clause was to bolster loyalty

---

[13] Two examples of these staff notes give their flavor: "Looking at '90 rates--and a deterent [sic] to joining other HMOs (like Healthcare)"; and "amend contract (sending this or next week) based on exclusivity. HMOs only (careful about restraint of trade) will be sent to even those in Healthcare already...."

and cost-cutting incentives. Motive can, of course, be a guide to expected effects, but effects are still the central concern of the antitrust laws, and motive is mainly a clue. This case itself suggests how far motives in business arrangement may be mixed, ambiguous, and subject to dispute. In any event, under *Tampa* the ultimate issue in exclusivity cases remains the issue of foreclosure and its consequences.

Absent a compelling showing of foreclosure of substantial dimensions, we think there is no need for us to pursue any inquiry into Healthsource's precise motives for the clause, the existence and measure of any claimed benefits from exclusivity, the balance between harms and benefits, or the possible existence and relevance of any less restrictive means of achieving the benefits. We are similarly spared the difficulty of assessing the   fact that the clause is limited to HMOs, a fact from which more than one inference may be drawn. The point is that proof of substantial foreclosure and of "probable immediate and future effects" is the essential basis under *Tampa* for an attack on an exclusivity clause. U.S. Healthcare has not supplied that basis.

* * *

Whether the law requires such a further showing of likely impact on consumers is open to debate. Our own case law is not crystal clear on this issue. Ultimately the issue turns upon antitrust policy, where a permanent tension prevails between the "no sparrow shall fall" concept of antitrust, see Klor's, 359 U.S. at 213 (violation "not to be tolerated merely because the victim is just one merchant whose business is so small that his destruction makes little difference to the economy"), and the ascendant view that antitrust protects "competition, not competitors". See *Brunswick Corp. v. Pueblo Bowl-O-Mat, Inc.*, 429 U.S. 477, 488 (1977). We need not confront this issue in a case where the cardinal requirement of a valid claim-- significant foreclosure unreasonably restricting competitors--has not been demonstrated.

Section 2

Exclusive contracts might in some situations constitute the wrongful act that is an ingredient in monopolization claims under section 2. The magistrate judge resolved these section 2 claims in favor of Healthsource primarily by defining the market broadly to include all health care financing in New Hampshire. So defined, Healthsource had a share of that market too small to support an attempt charge, let alone

190

one of actual monopolization. U.S. Healthcare argues, however, that the market was misdefined.

It may be unnecessary to consider this claim since, as we have already held, U.S. Healthcare has failed to show a substantial foreclosure effect from the exclusivity clause. After all, an act can be wrongful in the context of section 2 only where it has *598 or threatens to have a significant exclusionary impact. But a lesser showing of likely effect might be required if the actor were a monopolist or one within striking distance. More important, the magistrate judge dismissed the section 2 claims based on market definition and, if his definition were shown to be wrong, a remand might be required unless we were certain that U.S. Healthcare could never prevail.

There is no subject in antitrust law more confusing than market definition. One reason is that the concept, even in the pristine formulation of economists, is deliberately an attempt to oversimplify--for working purposes--the very complex economic interactions between a number of differently situated buyers and sellers, each of whom in reality has different costs, needs, and substitutes. Further, when lawyers and judges take hold of the concept, they impose on it nuances and formulas that reflect administrative and antitrust policy goals. This adaption is legitimate (economists have no patent on the concept), but it means that normative and descriptive ideas become intertwined in the process of market definition.

Nevertheless, rational treatment is assisted by remembering to ask, in defining the market, why we are doing so: that is, what is the antitrust question in this case that market definition aims to answer? This threshold inquiry helps resolve U.S. Healthcare's claim that the magistrate judge erred at the outset by directing his analysis to the issue whether HMOs or health care financing was the relevant product market. This approach, says U.S. Healthcare, mistakenly focuses on the sale of health care to buyers whereas its concern is Healthsource's buying power in tying up doctors needed by other HMOs in order to compete.

The magistrate judge's approach was correct. One can monopolize a product as either a seller or a buyer; but as a buyer of doctor services, Healthsource could never achieve a monopoly (monopsony is the technical term), because doctors have too many

191

alternative buyers for their services.[14]   Rather, the only way to cast Healthsource as a monopolist is to argue, as U.S. Healthcare apparently did, that HMO services (or even IPA HMOs) are a separate health care product sold to consumers such as employers and employees. If so, it might become possible (depending on market share and other factors) to describe Healthsource as a monopolist or potential monopolist in the sale of HMO (or IPA HMO) services in New Hampshire, using the exclusionary clause to foster or reinforce the monopoly.

Thus, the magistrate judge asked the right question. Even so U.S. Healthcare argues that he gave the wrong answer in finding that HMOs were not a separate market (it uses the phrase "submarket" but this does not alter the issue). This is a legitimate contention and U.S. Healthcare has at least some basis for it: HMOs are often cheaper than other care methods because they emphasize illness prevention and severe cost control. U.S. Healthcare also seeks to distinguish cases defining a broader "health care financing market"-- cases heavily relied on by the magistrate judge--as involving quite different types of antitrust claims. See, e.g., *Ball Memorial Hosp., Inc. v. Mutual Hosp. Ins., Inc.*, 784 F.2d 1325 (7th Cir.1986). Once again, we agree that the nature of the claim can affect the proper market definition.

The problem with U.S. Healthcare's argument is that differences in cost and quality between products create the possibility of separate markets, not the certainty. A car with more features and a higher price is, within some range, in the same market as one with less features and a lower price. In practice, the frustrating but routine question how to define the product market is answered in antitrust cases by asking expert economists to testify. Here, the issue for an economist would be whether a sole supplier of HMO services (or IPA HMOs if that is U.S. Healthcare's proposed market) could raise price far enough over cost, and for a long enough period, to enjoy monopoly profits. Usage patterns,

---

[14] U.S. Healthcare, of course, is not concerned with Healthsource's ability as a monopsonist to exploit doctors; it is concerned with its own ability to find doctors to serve it. The latter question--one of foreclosure-- depends on the available supply of doctors, the constraint imposed by the exclusivity clause, the prospect for entry of new doctors into the market, and similar issues. Whether U.S. Healthcare is foreclosed, however, does not depend on whether consumers treat HMOs as a part of health care financing or as a unique and separate product.

customer surveys, actual profit levels, comparison of features, ease of entry, and many other facts are pertinent in answering the question.

Once again, U.S. Healthcare has not made its case in this court. The (unquantified) cost advantage of HMOs is the only important fact supplied; consumers might, or might not, regard this benefit as just about offset by the limits placed on the patient's choice of doctors. To be sure, there was some expert testimony in the district court on both sides of the market definition issue. But if there is any case in which counsel has the obligation to cull the record, organize the facts, and present them in the framework of a persuasive legal argument, it is a sophisticated antitrust case like this one. Without such a showing on appeal, we have limited ability to reconstruct so complex a record ourselves and no basis for overturning the magistrate judge.

Absent the showing of a properly defined product market in which Healthsource could approach monopoly size, we have no reason to consider the geographic dimension of the market. If health care financing is the product market, as the magistrate judge determined, plainly Healthsource has no monopoly or anything close to it, given the number of other providers in New Hampshire, such as insurers, staff HMOs, Blue Cross/Blue Shield and individual doctors. This is equally so whether the geographic market is southern New Hampshire (as U.S. Healthcare claims) or the whole state (as the magistrate judge found).

* * *

CHAPTER 9.   HUMAN REPRODUCTION AND BIRTH

Insert at on page 931, following the Webster case:

PLANNED PARENTHOOD OF SOUTHEASTERN PENNSYLVANIA V. CASEY
Supreme Court of the United States, 1992
-U.S.-, 112 S. Ct. 2791, 120 L. Ed. 2d 674

Justice O'Connor, Justice Kennedy, and Justice Souter announced the judgment of the Court and delivered the opinion of the Court with respect to Parts I, II, III, V-A, V-C, and VI, an opinion with respect to Part V-E, in which Justice Stevens joins, and an opinion with respect to Parts IV, V-B, and V-D.

I.

Liberty finds no refuge in a jurisprudence of doubt. Yet 19 years after our holding that the Constitution protects a woman's right to terminate her pregnancy in its early stages, [ ] that definition of liberty is still questioned. * * *

At issue in these cases are five provisions of the Pennsylvania Abortion Control Act of 1982. * * * The Act requires that a woman seeking an abortion give her informed consent prior to the abortion procedure, and specifies that she be provided with certain information at least 24 hours before the abortion is performed.[ ] For a minor to obtain an abortion, the Act requires the informed consent of one of her parents, but provides for a judicial bypass option if the minor does not wish to or cannot obtain a parent's consent.[ ] Another provision of the Act requires that, unless certain exceptions apply, a married woman seeking an abortion must sign a statement indicating that she has notified her husband of her intended abortion.[ ] The Act exempts compliance with these three requirements in the event of a "medical emergency," which is defined in the Act.[ ] In addition to the above provisions regulating the performance of abortions, the Act imposes certain reporting requirements on facilities that provide abortion services.[ ]

* * *

After considering the fundamental constitutional questions resolved by *Roe*, principles of institutional integrity, and the rule of stare decisis, we are led to conclude this: the essential holding of *Roe v. Wade* should be retained and once again reaffirmed.

It must be stated at the outset and with clarity that *Roe's* essential holding, the holding we reaffirm, has three parts. First is a recognition of the right of the woman to choose to have an abortion before viability and to obtain it without undue interference from the State. Before viability, the State's interests are not strong enough to support a prohibition of abortion or the imposition of a substantial obstacle to the woman's effective right to elect the procedure. Second is a confirmation of the State's power to restrict abortions after fetal viability, if the law contains exceptions for pregnancies which endanger a woman's life or health. And third is the principle that the State has legitimate interests from the outset of the pregnancy in protecting the health of the woman and the life of the fetus that may become a child. These principles do not contradict one another; and we adhere to each.

II.

* * *

The inescapable fact is that adjudication of substantive due process claims may call upon the Court in interpreting the Constitution to exercise that same capacity which by tradition courts always have exercised: reasoned judgment. Its boundaries are not susceptible of expression as a simple rule. That does not mean we are free to invalidate state policy choices with which we disagree; yet neither does it permit us to shrink from the duties of our office.

* * *

Men and women of good conscience can disagree, and we suppose some always shall disagree, about the profound moral and spiritual implications of terminating a pregnancy, even in its earliest stage. Some of us as individuals find abortion offensive to our most basic principles of morality, but that cannot control our decision. Our obligation is to define the liberty of all, not to mandate our own moral code. The underlying constitutional issue is whether the State can resolve these philosophic questions in such a definitive way that a woman lacks all choice in the matter, except perhaps in those rare circumstances in which the pregnancy is itself a danger to her own life or health, or is the result of rape or incest. * * * Abortion is a unique act. It is an act fraught with consequences for others: for the woman who must live with the implications of her decision; for the persons who perform and assist in the procedure; for the spouse, family, and society which must confront the knowledge that these procedures exist, procedures some deem nothing short of an act of violence against innocent human life; and, depending on one's beliefs, for the life or potential life that is aborted. Though abortion is conduct, it does not follow that the State is entitled to proscribe it in all instances. That is because the liberty of the woman is at stake in a sense unique to the human condition and so unique to the law. The mother who carries a child to full term is subject to anxieties, to physical constraints, to pain that only she must bear. That these sacrifices have from the beginning of the human race been endured by woman with a pride that ennobles her in the eyes of others and gives to the infant a bond of love cannot alone be grounds for the State to insist she make the sacrifice. Her suffering is too intimate and personal for the State to insist, without more, upon its own vision of the woman's role, however dominant that vision has been in the course of our history and our culture. The destiny of the woman must be shaped to a large extent on her own conception of her spiritual imperatives and her place in society.

* * *

While we appreciate the weight of the arguments made on behalf of the State in the case before us, arguments which in their ultimate formulation conclude that *Roe* should be overruled, the reservations any of us may have in reaffirming the central holding of *Roe* are outweighed by the explication of individual liberty we have given combined with the force of stare decisis. We turn now to that doctrine.

III.

A.

[In this section, the court discussed the conditions under which it is appropriate for the Court to reverse its own precedent.]

So in this case we may inquire whether *Roe's* central rule has been found unworkable; whether the rule's limitation on state power could be removed without serious inequity to those who have relied upon it or significant damage to the stability of the society governed by the rule in question; whether the law's growth in the intervening years has left *Roe's* central rule a doctrinal anachronism discounted by society; and whether *Roe's* premises of fact have so far changed in the ensuing two decades as to render its central holding somehow irrelevant or unjustifiable in dealing with the issue it addressed.

* * *

The sum of the precedential inquiry to this point shows *Roe's* underpinnings unweakened in any way affecting its central holding. While it has engendered disapproval, it has not been unworkable. An entire generation has come of age free to assume *Roe's* concept of liberty in defining the capacity of women to act in society, and to make reproductive decisions; no erosion of principle going to liberty or personal autonomy has left *Roe's* central holding a doctrinal remnant; *Roe* portends no developments at odds with other precedent for the analysis of personal liberty; and no changes of fact have rendered viability more or less appropriate as the point at which the balance of interests tips. Within the bounds of normal stare decisis analysis, then, and subject to the considerations on which it customarily turns, the stronger argument is for affirming *Roe's* central holding, with whatever degree of personal reluctance any of us may have, not for overruling it.

B.

[The Court next distinguished the rule in the abortion cases from the rules in *Lochner* and the "separate but equal" cases, two areas in which the Supreme Court did reverse its well settled precedents this century. The Court also explained that it should not expend its political capital and put the public respect for the Court and its processes at risk by reversing *Roe.*]

The Court's duty in the present case is clear. In 1973, it confronted the already-divisive issue of governmental power to limit personal choice to undergo abortion, for which it provided a new resolution based on the due process guaranteed by the Fourteenth Amendment. Whether or not a new social consensus is developing on that issue, its divisiveness is no less today than in 1973, and pressure to overrule the decision, like pressure to retain it, has grown only more intense. A decision to overrule *Roe's* essential holding under the existing circumstances would address error, if error there was, at the cost of both profound and unnecessary damage to the Court's legitimacy, and to the Nation's commitment to the rule of law. It is therefore imperative to adhere to the essence of *Roe's* original decision, and we do so today.

IV.

From what we have said so far it follows that it is a constitutional liberty of the woman to have some freedom to terminate her pregnancy. We conclude that the basic decision in *Roe* was based on a constitutional analysis which we cannot now repudiate. The woman's liberty is not so unlimited, however, that from the outset the State cannot show its concern for the life of the unborn, and at a later point in fetal development the State's interest in life has sufficient force so that the right of the woman to terminate the pregnancy can be restricted.

That brings us, of course, to the point where much criticism has been directed at *Roe*, a criticism that always inheres when the Court draws a specific rule from what in the Constitution is but a general standard. We conclude, however, that the urgent claims of the woman to retain the ultimate control over her destiny and her body, claims implicit in the meaning of liberty, require us to perform that function. Liberty must not be extinguished for want of a line that is clear. And it falls to us to give some real substance to the woman's liberty to determine whether to carry her pregnancy to full term.

We conclude the line should be drawn at viability, so that before that time the woman has a right to choose to terminate her pregnancy. We adhere to this principle for two reasons. First, as we have said, is the doctrine of stare decisis. * * *

The second reason is that the concept of viability, as we noted in *Roe,* is the time at which there is a realistic possibility of maintaining and nourishing a life outside the womb, so that the independent existence of the second life can in reason and all fairness be the object of state protection that now overrides the rights of the woman. * * *

The woman's right to terminate her pregnancy before viability is the most central principle of *Roe v. Wade*. It is a rule of law and a component of liberty we cannot renounce.

* * *

Yet it must be remembered that *Roe v. Wade* speaks with clarity in establishing not only the woman's liberty but also the State's "important and legitimate interest in potential life."[ ] That portion of the decision in *Roe* has been given too little acknowledgement and

198

implementation by the Court in its subsequent cases. Those cases decided that any regulation touching upon the abortion decision must survive strict scrutiny, to be sustained only if drawn in narrow terms to further a compelling state interest.[ ] Not all of the cases decided under that formulation can be reconciled with the holding in *Roe* itself that the State has legitimate interests in the health of the woman and in protecting the potential life within her. In resolving this tension, we choose to rely upon *Roe,* as against the later cases.

Roe established a trimester framework to govern abortion regulations. Under this elaborate but rigid construct, almost no regulation at all is permitted during the first trimester of pregnancy; regulations designed to protect the woman's health, but not to further the State's interest in potential life, are permitted during the second trimester; and during the third trimester, when the fetus is viable, prohibitions are permitted provided the life or health of the mother is not at stake.[ ] Most of our cases since *Roe* have involved the application of rules derived from the trimester framework.

* * *

We reject the trimester framework, which we do not consider to be part of the essential holding of *Roe*.[ ] Measures aimed at ensuring that a woman's choice contemplates the consequences for the fetus do not necessarily interfere with the right recognized in *Roe*, although those measures have been found to be inconsistent with the rigid trimester framework announced in that case. A logical reading of the central holding in *Roe* itself, and a necessary reconciliation of the liberty of the woman and the interest of the State in promoting prenatal life, require, in our view, that we abandon the trimester framework as a rigid prohibition on all previability regulation aimed at the protection of fetal life.

* * *

Numerous forms of state regulation might have the incidental effect of increasing the cost or decreasing the availability of medical care, whether for abortion or any other medical procedure. The fact that a law which serves a valid purpose, one not designed to strike at the right itself, has the incidental effect of making it more difficult or more expensive to procure an abortion cannot be enough to invalidate it. Only where state regulation imposes an undue burden on a woman's ability to make this decision does the power of the State reach into the heart of the liberty protected by the Due Process Clause.

* * *

Roe v. Wade was express in its recognition of the State's "important and legitimate interests in preserving and protecting the health of the pregnant woman [and] in protecting the potentiality of human life."[ ] The trimester framework, however, does not fulfill Roe's own promise that the State has an interest in protecting fetal life or potential life. Roe began the contradiction by using the trimester framework to forbid any regulation of abortion designed to advance that interest before viability.[ ] Before viability, Roe and subsequent cases treat all governmental attempts to influence a woman's decision on behalf of the potential life within her as unwarranted. This treatment is, in our judgment, incompatible with the recognition that there is a substantial state interest in potential life throughout pregnancy.[ ]

The very notion that the State has a substantial interest in potential life leads to the conclusion that not all regulations must be deemed unwarranted. Not all burdens on the right to decide whether to terminate a pregnancy will be undue. In our view, the undue burden standard is the appropriate means of reconciling the State's interest with the woman's constitutionally protected liberty.

* * *

A finding of an undue burden is a shorthand for the conclusion that a state regulation has the purpose or effect of placing a substantial obstacle in the path of a woman seeking an abortion of a nonviable fetus. A statute with this purpose is invalid because the means chosen by the State to further the interest in potential life must be calculated to inform the woman's free choice, not hinder it. And a statute which, while furthering the interest in potential life or some other valid state interest, has the effect of placing a substantial obstacle in the path of a woman's choice cannot be considered a permissible means of serving its legitimate ends. * * *

Some guiding principles should emerge. What is at stake is the woman's right to make the ultimate decision, not a right to be insulated from all others in doing so. Regulations which do no more than create a structural mechanism by which the State, or the parent or guardian of a minor, may express profound respect for the life of the unborn are permitted, if they are not a substantial obstacle to the woman's exercise of the right to choose.[ ]

[The Justices then summarized their new undue burden test:]

(a) To protect the central right recognized by *Roe v. Wade* while at the same time accommodating the State's profound interest in potential life, we will employ the undue burden analysis as explained in this opinion. An undue burden exists, and therefore a provision of law is invalid, if its purpose or effect is to place a substantial obstacle in the path of a woman seeking an abortion before the fetus attains viability.

(b) We reject the rigid trimester framework of *Roe v. Wade*. To promote the State's profound interest in potential life, throughout pregnancy the State may take measures to ensure that the woman's choice is informed, and measures designed to advance this interest will not be invalidated as long as their purpose is to persuade the woman to choose childbirth over abortion. These measures must not be an undue burden on the right.

(c) As with any medical procedure, the State may enact regulations to further the health or safety of a woman seeking an abortion. Unnecessary health regulations that have the purpose or effect of presenting a substantial obstacle to a woman seeking an abortion impose an undue burden on the right.

(d) Our adoption of the undue burden analysis does not disturb the central holding of *Roe v. Wade,* and we reaffirm that holding. Regardless of whether exceptions are made for particular circumstances, a State may not prohibit any woman from making the ultimate decision to terminate her pregnancy before viability.

(e) We also reaffirm *Roe's* holding that "subsequent to viability, the State in promoting its interest in the potentiality of human life may, if it chooses, regulate, and even proscribe, abortion except where it is necessary, in appropriate medical judgment, for the preservation of the life or health of the mother."[ ]

* * *

V.

* * *

Because it is central to the operation of various other requirements, we begin with the statute's definition of medical emergency. Under the statute, a medical emergency is "that condition which, on the basis of the physician's good faith clinical judgment, so complicates the medical condition of a pregnant woman as to necessitate the immediate abortion of her pregnancy to avert her death or for which a delay will create serious risk of substantial and irreversible impairment of a major bodily function."[ ]

Petitioners argue that the definition is too narrow, contending that it forecloses the possibility of an immediate abortion despite some significant health risks.

[The Justices accepted the Court of Appeals interpretation of the statute, which assured that "abortion regulation would not in any way pose a significant threat to the life or health of a woman," and determined that the definition imposed no undue burden on a woman's right to an abortion.]

B.

We next consider the informed consent requirement.[ ] Except in a medical emergency, the statute requires that at least 24 hours before performing an abortion a physician inform the woman of the nature of the procedure, the health risks of the abortion and of childbirth, and the "probable gestational age of the unborn child." The physician or a qualified nonphysician must inform the woman of the availability of printed materials published by the State describing the fetus and providing information about medical assistance for childbirth, information about child support from the father, and a list of agencies which provide adoption and other services as alternatives to abortion. An abortion may not be performed unless the woman certifies in writing that she has been informed of the availability of these printed materials and has been provided them if she chooses to view them.

* * *

To the extent [our prior cases] find a constitutional violation when the government requires, as it does here, the giving of truthful, nonmisleading information about the nature of the procedure, the attendant health risks and those of childbirth, and the "probable gestational age" of the fetus, those cases go too far, are inconsistent with *Roe's* acknowledgment of an important interest in potential life, and are overruled. * * * If the information the State requires to be made available to the woman is truthful and not misleading, the requirement may be permissible.

We also see no reason why the State may not require doctors to inform a woman seeking an abortion of the availability of materials relating to the consequences to the fetus, even when those consequences have no direct relation to her health. * * * As we have made clear, we depart from the holdings of *Akron I* and *Thornburgh* to the extent that we permit a State to further its legitimate goal of protecting the life of the unborn by enacting legislation aimed at ensuring a decision that is mature and informed, even when in so doing the State expresses a preference for childbirth over abortion. In short, requiring that the woman be informed of the availability of information relating to fetal development and the assistance available should she decide to carry the pregnancy to full term is a reasonable measure to insure an informed choice, one which might cause the woman to choose childbirth over abortion. This requirement cannot be considered a substantial obstacle to obtaining an abortion, and, it follows, there is no undue burden.

* * *

All that is left of petitioners' argument is an asserted First Amendment right of a physician not to provide information about the risks of abortion, and childbirth, in a manner mandated by the State. To be sure, the physician's First Amendment rights not to speak are implicated,[ ] but only as part of the practice of medicine, subject to reasonable licensing and regulation by the State. We see no constitutional infirmity in the requirement that the physician provide the information mandated by the State here.

The Pennsylvania statute also requires us to reconsider the holding [ ] that the State may not require that a physician, as opposed to a qualified assistant, provide information relevant to a woman's informed consent.[ ] Since there is no evidence on this record that requiring a doctor to give the information as provided by the statute would amount in practical terms to a substantial obstacle to a woman seeking an abortion, we conclude that it is not an undue burden. Our cases reflect the fact that the Constitution gives the States broad latitude to decide that particular functions may be performed only by licensed professionals, even if an objective assessment might suggest that those same tasks could be performed by others.[ ]   Thus, we uphold the provision as a reasonable means to insure that the woman's consent is informed.

Our analysis of Pennsylvania's 24-hour waiting period between the provision of the information deemed necessary to informed consent and the performance of an abortion under the undue burden standard requires us to reconsider the premise behind the decision in *Akron I* invalidating a parallel requirement. In *Akron I* we said: "Nor are we convinced that the State's legitimate concern that the woman's decision be informed is reasonably served by requiring a 24-hour delay as a matter of course."[ ] We consider that conclusion to be wrong. The idea that important decisions will be more informed and deliberate if they follow some period of reflection does not strike us as unreasonable, particularly where the statute directs that important information become part of the background of the decision.* * *

Whether the mandatory 24-hour waiting period is nonetheless invalid because in practice it is a substantial obstacle to a woman's choice to terminate her pregnancy is a closer question. The findings of fact by the District Court indicate that because of the distances many women must travel to reach an abortion provider, the practical effect will often be a delay of much more than a day because the waiting period requires that a woman seeking an abortion make at least two visits to the doctor. * * *

These findings are troubling in some respects, but they do not demonstrate that the waiting period constitutes an undue burden. We do not doubt that, as the District Court held, the waiting period has the effect of "increasing the cost and risk of delay of abortions,"[ ] but the District Court did not conclude that the increased costs and potential delays amount to substantial obstacles.* * * In light of the construction given the statute's definition of medical emergency by the Court of Appeals, and the District Court's findings, we cannot say that the waiting period imposes a real health risk.

We also disagree with the District Court's conclusion that the "particularly burdensome" effects of the waiting period on some women require its invalidation. A particular burden is not of necessity a substantial obstacle. Whether a burden falls on a particular group is a distinct inquiry from whether it is a substantial obstacle even as to the women in that group. * * *

We are left with the argument that the various aspects of the informed consent requirement are unconstitutional because they place barriers in the way of abortion on demand. Even the broadest reading of *Roe*, however, has not suggested that there is a constitutional right to abortion on demand.[ ] Rather, the right protected by *Roe* is a right to decide to terminate a pregnancy free of undue interference by the State. Because the informed consent requirement facilitates the wise exercise of that right it cannot be classified as an interference with the right *Roe* protects. The informed consent requirement is not an undue burden on that right.

C.

[The] Pennsylvania's abortion law provides, except in cases of medical emergency, that no physician shall perform an abortion on a married woman without receiving a signed statement from the woman that she has notified her spouse that she is about to undergo an abortion.

* * *

This information and the District Court's findings reinforce what common sense would suggest. In well-functioning marriages, spouses discuss important intimate decisions such as whether to bear a child. But there are millions of women in this country who are the victims of regular physical and psychological abuse at the hands of their husbands. Should these women become pregnant, they may have very good reasons for not wishing to inform their husbands of their decision to obtain an abortion. Many may have justifiable fears of physical abuse, but may be no less fearful of the consequences of reporting prior abuse to the Commonwealth of Pennsylvania. Many may have a reasonable fear that notifying their husbands will provoke further instances of child abuse; these women are not exempt from [the] notification requirement. Many may fear devastating forms of psychological abuse from their husbands, including verbal harassment, threats of future violence, the destruction of possessions, physical confinement to the home, the withdrawal of financial support, or the disclosure of the abortion to family and friends. * * *

The spousal notification requirement is thus likely to prevent a significant number of women from obtaining an abortion. It does not merely make abortions a little more difficult or expensive to obtain; for many women, it will impose a substantial obstacle. We must not blind ourselves to the fact that the significant number of women who fear for their safety and the safety of their children are likely to be deterred from procuring an abortion as surely as if the Commonwealth had outlawed abortion in all cases.

Respondents attempt to avoid the conclusion that [the spousal notification provision] is invalid by pointing out that it imposes almost no burden at all for the vast majority of women seeking abortions.* * * Respondents argue that since some of [the 20% of women who seek abortions who are married] will be able to notify their husbands without adverse consequences or will qualify for one of the exceptions, the statute affects fewer than one percent of women seeking abortions. For this reason, it is asserted, the statute cannot be invalid on its face.[ ] We disagree with respondents' basic method of analysis.

The analysis does not end with the one percent of women upon whom the statute operates; it begins there. Legislation is measured for consistency with the Constitution by its impact on those whose conduct it affects.* * * [A]s we have said, [the Act's] real target is narrower even than the class of women seeking abortions * * *: it is married women seeking abortions who do not wish to notify their husbands of their intentions and who do not qualify for one of the statutory exceptions to the notice requirement. The unfortunate yet persisting conditions * * * will mean that in a large fraction of the cases * * *, [the statute] it will operate as a substantial obstacle to a woman's choice to undergo an abortion. It is an undue burden, and therefore invalid.

* * *

[The spousal notification provision] embodies a view of marriage consonant with the common-law status of married women but repugnant to our present understanding of marriage and of the nature of the rights secured by the Constitution. Women do not lose their constitutionally protected liberty when they marry.* * *

206

D.

* * *

Our cases establish, and we reaffirm today, that a State may require a minor seeking an abortion to obtain the consent of a parent or guardian, provided that there is an adequate judicial bypass procedure.[ ] Under these precedents, in our view, the [Pennsylvania] one-parent consent requirement and judicial bypass procedure are constitutional.

The only argument made by petitioners respecting this provision and to which our prior decisions do not speak is the contention that the parental consent requirement is invalid because it requires informed parental consent. For the most part, petitioners' argument is a reprise of their argument with respect to the informed consent requirement in general, and we reject it for the reasons given above. Indeed, some of the provisions regarding informed consent have particular force with respect to minors: the waiting period, for example, may provide the parent or parents of a pregnant young woman the opportunity to consult with her in private, and to discuss the consequences of her decision in the context of the values and moral or religious principles of their family.[ ]

E.

[The Justices upheld all of the recordkeeping and reporting requirements of the statute, except for that provision requiring the reporting of a married woman's reason for failure to give notice to her husband.]

VI.

Our Constitution is a covenant running from the first generation of Americans to us and then to future generations. It is a coherent succession. Each generation must learn anew that the Constitution's written terms embody ideas and aspirations that must survive more ages than one. We accept our responsibility not to retreat from interpreting the full meaning of the covenant in light of all of our precedents. We invoke it once again to define the freedom guaranteed by the Constitution's own promise, the promise of liberty.

* * *

[In addition to those parts of the statute found unconstitutional in the three-justice opinion, Justice Stevens would find unconstitutional the requirement that the doctor deliver state-produced materials to a woman seeking an abortion, the counseling requirements, and the 24-hour-waiting requirement. His "concurring and dissenting" opinion is omitted.]

Blackmun, J., concurring in part, concurring in the judgment in part, and dissenting in part.

* * *

Three years ago, in Webster [ ] four Members of this Court appeared poised to "cast into darkness the hopes and visions of every woman in this country" who had come to believe that the Constitution guaranteed her the right to reproductive choice.[ ] All that remained between the promise of *Roe* and the darkness of the plurality was a single, flickering flame. * * * But now, just when so many expected the darkness to fall, the flame has grown bright.

I do not underestimate the significance of today's joint opinion. Yet I remain steadfast in my belief that the right to reproductive choice is entitled to the full protection afforded by this Court before *Webster*. And I fear for the darkness as four Justices anxiously await the single vote necessary to extinguish the light.

I.

Make no mistake, the joint opinion of Justices O'Connor, Kennedy, and Souter is an act of personal courage and constitutional principle. In contrast to previous decisions in which Justices O'Connor and Kennedy postponed reconsideration of *Roe v. Wade*[ ], the authors of the joint opinion today join Justice Stevens and me in concluding that "the essential holding of *Roe* should be retained and once again reaffirmed."[ ] In brief, five Members of this Court today recognize that "the Constitution protects a woman's right to terminate her pregnancy in its early stages."[ ]

* * *

II.

Today, no less than yesterday, the Constitution and decisions of this Court require that a State's abortion restrictions be subjected to the strictest of judicial scrutiny. Our precedents and the joint opinion's principles require us to subject all non-de minimis abortion regulations to strict scrutiny. Under this standard, the Pennsylvania statute's provisions requiring content-based counseling, a 24-hour delay, informed parental consent, and reporting of abortion-related information must be invalidated.

* * *

A State's restrictions on a woman's right to terminate her pregnancy also implicate constitutional guarantees of gender equality. State restrictions on abortion compel women to continue pregnancies they otherwise might terminate. By restricting the right to terminate pregnancies, the State conscripts women's bodies into its service, forcing women to continue their pregnancies, suffer the pains of childbirth, and in most instances, provide years of maternal care. The State does not compensate women for their services; instead, it assumes that they owe this duty as a matter of course.

* * *

Chief Justice Rehnquist, with whom Justice White, Justice Scalia, and Justice Thomas join, concurring in the judgment in part and dissenting in part.

The joint opinion, following its newly-minted variation on stare decisis, retains the outer shell of *Roe v. Wade*,[ ] but beats a wholesale retreat from the substance of that case. We believe that *Roe* was wrongly decided, and that it can and should be overruled consistently with our traditional approach to stare decisis in constitutional cases. We would adopt the approach of the plurality in Webster [ ] and uphold the challenged provisions of the Pennsylvania statute in their entirety.

I.

[The Chief Justice reviewed the jurisprudence of abortion, both before and after the decision in *Roe v. Wade*.]

In *Roe v. Wade*, the Court recognized a "guarantee of personal privacy" which "is broad enough to encompass a woman's decision whether or not to terminate her pregnancy."[ ] We are now of the view that, in terming this right fundamental, the Court in *Roe* read the earlier opinions upon which it based its decision much too broadly. Unlike marriage, procreation and contraception, abortion "involves the purposeful termination of potential life."[ ] The abortion decision must therefore "be recognized as sui generis, different in kind from the others that the Court has protected under the rubric of personal or family privacy and autonomy."[ ] One cannot ignore the fact that a woman is not isolated in her pregnancy, and that the decision to abort necessarily involves the destruction of a fetus.[ ] * * *

Nor do the historical traditions of the American people support the view that the right to terminate one's pregnancy is "fundamental." * * *

We think, therefore, both in view of this history and of our decided cases dealing with substantive liberty under the Due Process Clause, that the Court was mistaken in *Roe* when it classified a woman's decision to terminate her pregnancy as a "fundamental right" that could be abridged only in a manner which withstood "strict scrutiny." * * *

II.

[The Chief Justice then explained why principles of stare decisis did not require that "any portion of the reasoning of *Roe* be kept intact."]

The end result of the joint opinion's paeans of praise for legitimacy is the enunciation of a brand new standard for evaluating state regulation of a woman's right to abortion -- the "undue burden" standard. As indicated above, *Roe v. Wade* adopted a "fundamental right" standard under which state regulations could survive only if they met the requirement of "strict scrutiny." While we disagree with that standard, it at least had a recognized basis in constitutional law at the time *Roe* was decided. The same cannot be said for the "undue burden" standard, which is created largely out of whole cloth by the authors of the joint opinion. It is a standard which even today does not command the support of a majority of this Court. And it will not, we believe, result in the sort of "simple limitation," easily applied, which the joint opinion anticipates.[ ] In sum, it is a standard which is not built to last.

In evaluating abortion regulations under that standard, judges will have to decide whether they place a "substantial obstacle" in the path of a woman seeking an abortion.[ ] In that this standard is based even more on a judge's subjective determinations than was the trimester framework, the standard will do nothing to prevent "judges from roaming at large in the constitutional field" guided only by their personal views.[ ]

* * *

The sum of the joint opinion's labors in the name of stare decisis and "legitimacy" is this: *Roe v. Wade* stands as a sort of judicial Potemkin Village, which may be pointed out to passers by as a monument to the importance of adhering to precedent. But behind the facade, an entirely new method of analysis, without any roots in constitutional law, is imported to decide the constitutionality of state laws regulating abortion. Neither stare decisis nor "legitimacy" are truly served by such an effort.

* * *

Justice Scalia, with whom The Chief Justice, Justice White, and Justice Thomas join, concurring in the judgment in part and dissenting in part.

* * *

The States may, if they wish, permit abortion-on-demand, but the Constitution does not require them to do so. The permissibility of abortion, and the limitations upon it, are to be resolved like most important questions in our democracy: by citizens trying to persuade one another and then voting. As the Court acknowledges, "where reasonable people disagree the government can adopt one position or the other."[ ] The Court is correct in adding the qualification that this "assumes a state of affairs in which the choice does not intrude upon a protected liberty,"[ ] -- but the crucial part of that qualification is the penultimate word. A State's choice between two positions on which reasonable people can disagree is constitutional even when (as is often the case) it intrudes upon a "liberty" in the absolute sense. Laws against bigamy, for example -- which entire societies of reasonable people disagree with -- intrude upon men and women's liberty to marry and live with one another. But bigamy happens not to be a liberty specially "protected" by the Constitution.

That is, quite simply, the issue in this case: not whether the power of a woman to abort her unborn child is a "liberty" in the absolute sense; or even whether it is a liberty of great importance to many women. Of course it is both. The issue is whether it is a liberty protected by the Constitution of the United States. I am sure it is not. I reach that conclusion not because of anything so exalted as my views concerning the "concept of existence, of meaning, of the universe, and of the mystery of human life."[ ] I reach it for the same reason I reach the conclusion that bigamy is not constitutionally protected -- because of two simple facts: (1) the Constitution says absolutely nothing about it, and (2) the longstanding traditions of American society have permitted it to be legally proscribed.

* * *

To the extent I can discern any meaningful content in the "undue burden" standard as applied in the joint opinion, it appears to be that a State may not regulate abortion in such a way as to reduce significantly its incidence. The joint opinion repeatedly emphasizes that an important factor in the "undue burden" analysis is whether the regulation "prevents a significant number of women from obtaining an abortion,"[ ] whether a "significant number of women . . . are likely to be deterred from procuring an abortion," [ ]; and whether the regulation often "deters" women from seeking abortions,[ ]. We are not told, however, what forms of "deterrence" are impermissible or what degree of success in deterrence is too much to be tolerated. If, for example, a State required a woman to read a pamphlet describing, with illustrations, the facts of fetal development before she could obtain an abortion, the effect of such legislation might be to "deter" a "significant number of women" from procuring abortions, thereby seemingly allowing a district judge to invalidate it as an undue burden. Thus, despite flowery rhetoric about the State's "substantial" and "profound" interest in "potential human life," and criticism of *Roe* for undervaluing that interest, the joint opinion permits the State to pursue that interest only so long as it is not too successful. As Justice BLACKMUN recognizes (with evident hope),[ ] the "undue burden" standard may ultimately require the invalidation of each provision upheld today if it can be shown, on a better record, that the State is too effectively "expressing a preference for childbirth over abortion,"[ ]. Reason finds no refuge in this jurisprudence of confusion.

* * *

The Court's reliance upon stare decisis can best be described as contrived. It insists upon the necessity of adhering not to all of *Roe*, but

212

only to what it calls the "central holding." It seems to me that stare decisis ought to be applied even to the doctrine of stare decisis, and I confess never to have heard of this new, keep what you want and throw away the rest version. I wonder whether, as applied to Marbury[ ], for example, the new version of stare decisis would be satisfied if we allowed courts to review the constitutionality of only those statutes that (like the one in Marbury) pertain to the jurisdiction of the courts.

I am certainly not in a good position to dispute that the Court has saved the "central holding" of *Roe*, since to do that effectively I would have to know what the Court has saved, which in turn would require me to understand (as I do not) what the "undue burden" test means. I must confess, however, that I have always thought, and I think a lot of other people have always thought, that the arbitrary trimester framework, which the Court today discards, was quite as central to *Roe* as the arbitrary viability test, which the Court today retains. It seems particularly ungrateful to carve the trimester framework out of the core of *Roe*, since its very rigidity (in sharp contrast to the utter indeterminability of the "undue burden" test) is probably the only reason the Court is able to say, in urging stare decisis, that *Roe* "has in no sense proven 'unworkable,'"[ ]. I suppose the Court is entitled to call a "central holding" whatever it wants to call a "central holding" -- which is, come to think of it, perhaps one of the difficulties with this modified version of stare decisis. I thought I might note, however, that the following portions of *Roe* have not been saved:

* Under *Roe*, requiring that a woman seeking an abortion be provided truthful information about abortion before giving informed written consent is unconstitutional, if the information is designed to influence her choice[ ]. Under the joint opinion's "undue burden" regime (as applied today, at least) such a requirement is constitutional[ ].

* Under *Roe*, requiring that information be provided by a doctor, rather than by nonphysician counselors, is unconstitutional[ ]. Under the "undue burden" regime (as applied today, at least) it is not[ ].

* Under *Roe*, requiring a 24-hour waiting period between the time the woman gives her informed consent and the time of the abortion is unconstitutional. Under the "undue burden" regime (as applied today, at least) it is not[ ].

* Under *Roe*, requiring detailed reports that include demographic data about each woman who seeks an abortion and various information about each abortion is unconstitutional[ ]. Under the "undue burden" regime (as applied today, at least) it generally is not[ ].

* * *

The Court's description of the place of *Roe* in the social history of the United States is unrecognizable. Not only did *Roe* not, as the Court suggests, resolve the deeply divisive issue of abortion; it did more than anything else to nourish it, by elevating it to the national level where it is infinitely more difficult to resolve. National politics were not plagued by abortion protests, national abortion lobbying, or abortion marches on Congress, before *Roe v. Wade* was decided. Profound disagreement existed among our citizens over the issue -- as it does over other issues, such as the death penalty -- but that disagreement was being worked out at the state level. As with many other issues, the division of sentiment within each State was not as closely balanced as it was among the population of the Nation as a whole, meaning not only that more people would be satisfied with the results of state-by-state resolution, but also that those results would be more stable. Pre-Roe, moreover, political compromise was possible.

Roe's mandate for abortion-on-demand destroyed the compromises of the past, rendered compromise impossible for the future, and required the entire issue to be resolved uniformly, at the national level. At the same time, *Roe* created a vast new class of abortion consumers and abortion proponents by eliminating the moral opprobrium that had attached to the act. ("If the Constitution guarantees abortion, how can it be bad?" -- not an accurate line of thought, but a natural one.) Many favor all of those developments, and it is not for me to say that they are wrong. But to portray *Roe* as the statesmanlike "settlement" of a divisive issue, a jurisprudential Peace of Westphalia that is worth preserving, is nothing less than Orwellian. *Roe* fanned into life an issue that has inflamed our national politics in general, and has obscured with its smoke the selection of Justices to this Court in particular, ever since. And by keeping us in the abortion-umpiring business, it is the perpetuation of that disruption, rather than of any *Pax Roeana*, that the Court's new majority decrees.

* * *

214

There is a poignant aspect to today's opinion. Its length, and what might be called its epic tone, suggest that its authors believe they are bringing to an end a troublesome era in the history of our Nation and of our Court. "It is the dimension" of authority, they say, to "call the contending sides of national controversy to end their national division by accepting a common mandate rooted in the Constitution."[ ]

There comes vividly to mind a portrait by Emanuel Leutze that hangs in the Harvard Law School: Roger Brooke Taney, painted in 1859, the 82d year of his life, the 24th of his Chief Justiceship, the second after his opinion in *Dred Scott*. He is all in black, sitting in a shadowed red armchair, left hand resting upon a pad of paper in his lap, right hand hanging limply, almost lifelessly, beside the inner arm of the chair. He sits facing the viewer, and staring straight out. There seems to be on his face, and in his deep-set eyes, an expression of profound sadness and disillusionment. Perhaps he always looked that way, even when dwelling upon the happiest of thoughts. But those of us who know how the lustre of his great Chief Justiceship came to be eclipsed by *Dred Scott* cannot help believing that he had that case -- its already apparent consequences for the Court, and its soon-to-be-played-out consequences for the Nation -- burning on his mind. I expect that two years earlier he, too, had thought himself "calling the contending sides of national controversy to end their national division by accepting a common mandate rooted in the Constitution."

It is no more realistic for us in this case, than it was for him in that, to think that an issue of the sort they both involved -- an issue involving life and death, freedom and subjugation -- can be "speedily and finally settled" by the Supreme Court, as President James Buchanan in his inaugural address said the issue of slavery in the territories would be. Quite to the contrary, by foreclosing all democratic outlet for the deep passions this issue arouses, by banishing the issue from the political forum that gives all participants, even the losers, the satisfaction of a fair hearing and an honest fight, by continuing the imposition of a rigid national rule instead of allowing for regional differences, the Court merely prolongs and intensifies the anguish.

We should get out of this area, where we have no right to be, and where we do neither ourselves nor the country any good by remaining.

NOTE: THE FREEDOM OF ACCESS TO CLINIC ENTRANCES ACT OF 1994

In May of 1994 the President signed the Freedom of Access to Clinic Entrances Act of 1994. The Act provides that

> Whoever --
> (1) by force or threat of force of by physical obstruction, intentionally injures, intimidates or interferes with or attempts to injure, intimidate or interfere with any person because that person is or has been, or in order to intimidate such person or any other person or any class of persons from, obtaining or providing reproductive health services; * * *
> (3) intentionally damages or destroys the property of a facility, or attempts to do so, because such facility provides reproductive health services * * *

shall be guilty of a crime and fined or imprisoned. 18 U.S.C. section 248 (a). The statute provides longer prison terms and larger fines for repeat offenders and shorter prison terms and smaller fines for offenses "involving exclusively a nonviolent physical instruction." 18 U.S.C. section 248(b). The term "reproductive health services" is expansively defined to include "medical, surgical, counselling or referral services * * * including services relating to * * * the termination of a pregnancy" whether those services are provided "in a hospital, clinic, physician's office, or other facility." 18 U.S.C. section 248(e)(5). In addition to its criminal sanctions, the Act provides for civil enforcement by the United States Attorney General and the attorneys general of the states.

The Act also extends the same protection that is accorded to those seeking access to clinics to those "seeking to exercise the First Amendment right of religious freedom at a place of religious worship." This additional protection was originally added by an amendment offered by Senator Hatch, who opposed the bill and thought (incorrectly) that this addition might kill it. While the Act explicitly provides that it is not to be construed to prohibit any "expressive conduct" protected by the First Amendment, 18 U.S.C. section 248(d)(1), abortion protesters filed suit seeking an injunction against enforcement of the statute, on First Amendment grounds, the day it was signed into law.

This Act is not the only weapon provided to those who are concerned about the blockading of clinics that perform abortions. Earlier in 1994 the United States Supreme Court declared that RICO could be applied against those who violate laws to blockade the clinics, and that created the possibility of substantial civil damage awards against organizations and individuals that encourage or participate in illegal conduct to limit the access of women to the clinics. See National Organization of Women v. Scheidler, 114 S. Ct. 798 (1994).

Replace on page 970, the Tennessee Court of Appeals opinion in *Davis v. Davis* with the following opinion of the Supreme Court of Tennessee:

DAVIS V. DAVIS
Supreme Court of Tennessee, 1992
842 S.W.2d 588

Daughtrey, J.:

This appeal presents a question of first impression, involving the disposition of the cryogenically-preserved product of in vitro fertilization (IVF), commonly referred to in the popular press and the legal journals as "frozen embryos." The case began as a divorce action, filed by the appellee, Junior Lewis Davis, against his then wife, appellant Mary Sue Davis. The parties were able to agree upon all terms of dissolution, except one: who was to have "custody" of the seven "frozen embryos" stored in a Knoxville fertility clinic that had attempted to assist the Davises in achieving a much-wanted pregnancy during a happier period in their relationship.

I. Introduction

Mary Sue Davis originally asked for control of the "frozen embryos" with the intent to have them transferred to her own uterus, in a post-divorce effort to become pregnant. Junior Davis objected, saying that he preferred to leave the embryos in their frozen state until he decided whether or not he wanted to become a parent outside the bounds of marriage.

Based on its determination that the embryos were "human beings" from the moment of fertilization, the trial court awarded "custody" to Mary Sue Davis and directed that she "be permitted the opportunity to bring these children to term through implantation." The Court of Appeals reversed, finding that Junior Davis has a "constitutionally protected right not to beget a child where no pregnancy has taken place" and holding that "there is no compelling state interest to justify [] ordering implantation against the will of either party." The Court of Appeals further held that "the parties share an interest in the seven fertilized ova" and remanded the case to the trial court for entry of an order vesting them with "joint control . . . and equal voice over their disposition."

Mary Sue Davis then sought review in this Court, contesting the validity of the constitutional basis for the Court of Appeals decision. We granted review, not because we disagree with the basic legal analysis utilized by the intermediate court, but because of the obvious importance of the case in terms of the development of law regarding the new reproductive technologies, and because the decision of the Court of Appeals does not give adequate guidance to the trial court in the event the parties cannot agree.

We note, in this latter regard, that their positions have already shifted: both have remarried and Mary Sue Davis (now Mary Sue Stowe) has moved out of state. She no longer wishes to utilize the "frozen embryos" herself, but wants authority to donate them to a childless couple. Junior Davis is adamantly opposed to such donation and would prefer to see the "frozen embryos" discarded. The result is, once again, an impasse, but the parties' current legal position does have an effect on the probable outcome of the case, as discussed below.

If we have no statutory authority or common law precedents to guide us [in this case], we do have the benefit of extensive comment and analysis in the legal journals. In those articles, medical-legal scholars and ethicists have proposed various models for the disposition of "frozen embryos" when unanticipated contingencies arise, such as divorce, death of one or both of the parties, financial reversals, or simple disenchantment with the IVF process. Those models range from a rule requiring, at one extreme, that all embryos be used by the gamete-providers or donated for uterine transfer, and, at the other extreme, that any unused embryos be automatically discarded. Other formulations would vest control in the female gamete-provider -- in every case, because of her greater physical and emotional contribution to the IVF process, or perhaps only in the event that she wishes to use them herself. There are also two "implied contract" models: one would infer from enrollment in an IVF program that the IVF clinic has authority to decide in the event of an impasse whether to donate, discard, or use the

218

"frozen embryos" for research; the other would infer from the parties' participation in the creation of the embryos that they had made an irrevocable commitment to reproduction and would require transfer either to the female provider or to a donee. There are also the so-called "equity models": one would avoid the conflict altogether by dividing the "frozen embryos" equally between the parties, to do with as they wish; the other would award veto power to the party wishing to avoid parenthood, whether it be the female or the male progenitor.

Each of these possible models has the virtue of ease of application. Adoption of any of them would establish a bright-line test that would dispose of disputes like the one we have before us in a clear and predictable manner. As appealing as that possibility might seem, we conclude that given the relevant principles of constitutional law, the existing public policy of Tennessee with regard to unborn life, the current state of scientific knowledge giving rise to the emerging reproductive technologies, and the ethical considerations that have developed in response to that scientific knowledge, there can be no easy answer to the question we now face. We conclude, instead, that we must weigh the interests of each party to the dispute, in terms of the facts and analysis set out below, in order to resolve that dispute in a fair and responsible manner.

* * *

III. The Scientific Testimony

In the record, and especially in the trial court's opinion, there is a great deal of discussion about the proper descriptive terminology to be used in this case. Although this discussion appears at first glance to be a matter simply of semantics, semantical distinctions are significant in this context, because language defines legal status and can limit legal rights. Obviously, an "adult" has a different legal status than does a "child." Likewise, "child" means something other than "fetus." A "fetus" differs from an "embryo." There was much dispute at trial about whether the four-to eight-cell entities in this case should properly be referred to as "embryos" or as "preembryos," with resulting differences in legal analysis.

* * *

219

Admittedly, this distinction is not dispositive in the case before us. It deserves emphasis only because inaccuracy can lead to misanalysis such as occurred at the trial level in this case. The trial court reasoned that if there is no distinction between embryos and preembryos, as [the appellant's expert] theorized, then [that expert] must also have been correct when he asserted that "human life begins at the moment of conception." From this proposition, the trial judge concluded that the eight-cell entities at issue were not preembryos but were "children in vitro." He then invoked the doctrine of parens patriae and held that it was "in the best interest of the children" to be born rather than destroyed. Finding that Mary Sue Davis was willing to provide such an opportunity, but that Junior Davis was not, the trial judge awarded her "custody" of the "children in vitro."

The Court of Appeals explicitly rejected the trial judge's reasoning, as well as the result. Indeed, the argument that "human life begins at the moment of conception" and that these four- to eight-cell entities therefore have a legal right to be born has apparently been abandoned by the appellant, despite her success with it in the trial court. We have nevertheless been asked by the American Fertility Society, joined by 19 other national organizations allied in this case as amici curiae, to respond to this issue because of its far-reaching implications in other cases of this kind. We find the request meritorious.

IV. The "Person" vs. "Property" Dichotomy

One of the fundamental issues the inquiry poses is whether the preembryos in this case should be considered "persons" or "property" in the contemplation of the law. The Court of Appeals held, correctly, that they cannot be considered "persons" under Tennessee law * * *.

Nor do preembryos enjoy protection as "persons" under federal law. * * *

Left undisturbed, the trial court's ruling would have afforded preembryos the legal status of "persons" and vested them with legally cognizable interests separate from those of their progenitors. Such a decision would doubtless have had the effect of outlawing IVF programs in the state of Tennessee. But in setting aside the trial court's judgment, the Court of Appeals, at least by implication, may have swung too far in the opposite direction.

To our way of thinking, the most helpful discussion on this point is found not in the minuscule number of legal opinions that have involved "frozen embryos, " but in the ethical standards set by The American Fertility Society, as follows:

Three major ethical positions have been articulated in the debate over preembryo status. At one extreme is the view of the preembryo as a human subject after fertilization, which requires that it be accorded the rights of a person. This position entails an obligation to provide an opportunity for implantation to occur and tends to ban any action before transfer that might harm the preembryo or that is not immediately therapeutic, such as freezing and some preembryo research.

At the opposite extreme is the view that the preembryo has a status no different from any other human tissue. With the consent of those who have decision-making authority over the preembryo, no limits should be imposed on actions taken with preembryos.

A third view -- one that is most widely held -- takes an intermediate position between the other two. It holds that the preembryo deserves respect greater than that accorded to human tissue but not the respect accorded to actual persons. The preembryo is due greater respect than other human tissue because of its potential to become a person and because of its symbolic meaning for many people. Yet, it should not be treated as a person, because it has not yet developed the features of personhood, is not yet established as developmentally individual, and may never realize its biologic potential.

* * *

In its report, the Ethics Committee then calls upon those in charge of IVF programs to establish policies in keeping with the "special respect" due preembryos and suggests:

Within the limits set by institutional policies, decision-making authority regarding preembryos should reside with the persons who have provided the gametes. . . . As a matter of law, it is reasonable to assume that the gamete providers have primary decision-making authority regarding preembryos in the absence of specific legislation on the subject. A person's liberty to procreate or to avoid procreation is directly involved in most decisions involving preembryos.[ ]

We conclude that preembryos are not, strictly speaking, either "persons" or "property," but occupy an interim category that entitles them to special respect because of their potential for human life. It follows that any interest that Mary Sue Davis and Junior Davis have in the preembryos in this case is not a true property interest. However, they do have an interest in the nature of ownership, to the extent that they have decision-making authority concerning disposition of the preembryos, within the scope of policy set by law.

V. The Enforceability of Contract

* * *

We believe, as a starting point, that an agreement regarding disposition of any untransferred preembryos in the event of contingencies (such as the death of one or more of the parties, divorce, financial reversals, or abandonment of the program) should be presumed valid and should be enforced as between the progenitors. This conclusion is in keeping with the proposition that the progenitors, having provided the gametic material giving rise to the preembryos, retain decision-making authority as to their disposition.

At the same time, we recognize that life is not static, and that human emotions run particularly high when a married couple is attempting to overcome infertility problems. It follows that the parties' initial "informed consent" to IVF procedures will often not be truly informed because of the near impossibility of anticipating, emotionally and psychologically, all the turns that events may take as the IVF process unfolds. Providing that the initial agreements may later be modified by agreement will, we think, protect the parties against some of the risks they face in this regard. But, in the absence of such agreed modification, we conclude that their prior agreements should be considered binding.

* * *

[In this case,] we are * * * left with this situation: there was initially no agreement between the parties concerning disposition of the

222

preembryos under the circumstances of this case; there has been no agreement since; and there is no formula in the Court of Appeals opinion for determining the outcome if the parties cannot reach an agreement in the future.

In granting joint custody to the parties, the Court of Appeals must have anticipated that, in the absence of agreement, the preembryos would continue to be stored, as they now are, in the Knoxville fertility clinic. One problem with maintaining the status quo is that the viability of the preembryos cannot be guaranteed indefinitely. Experts in cryopreservation who testified in this case estimated the maximum length of preembryonic viability at two years. Thus, the true effect of the intermediate court's opinion is to confer on Junior Davis the inherent power to veto any transfer of the preembryos in this case and thus to insure their eventual discard or self-destruction.

As noted in Section I of this opinion, the recognition of such a veto power, as long as it applies equally to both parties, is theoretically one of the routes available to resolution of the dispute in this case. Moreover, because of the current state of law regarding the right of procreation, such a rule would probably be upheld as constitutional. Nevertheless, for the reasons set out in Section VI of this opinion, we conclude that it is not the best route to take, under all the circumstances.

VI. The Right of Procreational Autonomy

Although an understanding of the legal status of preembryos is necessary in order to determine the enforceability of agreements about their disposition, asking whether or not they constitute "property" is not an altogether helpful question. As the appellee points out in his brief, "[as] two or eight cell tiny lumps of complex protein, the embryos have no [intrinsic] value to either party." Their value lies in the "potential to become, after implantation, growth and birth, children." Thus, the essential dispute here is not where or how or how long to store the preembryos, but whether the parties will become parents. The Court of Appeals held in effect that they will become parents if they both agree to become parents. The Court did not say what will happen if they fail to agree. We conclude that the answer to this dilemma turns on the parties' exercise of their constitutional right to privacy.

* * *

[The Court found there was a right to individual privacy in both Federal and Tennessee State law, and that this right to individual privacy encompassed the right of procreational autonomy.]

For the purposes of this litigation it is sufficient to note that, whatever its ultimate constitutional boundaries, the right of procreational autonomy is composed of two rights of equal significance -- the right to procreate and the right to avoid procreation. Undoubtedly, both are subject to protections and limitations.

The equivalence of and inherent tension between these two interests are nowhere more evident than in the context of in vitro fertilization. None of the concerns about a woman's bodily integrity that have previously precluded men from controlling abortion decisions is applicable here. We are not unmindful of the fact that the trauma (including both emotional stress and physical discomfort) to which women are subjected in the IVF process is more severe than is the impact of the procedure on men. In this sense, it is fair to say that women contribute more to the IVF process than men. Their experience, however, must be viewed in light of the joys of parenthood that is desired or the relative anguish of a lifetime of unwanted parenthood. As they stand on the brink of potential parenthood, Mary Sue Davis and Junior Lewis Davis must be seen as entirely equivalent gamete-providers.

It is further evident that, however far the protection of procreational autonomy extends, the existence of the right itself dictates that decisional authority rests in the gamete-providers alone, at least to the extent that their decisions have an impact upon their individual reproductive status. As discussed in Section V above, no other person or entity has an interest sufficient to permit interference with the gamete-providers' decision to continue or terminate the IVF process, because no one else bears the consequences of these decisions in the way that the gamete-providers do.

Further, at least with respect to Tennessee's public policy and its constitutional right of privacy, the state's interest in potential human life is insufficient to justify an infringement on the gamete-providers' procreational autonomy.

Certainly, if the state's interests do not become sufficiently compelling in the abortion context until the end of the first trimester, after very significant developmental stages have passed, then surely there is no state interest in these preembryos which could suffice to overcome the interests of the gamete-providers. The [Tennessee] abortion statute reveals that the increase in the state's interest is marked by each successive developmental stage such that, toward the end of a pregnancy, this interest is so compelling that abortion is almost strictly forbidden. This scheme supports the conclusion that the state's interest in the potential life embodied by these four- to eight-cell preembryos (which may or may not be able to achieve implantation in a uterine wall and which, if implanted, may or may not begin to develop into fetuses, subject to possible miscarriage) is at best slight. When weighed against the interests of the individuals and the burdens inherent in parenthood, the state's interest in the potential life of these preembryos is not sufficient to justify any infringement upon the freedom of these individuals to make their own decisions as to whether to allow a process to continue that may result in such a dramatic change in their lives as becoming parents. The unique nature of this case requires us to note that the interests of these parties in parenthood are different in scope than the parental interests considered in other cases. Previously, courts have dealt with the childbearing and child-rearing aspects of parenthood. Abortion cases have dealt with gestational parenthood. In this case, the Court must deal with the question of genetic parenthood. We conclude, moreover, that an interest in avoiding genetic parenthood can be significant enough to trigger the protections afforded to all other aspects of parenthood. The technological fact that someone unknown to these parties could gestate these preembryos does not alter the fact that these parties, the gamete-providers, would become parents in that event, at least in the genetic sense. The profound impact this would have on them supports their right to sole decisional authority as to whether the process of attempting to gestate these preembryos should continue. This brings us directly to the question of how to resolve the dispute that arises when one party wishes to continue the IVF process and the other does not.

VII. Balancing the Parties' Interests

Resolving disputes over conflicting interests of constitutional import is a task familiar to the courts. One way of resolving these disputes is to consider the positions of the parties, the significance of their interests, and the relative burdens that will be imposed by differing resolutions. In this case, the issue centers on the two aspects of procreational autonomy -- the right to procreate and the right to avoid procreation. We start by considering the burdens imposed on the parties

225

by solutions that would have the effect of disallowing the exercise of individual procreational autonomy with respect to these particular preembryos.

Beginning with the burden imposed on Junior Davis, we note that the consequences are obvious. Any disposition which results in the gestation of the preembryos would impose unwanted parenthood on him, with all of its possible financial and psychological consequences. The impact that this unwanted parenthood would have on Junior Davis can only be understood by considering his particular circumstances, as revealed in the record.

Junior Davis testified that he was the fifth youngest of six children. When he was five years old, his parents divorced, his mother had a nervous break-down, and he and three of his brothers went to live at a home for boys run by the Lutheran Church. Another brother was taken in by an aunt, and his sister stayed with their mother. From that day forward, he had monthly visits with his mother but saw his father only three more times before he died in 1976. Junior Davis testified that, as a boy, he had severe problems caused by separation from his parents. He said that it was especially hard to leave his mother after each monthly visit. He clearly feels that he has suffered because of his lack of opportunity to establish a relationship with his parents and particularly because of the absence of his father.

In light of his boyhood experiences, Junior Davis is vehemently opposed to fathering a child that would not live with both parents. Regardless of whether he or Mary Sue had custody, he feels that the child's bond with the non-custodial parent would not be satisfactory. He testified very clearly that his concern was for the psychological obstacles a child in such a situation would face, as well as the burdens it would impose on him. Likewise, he is opposed to donation because the recipient couple might divorce, leaving the child (which he definitely would consider his own) in a single-parent setting.

Balanced against Junior Davis's interest in avoiding parenthood is Mary Sue Davis's interest in donating the preembryos to another couple for implantation. Refusal to permit donation of the preembryos would impose on her the burden of knowing that the lengthy IVF procedures she underwent were futile, and that the preembryos to which she contributed genetic material would never become children. While this is not an insubstantial emotional burden, we can only conclude that

Mary Sue Davis's interest in donation is not as significant as the interest Junior Davis has in avoiding parenthood. If she were allowed to donate these preembryos, he would face a lifetime of either wondering about his parental status or knowing about his parental status but having no control over it. He testified quite clearly that if these preembryos were brought to term he would fight for custody of his child or children. Donation, if a child came of it, would rob him twice -- his procreational autonomy would be defeated and his relationship with his offspring would be prohibited.

The case would be closer if Mary Sue Davis were seeking to use the preembryos herself, but only if she could not achieve parenthood by any other reasonable means. We recognize the trauma that Mary Sue has already experienced and the additional discomfort to which she would be subjected if she opts to attempt IVF again. Still, she would have a reasonable opportunity, through IVF, to try once again to achieve parenthood in all its aspects -- genetic, gestational, bearing, and rearing.

Further, we note that if Mary Sue Davis were unable to undergo another round of IVF, or opted not to try, she could still achieve the child-rearing aspects of parenthood through adoption. The fact that she and Junior Davis pursued adoption indicates that, at least at one time, she was willing to forego genetic parenthood and would have been satisfied by the child-rearing aspects of parenthood alone.

VIII. Conclusion

In summary, we hold that disputes involving the disposition of preembryos produced by in vitro fertilization should be resolved, first, by looking to the preferences of the progenitors. If their wishes cannot be ascertained, or if there is dispute, then their prior agreement concerning disposition should be carried out. If no prior agreement exists, then the relative interests of the parties in using or not using the preembryos must be weighed. Ordinarily, the party wishing to avoid procreation should prevail, assuming that the other party has a reasonable possibility of achieving parenthood by means other than use of the preembryos in question. If no other reasonable alternatives exist, then the argument in favor of using the preembryos to achieve pregnancy should be considered. However, if the party seeking control of the preembryos intends merely to donate them to another couple, the objecting party obviously has the greater interest and should prevail.

But the rule does not contemplate the creation of an automatic veto, and in affirming the judgment of the Court of Appeals, we would not wish to be interpreted as so holding.

For the reasons set out above, the judgment of the Court of Appeals is affirmed, in the appellee's favor. This ruling means that the Knoxville Fertility Clinic is free to follow its normal procedure in dealing with unused preembryos, as long as that procedure is not in conflict with this opinion.

NOTE

In fact, the Knoxville Fertility Clinic could not "follow its normal procedure in dealing with unused preembryos" because its normal procedure was to provide those preembryos to infertile couples -- a procedure that would have been in conflict with the opinion. On rehearing directed to this issue, the Tennessee court looked to the report of the American Fertility Society's Ethics Committee, which authorizes the preembryos to be donated for research purposes (which would require the consent of both of the Davises) or to be discarded. See Davis v. Davis, Order on Petitions to Rehear, (Sup. Ct. Tenn., Nov. 23, 1992).

Insert at page 974, at the end of Note 3, the following:

For the first American judicial consideration of this matter, see *Johnson v. Calvert*, infra, in this supplement.

Insert at page 991 the following: The case discussed in note 8 was finally resolved by the California Supreme Court in 1993:

JOHNSON v. CALVERT
Supreme Court of California, 1993
5 Cal. 4th 84; 851 P.2d 776; 19 Cal. Rptr. 2d 494

Panelli, J.

In this case we address several of the legal questions raised by recent advances in reproductive technology. When, pursuant to a surrogacy agreement, a zygote formed of the gametes of a husband and wife is implanted in the uterus of another woman, who carries the resulting fetus to term and gives birth to a child not genetically related to her, who is the child's "natural mother" under California law? Does a determination that the wife is the child's natural mother work a deprivation of the gestating woman's constitutional rights? And is such an agreement barred by any public policy of this state?

We conclude that the husband and wife are the child's natural parents, and that this result does not offend the state or federal Constitution or public policy.

Mark and Crispina Calvert are a married couple who desired to have a child. Crispina was forced to undergo a hysterectomy in 1984. Her ovaries remained capable of producing eggs, however, and the couple eventually considered surrogacy. In 1989 Anna Johnson heard about Crispina's plight from a coworker and offered to serve as a surrogate for the Calverts.

On January 15, 1990, Mark, Crispina, and Anna signed a contract providing that an embryo created by the sperm of Mark and the egg of Crispina would be implanted in Anna and the child born would be taken into Mark and Crispina's home "as their child." Anna agreed she would relinquish "all parental rights" to the child in favor of Mark and Crispina. In return, Mark and Crispina would pay Anna $ 10,000 in a series of installments, the last to be paid six weeks after the child's birth. Mark and Crispina were also to pay for a $ 200,000 life insurance policy on Anna's life.

The zygote was implanted on January 19, 1990. Less than a month later, an ultrasound test confirmed Anna was pregnant.

Unfortunately, relations deteriorated between the two sides. Mark learned that Anna had not disclosed she had suffered several stillbirths and miscarriages. Anna felt Mark and Crispina did not do enough to obtain the required insurance policy. She also felt abandoned during an onset of premature labor in June.

In July 1990, Anna sent Mark and Crispina a letter demanding the balance of the payments due her or else she would refuse to give up the child. The following month, Mark and Crispina responded with a lawsuit, seeking a declaration they were the legal parents of the unborn child. Anna filed her own action to be declared the mother of the child, and the two cases were eventually consolidated. The parties agreed to an independent guardian ad litem for the purposes of the suit.

The child was born on September 19, 1990, and blood samples were obtained from both Anna and the child for analysis. The blood test results excluded Anna as the genetic mother. The parties agreed to a court order providing that the child would remain with Mark and Crispina on a temporary basis with visits by Anna.

At trial in October 1990, the parties stipulated that Mark and Crispina were the child's genetic parents. After hearing evidence and arguments, the trial court ruled that Mark and Crispina were the child's "genetic, biological and natural" father and mother, that Anna had no "parental" rights to the child, and that the surrogacy contract was legal and enforceable against Anna's claims. The court also terminated the order allowing visitation. Anna appealed from the trial court's judgment. The Court of Appeal affirmed. We granted review.

Discussion

Determining Maternity Under the Uniform Parentage Act

* * *

Passage of the [Uniform Parentage] Act clearly was not motivated by the need to resolve surrogacy disputes, which were virtually unknown in 1975 [when the uniform act became law in California]. Yet it facially applies to any parentage determination, including the rare case in which a child's maternity is in issue. We are invited to disregard the Act and decide this case according to other criteria, including constitutional precepts and our sense of the demands of public policy. We feel constrained, however, to decline the invitation. * * *

Anna, of course, predicates her claim of maternity on the fact that she gave birth to the child. The Calverts contend that Crispina's genetic relationship to the child establishes that she is his mother. Counsel for the minor joins in that contention and argues, in addition, that several of the presumptions created by the Act dictate the same result. * * * We conclude that presentation of blood test evidence is one means of establishing maternity, as is proof of having given birth * * *.

We turn to those few provisions of the Act directly addressing the determination of maternity. "Any interested party," presumably including a genetic mother, "may bring an action to determine the existence . . . of a mother and child relationship."[ ] [One section of the act] provides, in relevant part, that between a child and the natural mother a parent and child relationship "may be established by proof of her having given birth to the child, or under [the Act]."[ ] Apart from [that section], the Act sets forth no specific means by which a natural mother can establish a parent and child relationship. However, it declares that, insofar as practicable, provisions applicable to the father and child relationship apply in an action to determine the existence or nonexistence of a mother and child relationship.

Significantly for this case, [the] Evidence Code [ ] provides that blood testing may be ordered in an action when paternity is a relevant fact. When maternity is disputed, genetic evidence derived from blood testing is likewise admissible.[ ] The Evidence Code further provides that if the court finds the conclusions of all the experts, as disclosed by the evidence based on the blood tests, are that the alleged father is not the father of the child, the question of paternity is resolved accordingly.[ ] By parity of reasoning, blood testing may also be dispositive of the question of maternity. Further, there is a rebuttable presumption of paternity (hence, maternity as well) on the finding of a certain number of genetic markers.

Disregarding the presumptions of paternity that have no application to this case, then, we are left with the undisputed evidence that Anna, not Crispina, gave birth to the child and that Crispina, not Anna, is genetically related to him. Both women thus have adduced evidence of a mother and child relationship as contemplated by the Act.[ ] Yet for any child California law recognizes only one natural mother, despite advances in reproductive technology rendering a different outcome biologically possible.

We decline to accept the contention of amicus curiae * * * that we should find the child has two mothers. Even though rising divorce rates have made multiple parent arrangements common in our society, we see no compelling reason to recognize such a situation here. The Calverts are the genetic and intending parents of their son and have provided him, by all accounts, with a stable, intact, and nurturing home. To recognize parental rights in a third party with whom the Calvert family has had little contact since shortly after the child's birth would diminish Crispina's role as mother.

We see no clear legislative preference in [the statutory law] as between blood testing evidence and proof of having given birth.

* * *

Because two women each have presented acceptable proof of maternity, we do not believe this case can be decided without enquiring into the parties' intentions as manifested in the surrogacy agreement. Mark and Crispina are a couple who desired to have a child of their own genes but are physically unable to do so without the help of reproductive technology. They affirmatively intended the birth of the child, and took the steps necessary to effect in vitro fertilization. But for their acted-on intention, the child would not exist. Anna agreed to facilitate the procreation of Mark's and Crispina's child. The parties' aim was to bring Mark's and Crispina's child into the world, not for Mark and Crispina to donate a zygote to Anna. Crispina from the outset intended to be the child's mother. Although the gestative function Anna performed was necessary to bring about the child's birth, it is safe to say that Anna would not have been given the opportunity to gestate or deliver the child had she, prior to implantation of the zygote, manifested her own intent to be the child's mother. No reason appears why Anna's later change of heart should vitiate the determination that Crispina is the child's natural mother.

We conclude that although the Act recognizes both genetic consanguinity and giving birth as means of establishing a mother and child relationship, when the two means do not coincide in one woman, she who intended to procreate the child--that is, she who intended to bring about the birth of a child that she intended to raise as her own--is the natural mother under California law.[15]

---

[15] Thus, under our analysis, in a true "egg donation" situation, where a woman gestates and gives birth to a child formed from the egg of another woman with the intent to raise the child as her own, the birth mother is the natural mother under California law.

Anna urges that surrogacy contracts violate several social policies. Relying on her contention that she is the child's legal, natural mother, she cites the public policy embodied in [the] Penal Code[ ], prohibiting the payment for consent to adoption of a child. She argues further that the policies underlying the adoption laws of this state are violated by the surrogacy contract because it in effect constitutes a prebirth waiver of her parental rights.

We disagree. Gestational surrogacy differs in crucial respects from adoption and so is not subject to the adoption statutes. The parties voluntarily agreed to participate in in vitro fertilization and related medical procedures before the child was conceived; at the time when Anna entered into the contract, therefore, she was not vulnerable to financial inducements to part with her own expected offspring. As discussed above, Anna was not the genetic mother of the child. The payments to Anna under the contract were meant to compensate her for her services in gestating the fetus and undergoing labor, rather than for giving up "parental" rights to the child. Payments were due both during the pregnancy and after the child's birth. * * *

The dissent would decide parentage based on the best interests of the child. Such an approach raises the repugnant specter of governmental interference in matters implicating our most fundamental notions of privacy, and confuses concepts of parentage and custody. Logically, the determination of parentage must precede, and should not be dictated by, eventual custody decisions. The implicit assumption of the dissent is that a recognition of the genetic intending mother as the natural mother may sometimes harm the child. This assumption overlooks California's dependency laws, which are designed to protect all children irrespective of the manner of birth or conception. Moreover, the best interests standard poorly serves the child in the present situation: it fosters instability during litigation and, if applied to recognize the gestator as the natural mother, results in a split of custody between the natural father and the gestator, an outcome not likely to benefit the child. Further, it may be argued that, by voluntarily contracting away any rights to the child, the gestator has, in effect, conceded the best interests of the child are not with her.

It has been suggested that gestational surrogacy may run afoul of prohibitions on involuntary servitude.[ ] We see no potential for that evil in the contract at issue here, and extrinsic evidence of coercion or duress is utterly lacking.

Finally, Anna and some commentators have expressed concern that surrogacy contracts tend to exploit or dehumanize women, especially women of lower economic status. Anna's objections center around the psychological harm she asserts may result from the gestator's relinquishing the child to whom she has given birth. Some have also cautioned that the practice of surrogacy may encourage society to view children as commodities, subject to trade at their parents' will.

We are unpersuaded that gestational surrogacy arrangements are so likely to cause the untoward results Anna cites as to demand their invalidation on public policy grounds. Although common sense suggests that women of lesser means serve as surrogate mothers more often than do wealthy women, there has been no proof that surrogacy contracts exploit poor women to any greater degree than economic necessity in general exploits them by inducing them to accept lower-paid or otherwise undesirable employment. We are likewise unpersuaded by the claim that surrogacy will foster the attitude that children are mere commodities; no evidence is offered to support it.

The argument that a woman cannot knowingly and intelligently agree to gestate and deliver a baby for intending parents carries overtones of the reasoning that for centuries prevented women from attaining equal economic rights and professional status under the law. To resurrect this view is both to foreclose a personal and economic choice on the part of the surrogate mother, and to deny intending parents what may be their only means of procreating a child of their own genes.

* * *

Constitutionality of the Determination that Anna Johnson is not the Natural Mother

Anna argues at length that her right to the continued companionship of the child is protected under the federal Constitution.

* * *

234

Anna relies mainly on theories of substantive due process, privacy, and procreative freedom, citing a number of decisions recognizing the fundamental liberty interest of natural parents in the custody and care of their children.[ ] These cases do not support recognition of parental rights for a gestational surrogate.

Anna's argument depends on a prior determination that she is indeed the child's mother. Since Crispina is the child's mother under California law because she, not Anna, provided the ovum for the in vitro fertilization procedure, intending to raise the child as her own, it follows that any constitutional interests Anna possesses in this situation are something less than those of a mother. As counsel for the minor points out, the issue in this case is not whether Anna's asserted rights as a natural mother were unconstitutionally violated, but rather whether the determination that she is not the legal natural mother at all is constitutional.

Anna relies principally on the decision of the United States Supreme Court in *Michael H. v. Gerald D.*[ ] to support her claim to a constitutionally protected liberty interest in the companionship of the child, based on her status as "birth mother." In that case, a plurality of the court held that a state may constitutionally deny a man parental rights with respect to a child he fathered during a liaison with the wife of another man, since it is the marital family that traditionally has been accorded a protected liberty interest, as reflected in the historic presumption of legitimacy of a child born into such a family. The reasoning of the plurality in *Michael H.* does not assist Anna. Society has not traditionally protected the right of a woman who gestates and delivers a baby pursuant to an agreement with a couple who supply the zygote from which the baby develops and who intend to raise the child as their own; such arrangements are of too recent an origin to claim the protection of tradition. To the extent that tradition has a bearing on the present case, we believe it supports the claim of the couple who exercise their right to procreate in order to form a family of their own, albeit through novel medical procedures.

Moreover, if we were to conclude that Anna enjoys some sort of liberty interest in the companionship of the child, then the liberty interests of Mark and Crispina, the child's natural parents, in their procreative choices and their relationship with the child would perforce be infringed. Any parental rights Anna might successfully assert could come only at Crispina's expense.

* * *

The judgment of the Court of Appeal is affirmed.

[Arabian, J., concurred with the majority's Uniform Parentage Act analysis, but would leave the issue of whether surrogacy contracts could be consistent with public policy to the legislature.]

Kennard, J., dissenting.

When a woman who wants to have a child provides her fertilized ovum to another woman who carries it through pregnancy and gives birth to a child, who is the child's legal mother? Unlike the majority, I do not agree that the determinative consideration should be the intent to have the child that originated with the woman who contributed the ovum. In my view, the woman who provided the fertilized ovum and the woman who gave birth to the child both have substantial claims to legal motherhood. Pregnancy entails a unique commitment, both psychological and emotional, to an unborn child. No less substantial, however, is the contribution of the woman from whose egg the child developed and without whose desire the child would not exist.

For each child, California law accords the legal rights and responsibilities of parenthood to only one "natural mother." When, as here, the female reproductive role is divided between two women, California law requires courts to make a decision as to which woman is the child's natural mother, but provides no standards by which to make that decision. The majority's resort to "intent" to break the "tie" between the genetic and gestational mothers is unsupported by statute, and, in the absence of appropriate protections in the law to guard against abuse of surrogacy arrangements, it is ill-advised. To determine who is the legal mother of a child born of a gestational surrogacy arrangement, I would apply the standard most protective of child welfare--the best interests of the child.

* * *

II. This Opinion's Approach

The determination of a question of parental rights to a child born of a surrogacy arrangement was before the New Jersey Supreme Court in *Matter of Baby M.*[ ] a case that received worldwide attention. But in

236

the surrogacy arrangement at issue there the woman who gave birth to the child, Marybeth Whitehead, had been impregnated by artificial insemination with the sperm of the intending father, William Stern. Whitehead thus provided the genetic material and carried the fetus to term. This case is different, because here those two aspects of the female role in reproduction were divided between two women. This process is known as "gestational" surrogacy, to distinguish it from the surrogacy arrangement involved in *Baby M*.

In this opinion, I first discuss gestational surrogacy in light of the medical advances that have made it a reality. I next consider the wider social and philosophical implications of using gestational surrogacy to give birth to a child, and set out some of the suggested models for deciding the child's parentage in this situation. I then review a comprehensive model legislative scheme, not enacted in California, designed to accommodate the interests of all participants in surrogacy arrangements. I next turn to California's Uniform Parentage Act, and critique the majority's reliance on "intent" as the determinative factor under that act in deciding who is the "natural," and thus legal, mother of a child born of a gestational surrogacy arrangement. Finally, I explain why, in the absence of legislation designed to address the unique problems of gestational surrogacy, courts deciding who is the legal mother of a child born of gestational surrogacy should look to the best interests of that child.

III. Gestational Surrogacy

* * *

The division of the female reproductive role in gestational surrogacy points up the three discrete aspects of motherhood: genetic, gestational and social. The woman who contributes the egg that becomes the fetus has played the genetic role of motherhood; the gestational aspect is provided by the woman who carries the fetus to term and gives birth to the child; and the woman who ultimately raises the child and assumes the responsibilities of parenthood is the child's social mother.[ ]

IV. Policy Considerations

* * *

Surrogacy proponents generally contend that gestational surrogacy, like the other reproductive technologies that extend the ability to procreate to persons who might not otherwise be able to have children, enhances "individual freedom, fulfillment and responsibility."[ ] Under this view, women capable of bearing children should be allowed to freely agree to be paid to do so by infertile couples desiring to form a family.[ ] The "surrogate mother" is expected "to weigh the prospective investment in her birthing labor" before entering into the arrangement, and, if her "autonomous reproductive decision" is "voluntary," she should be held responsible for it so as "to fulfill the expectations of the other parties . . .."[ ]

One constitutional law scholar argues that the use of techniques such as gestational surrogacy is constitutionally protected and should be restricted only on a showing of a compelling state interest.

* * *

Surrogacy critics, however, maintain that the payment of money for the gestation and relinquishment of a child threatens the economic exploitation of poor women who may be induced to engage in commercial surrogacy arrangements out of financial need.[ ] Some fear the development of a "breeder" class of poor women who will be regularly employed to bear children for the economically advantaged.[ ] Others suggest that women who enter into surrogacy arrangements may underestimate the psychological impact of relinquishing a child they have nurtured in their bodies for nine months.[ ]

Gestational surrogacy is also said to be "dehumanizing"[ ] and to "commodify" women and children by treating the female reproductive capacity and the children born of gestational surrogacy arrangements as products that can be bought and sold.[ ]. The commodification of women and children, it is feared, will reinforce oppressive gender stereotypes and threaten the well-being of all children.* * *

Whether surrogacy contracts are viewed as personal service agreements or agreements for the sale of the child born as the result of the agreement, commentators critical of contractual surrogacy view these contracts as contrary to public policy and thus not enforceable.[ ]

* * *

238

The policy statement of the New York State Task Force on Life and the Law sums up the broad range of ethical problems that commercial surrogacy arrangements are viewed to present:

"The gestation of children as a service for others in exchange for a fee is a radical departure from the way in which society understands and values pregnancy. It substitutes commercial values for the web of social, affective and moral meanings associated with human reproduction.* * * This transformation has profound implications for child-bearing, for women, and for the relationship between parents and the children they bring into the world.* * * Surrogate parenting allows the genetic, gestational and social components of parenthood to be fragmented, creating unprecedented relationships among people bound together by contractual obligation rather than by the bonds of kinship and caring. * * * Surrogate parenting alters deep-rooted social and moral assumptions about the relationship between parents and children. [It] is premised on the ability and willingness of women to abdicate [their parental] responsibility without moral compunction or regret [and] makes the obligations that accompany parenthood alienable and negotiable."

Proponents and critics of gestational surrogacy propose widely differing approaches for deciding who should be the legal mother of a child born of a gestational surrogacy arrangement. Surrogacy advocates propose to enforce pre-conception contracts in which gestational mothers have agreed to relinquish parental rights, and, thus, would make "bargained-for intentions determinative of legal parenthood."[ ] Professor Robertson, for instance, contends that "The right to noncoital, collaborative reproduction also includes the right of the parties to agree how they should allocate their obligations and entitlements with respect to the child. Legal presumptions of paternity and maternity would be overridden by this agreement of the parties."[ ]

Surrogacy critics, on the other hand, consider the unique female role in human reproduction as the determinative factor in questions of legal parentage. They reason that although males and females both contribute genetic material for the child, the act of gestating the fetus falls only on the female.[ ]

Accordingly, in their view, a woman who, as the result of gestational surrogacy, is not genetically related to the child she bears is like any other woman who gives birth to a child. In either situation the woman giving birth is the child's mother. Under this approach, the laws governing adoption should govern the parental rights to a child born of gestational surrogacy. Upon the birth of the child, the gestational mother can decide whether or not to relinquish her parental rights in favor of the genetic mother.

[The dissent's discussion of the Uniform Status of Children of Assisted Conception Act and the Uniform Parentage Act is omitted.]

VII. Analysis of the Majority's "Intent" Test

Faced with the failure of current statutory law to adequately address the issue of who is a child's natural mother when two women qualify under the UPA, the majority breaks the "tie" by resort to a criterion not found in the UPA--the "intent" of the genetic mother to be the child's mother.

* * *

The majority offers four arguments in support of its conclusion to rely on the intent of the genetic mother as the exclusive determinant for deciding who is the natural mother of a child born of gestational surrogacy. Careful examination, however, demonstrates that none of the arguments mandates the majority's conclusion.

The first argument that the majority uses in support of its conclusion that the intent of the genetic mother to bear a child should be dispositive of the question of motherhood is "but-for" causation. Specifically, the majority relies on a commentator who writes that in a gestational surrogacy arrangement, " 'the child would not have been born but for the efforts of the intended parents."[ ]

The majority's resort to "but-for" causation is curious. The concept of "but-for" causation is a "test used in determining tort liability * * *." In California, the test for causation is whether the conduct was a "substantial factor" in bringing about the event.[ ] Neither test for causation assists the majority * * *.

The proposition that a woman who gives birth to a child after carrying it for nine months is a "substantial factor" in the child's birth cannot reasonably be debated. Nor can it reasonably be questioned that "but for" the gestational mother, there would not be a child. Thus, the majority's reliance on principles of causation is misplaced. Neither the "but for" nor the "substantial factor" test of causation provides any basis for preferring the genetic mother's intent as the determinative factor in gestational surrogacy cases: Both the genetic and the gestational mothers are indispensable to the birth of a child in a gestational surrogacy arrangement.

Behind the majority's reliance on "but-for" causation as justification for its intent test is a second, closely related argument. The majority draws its second rationale from a student note: "'The mental concept of the child is a controlling factor of its creation, and the originators of that concept merit full credit as conceivers.'"[ ]

The "originators of the concept" rationale seems comfortingly familiar. The reason it seems familiar, however, is that it is a rationale that is frequently advanced as justifying the law's protection of intellectual property. * * *

The problem with this argument, of course, is that children are not property. Unlike songs or inventions, rights in children cannot be sold for consideration, or made freely available to the general public. Our most fundamental notions of personhood tell us it is inappropriate to treat children as property. Although the law may justly recognize that the originator of a concept has certain property rights in that concept, the originator of the concept of a child can have no such rights, because children cannot be owned as property. * * *

Next, the majority offers as its third rationale the notion that bargained-for expectations support its conclusion regarding the dispositive significance of the genetic mother's intent. Specifically, the majority states that "'intentions that are voluntarily chosen, deliberate, express and bargained-for ought presumptively to determine legal parenthood.'"

* * * But the courts will not compel performance of all contract obligations.[ ] The unsuitability of applying the notion that, because contract intentions are "voluntarily chosen, deliberate, express and bargained-for," their performance ought to be compelled by the courts is even more clear when the concept of specific performance is used to determine the course of the life of a child. Just as children are not the intellectual property of their parents, neither are they the personal property of anyone, and their delivery cannot be ordered as a contract

remedy on the same terms that a court would, for example, order a breaching party to deliver a truckload of nuts and bolts.

* * *

To summarize, the woman who carried the fetus to term and brought a child into the world has, like the genetic mother, a substantial claim to be the natural mother of the child. The gestational mother has made an indispensable and unique biological contribution, and has also gone beyond biology in an intangible respect that, though difficult to label, cannot be denied. Accordingly, I cannot agree with the majority's devaluation of the role of the gestational mother.

I find the majority's reliance on "intent" unsatisfactory for yet another reason. By making intent determinative of parental rights to a child born of a gestational surrogacy arrangement, the majority would permit enforcement of a gestational surrogacy agreement without requiring any of the protections that would be afforded by the Uniform Status of Children of Assisted Conception Act. Under that act, the granting of parental rights to a couple that initiates a gestational surrogacy arrangement would be conditioned upon compliance with the legislation's other provisions. They include court oversight of the gestational surrogacy arrangement before conception, legal counsel for the woman who agrees to gestate the child, a showing of need for the surrogacy, medical and mental health evaluations, and a requirement that all parties meet the standards of fitness of adoptive parents.[ ]

In my view, protective requirements such as those set forth in the USCACA are necessary to minimize any possibility in gestational surrogacy arrangements for overreaching or abuse by a party with economic advantage. As the New Jersey Supreme Court recognized, it will be a rare instance when a low income infertile couple can employ an upper income surrogate. The model act's carefully drafted provisions would assure that the surrogacy arrangement is a matter of medical necessity on the part of the intending parents, and not merely the product of a desire to avoid the inconveniences of pregnancy, together with the financial ability to do so. Also, by requiring both pre-conception psychological counseling for all parties and judicial approval, the model act would assure that parties enter into a surrogacy arrangement only if they are legally and psychologically capable of doing so and fully understand all the risks involved, and that the surrogacy arrangement would not be substantially detrimental to the interests of any individual.

242

Moreover, by requiring judicial approval, the model act would significantly discourage the rapid expansion of commercial surrogacy brokerage and the resulting commodification of the products of pregnancy. In contrast, here the majority's grant of parental rights to the intending mother contains no provisions for the procedural protections suggested by the commissioners who drafted the model act. The majority opinion is a sweeping endorsement of unregulated gestational surrogacy.

The majority's final argument in support of using the intent of the genetic mother as the exclusive determinant of the outcome in gestational surrogacy cases is that preferring the intending mother serves the child's interests, which are "'[u]nlikely to run contrary to those of adults who choose to bring [the child] into being.'"[ ]

I agree with the majority that the best interests of the child is an important goal * * *. The problem with the majority's rule of intent is that application of this inflexible rule will not serve the child's best interests in every case.

* * *

VIII. The Best Interests of the Child

* * *

In the absence of legislation that is designed to address the unique problems of gestational surrogacy, this court should look not to tort, property or contract law, but to family law, as the governing paradigm and source of a rule of decision. The allocation of parental rights and responsibilities necessarily impacts the welfare of a minor child. And in issues of child welfare, the standard that courts frequently apply is the best interests of the child.[ ] This "best interests" standard serves to assure that in the judicial resolution of disputes affecting a child's well-being, protection of the minor child is the foremost consideration. Consequently, I would apply "the best interests of the child" standard to determine who can best assume the social and legal responsibilities of motherhood for a child born of a gestational surrogacy arrangement.

* * *

Factors that are pertinent to good parenting, and thus that are in a child's best interests, include the ability to nurture the child physically

243

and psychologically [ ] and to provide ethical and intellectual guidance.[ ] Also crucial to a child's best interests is the "well recognized right" of every child "to stability and continuity."[ ] The intent of the genetic mother to procreate a child is certainly relevant to the question of the child's best interests; alone, however, it should not be dispositive.

* * *

CONCLUSION

* * *

In this opinion, I do not purport to offer a perfect solution to the difficult questions posed by gestational surrogacy; perhaps there can be no perfect solution. But in the absence of legislation specifically designed to address the complex issues of gestational surrogacy and to protect against potential abuses, I cannot join the majority's uncritical validation of gestational surrogacy.

I would reverse the judgment of the Court of Appeal, and remand the case to the trial court for a determination of disputed parentage on the basis of the best interests of the child.

NOTE

1. All of the justices agreed that the child could not have two mothers. Is this conclusion a good one? From the perspective of law? From the perspective of public policy? In these days of blended families, is the two parent (one father; one mother) family an anachronism? How could the Court have dealt with the ultimate disposition of this case if it had decided that both Ms. Johnson and Ms. Calvert had maternal rights?

2. Gestational surrogacy has been the subject of two other reported cases. In McDonald v. McDonald, 608 N.Y.S.2d 477 (A.D. 1944), a "true 'egg donation'" case, the New York Supreme Court, Appellate Division, determined that a woman who gestated a child produced through the fertilization of another woman's ovum with her husband's sperm was to be considered the mother of the child that resulted. The New York court depended heavily on the reasoning of *Johnson v. Calvert*. On the other hand, the Court of Common Pleas of Ohio rejected the *Johnson* reasoning

in an uncontested case initiated to determine who was to be listed as the mother on the birth certificate in the case of gestational surrogacy. In Belsito v. Clark, 644 N.E.2d 760 (Ohio Comm. Pl. 1994), the court determined that parentage was to be determined by genetic contribution, not by the intent-to-procreate of the parties to the original surrogacy agreement. The court found *Johnson* unpersuasive "for the following three important reasons: (1) the difficulty in applying the *Johnson* intent test; (2) public policy; and (3) *Johnson's* failure to recognize and emphasize the genetic provider's right to consent to procreation and to surrender potential parental rights."

CHAPTER 10.   DEFINING DEATH

Insert at page 1051 at the end of Note the following:

The question of whether anencephalic infants should be maintained or "allowed to die" arises in contexts other than the availability of transplantation of organs, as the following case suggests.

IN THE MATTER OF BABY "K"
United States Court of Appeals, Fourth Circuit, 1994
16 F.3d 590

Wilkins, J.:

The Hospital instituted this action against Ms. H, Mr. K, and Baby "K", seeking a declaratory judgment that it is not required under the Emergency Medical Treatment and Active Labor Act (EMTALA), [ ],[16] to provide treatment other than warmth, nutrition, and hydration to Baby "K", an anencephalic infant. Because we agree with the district court that EMTALA gives rise to a duty on the part of the Hospital to provide respiratory support to Baby "K" when she is presented at the Hospital in respiratory distress and treatment is requested for her, we affirm.

I.

Baby "K" was born at the Hospital in October of 1992 with anencephaly, a congenital malformation in which a major portion of the brain, skull, and scalp are missing. While the presence of a brain stem

---

[16] The Hospital also sought declaratory relief under Section 794 of the Rehabilitation Act of 1973; the Americans with Disabilities Act of 1990; the Child Abuse Prevention and Treatment Act, and the statutes and common law of Virginia. In addressing these provisions, the district court concluded that a failure to provide respiratory support to Baby K because of her condition of anencephaly would constitute discrimination in violation of the ADA and the Rehabilitation Act but declined to rule on the application of the Child Abuse Act or Virginia law. Because we conclude that the Hospital has a duty to render stabilizing treatment under EMTALA, we need not address its obligations under the remaining federal statutes or the laws of Virginia.

does support her autonomic functions and reflex actions, because Baby "K" lacks a cerebrum, she is permanently unconscious. Thus, she has no cognitive abilities or awareness. She cannot see, hear, or otherwise interact with her environment.

When Baby "K" had difficulty breathing on her own at birth, Hospital physicians placed her on a mechanical ventilator. This respiratory support allowed the doctors to confirm the diagnosis and gave Ms. H, the mother, an opportunity to fully understand the diagnosis and prognosis of Baby "K"'s condition. The physicians explained to Ms. H that most anencephalic infants die within a few days of birth due to breathing difficulties and other complications. Because aggressive treatment would serve no therapeutic or palliative purpose, they recommended that Baby "K" only be provided with supportive care in the form of nutrition, hydration, and warmth. Physicians at the Hospital also discussed with Ms. H the possibility of a "Do Not Resuscitate Order" that would provide for the withholding of lifesaving measures in the future.

The treating physicians and Ms. H failed to reach an agreement as to the appropriate care. Ms. H insisted that Baby "K" be provided with mechanical breathing assistance whenever the infant developed difficulty breathing on her own, while the physicians maintained that such care was inappropriate. As a result of this impasse, the Hospital sought to transfer Baby "K" to another hospital. This attempt failed when all of the hospitals in the area with pediatric intensive care units declined to accept the infant. In November of 1992, when Baby "K" no longer needed the services of an acute-care hospital, she was transferred to a nearby nursing home.

Since being transferred to the nursing home, Baby "K" has been readmitted to the Hospital three times due to breathing difficulties. Each time she has been provided with breathing assistance and, after stabilization, has been discharged to the nursing home. Following Baby "K"'s second admission, the Hospital filed this action to resolve the issue of whether it is obligated to provide emergency medical treatment to Baby "K" that it deems medically and ethically inappropriate. Baby "K"'s guardian ad litem and her father, Mr. K, joined in the Hospital's request for a declaration that the Hospital is not required to provide respiratory support or other aggressive treatments. Ms. H contested the Hospital's request for declaratory relief. * * * [The district court denied the hospital the requested relief and the Petitioners appealed to the Court of Appeals.]

II.

Congress enacted EMTALA in response to its "concern that hospitals were 'dumping' patients [who were] unable to pay, by either refusing to provide emergency medical treatment or transferring patients before their emergency conditions were stabilized." [ ]   Through EMTALA, Congress sought "to provide an 'adequate first response to a medical crisis' for all patients," [ ] by imposing two duties on hospitals that have entered into Medicare provider agreements.

First, those hospitals with an emergency medical department must provide an appropriate medical screening to determine whether an emergency medical condition exists for any individual who comes to the emergency medical department requesting treatment.[ ] A hospital fulfills this duty if it utilizes identical screening procedures for all patients complaining of the same condition or exhibiting the same symptoms.[ ]

An additional duty arises if an emergency medical condition is discovered during the screening process. [ ]   EMTALA defines an "emergency medical condition" as including:

> a medical condition manifesting itself by acute symptoms of sufficient severity (including severe pain) such that the absence of immediate medical attention could reasonably be expected to result in--
>
> * * *
>
> (ii) serious impairment to bodily functions[.]
>   * * *

When an individual is diagnosed as presenting an emergency medical condition:

the hospital must provide either--

(A) within the staff and facilities available at the hospital, for such further medical examination and such treatment as may be required to stabilize the medical condition, or

248

(B) for the transfer of the individual to another medical facility * * *.

The treatment required "to stabilize" an individual is that treatment "necessary to assure, within reasonable medical probability, that no material deterioration of the condition is likely to result from or occur during the transfer of the individual from a facility." [ ]. Therefore, once an individual has been diagnosed as presenting an emergency medical condition, the hospital must provide that treatment necessary to prevent the material deterioration of the individual's condition or provide for an appropriate transfer to another facility.

In the application of these provisions to Baby "K", the Hospital concedes that when Baby "K" is presented in respiratory distress a failure to provide "immediate medical attention" would reasonably be expected to cause serious impairment of her bodily functions. [ ] Thus, her breathing difficulty qualifies as an emergency medical condition, and the diagnosis of this emergency medical condition triggers the duty of the hospital to provide Baby "K" with stabilizing treatment or to transfer her in accordance with the provisions of EMTALA. Since transfer is not an option available to the Hospital at this juncture, the Hospital must stabilize Baby "K"'s condition.

The Hospital acknowledged in its complaint that aggressive treatment, including mechanical ventilation, is necessary to "assure within a reasonable medical probability, that no material deterioration of Baby "K"'s condition is likely to occur." Thus, stabilization of her condition requires the Hospital to provide respiratory support through the use of a respirator or other means necessary to ensure adequate ventilation. In sum, a straightforward application of the statute obligates the Hospital to provide respiratory support to Baby "K" when she arrives at the emergency department of the Hospital in respiratory distress and treatment is requested on her behalf.

III.

In an effort to avoid the result that follows from the plain language of EMTALA, the Hospital offers four arguments. The Hospital claims: (1) that this court has previously interpreted EMTALA as only requiring uniform treatment of all patients exhibiting the same condition; (2) that in prohibiting disparate emergency medical treatment Congress did not intend to require physicians to provide treatment outside the

249

prevailing standard of medical care; (3) that an interpretation of EMTALA that requires a hospital or physician to provide respiratory support to an anencephalic infant fails to recognize a physician's ability, under Virginia law, to refuse to provide medical treatment that the physician considers medically or ethically inappropriate; and (4) that EMTALA only applies to patients who are transferred from a hospital in an unstable condition. We find these arguments unavailing.

A.

* * *

If, as the Hospital suggests, it were only required to provide uniform treatment, it could provide any level of treatment to Baby "K", including a level of treatment that would allow her condition to materially deteriorate, so long as the care she was provided was consistent with the care provided to other individuals.[ ] The definition of stabilizing treatment advocated by the Hospital directly conflicts with the plain language of EMTALA.

As we have previously stated, "it is not our role to rewrite legislation passed by Congress. When a statute is clear and unambiguous, we must apply its terms as written."[ ] The terms of EMTALA as written do not allow the Hospital to fulfill its duty to provide stabilizing treatment by simply dispensing uniform treatment. Rather, the Hospital must provide that treatment necessary to prevent the material deterioration of each patient's emergency medical condition. In the case of Baby "K", the treatment necessary to prevent the material deterioration of her condition when she is in respiratory distress includes respiratory support.

Even if this court were to interpret EMTALA as requiring hospitals to provide uniform treatment for emergency medical conditions, we could not find that the Hospital is only required to provide Baby "K" with warmth, nutrition, and hydration. * * * It is bradypnea or apnea, not anencephaly, that is the emergency medical condition that brings Baby "K" to the Hospital for treatment. Uniform treatment of emergency medical conditions would require the Hospital to provide Baby "K" with the same treatment that the Hospital provides all other patients experiencing bradypnea or apnea. The Hospital does not allege that it would refuse to provide respiratory support to infants experiencing bradypnea or apnea who do not have anencephaly. * * *

250

B.

The second argument of the Hospital is that, in redressing the problem of disparate emergency medical treatment, Congress did not intend to require physicians to provide medical treatment outside the prevailing standard of medical care. The Hospital asserts that, because of their extremely limited life expectancy and because any treatment of their condition is futile, the prevailing standard of medical care for infants with anencephaly is to provide only warmth, nutrition, and hydration. Thus, it maintains that a requirement to provide respiratory assistance would exceed the prevailing standard of medical care. However, the plain language of EMTALA requires stabilizing treatment for any individual who comes to a participating hospital, is diagnosed as having an emergency medical condition, and cannot be transferred. * * * We recognize the dilemma facing physicians who are requested to provide treatment they consider morally and ethically inappropriate, but we cannot ignore the plain language of the statute because "to do so would 'transcend our judicial function.'" [ ] The appropriate branch to redress the policy concerns of the Hospital is Congress.

C.

The Hospital further argues that EMTALA cannot be construed to require it to provide respiratory support to anencephalics when its physicians deem such care inappropriate, because Virginia law permits physicians to refuse to provide such care.

* * *

It is well settled that state action must give way to federal legislation where a valid "act of Congress, fairly interpreted, is in actual conflict with the law of the state,"[ ] and EMTALA provides that state and local laws that directly conflict with the requirements of EMTALA are preempted.

D.

[The Court found the hospital's claim that EMTALA applies only to those transferred from a hospital in an unstable condition inconsistent with the language of the statute.]

IV.

It is beyond the limits of our judicial function to address the moral or ethical propriety of providing emergency stabilizing medical treatment to anencephalic infants. We are bound to interpret federal statutes in accordance with their plain language and any expressed congressional intent. Congress rejected a case-by-case approach to determining what emergency medical treatment hospitals and physicians must provide and to whom they must provide it; instead, it required hospitals and physicians to provide stabilizing care to any individual presenting an emergency medical condition. EMTALA does not carve out an exception for anencephalic infants in respiratory distress any more than it carves out an exception for comatose patients, those with lung cancer, or those with muscular dystrophy--all of whom may repeatedly seek emergency stabilizing treatment for respiratory distress and also possess an underlying medical condition that severely affects their quality of life and ultimately may result in their death. Because EMTALA does not provide for such an exception, the judgment of the district court is affirmed.

Sprouse, J., dissenting:

* * * I simply do not believe * * *, that Congress, in enacting EMTALA, meant for the judiciary to superintend the sensitive decision-making process between family and physicians at the bedside of a helpless and terminally ill patient under the circumstances of this case. Tragic end-of-life hospital dramas such as this one do not represent phenomena susceptible of uniform legal control. In my view, Congress, even in its weakest moments, would not have attempted to impose federal control in this sensitive, private area.

I also submit that EMTALA's language concerning the type and extent of emergency treatment to be extended to all patients was not intended to cover the continued emergencies that typically attend patients like Baby "K". * * * The hospital argues that anencephaly, not the subsidiary respiratory failure, is the condition that should be reviewed in order to judge the applicability vel non of EMTALA. I agree. I would consider anencephaly as the relevant condition and the respiratory difficulty as one of many subsidiary conditions found in a patient with the disease. EMTALA was not designed to reach such circumstances.

The tragic phenomenon Baby "K" represents exemplifies the need to take a case-by-case approach to determine if an emergency episode is governed by EMTALA. Baby "K"'s condition presents her parents and doctors with decision-making choices that are different even from the difficult choices presented by other terminal diseases. * * * Given this unique medical condition, whatever treatment is appropriate for her unspeakably tragic illness should be regarded as a continuum, not as a series of discrete emergency medical conditions to be considered in isolation. Humanitarian concerns dictate appropriate care. However, if resort must be had to our courts to test the appropriateness of the care, the legal vehicle should be state malpractice law.

In my view, considering the discrete factual circumstances of Baby "K"'s condition and previous treatment, if she is transferred again from the nursing home to the hospital in respiratory distress, that condition should be considered integral to the anencephalic condition, and I would hold that there has been no violation of EMTALA. * * *

NOTES

1.   The original petitioners were not certain whether they should seek United States Supreme Court review of this case, or whether they should seek Congressional action modifying EMTALA instead. What are the advantages and disadvantages of each approach? Which would you recommend?

In the end, those who lost in the Fourth Circuit did seek review in the United States Supreme Court, but their petition for certiorari was denied on October 3, 1994. In re Baby "K", 115 S. Ct. 91 (1994).

2.   How would the Baby "K" analysis of EMTALA be applied in other cases? The dissenting judge pointed out:

> I emphasize that this view contemplates a case-by-case determination. Individual cases involving victims of trauma, cancer, heart attack, or other catastrophic illness, who are denied potentially life-saving treatments, may well require different analyses.

Does the majority contemplate case-by-case analysis?

For a thorough discussion of EMTALA, and another Fourth Circuit approach to that statute, see Chapter III, section A(2)(b), on pages 616-628 and the corresponding pages of the supplement.

3.   Baby "K" was shuffled back and forth between the nursing home and the hospital six times until she died, shortly after her second birthday, on April 15, 1995. Upon her death her mother, who had fought so hard to keep her alive, said, "She's in heaven. She's in peace. Knowing that she's with god is a comfort." See M. Tousignant, Death of Baby "K" Leaves a Legacy of Legal Precedents, Washington Post, April 7, 1995, p. 8. Baby "K", who was known by her real name, Stephanie, when she died, amassed medical bills of $500,000 during her short life. The hospital bill, which itself ran $250,000, was fully paid by Stephanie's mother's insurance and by Medicaid. Is the cost of her care relevant in determining what care is proper? How would you use that information in making a general policy decision about the treatment that ought to be afforded anencephalic infants? About the treatment that ought to be afforded Stephanie herself?

CHAPTER 11.   LIFE AND DEATH DECISIONS

Insert on page 1128 before the note on the Patient Self-Determination Act, the following:

NOTE: THE UNIFORM HEALTH CARE DECISIONS ACT

The Uniform Health Care Decisions Act (UHCDA), which could replace the Uniform Rights of the Terminally Ill Act, state durable powers acts and parts of the Uniform Anatomical Gifts Act, was approved by the National Conference of Commissioners on Uniform State Laws in 1993 and by the American Bar Association House of Delegates in 1994. While only one state had adopted the UHCDA as of June of 1995, it is expected to be considered by several other state legislatures in 1995 and 1996. The UHCDA would substantially alter the form and utility of living wills and durable powers, and it would provide a method of making health care decisions for incompetent patients who do not have advance directives.

The proposed act takes a comprehensive approach by placing the living will (which is retitled the "individual instruction"), the durable power of attorney (now called the "power of attorney for health care"), a family consent law, and some provisions concerning organ donation together in one statute. Further, the statute integrates the current living will and durable power (and statement of desire to donate organs) into a single document. The UHCDA provides a statutory form, but it also explicitly declares that the form is not a mandatory one, and that individuals may draft their own form that includes only some of the kinds of instructions permitted in the unified form.

The UHCDA substantially broadens the role of the living will. The new "individual instruction" can apply to virtually any health care decision, not just the end of life decisions to which living wills are typically applicable. The individual instruction part of the unified form directly addresses several issues, and, of course, it can be modified in any way any person signing it may wish. The form specifically permits the person signing it to check off "choice not to prolong life" or "choice to prolong life." The "choice not to prolong life" is described in the following language: "I do not want my life to be prolonged if (i) I have an incurable and irreversible condition that will result in my death within a relatively short time, (ii) I become unconscious and, to a reasonable degree of medical certainty, I will not regain consciousness, or (iii) the likely risks and burdens of treatment would outweigh the expected benefits." The "choice to prolong life," on the other hand, is described as follows: "I want my life to be prolonged as long as possible within the limits of generally accepted health-care standards."

The UHCDA makes far less substantial changes in the documents traditionally available for appointing health care decisionmaking agents and for donating organs, although it does provide that the durable power can become effective at any time specified by the signatory, not just upon that person's incompetency. The proposed act also makes the execution of the unified document very easy. It has no witness requirement, and it does not require that the document be notarized. The drafters of the proposed act concluded that the formalities often associated with living wills and durable powers served to discourage their execution more than to deter fraud.

The residual decisionmaking portion of the act is very much like the family consent statutes that have now been adopted in a majority of states, and this section of the act applies only if there is no applicable individual instruction or appointed agent. While it provides for a common family hierarchy of decisionmakers for decisionally incapacitated patients, it also provides that the family can be trumped by an "orally designated surrogate," who may be appointed by a patient informing her "supervising physician" that the surrogate is entitled to make health care decisions on her behalf. In the same manner a patient may orally disqualify someone who otherwise would be entitled to make decisions on her behalf.

The UHCDA includes the normal raft of recordkeeping provisions, limitations on the reach of the criminal law, assurances regarding the insurance rights of those who execute the documents, and restrictions on the liability of those act under the statute in good faith. The proposed act does not work any changes in substantive state law, and it does not permit any action that is otherwise prohibited by the law. Further, the proposed act applies only to adults.

While there does not appear to be any strong opposition to the general intent and structure of the UHCDA, some advocates for the elderly and the disabled are worried by some parts of the proposed statute. They are worried that the streamlined procedures for execution of a document allow a greater opportunity for fraud to be perpetrated against those who wish to sign, and they are concerned about the virtually unrestrained authority the proposed act gives to physicians to make determinations of when a patient lacks decisional capacity. In addition, there is some concern that any substantial change in the law will undercut the significant amounts of community education that have been directed to the current law over the past few years. The one state to adopt a version of the uniform act in 1995 modified it to provide greater due process protection for patients who believe they have been improperly determined to be decisionally incapacitated, and that state statute explicitly provides that its living will and durable power statutes remain in full force and effect. Thus, in that state a patient may sign a living will (or "individual instruction")or a durable power under either of two different statutes. The patient who really wants to be safe can sign different (but, presumably, consistent) advance directives and cover himself under all of the statutes dealing with advance directives.

Insert at page 1180, at the end of the section on suicide and assisted suicide, just before the poem, the following:

NOTE: THE KEVORKIAN CASES

Over the past four years the issue of physician assisted suicide has become the subject of intense public debate, in large part because of the activities of Dr. Jack Kevorkian. Dr. Kevorkian employed a "suicide machine" that allowed patients -- sometimes young and still relatively healthy patients -- to end their lives. Dr. Kevorkian chose Michigan for his practice because assisted suicide was not a crime in Michigan. On the other hand, an early Michigan case, *People v. Roberts*, 178 N.W. 690 (Mich. 1920) had determined that assisting suicide could constitute murder. In that case a husband pleaded guilty to murder after he placed a poisonous mixture next to his wife, who was suffering from multiple sclerosis, was in excruciating pain, and had begged her husband to help her end her misery. The Michigan court determined that murder by poison, a form of first degree murder, was the proper charge.

In 1990 prosecutors in Michigan indicted Dr. Kevorkian on homicide charges, which were subsequently dismissed. As a direct result of Kevorkian's activities, in 1992 the Michigan legislature created the crime of assistance to suicide, which renders one criminally liable if one "provides the physical means by which the other person attempts or commits suicide" or participates in the physical act of the suicide. Mich. Comp. Laws Ann. section 752-1027.

Just before Michigan's new assisted suicide statute became law, Dr. Kevorkian was indicted for murder and for the delivery of drugs for an unauthorized purpose. Dr. Kevorkian was bound over for trial on the murder charge, which was subsequently dismissed by the circuit court. As soon as the new assisted suicide statute was passed several terminally ill patients and some health care providers brought a declaratory judgment action seeking to have the new statute declared void because it violated due process protections afforded to the petitioners, and because it passed the legislature in a bill that did not have "a single object," because the purpose of the bill changed during the course of its consideration in the Michigan legislature, and because it was inadequately titled, all in violation of the Michigan constitution. Ultimately the circuit court found the statute unconstitutional. It was not long before Dr. Kevorkian was charged under the new assisted suicide statute -- twice, in fact, once in Wayne County and once in Oakland County. In both cases the circuit court dismissed the actions because they found the new assisted suicide statute to be unconstitutional.

All four cases (the second murder case, the two assisted suicide cases and the declaratory judgment case) were appealed to the Michigan Supreme Court, which consolidated them. In December of 1994 a divided Michigan Supreme Court issued a brief per curiam memorandum opinion and a series of separate opinions dealing with the various issues raised by the four appeals. The court decided that (1) there was no technical problem in the form of the bill passed by the legislature (by unanimous vote), (2) a criminal statute penalizing assisted suicide does not violate the United States Constitution (5-2 vote), (3) *People v. Roberts* should be overruled; merely intentionally providing the means for another to commit suicide does not, as a general matter, constitute murder (5-2 vote) and (4) whether there was sufficient evidence to prosecute Dr. Kevorkian for murder should be reconsidered by the circuit court (4-3 vote). See *People v. Kevorkian,* 527 N.W. 2d 714 (Mich. 1994) for the lengthy, thoughtful and heartfelt opinions on all sides of all of these issues.

Another prosecution for murder ended in a jury verdict of acquittal for Dr. Kevorkian -- and the acquittal, even more than the formal legal challenge to the constitutionality of the new Michigan statute, may discourage prosecutors from commencing actions against physicians who assist in their patients' suicides, at least when the patients are terminally ill or in intractable pain. Indeed, an exceptionally large number of cases of jury nullification -- where the jury simply ignores the

258

law to acquit the defendant -- are "mercy killing" cases where the defendant is accused of bringing death to a terminally ill person suffering some form of intractable pain. See Margaret Otlowski, <u>Euthanasia in Australia</u> (1992).

"DEATH WITH DIGNITY" INITIATIVES

The debate over the proper role of physicians in assisting their patients in death has been carried on through the legislative and citizen initiative processes also. While "Death with Dignity" initiatives were narrowly defeated in California in 1991 and in Washington in 1992, Measure 16, the Oregon "Death with dignity" initiative, was approved by voters in the November, 1994 election, and it thus became part of the statute law of Oregon. The substantive provisions are reprinted here:

THE OREGON
DEATH WITH DIGNITY ACT

SECTION 1
GENERAL PROVISIONS

§ 1.01 DEFINITIONS

The following words and phrases, whenever used in this Act, shall have the following meanings:

(1) "Adult" means an individual who is 18 years of age or older.

(2) "Attending physician" means the physician who has primary responsibility for the care of the patient and treatment of the patient's terminal disease.

(3) "Consulting physician" means a physician who is qualified by specialty or experience to make a professional diagnosis and prognosis regarding the patient's disease.

(4) "Counseling" means a consultation between a state licensed psychiatrist or psychologist and a patient for the purpose of determining whether the patient is suffering from a psychiatric or psychological disorder, or depression causing impaired judgment.

(5) "Health care provider" means a person licensed, certified, or otherwise authorized or permitted by the law of this State to administer health care in the ordinary course of business or practice of a profession, and includes a health care facility.

(6) "Incapable" means that in the opinion of a court or in the opinion of the patient's attending physician or consulting physician, a patient lacks the ability to make and communicate health care decisions to health care providers, including communication through persons familiar with the patient's manner of communicating if those persons are available. Capable means not incapable.

(7) "Informed decision" means a decision by a qualified patient, to request and obtain a prescription to end his or her life in a humane and dignified manner, that is based on an appreciation of the relevant facts and after being fully informed by the attending physician of:

(a) his or her medical diagnosis;

(b) his or her prognosis;

(c) the potential risks associated with taking the medication prescribed;

(d) the probable result of taking the medication to be prescribed;

(e) the feasible alternatives, including, but not limited to, comfort care, hospice care and pain control.

(8) "Medically confirmed" means the medical opinion of the attending physician has been confirmed by a consulting physician who has examined the patient and the patient's relevant medical records.

(9) "Patient" means a person who is under the care of a physician.

(10) "Physician" means a doctor of medicine or osteopathy licensed to practice medicine by the Board of Medical Examiners for the State of Oregon.

(11) "Qualified patient" means a capable adult who is a resident of Oregon and has satisfied the requirements of this Act in order to obtain a prescription for medication to end his or her life in a humane and dignified manner.

(12) "Terminal disease" means an incurable and irreversible disease that has been medically confirmed and will, within reasonable medical judgment, produce death within six (6) months.

SECTION 2
WRITTEN REQUEST FOR MEDICATION
TO END ONE'S LIFE
IN A HUMANE AND DIGNIFIED MANNER

§ 2.01 WHO MAY INITIATE A WRITTEN REQUEST FOR MEDICATION

An adult who is capable, is a resident of Oregon, and has been determined by the attending physician and consulting physician to be suffering from a terminal disease, and who has voluntarily expressed his or her wish to die, may make a written request for medication for the purpose of ending his or her life in a humane and dignified manner in accordance with this Act.

§ 2.02 FORM OF THE WRITTEN REQUEST

(1) A valid request for medication under this Act shall be in substantially the form described in Section 6 of this Act, signed and dated by the patient and witnessed by at least two individuals who, in the presence of the patient, attest that to the best of their knowledge and belief the patient is capable, acting voluntarily, and is not being coerced to sign the request.

(2) One of the witnesses shall be a person who is not:

    (a) A relative of the patient by blood, marriage or adoption;

    (b) A person who at the time the request is signed would be entitled to any portion of the estate of the qualified patient upon death under any will or by operation of law; or

    (c) An owner, operator or employee of a health care facility where the qualified patient is receiving medical treatment or is a resident.

(3) The patient's attending physician at the time the request is signed shall not be a witness.

(4) If the patient is a patient in a long term care facility at the time the written request is made, one of the witnesses shall be an individual designated by the facility and having the qualifications specified by the Department of Human Resources by rule.

SECTION 3
SAFEGUARDS

§ 3.01 ATTENDING PHYSICIAN RESPONSIBILITIES

The attending physician shall:

(1) Make the initial determination of whether a patient has a terminal disease, is capable, and has made the request voluntarily;

(2) Inform the patient of:

    (a) his or her medical diagnosis;

    (b) his or her prognosis;

    (c) the potential risks associated with taking the medication to be prescribed;

    (d) the probable result of taking the medication to be prescribed;

    (e) the feasible alternatives, including, but not limited to, comfort care, hospice care and pain control.

(3) Refer the patient to a consulting physician for medical confirmation of the diagnosis, and for a determination that the patient is capable and acting voluntarily;

(4) Refer the patient for counseling if appropriate pursuant to Section 3.03;

(5) Request that the patient notify the next of kin;

(6) Inform the patient that he or she has an opportunity to rescind the request at any time and in any manner, and offer the patient an opportunity to rescind at the end of the 15 day waiting period pursuant to Section 3.06;

(7) Verify, immediately prior to writing the prescription for medication under this Act, that the patient is making an informed decision:

(8) Fulfill the medical record documentation requirements of Section 3.09;

(9) Ensure that all appropriate steps are carried out in accordance with this Act prior to writing a prescription for medication to enable a qualified patient to end his or her life in a humane and dignified manner.

§ 3.02 CONSULTING PHYSICIAN CONFIRMATION

Before a patient is qualified under this Act, a consulting physician shall examine the patient and his or her relevant medical records and confirm, in writing, the attending physician's diagnosis that the patient is suffering from a terminal disease, and verify that the patient is capable, is acting voluntarily and has made an informed decision.

§ 3.03 COUNSELING REFERRAL

If in the opinion of the attending physician or the consulting physician a patient may be suffering from a psychiatric or psychological disorder, or depression causing impaired judgment, either physician shall refer the patient for counseling. No medication to end a patient's life in a humane and dignified manner shall be prescribed until the person performing the counseling determines that the patient is not suffering from a psychiatric or psychological disorder, or depression causing impaired judgment.

§ 3.04 INFORMED DECISION

No person shall receive a prescription for medication to end his or her life in a humane and dignified manner unless he or she has made an informed decision as defined in Section 1.01(7). Immediately prior to writing a prescription for medication under this Act, the attending physician shall verify that the patient is making an informed decision.

§ 3.05 FAMILY NOTIFICATION

The attending physician shall ask the patient to notify next of kin of his or her request for medication pursuant to this Act. A patient who declines or is unable to notify next of kin shall not have his or her request denied for that reason.

§ 3.06 WRITTEN AND ORAL REQUESTS

In order to receive a prescription for medication to end his or her life in a humane and dignified manner, a qualified patient shall have made an oral request and a written request, and reiterate the oral request to his or her attending physician no less than fifteen (15) days after making the initial oral request. At the time the qualified patient makes his or her second oral request, the attending physician shall offer the patient an opportunity to rescind the request.

§ 3.07 RIGHT TO RESCIND REQUEST

A patient may rescind his or her request at any time and in any manner without regard to his or her mental state. No prescription for medication under this Act may be written without the attending physician offering the qualified patient an opportunity to rescind the request.

§ 3.08 WAITING PERIODS

No less than fifteen (15) days shall elapse between the patient's initial oral request and the writing of a prescription under this Act. No less than 48 hours shall elapse between the patient's written request and the writing of a prescription under this Act.

§ 3.09 MEDICAL RECORD DOCUMENTATION REQUIREMENTS

The following shall be documented or filed in the patient's medical record:
(1) All oral requests by a patient for medication to end his or her life in a humane and dignified manner;

(2) All written requests by a patient for medication to end his or her life in a humane and dignified manner;

(3) The attending physician's diagnosis and prognosis, determination that the patient is capable, acting voluntarily and has made an informed decision;

(4) The consulting physician's diagnosis and prognosis, and verification that the patient is capable, acting voluntarily and has made an informed decision;

(5) A report of the outcome and determinations made during counseling, if performed;

(6) The attending physician's offer to the patient to rescind his or her request at the time of the patient's second oral request pursuant to Section 3.06; and

(7) A note by the attending physician indicating that all requirements under this Act have been met and indicating the steps taken to carry out the request, including a notation of the medication prescribed.

§ 3.10 RESIDENCY REQUIREMENT

Only request made by Oregon residents, under this Act, shall be granted.

§ 3.11 REPORTING REQUIREMENTS

(1) The Health Division shall annually review a sample of records maintained pursuant to this Act.

(2) The Health Division shall make rules to facilitate the collection of information regarding compliance with this Act. The information collected shall not be a public record and may not be made available for inspection by the public.

(3) The Health Division shall generate and make available to the public an annual statistical report of information collected under Section 3.11(2) of this Act.

§ 3.12 EFFECT ON CONSTRUCTION OF WILLS, CONTRACTS AND STATUTES

(1) No provision in a contract, will or other agreement, whether written or oral, to the extent the provision would affect whether a person may make or rescind a request for medication to end his or her life in a humane and dignified manner, shall be valid.

(2) No obligation owing under any currently existing contract shall be conditioned or affected by the making or rescinding of a request, by a

person, for medication to end his or her life in a humane and dignified manner.

§ 3.13 INSURANCE OR ANNUITY POLICIES

The sale, procurement, or issuance of any life, health, or accident insurance or annuity policy or the rate charged for any policy shall not be conditioned upon or affected by the making or rescinding of a request, by a person, for medication to end his or her life in a humane and dignified manner. Neither shall a patient's act of ingesting medication to end his or her life in a humane and dignified manner have an effect upon a life, health, or accident insurance or annuity policy.

§ 3.14 CONSTRUCTION OF ACT

Nothing in this Act shall be construed to authorize a physician or any other person to end a patient's life by lethal injection, mercy killing or active euthanasia. Actions taken in accordance with this Act shall not, for any purpose, constitute suicide, assisted suicide, mercy killing or homicide, under the law.

SECTION 4
IMMUNITIES AND LIABILITIES

§ 4.01 IMMUNITIES

Except as provided in Section 4.02:
(1) No person shall be subject to civil or criminal liability or professional disciplinary action for participating in good faith compliance with this Act. This includes being present when a qualified patient takes the prescribed medication to end his or her life in a humane and dignified manner.
(2) No professional organization or association, or health care provider, may subject a person to censure, discipline, suspension, loss of license, loss of privileges, loss of membership or other penalty for participating or refusing to participate in good faith compliance with this Act.
(3) No request by a patient for or provision by an attending physician of medication in good faith compliance with the provisions of this Act shall constitute neglect for any purpose of law or provide the sole basis for the appointment of a guardian or conservator.
(4) No health care provider shall be under any duty, whether by contract, by statute or by any other legal requirement to participate in the provision

to a qualified patient of medication to end his or her life in a humane and dignified manner. If a health care provider is unable or unwilling to carry out a patient's request under this Act, and the patient transfers his or her care to a new health care provider, the prior health care provider shall transfer, upon request, a copy of the patient's relevant medical records to the new health care provider.

§ 4.02 LIABILITIES

(1) A person who without authorization of the patient willfully alters or forges a request for medication or conceals or destroys a rescission of that request with the intent or affect of causing the patient's death shall be guilty of a Class A felony.

(2) A person who coerces or exerts undue influence on a patient to request medication for the purpose of ending the patient's life, or to destroy a rescission of such a request, shall be guilty of a Class A felony.

(3) Nothing in this Act limits further liability for civil damages resulting from other negligent conduct or intentional misconduct by any person.

(4) The penalties in this Act do not preclude criminal penalties applicable under the law for conduct which is inconsistent with provisions of this Act.

SECTION 5
SEVERABILITY

§ 5.01 SEVERABILITY

Any section of this Act being invalid as to any person or circumstance shall not affect the application of any other section of this Act which can be given full effect without the invalid section or application.

SECTION 6
FORM OF THE REQUEST

§ 6.01 FORM OF THE REQUEST

A request for a medication as authorized by this act shall be in substantially the following form:

REQUEST FOR MEDICATION
TO END MY LIFE IN A HUMANE AND DIGNIFIED MANNER

I, _____, am an adult of sound mind.

I am suffering from _____, which my attending physician has determined is a terminal disease and which has been medically confirmed by a consulting physician.

I have been fully informed of my diagnosis, prognosis, the nature of medication to be prescribed and potential associated risks, the expected result, and the feasible alternatives, including comfort care, hospice care and pain control.

I request that my attending physician prescribe medication that will end my life in a humane and dignified manner.

INITIAL ONE:

_____ I have informed my family of my decision and taken their opinions into consideration.

_____ I have decided not to inform my family of my decision.

_____ I have no family to inform of my decision.

I understand that I have the right to rescind this request at any time.

I understand the full import of this request and I expect to die when I take the medication to be prescribed.

I make this request voluntarily and without reservation, and I accept full moral responsibility for my actions.

Signed: _____

Dated: _____

DECLARATION OF WITNESSES

We declare that the person signing this request:

(a) Is personally known to us or has provided proof of identity;

(b) Signed this request in our presence;

(c) Appears to be of sound mind and not under duress, fraud or undue influence;

(d) Is not a patient for whom either of us is attending physician.

_____ Witness 1/Date

_____ Witness 2/Date

NOTE: One witness shall not be a relative (by blood, marriage or adoption) of the person signing this request, shall not be entitled to any portion of the person's estate upon death and shall not own, operate or be employed at a health care facility where the person is a patient or resident. If the patient is an inpatient at a health care facility, one of the witness shall be an individual designated by the facility.

NOTES ON THE "DEATH WITH DIGNITY" MOVEMENT

1. As soon as the Oregon measure was approved, those who had opposed it in the political arena -- right to life groups, some medical associations, some religious groups, and some disability advocacy organizations -- sought to enjoin it from going into effect. They based their legal arguments on the equal protection and due process clauses of the United States Constitution as well as the Americans With Disabilities Act and the religion and association clauses of the First Amendment. A United States District Court judge in Oregon issued a preliminary injunction against enforcing the initiative in *Lee v. Oregon*, 869 F. Supp. 1491 (D. Or. 1994) on December 27, 1994, because he found the following "serious questions" which deserved full hearing:

As to the equal protection clause challenge:

(1) Must the state show only that Measure 16 is rationally related to a legitimate state interest?
(2) The state has identified its interest in Measure 16 as preventing continued pain and suffering of competent terminally ill patients and support of Oregon voters' rights to participate in the democratic process. However, "pain and suffering" is not contained in the terms of Measure 16.
(3) Is there a rational basis for the classification of "terminally ill" patient if, as patients claim,
(a) Physicians often misdiagnose terminal illness [], or
(b) A physician';s prognosis of six months to live is often fallible,[] or,
(c) It may be contrary to reasoned medical judgment to include a patient who can live a normal life span with medication, i.e., a diabetic taking insulin, but not without it.
(4) Is it a legitimate state interest to provide that only competent individuals can receive a lethal dosage, but remain

silent about whether only competent individuals can take that lethal dosage?

> (5) Are persons who have a terminal disease disabled for purposes of the Americans With Disabilities Act and if so, does this mean they are a suspect class?

> (6) Must Measure 16 serve a compelling state interest?

> (7) Does Measure 16 "deny" terminally ill patients the protections of Oregon's criminal and civil commitment statutes or does it give them the benefit of opting out of coverage under those laws?

Id. at 1497.

As to the due process clause challenge:

> (1) Does Measure 16 deprive a person of constitutional rights? Before a state can allow an individual to waive a federal constitutional right, must it also ensure that the waiver is voluntary and informed?

> (2) A state does not have a constitutional duty to protect members of the general public, with a few exceptions. [] Does this rule apply when the state enacts a law and allows a state operated facility [i.e., the medical school] to implement the law on its premises?

> (3) Is plaintiff's due process claim, in essence, a facial constitutional challenge to Measure 16 and if so, what is the appropriate test to determine the constitutionality of Measure 16?

> (4) If Measure 16 implicates a terminally ill person's liberty interest, does that interest outweigh that of the state?

Id. at 1498-1499.

The court also found questions under the Americans With Disabilities Act and it determined that

> [i]f a health care provider or physician is required to perform acts to facilitate or accommodate a request for assisted suicide and based on sincerely held religious convictions, reasonably believes that their participation constitutes "complicity" in the suicide, there is a serious question regarding an infringement on religious beliefs against such conduct.

Id. at 1500. The judge held the trial on the issue of the permanent injunction in April of 1995, and his decision was presumed to be imminent as this supplement went to press.

2. If you could rewrite Initiative 16, how would you do it? Would you narrow its coverage to avoid abuse? Would you broaden its coverage (and, perhaps, extend it to euthanasia as well as assisted suicide)? How would you redraft the statute to meet the objections of the petitioners in Lee v. Oregon?

3. Emboldened by the success in Oregon, many "Death With Dignity" groups have sought state statutes that would accomplish what Initiative 16 sought to do. In 1995 a New Mexico bill that would have made euthanasia legal under some circumstances was passed out of one legislative committee before it was killed by a combination of religious and hospice opposition; its proponents predict a greater chance for success next time around. Similar bills have been introduced in several other states, and a floor debate and vote on one of the bills is expected in Maine in 1995.

4. The public interest in this issue is not limited to the United States. For a discussion of the law in the Netherlands, see the main text, pages 1176-77. In addition, on May 25, 1995 Australia's Northern Territory's parliament passed The Rights of the Terminally Ill Bill (1995), which permits what some have called "voluntary euthanasia" under some limited circumstances. Other Australian states are considering similar bills.

———————

Those who believe that laws prohibiting assisting suicide are hindering proper care of some terminally ill patients have not been limited to the legislative and initiative processes. A few have also decided to mount judicial challenges to the statutes.

COMPASSION IN DYING V. WASHINGTON
United States Court of Appeals for the Ninth Circuit, 1995
49 F.3d 586

Noonan, Circuit Judge:

The State of Washington (Washington) appeals the decision of the district court holding unconstitutional Washington's statute on promoting a suicide attempt. Finding no basis for concluding that the statute violates the Constitution, we reverse the district court.

THE STATUTE

The challenged statute reads as follows:

Promoting a suicide attempt

(1) A person is guilty of promoting a suicide attempt when he knowingly causes or aids another person to attempt suicide.

(2) Promoting a suicide is a Class C felony. Wash. Rev. Code 9A.36.060.

THE PLAINTIFFS

Compassion in Dying is a nonprofit incorporated in the state of Washington. Its avowed purpose is to assist persons described by it as "competent" and "terminally ill" to hasten their deaths by providing them information, counselling, and emotional support but not by administering fatal medication.

Three individuals were plaintiffs in their own right. Their identities are cloaked by an order permitting them to litigate under pseudonyms. They are now deceased. Jane Roe was a 69-year-old physician, suffering from cancer; she had been bedridden for seven months at the time the suit was brought and died before judgment was entered by the district court. John Doe was a 44-year-old artist, who was partially blind at the time of suit and was also suffering from AIDS; he had been advised that his disease was incurable; he died prior to judgment. James Poe was a 69-year-old patient suffering from chronic obstructive pulmonary disease; he was connected to an oxygen tank at all times. He died after judgment but prior to the hearing of this appeal.

Four physicians also joined the suit asserting their own rights and those of their patients. * * *

PROCEEDINGS

On January 29, 1994, the plaintiffs brought suit against Washington, seeking a declaration that the statute violated 42 U.S.C. §

271

1983 and the Constitution of the United States; additionally, they asked that enforcement of the statute be enjoined.

* * *

The plaintiffs moved for summary judgment, and the defendants made a cross-motion for summary judgment. On May 3, 1994, the district court ruled on these motions. It denied the motion of the four physician plaintiffs asserting their own claims "on the grounds that the basis for those claims has not been adequately addressed." It denied Compassion in Dying's claim on its own behalf "for the same reason." It denied the cross-motion of Washington. It granted the motion for summary judgment of Jane Roe, John Doe and James Poe and the similar motion of the physician plaintiffs "on behalf of their terminally ill patients." The court declined to enjoin enforcement of the statute but declared the statute to violate the Constitution of the United States.

The district court reached its conclusion as to unconstitutionality on two grounds. First, the court held that the statute violated the liberty guaranteed by the Fourteenth Amendment against deprivation by a state. The court reached this conclusion by noting "a long line of cases" protecting "personal decisions relating to marriage, procreation, contraception, family relationships, child rearing and education." The court quoted as the explanation of this line the statement made in *Planned Parenthood v. Casey*, [ ]: "These matters, including the most intimate and personal choices a person may make in a lifetime, choices central to personal dignity and autonomy, are central to the liberty protected by the Fourteenth Amendment. At the heart of the liberty is the right to define one's own concept of existence, of meaning, of the universe, and of the mystery of human life. Beliefs about these matters could not define the attributes of personhood were they formed under compulsion of the State."

The district court analogized the "terminally ill person's choice to commit suicide" to the choice of abortion protected by *Casey*, stating: "this court finds the reasoning in *Casey* highly instructive and almost prescriptive." Like the abortion decision, the court found the decision by a terminally ill person to end his or her life to be one of the most intimate and personal that could be made in a lifetime and a choice central to personal autonomy and dignity.

The district court also found *Cruzan v. Director, Missouri Dept. of Health*, [ ] to be "instructive." It quoted that case's reference to "the recognition of a general liberty interest in refusing medical treatment," [ ] and the assumption for purposes of the decision in *Cruzan* "that the United States Constitution would grant a competent person a constitutionally protected right to refuse lifesaving hydration and nutrition." [ ] The district court stated that it did not believe that a distinction of constitutional significance could be drawn "between refusing life-sustaining medical treatment and physician-assisted suicide by an uncoerced, mentally competent, terminally ill adult." Combining its exegesis of *Casey* and *Cruzan*, the district court reached its conclusion that there was a constitutional right to physician-assisted suicide.

The district court then reviewed the statute to determine whether, on its face, it imposed an "undue burden" on a personal right of the *Casey* kind. See *Casey* [ ] (concluding that a statute regulating abortion was invalid on its face because "in a large fraction of the cases" in which the statute would operate it would "operate as a substantial obstacle to a woman's choice to undergo an abortion" and therefore placed "an undue burden"). The district court declared that there was "no question" that the "total ban" on physician-assisted suicide for the terminally ill was "an undue burden" on the constitutional right that the district court had discovered. Consequently, the statute was invalid.

Secondly, the district court held that the statute violated the Equal Protection Clause of the Fourteenth Amendment, requiring that all similarly situated persons be treated alike. * * * The district court could see no constitutional distinction between the terminally ill able to direct the withdrawal or withholding of life support [which is explicitly permitted by Washington Law] and the terminally ill seeking medical aid to end their lives. Accordingly, it found an unequal application of the laws.

Washington appeals.

ANALYSIS

The conclusion of the district court that the statute deprived the plaintiffs of a liberty protected by the Fourteenth Amendment and denied them the equal protection of the laws cannot be sustained.

First. The language taken from *Casey*, on which the district court pitched its principal argument, should not be removed from the context in which it was uttered. Any reader of judicial opinions knows they often attempt a generality of expression and a sententiousness of phrase that extend far beyond the problem addressed. It is commonly accounted an error to lift sentences or even paragraphs out of one context and insert the abstracted thought into a wholly different context. To take three sentences out of an opinion over thirty pages in length dealing with the highly charged subject of abortion and to find these sentences "almost prescriptive" in ruling on a statute proscribing the promotion of suicide is to make an enormous leap, to do violence to the context, and to ignore the differences between the regulation of reproduction and the prevention of the promotion of killing a patient at his or her request.

The inappropriateness of the language of *Casey* in the situation of assisted suicide is confirmed by considering what this language, as applied by the district court, implies. * * * The depressed twenty-one year old, the romantically-devastated twenty-eight year old, the alcoholic forty-year old who choose suicide are also expressing their views of the existence, meaning, the universe, and life; they are also asserting their personal liberty. If at the heart of the liberty protected by the Fourteenth Amendment is this uncurtailable ability to believe and to act on one's deepest beliefs about life, the right to suicide and the right to assistance in suicide are the prerogative of at least every sane adult. The attempt to restrict such rights to the terminally ill is illusory. If such liberty exists in this context, as *Casey* asserted in the context of reproductive rights, Every man and woman in the United States must enjoy it.[ ] The conclusion is a reductio ad absurdum.

Second. While *Casey* was not about suicide at all, *Cruzan* was about the termination of life. The district court found itself unable to distinguish between a patient refusing life support and a patient seeking medical help to bring about death and therefore interpreted *Cruzan's* limited acknowledgment of a right to refuse treatment as tantamount to an acceptance of a terminally ill patient's right to aid in self-killing. The district court ignored the far more relevant part of the opinion in *Cruzan* that "there can be no gainsaying" a state's interest "in the protection and preservation of human life" and, as evidence of that legitimate concern, the fact that "the majority of States in this country have laws imposing criminal penalties on one who assists another to commit suicide." *Cruzan* [ ]. * * *

274

Third. Unsupported by the gloss on "liberty" written by *Casey*, a gloss on a gloss, inasmuch as *Casey* developed an interpretation of "liberty" first elaborated in *Eisenstadt v. Baird*,[ ] and implicitly controverted by *Cruzan*, the decision of the district court lacks foundation in recent precedent. It also lacks foundation in the traditions of our nation.[ ] In the two hundred and five years of our existence no constitutional right to aid in killing oneself has ever been asserted and upheld by a court of final jurisdiction. Unless the federal judiciary is to be a floating constitutional convention, a federal court should not invent a constitutional right unknown to the past and antithetical to the defense of human life that has been a chief responsibility of our constitutional government.

Fourth. [Here the court said that any facial challenge to the Washington statute must fail because, even the plaintiffs agreed, there were some circumstances in which it could be constitutionally applied.]

Fifth. The district court declared the statute unconstitutional on its face without adequate consideration of Washington's interests that, individually and convergently, outweigh any alleged liberty of suicide. [Since the district court ruled, reports of Commissions established by New York or Michigan to address this issue have become available to this court]. In the light of all these materials, Washington's interests are at least these:

1. The interest in not having physicians in the role of killers of their patients. "Physician-assisted suicide is fundamentally incompatible with the physician's role as healer," declares the American Medical Association's Code of Medical Ethics (1994) §2.211. * * *

Not only would the self-understanding of physicians be affected by removal of the state's support for their professional stance; the physician's constant search for ways to combat disease would be affected, if killing were as acceptable an option for the physician as curing. * * *

2. The interest in not subjecting the elderly and even the not-elderly but infirm to psychological pressure [that inevitably will come from physicians] to consent to their own deaths. * * *

3. The interest in protecting the poor and minorities from exploitation. The poor and minorities would be especially open to manipulation in a regime of assisted suicide for two reasons: Pain is a

significant factor in creating a desire for assisted suicide, and the poor and minorities are notoriously less provided for in the alleviation of pain.
* * *

4. The interest in protecting all of the handicapped from societal indifference and antipathy. * * * The vulnerability of such persons to physician-assisted suicide is foreshadowed in the discriminatory way that a seriously-disabled person's expression of a desire to die is interpreted. When the nondisabled say they want to die, they are labelled as suicidal; if they are disabled, it is treated as "natural" or "reasonable". An insidious bias against the handicapped - again coupled with a cost-saving mentality - makes them especially in need of Washington's statutory protection.

5. An interest in preventing abuse similar to what has occurred in the Netherlands. * * *

Sixth. The scope of the district court's judgment is, perhaps necessarily, indefinite [because it gives a right to the "terminally ill" without providing any meaningful definition of who is terminally ill]. Consequently, an amorphous class of beneficiaries has been created in this non-class action; and the district court has mandated Washington to reform its law against the promotion of suicide to safeguard the constitutional rights of persons whom the district court has not identified.

Seventh. At the heart of the district court's decision appears to be its refusal to distinguish between actions taking life and actions by which life is not supported or ceases to be supported. This refusal undergirds the district court's reading of Cruzan as well as its holding that the statute violates equal protection. The distinction, being drawn by the legislature not on the basis of race, gender or religion or membership in any protected class and not infringing any fundamental constitutional right, must be upheld unless the plaintiffs can show "that the legislature's actions were irrational."[ ] The plaintiffs have not sustained this burden.

* * * Protected by the law of torts, you can have or reject such medical treatment as you see fit. You can be left alone if you want. Privacy in the primordial sense in which it entered constituted parlance - "the right to be let alone" - is yours.[ ]

Tort law and criminal law have never recognized a right to let others enslave you, mutilate you, or kill you. When you assert a claim that another - and especially another licensed by the state - should help you bring about your death, you ask for more than being let alone; you ask that the state, in protecting its own interest, not prevent its licensee from killing. The difference is not of degree but of kind. You no longer seek the ending of unwanted medical attention. You seek the right to have a second person collaborate in your death. To protect all the interests enumerated under Fifth above, the statute rightly and reasonably draws the line.

* * *

Compassion is a proper, desirable, even necessary component of judicial character; but compassion is not the most important, certainly not the sole law of human existence. * * * Justice, prudence, and fortitude are necessary too. Compassion cannot be the compass of a federal judge. That compass is the Constitution of the United States. Where, as here in the case of Washington, the statute of a state comports with that compass, the validity of the statute must be upheld.

Wright, Circuit Judge, Dissenting:

This case involves the state's power arbitrarily to deprive terminally ill, mentally competent adults of the right to choose how to die. Because [the Washington assisted suicide statute] violates plaintiffs' privacy and equal protection rights, I dissent. The majority's approach subjects such patients to unwanted and needless suffering.[ ]

The majority views the asserted right as illimitable because it depends upon the meaning of "terminally ill." But if we were to affirm, our task would not be to specify the parameters of the right. We are limited, as was the district court, to the dispute before us. The majority's "depressed twenty-one year old" is not a party before us. The deceased plaintiff patients were terminally ill, mentally competent adults, entitled to be free from unwarranted state interference in their last days.

A. Due Process

1. Privacy Right

Planned Parenthood v. Casey, [ ] defines the scope of protected liberty interests.

The majority contends that this language is out of context in this case. Yet that general language was not tailored specifically for the abortion context but derived from well-established Supreme Court precedent. The same paragraph explains:

> Our law affords constitutional protection to personal decisions relating to marriage, procreation, contraception, family relationships, child rearing, and education.[ ]

The district court's application of *Casey* hardly amounts to "an enormous leap" that does "violence to the context."

* * *

The right to die with dignity falls squarely within the privacy right recognized by the Supreme Court. The decision by a terminally ill, mentally competent adult to request physician assistance in hastening death is a highly personal one, directly implicating the right to privacy. * * *

A constitutional distinction cannot be drawn between refusing life-sustaining medical treatment and accepting physician assistance in hastening death. * * * Such a distinction yields patently unjust results. For example, a respirator-dependent patient may demand that the respirator be removed when the pain becomes unbearable. Terminally ill patients not dependent on such life support, however, cannot receive physician assistance to end unwanted agony. So says the majority opinion.

Along with established precedent, "this Nation's history and tradition" help to define the content of substantive due process.[ ] Because medicine is constantly evolving and presenting new legal questions, whether American history and tradition support the right asserted must be answered at a more abstract level than the majority would permit. * * *

Likewise, we must ask whether American history and tradition reflect the values of self-determination and privacy regarding personal decisions. In the late nineteenth century, the Court wrote: "No right is held more sacred, or is more carefully guarded, by the common law, than the right of every individual to the possession and control of his own person, free

278

from all restraint or interference of others unless by clear and unquestioned authority of law."[ ] The right to die with dignity accords with the American values of self-determination and privacy regarding personal decisions.

2. Standard of Review

The applicable standard of review is strict scrutiny. Because a fundamental right is involved, the statute that limits this right can be justified only by a "compelling state interest,"[ ].

3. The Statute is Invalid as Applied

The state has an interest in preserving the lives of its citizens. But the state's interest weakens and the individual's right to privacy grows as natural death approaches.[ ]

The Washington Legislature is capable of enacting regulations that serve the state's interest in preserving human life, while protecting the fundamental liberties of terminally ill, mentally competent adults. As Washington law now stands, the statute prevents all terminally ill, mentally competent adults from exercising their right to physician-hastened death. Because the legislature can draft laws that would protect plaintiffs' right to privacy, the existing legislation is not narrowly tailored.

* * *

B. Equal Protection

Washington law permits terminally ill persons to obtain medical assistance in withdrawing life-sustaining treatment.[ ] Yet it prohibits other forms of physician-hastened death for terminally ill, mentally competent adults. Because Washington's laws abrogate the fundamental rights of one group, but not those of a similarly situated group, they must be subjected to strict scrutiny and upheld only if the classifications are suitably tailored to serve a compelling state interest.[ ]

The two groups of patients are similarly situated because they are both comprised of terminally ill, mentally competent adults. As observed by the district court, "both [groups of] patients may be terminally ill, suffering pain and loss of dignity and subjected to a more extended dying

279

process without some medical intervention, be it removal of life support systems or the prescription of medication to be self-administered."[ ] There is but one difference: one group can hasten death through withdrawal of life support; the other can do so only with affirmative medical assistance. Washington's disparate treatment drawn on this difference is not suitably tailored to serve a compelling state interest. * * *

* * *

I dissent.

NOTE

The Ninth Circuit is not the only court to hear this issue. Challenges to assisting suicide statutes were also turned back in New York, *Quill v. Koppel,* 870 F.Supp. 78 (S.D.N.Y. 1994), and, of course, in Michigan in the *Kevorkian* case, discussed in this supplement. The thoughtful District Court opinion in *Compassion in Dying* is found at 850 F. Supp. 1454 (W.D. Wash. 1994). For a thorough account of all of the arguments raised in challenges to assisted suicide statutes, see Robert Sedler, Constitutional Challenges to Bans on "Assisted Suicide": The View From Without and Within, 21 Hastings Const. L.Q. 777 (1994).